THE THORNS OF MEMORY

THE THORNS OF MEMORY

Memoirs

by

PETER KEMP

SINCLAIR-STEVENSON

To Liz
To acknowledge a debt
I can never hope to repay

First published in Great Britain by
Sinclair-Stevenson Limited
7/8 Kendrick Mews
London SW7 3HG, England

British Library Cataloguing in Publication Data

Kemp, Peter
The thorns of memory.
I. Title
940.548641
ISBN 1-85619-011-0

Photoset by Rowland Phototypesetting Limited
Bury St Edmunds, Suffolk
Printed and bound in Great Britain by
Clays Limited, St Ives plc

Contents

Acknowledgements

Among many kind friends who have helped me in my work on this book I would like to mention:

Elizabeth Moore and Cynthia Hurt for indispensable help in the preparation of my manuscript; Vane Ivanović, Daška McLean, Liz and Bill McCelland, Xan and Magouche Fielding, and Christine, Lady Hesketh for their encouragement and lavish hospitality while I was writing it; Professor Stuart Simmonds for his expert advice on South East Asia and instruction in the Laotian language; and the Winston Churchill Memorial Trust, from whom a travelling fellowship in 1972 made my last trip to Laos possible.

To all of them I wish to express my warmest thanks.

Peter Kemp
London, May 1990

And on the thorns of memory rest uneasy

Camoens (translated by
Roy Campbell)

PART ONE
SPAIN

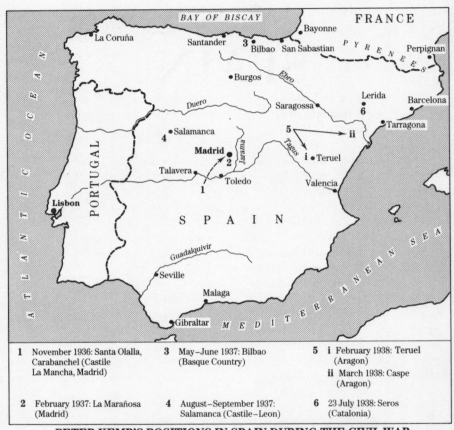

1	November 1936: Santa Olalla, Carabanchel (Castile La Mancha, Madrid)	3	May–June 1937: Bilbao (Basque Country)	5	i February 1938: Teruel (Aragon)
					ii March 1938: Caspe (Aragon)
2	February 1937: La Marañosa (Madrid)	4	August–September 1937: Salamanca (Castile–Leon)	6	23 July 1938: Seros (Catalonia)

PETER KEMP'S POSITIONS IN SPAIN DURING THE CIVIL WAR

Chapter 1

I HATE BEING SHOT at. I am not the stuff of which heroes are made. This dismal thought came to me in the early hours of 16 March 1938 as I stood in an olive grove near the little town of Caspe on the borders of Aragon and Catalonia, while shell splinters from the guns of Russian tanks lopped branches off the trees overhead and scattered on the ground nearby. Around me stood or crouched the officers and men of the 14th Bandera of the Spanish Foreign Legion, all of us waiting for the battle to develop in the approaching daylight.

I had been nearly eighteen months in Spain and so had already seen action. But vitality and courage are at their lowest around dawn, and the prospect of having to repel a spirited enemy counter-attack was doing nothing to raise mine. I was not looking forward to the day. It was going to be rough.

I had never been intended for a military career although I had spent four years at Wellington. In 1933, aged eighteen, I had gone up to Trinity, Cambridge, where I had scraped a degree in Classics and Law, and passed a few Bar exams. My father, who had spent thirty-five years in India before retiring as Chief Justice of Bombay, had wanted me to become a lawyer, like himself and his brother, or else to go into the Indian Civil or the Sudan Colonial Services; we were far from rich, so there was no question of my practising at the Bar in England.

Nevertheless, since my early childhood I had been brought up to admire, and try to emulate, the military virtues of patriotism, loyalty and courage. My only brother, five years older than myself and the best friend I ever had, was now a lieutenant in the Fleet Air Arm, having entered the Royal Navy through Dartmouth at the age of thirteen. The Navy was his whole life and its values were his creed: because I always looked up to him, those values meant a lot to me too. My father, for whom I felt enormous respect and a good deal of awe, was an austere Scotsman with a strong sense of duty and a ferocious capacity for hard work. He had retired in 1931, when I was approaching sixteen. Outside his work his great enthusiasm was for sport, particularly what he called the 'manly sports' of rugger and boxing. 'Manliness' and a serious attitude to work were the qualities he looked for, and sadly failed to find, in his younger son; he considered me feckless, indolent and feeble. One of the reasons – by no means the only one – why I had come to Spain was to make him change this opinion.

Although I was born in Bombay my first clear memories are of Karachi, where I remember being taken for walks in the guava gardens, along paths overhung with deep green foliage, while the heavy air pulsated with the continuous thud of engine wells. I came home to England at the age of four and saw no more of India until 1945, when I passed through on my way to be dropped into Thailand to work against the Japanese.

In England I went through a conventional middle-class education: a prep school situated in beautiful country on the Battle ridge behind Hastings, which I enjoyed, and Wellington, where I was often bored but seldom unhappy. I endured rather than enjoyed the obligatory games and did well enough at my work to avoid unpleasantness. I think I must have been a dull fellow, showing neither initiative nor eccentricity. My performance was summarised in one of my school-reports which stated simply: 'Gives no trouble and takes none.'

At Cambridge, unlike Wellington, I was seldom bored, but just as idle. In fact, if the Tripos in those days had been anywhere near as hard as it is today I doubt if I would have scraped that degree. Social life occupied too much of my time, with parties at Cambridge and in London; politics also absorbed my keen but unsophisticated interest and I spoke regularly in debates at the Union, said to be, with Oxford, the most critical audience in the country. I never held office there, but I enjoyed myself, undismayed by the good-natured ribaldry that invariably greeted every declaration of my unfashionable Tory faith.

Cambridge in the Thirties is often depicted as a nursery of communism. This is not my impression. There was at the university a small though active branch of the Party, but few outside their own group took them seriously. One or two became notorious, among them Guy Burgess, whom I used to meet occasionally then and over the years; he gave shits a bad name. Philby had gone down the year before I went up, but I knew him later in Spain, where he was *The Times* correspondent with the Nationalists. The local Party

Secretary was a highly intelligent undergraduate, James Klugman, whom I met again briefly in the war, when he occupied, to my surprise, a very sensitive post as intelligence officer in the Cairo office of SOE; after the war he became a member of the British Party Politburo.

An old master who taught me English at Wellington used to describe undergraduate life as 'three years of glorious irresponsibility'. It certainly was for for me. Although I didn't learn very much – least of all the habit of hard work – I thoroughly enjoyed it and I made some wonderful friends; those of them who survived the Second World War remained valued friends for life. But when, in June 1936, I came down from Cambridge to enter the real world I had no qualifications to make my way in it, apart from a modest degree, and I had no idea what I was going to do.

I remember very well the morning I left London. It was a raw day in early November 1936; in the gardens of the Temple, where I had been sharing a flat with two barristers, the bare branches of the trees swayed mournfully in the chill wind and driving rain. The time was 8.30, and I was waiting for a Cambridge friend to pick me up in his car and drive me to Newhaven, where I would take the cross-channel boat on the first leg of my journey to Spain. I was packed and ready, and despite the gloomy day outside I was feeling elated at the prospect of my adventure.

In August I had spent my twenty-first birthday with my parents in Argyllshire and since September I had been in London reading for the Bar. Now I had passed my preliminary exams and only the Bar finals remained. They would have to wait. They are still waiting. After a good deal of thought I had made up my mind to go and fight for the Nationalists in Spain, a decision, though I couldn't know it then, that would alter radically the whole course of my life. I had almost no money for the journey or living expenses but my brother Neil, who was enthusiastic over my plans, had generously sent me £15 – he supplemented his naval pay by writing for service publications – and that sum would at least get me to Spain.

I wrote to my father asking not for money but only for his blessing. My mind was made up, I told him, and I could just manage for money but I didn't want to leave without his good will. Well aware of his habitual – and often justified – disapproval of what I did, I feared an explosion; instead I received back by return of post the warmest letter I ever had from him. 'Of course you have my blessing,' he concluded. 'But no son of mine is going on such a venture with only £15.' He was opening an account for me at a bank in Burgos, the Nationalist headquarters at that time. From my mother I had a sweet letter, wishing me well; but I knew she was desperately worried.

My father insisted on coming up from Sussex to London to help me choose 'the right kit for this sort of thing'. We spent an extravagant afternoon in the Army and Navy Stores where we bought, among other things, a bulky leather 'medicine chest' like those my father used on *shikari* in India: it contained chiefly quinine, iodine and cascara, and was too bulky to carry in a haversack; I lost it soon after my arrival in Spain. I rejected my father's offer of his valuable .275 Männlicher sporting carbine, but accepted from an old friend a prismatic compass and an enormous .44 service revolver of 1918 vintage, which I had difficulty in concealing on me whenever I passed through customs. To help me with the language I had bought Hugo's *Spanish in Three Months Without a Master*, to prove indispensable over the next two years.

Not everyone was so enthusiastic as my father and Neil. Shortly before I left I was having tea with a girlfriend, when her father came in; he was an old regular soldier who had fought in the First World War and several lesser wars before it, and was now very deaf.

'Daddy!' she shouted. 'Peter is off to the Civil War in Spain!'

'What? What?' the Colonel shouted back. He turned to me. 'You're going to Spain to fight?'

'Yes, sir.'

'You damned young fool! You know what fighting means? It's hell! You bloody young idiot! Ever read Napier's *Peninsular War*? You damn well read it! Icicles hanging from their noses! Icicles, frostbite, hunger! It's hell, I tell you! You make me sick.'

I've often been asked what made me take part in the Spanish Civil War and why on the Nationalist side. I had a variety of motives; I have already mentioned one of them,* but even today I'm not sure which of them was the strongest. Possibly it was a feeling for adventure, the desire to be on my own and independent – hitherto I had been much too well looked after; also the wish to see a new country, get to know the people and learn to speak their language. I find this urge has not yet left me. I felt strongly, too, that as a Tory who had spoken frequently and at length in debates at the Cambridge Union I should be prepared now to stick my neck out in support of my views.

But I had other motives, just about as strong. One of them was

* See p.4

a deep-seated hatred and fear of communism and what it might do to Britain and Europe. Although I knew very little about Spain I had studied carefully the early, uncensored press reports from Republican Madrid. They gave lurid accounts of mob violence throughout Republican territory: churches burned, priests and nuns done to death simply because they were priests and nuns, people murdered because they had a little money or property. Surely it must be right to fight against such barbarism? Later, when I was in Spain, I heard plenty of such stories from eyewitnesses and from relations of the victims. Inevitably in a civil war, there were atrocities on both sides but it wasn't until much later that I came to recognise this sombre truth. Daily reports in the British press of the recruitment, directed by the Comintern,* of the International Brigades throughout Europe and America had convinced me that the communists were making a bid to take over Spain. If they succeeded, I thought, Britain would be in an extremely perilous situation, with a *Front Populaire* government in France under strong communist influence.

I still believe that if the Republicans had won Spain would have emerged as a communist state. Of course many, indeed most, of those who fought for the Republic were not communists; many were deeply suspicious of communism. But arms for the Republicans came almost entirely from Russia, and as the war developed, the Russians controlled more and more their supply and distribution; they ensured that the arms went to communist-controlled units of the Army and their 'advisers' came to dictate the policies of the Republic, so much so that in 1937 they liquidated the communist, anti-Stalinist POUM and the anarchist leadership as well, although both were staunch allies of the Republic. At the end of the war I was shown the torture chambers in Barcelona where so many of those poor people met a horrible end. I dream about them still.

The International Brigades, incomparably the best troops in the Republican Army, were under communist leadership from the beginning, with a political commissar attached to each unit down to battalion, if not company level. Their chief political commissar was the veteran French revolutionary, André Marty; he had led a mutiny in the French fleet supporting the Tsarist forces in the Black Sea during the Russian Civil War. Now in Spain he was quite ruthless in eliminating dissidents. Promotion, according to a company commander of the British battalion whom I spoke to after

* Communist International, the organisation that directed Communist Party activities outside Russia; it was disbanded, in name only, by Stalin in 1942.

the war,* depended on Party membership. Like so many, he was not a communist, but 'I joined the Party to get out of the ranks; otherwise I'd have stayed a private for the duration, digging trenches.'

I know that many of my contemporaries, including friends of mine from Cambridge, fought for the Republic from motives at least as idealistic as mine. They feared and hated fascism, and they were surely right to. I was no fascist myself; as a radical Tory I hated fascism as much as communism – two sides of an odious coin. But I wasn't going to fight for the fascist Falange; I was going to fight against communism. Moreover, in 1936 German and Italian help to the Nationalists – of which I shall have more to say – was neither so extensive nor so evident, at least to me, as help to the Republicans from the Comintern.

Having decided to join the Nationalists I had no idea how to set about it. I spoke not a word of Spanish and I had no Spanish contacts. Had I wished to join the International Brigades there would have been no problem; in every country there were organisations to attract volunteers. But the Nationalists showed no interest in recruiting in Britain.

At this point, in October, I received an introduction through a much older friend to the Marqués del Moral, who ran the Nationalist Agency in London.† A tall, spare figure with a deeply lined face, del Moral was by birth an Englishman, who had served with distinction in the British Army in South Africa. His greeting was reserved, even severe.

'Philip tells me you want to go to Spain. Why?'

'To fight, sir.'

His severity relaxed a little.

'Good. I can give you a letter to a friend of mine in Biarritz who runs a courier service across the frontier and I daresay he'd send you as far as Burgos.'

He advised me to get some accreditation from a newspaper, to avoid complications with the French authorities at the frontier, then handed me his letter and warmly wished me luck.

I went immediately to my good friend Collin Brooks, Editor of the *Sunday Dispatch*, whom I had met when he came to Cambridge, who willingly gave me a note authorising me to 'collect news and transmit articles from the Spanish fronts of war'.

* Captain Davidson. Members of the Brigades had to hand over their passports to the organisers when they entered Spain. If they were killed, I understand the Russians made use of their passports for their agents.

† Until very late in the war, the British did not recognise the Nationalist government. Therefore the Nationalist Agency filled the place of an Embassy.

My Cambridge friend had arrived punctually to collect me from the Temple. I sat beside him in his small green sportscar as we battered our way to the coast in the teeth of the storm and tried to answer his questions about my motives for going to Spain.

'You're not going to be very popular in England when you get back. How long do you think you'll be gone?'

'Oh, not more than six months.' I was yet to learn that it is much easier to get into a war than out; also, more significantly, that in any war, what you think you're fighting for is not what emerges at the end, even from victory.

At the jetty in Newhaven harbour I found my mother and father, who had driven from Cooden to see me off. None of us liked prolonged farewells, especially now when I realised that what to me was the prelude to an exciting adventure was for them the start of a period of separation and anxiety. I was deeply moved by the way they faced up to it; by my mother's appearance of cheerful courage and my father's acceptance of an idea that must have seemed to him quite crazy. We said, or rather shouted, goodbyes above the roar of the wind and sea, and as I walked away I turned once to look back at them. I still remember my father's stocky figure in his dripping mackintosh and old fishing hat, standing by the door of their car, his stern, sad face gazing intently after me. I never saw him again.

Five days later I arrived in Burgos. I stopped off on the way in Biarritz, while del Moral's friend applied for my *salvoconducto*, and laid on a car and courier to take me. Still posing as a journalist I crossed the frontier at Hendaye with little delay, thanks to the efforts of my Spanish courier, Pascual Vicuña, who spoke perfect French and English. Once over the frontier I told him my real purpose. He was delighted and promised to introduce me in Burgos to friends of his on the Nationalist general staff. A great admirer of the British and their way of life, he told me he regretted there was so little understanding of the Nationalists in Britain – entirely because of 'red propaganda', he believed; I could be assured of a warm welcome in the Nationalist ranks.

Soon after leaving the border we came to the blackened and gutted houses that had been the town of Irun, scene of some of the bitterest fighting of the year. In early September the Nationalist forces under General Mola, most of them Carlists, had stormed the forts on the hills that commanded the town and the western gateway through the Pyrenees. It was a long and bloody battle, and the Nationalists paid dearly for their success with heavy losses, particularly among the gallant and devoted Carlists from Navarre and Alava, where the Carlist tradition was strongest. They had rallied to a man to Mola's colours as soon as the war broke out – old men who remembered the Carlist Wars of the last century, and boys of fifteen who learned to load and fire their rifles as they travelled in lorries to the front. With reckless courage and no military training they died in hundreds on the steep, bare slopes of the almost impregnable fortress of San Marcial.

Some of the defenders – Basque Republicans and Asturian miners – escaped into France; others retreated westward, after burning and dynamiting Irun, to San Sebastian, only to be driven out nine days later. The fall of Irun cut the overland supply route from France to the northern Republican provinces of Vizcaya, Santander and Asturias; supplies for them would now have to come by sea in the face of a blockade by the Nationalists, who had command of the sea. It was the beginning of the end for the Basque Republic.

We stopped in San Sebastian at about two o'clock, in good time for a drink and lunch according to Spanish hours. San Sebastian showed no signs of war damage, the only reminders being the uniforms in the streets and the slogans on the walls – the '*Alistaos a la Falange*' ('Join the Falange') of the fascists, and the '*Dios, Fueros, Patria y Rey*' ('God, Privileges, Country and King') of the Carlists. After lunch our road led inland, rising gently at first among wooded hills with white, red-roofed villas and farmhouses on the slopes, and then climbing steeply on a winding road through the deep gorges and thick pine forests of the Cantabrian Range until we emerged on to the *meseta*, the great plateau of central Spain. We were stopped frequently at control posts manned by very young Carlist soldiers, smart and self-important in their red berets and neat khaki uniforms, who politely asked to see our passes, or by police of the Guardia Civil in green uniforms and shining black tricorn hats. Every few miles we passed placards hung beside the road, exhorting us to join the Falange or the Carlists, or to 'Ask always for Domecq wines and brandy'. Around seven we entered Burgos, where Vicuña took me to the Hotel Norte y Londres; they had no room available, but found one for me in a clean and comfortable house nearby which smelt strongly of cheese.

Outside the air was crisp and dry, with an icy wind to herald the approaching bitter winter of the high Castilian plains. Thankfully I returned to the warmth of the overcrowded hotel to wait for Vicuña. I sat down and watched the chattering, animated crowd –

men in smart Army uniforms or civilian suits with red *Requeté**
berets or, occasionally, the blue tasselled forage cap of the Falange,
and women wearing some medallion or badge attached by a ribbon
in the red and yellow colours of Nationalist Spain. After a few
minutes a tall, heavily built man with a florid complexion sat down
beside me.

'May I join you? I see you're English. So am I. Rupert Belville.'

I had already heard of him as an expert on Spain, a keen *aficionado*
of bullfighting and a skilled amateur pilot who flew his own aircraft.
The outbreak of the war had found him near Jerez in the South, where
he had joined a Falange unit fighting in Andalusia. He had soon left
it. Although sickened by communist and anarchist atrocities in the
country villages of that poverty-stricken region, he had also been
deeply shocked by Falange executions of enemy prisoners.

The shooting of prisoners was one of the nastiest features of this
war; both sides were guilty of it, especially in the early months. Not
only prisoners taken in battle but thousands of civilians died in front
of firing squads. There were two main reasons: first, the firm
conviction of each side that their opponents were 'traitors' to Spain
– the Nationalist view – or 'class enemies,' as the Republicans
believed, and that they fully deserved to die; second, the fear of
each side that its opponents would take the first opportunity to rise
against them. Later on, the Nationalists tended to spare their
prisoners, except officers and members of the International Brigades, for whom they felt a particular hatred.

'I've got my plane here in Burgos,' Belville told me. 'But I can't
get permission to fly it anywhere near the front. I'm not staying
here. It's full of nothing but wives and sweethearts sitting on their
bums and exchanging rumours and gossip.'

The following September Belville made headlines in the international press. The Nationalists were attacking Santander, whose
fall was expected at any moment. Misled by a false report of its
capture, he and a Spanish friend from one of the great sherry houses
in Jerez loaded up his aircraft with wine and brandy, and flew from
San Sebastian to Santander. On the airfield there they met a group
of Republican militiamen and, mistaking their blue overalls for
Falange uniforms, produced their liquor with enthusiastic cries of
'*¡Viva Franco!*' and '*¡Arriba España!*' They were bundled roughly off
to prison and were very lucky not to be shot. Eventually, after an
anxious and uncomfortable captivity, they were exchanged for two
Republican Army officers.

---

* *Requeté* is a Catalan word, first used in the Carlist Wars of the last century,
when Carlism was strong in Catalonia.

Vicuña rejoined me for dinner accompanied by his friends, a major on the general staff and three captains, one of whom spoke English. They were delighted to hear I wanted to fight, but pointed out that the only Nationalist units open to a foreigner were the *Tercio*, or Foreign Legion, and the Falange and *Requeté* militias. They strongly advised me not to enlist as a private in the Legion, advice which I'm heartily glad I took; I rejected without hesitation any idea of joining the Falange. The *Requetés* were for me an obvious choice – although they were intensely Catholic and I was Church of England; their monarchist and traditionalist ideas, however, appealed to me strongly. Being monarchists themselves, my friends warmly approved; they would give me letters to the Carlist leaders in Avila with a military *salvoconducto* for the journey and one of their cars would call for me at the hotel the following afternoon.

As we dined on river trout, washed down with local *rosado*, one of them told me:

'The military situation of the Reds is most precarious. Any day now Madrid will be in our hands.'

He had reckoned without the International Brigades.

The military situation of the Republicans was indeed precarious. In fact, for a time I wondered whether I had arrived in Spain too late to take part in the war. The Nationalists, after some initial reverses in the Peninsula, had succeeded in transporting the Army of Africa, comprising their best professional soldiers, across the Straits of Gibraltar and advanced rapidly to the gates of Madrid; while General Mola had rallied the *Requetés* and some Army units to take control of the provinces of Navarre and Alava, and all of Old Castile and Leon.

It seems now that ever since the Spanish elections of February 1936, which brought to power a Popular Front government, both the extreme Left and the extreme Right had been preparing to take power by force.* The Right had the support of the majority of sernior Army officers, who were increasingly concerned at the lawlessness and near chaos to which the impotence of the new government was rapidly reducing the country, and at the growing threat of a communist coup.†

* So much has been written since 1936 about the origins and causes of the Civil War that it is superfluous for me to go into details here. But a very brief summary may help those readers who have not seen the published literature.

† See for example *Spain* (pp 351 and 369) by Salvador de Madariaga, a liberal historian by no means sympathetic to the Nationalists.

On 17 July the garrison of Melilla in Spanish Morocco revolted, followed immediately by the rest of the Army of Africa, consisting chiefly of the Spanish Foreign Legion and the *Regulares* – Moorish crack troops recruited by the Spanish government and officered by Spaniards. Although foreigners could enlist in it, the Spanish Foreign Legion, unlike the French, was composed almost entirely of Spaniards – some ninety per cent of the legionnaires and virtually all the officers were Spanish, the remainder being mostly Portuguese; dedicated professionals and the best trained and equipped troops in the Spanish Army, they were deployed as shock troops in difficult and dangerous operations.

On the afternoon of the 17th General Franco arrived by air from the Canary Islands, where he had been governor and commander-in-chief, and immediately took command of the rebels; two months later he was proclaimed commander-in-chief of the Nationalist Armies.

On 18 July the *Movimiento*, as the Nationalists called their rising, exploded throughout the Spanish Peninsula. At first it went badly wrong. The big cities, Madrid, Barcelona and Bilbao, remained in Republican hands, along with all of Catalonia and New Castile, the eastern half of Aragon, much of the Basque country, the entire Biscay coast from the French frontier to the borders of Galicia and almost all of southern Spain. The Basque provinces of Guipuzcoa and Vizcaya would not have declared for the Republicans but for the attitude of the Basque Separatist leaders. The Basques were deeply religious Catholics, with no sympathy for the communist miners of Asturias or the anticlerical unions of Santander. But in the hope that they could obtain a greater measure of autonomy from the Madrid government than from the Nationalists, they declared an independent Basque Republic allied to Madrid and so opposed their fellow Basques, the *Requetés* of Navarre. At the end of 1936 a young Navarrese officer with whom I was serving told me: 'For me the saddest thing about this war is not only that Spaniard is fighting Spaniard, but Basque is fighting Basque.'

Worst of all for the Nationalists, a sizeable portion of the fleet, based at Cartagena in the South East, declared for the Republicans – the crews, under communist leadership, mutinied against their officers, killed them and threw their bodies into the sea. This success should have given the Republicans control of the vital Straits of Gibraltar and prevented the passage of Franco's army from Africa to the mainland. However the sailors, having killed their officers, had little idea themselves how to handle their ships; and so the few small warships remaining to Franco in that area were able to convey his troops across the Straits with little interference. Franco also used for this purpose six Junkers-52 transport aircraft leased from the Germans.

The Nationalists, who disposed of strong naval forces from the important base of El Ferrol in the extreme North West, very soon confined the incompetent Republican Navy to port, and established an effective blockade on the entire Spanish coastline. The Spanish Air Force was very small at the outbreak of the war; most of its aircraft were based in Republican territory and so the Republicans had command of the air, at least until 1937. It was not, however, a decisive factor in the war at that time.

In the Peninsular Army most of the officers who were free to do so joined the Nationalists; but those who found themselves, or their families, in Republican territory had little choice but to serve the Republicans. Of the police forces, the traditional Guardia Civil was almost all in favour of the Nationalists, whereas the Guardia de Asalto, the newer 'Shock Police', and the *Carabineros*, or Frontier Police, usually joined the Republicans, providing them with a useful core of trained officers and NCOs.

Both sides depended, particularly in the early days, largely on volunteer paramilitary militias raised from the various political parties. On the Republican side the *milicianos* were recruited chiefly by the trades unions – communist, Marxist (the POUM with which George Orwell fought in Catalonia), socialist and anarchist. The *milicianos* had plenty of enthusiasm and courage but no military training or organisation; each unit would elect its own commander, who would usually act independently, with no regard for any central command or overall plan. The result in battle was chaos, and the professionals of the Nationalist Armies found little difficulty in outmanoeuvering the disorganised Republican resistance and driving the defenders back from one position to the next.

Women, too, joined these Republican militias, fighting alongside the men with equal courage and often greater ferocity. They were also employed as gaolers to guard woman civilians held in Republican prisons, many of whom have told me they suffered much worse treatment from these *milicianas* than from the men.

When the Civil War began, the Republican government not only distributed arms from the state arsenals to the workers' unions but, unwisely, threw open the prisons and drafted the inmates into the militias. Since all purely political prisoners had already been released under an amnesty, the prisons contained only common criminals; issued with arms and uniforms, they were responsible for many of the vicious and violent crimes that in the early months disfigured Republican Spain.

On the Nationalist side the two militias were those of the Falange, or Fascist Party, and the *Requetés*, or Carlists. The *falangistas*, who only numbered a few thousand at the beginning of the war, did some fighting in Andalusia in the early days. But they seemed to be of more use to the Republicans as propaganda targets than to the Nationalists as soldiers; indeed, their fighting qualities were regarded with derision, especially by their *Requeté* rivals and the professionals of the Foreign Legion. However, by concentrating on placing their bright young men in key administrative posts they soon acquired a political influence out of all proportion to their military value. Later in the war I found it interesting to observe that where our troops occupied a Republican area, the Falange had no difficulty in finding new recruits from former communists, who found the transition less than painful.

The Carlist movement drew its main strength from the Basque provinces, especially Navarre, although it had followers throughout the Peninsula. Its origins were in the dynastic quarrels of the last century, following the death of Fernando VII in 1833, between the staunchly pro-clerical Conservatives, under their claimant to the throne, the King's brother Don Carlos – hence their name – and the anticlerical *Liberales*. After a series of bloody and cruelly fought wars between 1833 and 1876 the Carlists were defeated, largely through the jealousies and incompetence of their political leaders; but Carlism remained a powerful influence in the North, especially Navarre, until and during the Spanish Civil War.

Carlism, particularly among the Navarrese, was much more than a political movement; it was a faith, '*el ideal*', based not only on a paternalist and traditionalist conservatism – the Carlists were often called *tradicionalistas* – but on deep devotion to the Catholic faith. Throughout the years between 1876 and 1936, in almost every Navarre home – country house, farmstead, or cottage – there would be hanging on the wall a faded red beret and old musket or rifle handed down from some forebear who had marched with Ramón Cabrera or Zumala Carregui.

During the period of disorder and rising tension that followed the elections of 1936 the *Requetés* prepared for another war. Throughout Navarre the old and obselete weapons came down from the walls, to be cleaned and made ready for action. Within three weeks of the outbreak of war thirty thousand *Requetés* rallied to Mola; even the women enlisted as '*Margaritas*' – for nursing and other duties short of bearing arms. Only the very young and the very old remained to carry on the work of the countryside.

The *Requetés* were formed into *tercios* of about five hundred men, with four companies in each, and every company had its chaplain; even the mildest swearing attracted a fine, but in other respects discipline was inclined to be casual. In time, however, the Nationalist command, rating them very highly in the field, sent the *Requeté* units some of their best officers.

Meanwhile, so great was the urgency and so serious the shortage of troops that they were thrown into battle immediately, with no training and very few modern arms, to storm the fortresses guarding Irun and San Sebastian, and the passes over the Guadarrama mountains north of Madrid. It was a glorious thing to die in battle for *la tradición* and they died in their hundreds, holding their lives cheap and taking no care to protect themselves from enemy fire. In each company the first into the attack were the captain and the chaplain, the one with his pistol, the other with his missal and his red beret with its purple tassel streaming behind. They made superb targets. And so in the first few months perished some of the finest men in Spain.

Within a few weeks of its successful crossing of the Straits of Gibraltar the Army of Africa had occupied all of Andalusia from the Portuguese border in the West as far as Granada in the East, including Seville, Jerez and Cordoba, though not, as yet, Malaga. By the middle of August it had secured the towns of Merida and Badajoz on the frontier with Portugal, and joined forces with Mola's northern army. The Nationalists advanced rapidly eastwards towards Madrid, delayed only by a diversion to Toledo to relieve the hard-pressed garrison of the Alcazar; this diversion, probably necessary in terms of prestige and military honour, almost certainly cost them Madrid. If they had ignored Toledo and advanced directly on the capital, they would most probably have taken it with little difficulty and ended the war; as it was, the fighting was to continue for over two more years. On 7 November 1936, Nationalist troops were deployed along the Manzanares river and a few had even penetrated the city as far as the Puerta del Sol. The next day their attack was thrown back in confusion; only a prompt withdrawal across the river saved them from envelopment and probable annihilation. The International Brigades had arrived.

Chapter 2

B Y THE TIME I reached them the Spanish 'fronts of war' were already stabilised; position warfare had temporarily taken the place of the war of movement. With the arrival of the International Brigades the stage of foreign intervention had begun.

To meet this new threat as well as the increase in French help to the Republicans, Franco called for assistance from Germany and Italy. They were quick to respond. Contrary to Republican propaganda, the Germans sent no fighting troops. Their help was chiefly technical – experts in signals and other communications, a few artillery instructors and, in the early days, pilots to train the very small but growing Nationalist Air Force;* one or two squadrons of bombers, with their fighter escorts, were flown by Germans throughout the war. The Italians maintained two Army divisions with all supporting arms and armour, and officers for two more 'mixed divisions' of Italians and Spaniards. The Italians were not popular with their Spanish allies, who despised their military qualities and resented their arrogance. Italian bombers operated from the Balearics throughout the war, attacking Madrid and the Republican Mediterranean ports.

The French gave or sold to the Republicans aircraft, artillery and small arms, but sent no fighting troops apart from the French components of the International Brigades. It is worth mentioning here that virtually all the foreign war material used by both sides in Spain was obsolete – but quite adequate for its purpose in the Civil War. With the Soviet contribution to the Republicans, and the price exacted for it, I have already dealt. For their help, however, the Germans were unable to obtain any control over Nationalist policy. When they tried it in 1937, by encouraging a Falange plot against Franco, he sent the Falange ringleaders to prison for thirty years and demanded the recall of the German Ambassador. Whatever his

* There were so few Spanish pilots that at first both sides had to use foreigners, who were usually replaced by Spaniards as the war progressed.

faults, Franco was an intensely patriotic Spaniard, who would never agree to foreign control over his country.

As we drove south-west from Burgos the next afternoon I gazed for the first time on the harsh grandeur of the Castilian landscape, the heartland of Spain, which seems to have moulded so much of Spanish character, art and literature. The bare, brown plain, flushed golden in the clear light of the declining sun, its sombre colour lightened only by the green of the tamarisks on the river bank to our left, stretched away to the horizon where the sharp contours of a steep and treeless plateau stood out stark against the evening sky.

It was night when we drove through a gateway in the great medieval walls of Avila. At the *comandancia militar* the duty officer, an amiable old major with pince-nez and a sallow face creased like a prune, told me the Carlist command had moved south to Toledo, which was now the base for the assault on Madrid. When he had given me another *salvoconducto* and letters to the Carlist leaders in Toledo, and arranged for my journey there by car, I went in search of a room for the night. The hotels were full, but with the help of the Hotel Inglés – appropriately enough – I found a room in a house on the cathedral square.

Avila, now some twenty miles from the front, had fallen into Nationalist hands without any fighting in the first weeks of the war and so had suffered no damage; but there were occasional raids on the airfield by Republican planes and so a blackout was in force. In the Hotel Inglés I met a group of British and American journalists, who invited me to join them for dinner. Among them was the *Daily Mail* correspondent, Harold Cardozo, an old friend of Collin Brooks and a veteran among war correspondents. After distinguished Army service in the First World War he had joined the staff of the *Continental Daily Mail* and was now covering the Nationalist side in this war for the Rothermere newspapers. As a devout Catholic he had a particular sympathy for the *Requetés* and always wore their scarlet beret in Spain.

'You will find the fighting down there is conducted along established textbook lines,' he told me. 'A copy of *Field Service Regulations* might even be useful.'

With the journalists I also met their conducting officer, a middle-aged cavalry captain who looked, in spite of his smart uniform, worn and dejected; he hardly spoke a word all evening.

'He seems to have a secret sorrow,' I commented to the American sitting on my right.

'He has a sorrow,' he answered, 'but not so secret, because he never stops telling people about it. He used to live in Biarritz, where he had a very glamorous girlfriend – some titled Spaniard. I guess she used to put the horns on him too. Anyway, just after the war began she finally gave him the bird – said it was all over between them. So he came to Spain to mend his broken heart here in the hell and shell holes of Avila.' He chuckled. 'What got me was his story of their parting scene. "Do they mean nothing to you," he asked her, "all those nights of love we spent together?" "Don't be stupid," she said. "Sleeping with you was just like sleeping with my brother."'

This officer, unhappily, was typical of the kind of dug-out cavalry-men – some of them from the days of the Morocco campaigns – whom the Nationalists would appoint to look after foreign journalists. Their attitude to journalists, like that of the high command, was a blend of suspicion and contempt: at best they were an unnecessary nuisance, at worst they were spies; in no event should they be allowed to see anything of interest. To be fair, there were a few intelligent and able civilians in the Ministry of Press and Propaganda, but they were constantly frustrated by their military masters. The latter believed, like good Spaniards, that their cause was so manifestly just that only criminals, communists, or lunatics could fail to support it; and so, with a war to fight, why should they bother with interfering newshounds? Let them be content with the official communiqués and handouts. Yet the Nationalists never ceased complaining about the bad press they received in Britain, France and America.

By contrast, the Republicans concentrated very seriously on promoting a favourable image abroad, and spent considerable sums of money and enormous effort on their propaganda. Their handling of foreign journalists was brilliant. With the resources of the Comintern behind them they had a wealth of skill and experience to draw on, and almost unlimited funds. When I returned to England on convalescent leave two years later I felt the full impact of their success.

I shared my lodgings that night with another Englishman, James Walford. A quiet, sardonic young man, by profession an artist, he had a Spanish mother and so spoke the language perfectly. He wanted to do some sketches of the war and was on his way to the front; he too would join the *Requetés* because, he told me, 'Three of my relatives have already been murdered in Madrid.'

Avila, *tierra de cantos y santos*, land of stones and saints, stands on a rise in the centre of a broad plain. Walking next morning along the battlements of the huge eleventh-century walls, we could see, far to the south, the high peaks of the Gredos mountains, as yet only lightly dusted with snow, which formed the barrier between

Old Castile and the Tagus valley. We left at about 9.30 in bright sunlight. The northern approach to the pass was bare rock, but the southern slopes were thick with pine and fir, and as we descended steeply the sun lit them in brilliant green, flashed on torrents and waterfalls, and glistened on patches of bare, wet rock. The gravel and dirt road dropped frighteningly in hairpin bends and blind corners flanked by sheer precipices, which our chauffeur took with sublime contempt. An experienced Spanish driver once explained to me that he made it a rule on this route to drive round corners on the wrong side, because all Spaniards did the same.

'Of course,' he added, 'if you were to meet a foreigner on the corner you would collide.'

We awoke next morning in Toledo, to a dismal day of cloud, rain and cold, but even the weather failed to dampen my spirits as we made our way through the narrow cobbled streets to *Requeté* headquarters. At last I was in the war zone. The road from Talavera along which we had driven the night before had been pocked with shell holes from September's fighting, the roadside littered with burnt-out cars and lorries; Toledo itself was full of soldiers, on leave from the front or on their way there. At *Requeté* headquarters we met a cousin of Walford's, an old friend of the Carlist commanders, and with his help we swept through the crowd of guards, secretaries and hangers-on who thronged their anteroom, and walked into their office.

Enlistment in the *Requetés* proved easy. I had brought with me my Certificates 'A' and 'B' from the Wellington and Cambridge Officers Training Corps, which in theory qualified me for a commission in the British Army in the event of war and they seemed to impress the military commander, Zamanillo.

'However,' he told me, 'I don't think we can accept you as an officer until you speak some Spanish.'

I assured him I should be happy to join in the ranks. Thereupon Walford and I each signed an application form, which Zamanillo endorsed, and we became soldiers in the Carlist militia. I elected to join a squadron of irregular cavalry which the *Requetés* were forming under a White Russian colonel and left a few days later for the village of Santa Olalla on the Talavera road, where it was based. Walford joined a new *Requeté* infantry *tercio*, the 'Alcazar', in the Casa del Campo on the outskirts of Madrid, where I heard he acquitted himself well in some fierce fighting there. I never saw him again; without him I don't know how I could have managed in those early days.

Returning to the small, run-down hotel which was the best Toledo could offer, we found among our fellow guests several British journalists and one or two Americans. They were thoroughly disgruntled at their treatment by the military, who obstinately declined to let them visit the Madrid front and paid no attention to their repeated protests. Among the British journalists was George Steer, whom I had already met in England, a truly adventurous man of great initiative and charm, but a natural rebel whose utter contempt for authority and the pomposity that too often went with it was bound to land him in trouble. His perversity, inflamed by understandable fury at Spanish plumbing, was soon to lead to his expulsion by the Nationalists.

It seems the military at last decided to listen to the journalists' pleas and arranged for them a conducted tour of the front, starting at 8.30 one morning from Toledo. All the journalists – British, American, French, Italian, German and even some Latin Americans – were assembled in the square outside the hotel, ready to leave on time. Only Steer was missing. After waiting more than half an hour in a jitter of impatience, the officers and newsmen were on the point of leaving without him when Steer appeared on the hotel steps, his expression grim, his face suffused with rage. He addressed the assembly, speaking slowly, loud and clear.

'You pull, you pull, and nothing happens. You pull again, and the shit slowly rises. There's Spain for you,' he roared, 'in a nutshell!'

The morning after our arrival Walford and I plodded up the hill through the rain to see the ruins of the Alcazar, once a fortress but later converted into a military academy for cadets. Its heroic defence in the first two months of the war by a small force of officers and cadets under Colonel Moscardó had aroused the admiration of the world. Now it was a vast pile of rubble exuding a foul stench of ordure and decay; the houses round the square in front of the ruins were pockmarked with bullet holes, their windows shattered.

Not far away stood the house said to be once occupied by El Greco. We were warned to approach it with care because the streets around were exposed to sniper fire from Republican positions a short distance away, across the Tagus, and there had been casualties. The house was closed to visitors but we dug out the custodian, a tiny, wizened creature who stood as high as my waist, and persuaded him to show us around. Inside we came upon an extraordinary sight: in every room, stacked against the walls like old lumber, were El Greco's wonderful paintings, which the Republicans had assembled and intended to send to Madrid for sale abroad, but had abandoned in their precipitous flight from Toledo.

We weren't issued with any uniforms and so we went shopping in the town for suitable clothing. I bought a scarlet *Requeté* beret, some poor quality khaki shirts and a shaggy *cazadora*, similar to a battledress blouse, on which I had sewn, over the left breast pocket, the Carlist emblem – a red St Andrew cross (the 'cross of Burgundy') surmounted by the Habsburg double eagle under the Spanish crown.*

Reporting to Zamanillo for my *salvoconducto* to travel to Santa Olalla, I found with him a squat, paunchy officer with a pasty complexion and a face like a frog. He wore on his beret the two gold fleurs-de-lys of a *Requeté* lieutenant-colonel and proved to be the White Russian colonel who was nominally in command of the cavalry squadron I was joining. I say 'nominally' because he only visited the squadron once while I was there, spending the rest of his time in the comparative comfort of Seville. When told I was British he shook his head sadly. It turned out he had never forgiven the British for their refusal, or failure, to rescue his Tsar from the Bolsheviks. A compatriot and friend of his who felt the same way once told me he was so disgusted by the British behaviour that since those days he had never drunk a drop of whisky.

Santa Olalla, never a very clean or tidy village, had suffered severe damage from the fighting in September; now it was a depressing picture of ruins and neglect. About a dozen private houses and two or three small taverns were all that remained more or less intact. In a small house which served as the squadron headquarters and officers' mess I reported to the acting commanding officer.

Captain Carlos Llancia, Marqués de Cocuhuella, was one of the tallest and most powerfully built men I ever met. He seemed to flicker with nervous energy. His thin moustache and cold, dark eyes gave a ruthless expression to his handsome face, but in his treatment of his men he showed much kindliness as well as occasional ferocity; to me he was invariably considerate and helpful. He greeted me warmly and in fair English, and introduced me to the squadron doctor, who had been talking with him when I arrived. The doctor was a fat little man of about forty, with a sallow complexion and an expression of deep gloom, which he never seemed to shed. He had been a prisoner of the Republican *milicianos* in Ronda, in Andalusia, until freed by the Nationalists when they took the town at the end of August, and he could still hardly believe he was alive; I never saw him smile and he hardly ever spoke; about his experiences in prison never.

The squadron was well below strength, Llancia explained to me – a bare hundred sabres at present, in three troops. But he was expecting reinforcements. We were on protection duties along this sector of the Talavera-Toledo road, a vital line of communication between the Nationalist rear bases and the troops assaulting Madrid.

* While serving in the Carlist ranks I received no pay, only my keep. Later as an ensign I drew a ration allowance to cover my mess bill and pay equivalent to just under £1 a week.

The road ran a few miles from the Tagus, on its northern bank, and the Republicans controlled all the country south of the river; they also had scattered forces in the mountains to the north. If they could mount a combined attack from both directions and cut the road, they might inflict a serious blow on the Nationalists, at a decisive period of the Madrid battle. The Nationalists had very few troops deployed to hold the road; apart from ourselves, there was only a small Army garrison in Talavera, a company of soldiers a few miles to the east of us and a company of Falange militia in Santa Olalla – Canary Islanders who had no discernible discipline, although they were a happy and friendly crowd, and sang beautifully to their guitars and mouth organs.

The squadron was required to mount pickets by night and send out patrols by day between these garrisons; to deal with enemy raiding parties, if any; to give warning of enemy movements and to act as a mobile reserve in the event of attack.

'It is hard work for so few men,' sighed Llancia. 'Especially when they are not even half-trained. But what can we do? All the troops are engaged around Madrid.'

There were two other officers, besides Llancia and the doctor, with the squadron: a tall, slim lieutenant with a sparse moustache, and a cheerful little cornet with a childlike smile and a high, squeaky voice. Both came from Seville. Llancia himself was Catalan.

'The troopers,' Llancia went on, 'are all *andaluces* and very simple peasants. They are very like children, though most are in their thirties – usually cheerful, but easily depressed. I'm afraid they are rather inefficient and very lazy. But they are all volunteers and so it is not easy to enforce discipline.' But a few evenings later I saw him use his bare fists and a riding crop in front of the assembled squadron, to beat up two of these volunteers convicted of drunkenness. He never had to repeat the lesson.

For the first few nights I shared sleeping quarters with the other troopers, in a barn with plenty of straw on the floor; it was warm inside and I was issued with a couple of blankets as well as an Army *capote* – basically a blanket with a hole for the head – to replace my teddybear overcoat when on duty. Once I had learned to arrange it, I found it surprisingly good protection from the wind and cold, and much easier for riding. Later Llancia kindly found me a small room in a house nearby, with a bedstead and mattress, to sleep in. But I continued to mess with the men. The food was usually a stew of *alubias*, white beans, which we collected in our messtins from a huge cauldron, and a mug of red wine for each of us. We went early to bed, but at first I took a while to get to sleep, partly from excitement at my new circumstances and partly from the series of explosions repeated through the night as my companions broke wind.

I was given a horse, a great powerful, black beast with a beautiful mouth, which at first I had difficulty in mounting in a hurry; I also received an old Mauser carbine and a sabre of very poor quality steel which would never withstand much of an impact – and luckily never had to. The squadron possessed no automatic weapons except an old Hotchkiss light machine gun; I believe, though I'm not sure, there were two men in the squadron who understood its mechanism.

For the first week I was not allowed out on patrol, but spent the time working at my Spanish with the invaluable help of my Hugo and studying – though hardly mastering – a Spanish cavalry training manual of Llancia's. I read Spanish newspapers and tried to converse with my companions – a difficult task because their broad *andaluz* patois was almost impossible to hear, let alone follow. But they were so determined to make me welcome that I soon felt at home. As for words of command, on parade or on patrol later, I quickly learned to follow the movements of the others.

Llancia was certain, and convinced us all, that the great assault on Madrid was about to start; then, he was assured, the squadron would have an important role as part of a mobile column. Meanwhile training, mounted and dismounted, filled most of our time that wasn't taken up in guard duties and patrols, and we certainly needed the training; in our present state we could only hope that if we met an enemy in battle he would be as unprepared and ill-equipped as ourselves. My most exacting duty was standing guard at night. Now that winter was setting in, even two hours of standing still on a freezing night in a piercing wind would leave me numb and downcast.

Sunday was a day of rest, apart from Mass at noon, which was a parade and which I attended with the others. The service was celebrated by the chaplain of the Falange company; we were on excellent terms with all these *falangistas*, who refused to treat seriously either politics or the war. The villagers also attended this Mass and I wondered why they had no priest of their own.

The villagers were very friendly and often invited us into their houses – the few that remained – for a glass of wine or a meal. They told me what had happened to their priest. In August, they said, *milicianos* from Madrid descended on Santa Olalla – all of them strangers. After shooting the more prominent villagers, they crucified the priest in front of the others.

'He was a good man,' they told me, 'but we could do nothing to save him from those armed bandits. In Alcabon, five kilometres from here, they burned the priest alive.'

Many if not most of these atrocities were the work of armed gangs from the cities, not of the local peasants.

Around the end of November I began to accompany my troop on mounted patrols, which I found much the most satisfying part of my work. Riding out in the clear, keen air of a December dawn I delighted in the glory of the sunrise flushing with rosy fingers the snowy peaks of the Gredos away to the north. Usually we patrolled southward across the brown fields and through the olive groves towards the valley of the Tagus. As the sun climbed, the rolling landscape unfolded in a clear brilliant pattern of tawny earth, silvery olives, sunlit hillocks and blue-shadowed ravines, dipping gently towards the river, beyond which rose the mountains of enemy territory. But the enemy might not stay there quietly and so we had to watch out all the time for an ambush. After spending most of the day in the saddle we would trot home to Santa Olalla in the dusk.

About three o'clock one morning in mid-December I awoke to the sound of shouting outside and gunfire in the distance: the enemy, I heard, had crossed the Tagus with a force of unknown strength and were attacking a guard post on the road to Talavera, while their artillery shelled the town. After a short fight they were retreating, and we were to try and cut them off from the river. We mounted in haste and, after hanging around for orders, we moved off at about seven, one troop to the north in case the enemy made for the Gredos, the other two, including mine, south towards the Tagus.

We split into sections and had patrolled for several hours without seeing anyone when one of our scouts galloped back in breathless excitement to report sighting the enemy. We rejoined the troop on a small hill, where my companions pointed out to me a mass of dark specks moving slowly across a wide ravine some distance away to the right. This *must* be our enemy! Drawing our sabres, we formed line abreast and cantered down our hill and up the opposite slope. As we came over the crest our sergeant shouted, 'Charge!' Putting spurs to our horses, we swept downhill in a cheering line, leaning forward with our sabres pointed. Carried away with mad exhilaration, I saw myself as one of Subotai's Tartar horsemen or Tamerlane's *bahadurs*. Whoever said there was no more use for cavalry in war? What with these wild dreams and my efforts to keep station, I never thought of taking a look at the enemy ahead. Nor, apparently, did anyone else. The next thing I knew, we were in the midst of a bleating, panic-stricken herd of goats in the charge of three terrified herdsmen. So ended my first and only cavalry charge.

Chapter 3

I T WAS BECOMING clear to us all that the expected assault
on Madrid was not going to happen, at least not for a long time.
Stiffened by the support of the International Brigades and the
arrival of arms, armour and aircraft from France and the Soviet
Union, the Republican resistance had hardened and frustrated every
Nationalist attempt to penetrate the city's defences. Madrid was still
the main Nationalist objective, but operations were bogged down
in trench warfare and street fighting, where cavalry would have no
part to play; if I wanted to see any fighting I must arrange a transfer
to the infantry.

Visiting Toledo one day on leave from the squadron, I dined with
a party of six British Conservative MPs, touring the battle areas
with their Spanish conducting officer. The latter, a former regular
cavalry officer who had fought in the Moroccan wars of the 1920s,
had been at school in England and spoke perfect English – though
his character and temperament were wholly Spanish. I asked him
about a transfer.

'I'll fix it for you,' he assured me. 'I'm taking these MPs to look
at the front tomorrow and I'll have a word with my friend Colonel
Rada. He commands the central sector *and* he's Inspector General
of the *Requetés* as well.'

He was as good as his word. I spent Christmas with the squadron,
enlivened by my promotion to sergeant. On Boxing Day I set off
for Colonel Rada's headquarters in the Madrid suburb of Getafe.

I spent that night in Toledo and arrived at Getafe next evening
in the middle of an artillery bombardment. Climbing down from
the back of the lorry I trudged with my suitcase along the deserted
main street, stumbling over the chunks of debris that littered the
road, until I reached Rada's headquarters in a villa on a side street;
a *Requeté* lieutenant who spoke some English introduced me to the
Colonel. Rada was a cheerful, tubby little man who spoke with a
strong *andaluz* accent, making it almost impossible for me to
understand a word. However, he explained through the lieutenant

that he was sending me to the suburbs of Carabanchel Bajo, where our positions were very close to the enemy.

'You should see some action there,' he assured me.

Next morning I found him talking to a tall, slim young Army officer, of gaunt appearance, whom he introduced as Lieutenant Urmaneta and who, luckily, spoke some English.

'We can go now to Carabanchel Bajo,' Urmaneta said to me, 'and I will present you to our commanding officer, Major López Ibañez.'

I thanked Colonel Rada for his help. He smiled. 'Go with God.'

The lorry stopped suddenly and I banged my head on the windscreen. Urmaneta, beside me in the driver's cabin, grinned as we climbed down on to the street in a steady drizzle of chilly rain. Ahead of us the road ended in a high barricade of sandbags with a sentry crouched behind it. It was a gloomy scene: bare, crumbling, red-brick houses and a street torn with shell holes and littered with rubble. The only sounds were the occasional smack of a bullet on masonry and the faint rumble of gunfire in the north.

To the right of the barricade stood a small wooden hut reinforced with sandbags; inside, the smell of gun oil blended with the reek of cheap cigarettes, wet clothes and unwashed men. Three soldiers sprawled around a pre-1914 Hotchkiss machine gun whose barrel pointed through a hole in the parapet of thick wood beams and sandbags. Through the hole I saw a patch of open grassland and beyond it, several hundred metres away, more houses and another barricade which concealed the enemy.

'It seems quiet, yes?' said Urmaneta. 'But don't show your head, or you'll lose it. Men get careless, and' – we all ducked as there came a brief, high-pitched whirr followed at once by an explosion and the sound of spattering fragments.

'Mortar bomb,' he explained. 'We have them all the time and you can't hear them coming. Let's go for lunch.'

Picking our way through the debris of ruined houses and along narrow, winding trenches, we came to the dugout where Urmaneta had his platoon headquarters; we passed several strong-points, each with an old heavy machine gun or a light Hotchkiss, where a sentry crouched on duty and other soldiers were eating, smoking or sleeping near him. The posts were strengthened by sandbags shored with stout wooden beams, and roofed with iron bedsteads and pieces of furniture against mortar bombs. In other places the defences were sometimes shallow trenches, where we had almost to crawl, or rough barricades constructed of sandbags, bedsteads, mattresses, bits of furniture and, in one place, an old violin; or, more often, the walls of houses with the windows bricked up or blocked with sandbags, leaving only a loophole for a rifle.

By this time, Urmaneta explained over lunch, the assault on Madrid had developed into a siege – it was to last for more than two years. The Nationalists had taken up positions in the University City, the Casa del Campo, and the suburbs of Carabanchel and Usera, scenes of bloody and wasteful fighting over the next few months as each side tried to gain a little ground.

Our platoon formed part of the 8th Battalion of the 27th Infantry Regiment of Argel (Algeria), which was holding most of Carabanchel Bajo. Urmaneta's sector wound among the houses and streets in a bewildering series of salients and re-entrants which I could never master; in some places our positions were six hundred metres from the enemy, in others a mere ten. On fine days, the houses, domes and spires of Madrid were clearly visible, gleaming wetly through the mist. Conspicuous among them stood the tall Telefonica building, where the Republicans had an observation post for their artillery.

The men of our platoon were nearly all conscripts, or *pipis* in Army slang, with a leavening of regular NCOs, and most of them came from the western province of Estremadura, where the battalion had its depot; they were good soldiers, cheerful, willing and cool in danger, and they showed little of the strain of prolonged street fighting. Their high morale was largely due to Urmaneta himself, whom they seemed to look on almost as a father; although he was about the same age as they – and me – he had a maturity and sense of responsibility far beyond his years. In moments of danger he was quite imperturbable and always in control of the situation, and his air of confidence infected them all.

In the afternoon he introduced me to the CO, Major López Ibañez. On the way to battalion HQ we had to pass through a coppice which Urmaneta warned me was dangerously exposed to enemy fire. Crouching behind a wall, he whispered, 'This is where we must run. Keep well down and don't stop running till we reach that wall on the other side.' We had gone only a few yards when bullets started to fly around us, hissing through the branches above and slapping against the trees close by. The Major, a dark, thick-set man with a short moustache, radiated self-confidence and gruff good humour.

'Where would you like to go?' he bayed at me. 'We have all sorts of positions here. You can go to a quiet place, or' – he indicated Urmaneta – 'you can stay with this officer.' From preference at least as much as politeness I chose the last and was pleased to note that Urmaneta himself looked happy.

On New Year's Eve a runner arrived with orders for Urmaneta to report to company headquarters. When he returned he looked grave.

'We must move tonight to a very bad position, right in the middle of the enemy. Are you sure you want to come?'

It was near midnight when, after handing over to the relieving platoon, we left our position, formed up in the street and moved off quickly on foot. I remember well even now the silent darkness and the bitter cold of that journey, the stars twinkling frostily above, the whispered orders passed down the column, the muffled clink of weapons, the occasional clatter and muttered curses as someone kicked a fallen tile, and at intervals the brief flash of Urmaneta's torch ahead. Not exactly the kind of New Year's Eve my friends would be celebrating at home.

In the darkness it was impossible for me to keep any sense of direction; it was difficult enough just to follow the man in front. There was a faint grey light in the sky when Urmaneta halted us and went ahead to see the company commander. When he returned half an hour later he told me, 'Stay here with platoon headquarters while I settle the men into their new positions.' They shuffled off into the gloom.

It was daylight when he came back.

'Let's go. Keep close to me. When you see me duck do the same and run like hell when I tell you; some places are dangerous to cross in daylight. Above all, when we reach our position don't speak, except in whispers. The enemy are *very* near.'

I kept behind him, followed by his batman and his two runners. We were fired on twice – I didn't stop to find out from where – but we reached the first house of our new position without loss. It was a small, one-storey building with a patio that opened off the street and we were holding it with one of the two sections of our platoon.* We stopped for a rest, while Urmaneta talked to the sergeant in command.

Between this and the other house in our position ran a wide,

---

* A Spanish infantry platoon contains two half-platoons, each of twenty to twenty-five men under a sergeant. But the Spanish term for a platoon is, confusingly, *sección*, while a half-platoon is *pelotón*. A *pelotón* contains three *escuadras*, squads, each under a corporal.

straight street, both ends of which were held by the enemy. We had
to cross it by a narrow tunnel on the surface, formed by a double
line of loopholed sandbags, and roofed with more sandbags and
heavy planks. Two light machine guns defended it, one pointing in
each direction of the street; it was just high enough for a man to
edge past the defenders, though with difficulty.

Crawling through it we came to the main position and the remaining section of our platoon which occupied it. It had two storeys and
a patio. A gallery, approached from the patio by an open staircase,
encircled the upper storey; its windows were barricaded and loopholed. Downstairs Urmaneta established his office and sleeping
quarters in two adjacent rooms leading from the patio; the one
where we ate as well as slept was a bare room about thirteen foot
square, lit by one smelly carbide lamp. The furniture consisted of
a deal table and a few chairs, with six mattresses scattered round
the floor, on which slept Urmaneta, his servant, his two runners
and batman, and myself. A *pelotón* of Moors – *Regulares* – occupied
two rooms of a ruined house next to us; they were not involved in
the defence of our position but were there for sniping, reconnaissance and an occasional swift raid. They were giggly little men who
soon became good friends and would bring us cups of their sweet
mint tea. Some of them, I noticed, were of fairer complexion than
my own and one had red hair.

Our only line of communication with company HQ was by the
tunnel, through which had to come all our food, water, ammunition
and other supplies, and through which, also, we must evacuate our
wounded. The last was a difficult and often tragic operation. It
could only take place at night and so a badly wounded man might,
and sometimes did, die before he could get proper attention; we
had no doctor, not even a trained medic. Our food, mostly mule
steak or dried codfish, was cooked at company HQ, and so reached
us cold and unappetising as well as tough; however, hunger soon
took care of our appetites. Water was so scarce that washing, or
even cleaning our teeth, was out of the question. Within a very few
days we were all infested with lice.

The Republicans held houses encircling us on three sides, at
distances of between ten and thirty metres. They had long ago
targeted our position, and harassed us with mortar bombs and hand
grenades by day and night; any conversation above a whisper would
bring a shower of bombs around us, uncomfortably close. Moreover,
the enemy appeared to have pinpointed our latrine in an exposed
and shattered room in one corner of the patio, which we visited as
seldom and as briefly as we could.

The Spanish temperament seems to find hardship and danger

something of a stimulant; throughout the next two weeks we all remained surprisingly cheerful. We would take real pleasure in the smallest comforts – the arrival of an unexpected bottle of brandy or a box of cigarettes would raise our spirits out of all proportion.

But we suffered a daily drain of casualties. Mortar bombs and grenades couldn't penetrate the roofs and ceilings, strengthened as they were with wood and sandbags, but they were devastating to anyone crossing the patio, as we all had to do from time to time. Too often we would hear an explosion outside, followed after a moment's silence by a pathetic sound of scuffling and childlike whimpers. We would run out to pick up a torn, bleeding figure, which we would carry as gently as possible into the office and on to a mattress. He would lie there until nightfall in pain – we had no anaesthetics – if he didn't die before. Even our dead had to leave by the tunnel, for we had nowhere to bury them.

Sniping also cost us serious casualties; I think the Republicans had machine guns trained on our more vulnerable points. Our men, too, were keen snipers and would sometimes expose themselves to enemy fire, with fatal consequences. At first Urmaneta didn't discourage their sniping, believing it maintained morale. But early one morning they carried into the office our senior corporal, with a ragged red hole in his forehead and a small white dribble of brain oozing from the back of his head. He had been a cheerful, blond young man, a fine soldier and very popular with everyone. Although he was obviously unconscious, he seemed to be trying to speak; but all we could hear was a continuous, low-pitched, snuffling moan. Urmaneta bent over him, reciting the prayers for absolution and holding his own gold crucifix to the foam-flecked lips. As he straightened up I heard one of the soldiers murmur, 'Mateo was always too confident, he wouldn't keep under cover.'

I often wondered why we tried to hold such a precarious position, seeing that it cost us so much more than its worth. I still don't know the answer, but throughout the war both sides would defend with grim tenacity and at great cost some of the most dangerous and useless positions.

The previous two months' fighting had convinced both sides of the folly of attacking fortified streets and houses by day; but we had to repel frequent night assaults. At about 8.30 on the night of 2 January Urmaneta and his sergeant were sitting with me at our table after giving me a Spanish lesson in whispers; outside, all was quiet. Suddenly there was a burst of fire from one of our machine guns upstairs, followed by a series of explosions above and round us. In a moment the whole house was shaking with the blast of mortars and grenades; the night split into a cacophonous chattering of machine guns and rifle fire. I snatched up my rifle, and followed Urmaneta and the sergeant through the door. In the few hideous moments of danger as we raced across the patio and up the stairway to the gallery I saw the darkness lit all around with flashes. Taking my post at a loophole, I became aware also of a sound like hail as bullets smashed into the walls in front of me.

At first I could make out no target in the darkness and confined myself to aiming at the enemy rifle flashes; below, our men were lobbing grenades and soon I could see, in the light of the explosions, shadowy figures on the ground beneath and on neighbouring roof-tops and balconies – brief glimpses hardly enough for a snapshot. I continued to blaze away until it struck me that we must all be wasting a lot of ammunition. Urmaneta evidently thought the same, for he shouted from behind me, 'Don't shoot unless you can see your targets! That goes for grenades too. We must conserve our ammunition.' I had lobbed a few grenades, more for practice and to give myself the feeling I was actually doing something than for any likely effect; but for every grenade we threw, the enemy threw back a dozen at us. Luckily the standard grenade used by both sides was the old percussion Lafite, a metal cylinder like a modern beercan, filled with explosive; once the pin had been withdrawn, a weighted safety-tape would unwind in the course of flight and activate the grenade, which would thus explode on the slightest impact. But the casing was so thin that there was very little danger from its fragments and the blast effect was limited to a few feet. This wasn't the last occasion in the Civil War when I was thankful that the lethal Mills grenade of the First World War wasn't in use – or at least never came my way.

The battle – or the firing – went on for two hours, then died as quickly as it had begun. We tended our casualties – only four wounded, one of them seriously – posted guards and went to bed.

It's unlikely the enemy suffered more casualties than we did. But had they pressed their attack and forced an entry I don't see how we could have survived, for they outnumbered us heavily. Almost every other night that followed we had these alarms. Sometimes they were genuine attacks, like this one; more often I think they began with a jittery sentry or machinegunner, on one side or the other, loosing off at a shadow and starting a general alarm. It was a great waste of ammunition, but men whose nerves are raw from constant danger and lack of sleep tend to see shadows.

One morning in the second week of January Urmaneta came into the office after talking with his sergeant. Whispering at us to keep very still, he put his ear to the floor and stayed there for a full minute, listening; then he motioned to the NCO to join him.

Getting up, he scribbled a note for a runner to take to the company commander.

'What's wrong, Miguel?' I asked him, for he looked very worried.

'I'm afraid the enemy are mining below us. I heard their picks just now. I fear they will soon be right underneath this house.'

A new kind of warfare was beginning round Madrid. The Republicans were using skilled miners from Asturias and Pozoblanco to run mines under the Nationalist positions in Carabanchel and the University City, and they proved very good at it. In this way the Republicans inflicted serious losses on the Nationalists, even forcing them to abandon some positions, at very little cost to themselves. Although the Nationalists employed experienced engineers from Italy and Germany to stop the mining, they could do little more than limit its effect. The Nationalists, in their turn, began to use flamethrowers to blast the Republicans out of their positions. Their effect at close quarters, witnesses have told me, was devastating.

Happily we had to endure only a few more days of this unnerving tension. On the afternoon of 13 January we received orders to move out and soon after dusk we handed over to our relief, a platoon from another regiment – for whom I felt heartily sorry. With good reason, as it turned out, because two weeks later this position at Carabanchel was blown up by a mine; an entire company perished.

Chapter 4

W E SPENT THAT night and most of the next morning
sleeping in comparative comfort in the barracks at Getafe. In
the afternoon I received orders to report to Colonel Rada, who
greeted me very warmly and told me to put on my beret the silver
fleur-de-lys of a *Requeté* second lieutenant, or *alférez*.

But two days later, on 16 January, I had a telegram from an aunt:
'Your father sinking fast. Come at once.'

I was stunned. Just before Christmas I had received a letter from
my mother saying that my father was ill in bed; but only a week
ago another letter had told me he was much better. He had always
taken the greatest pride in his physical fitness and I could scarcely
believe his condition had deteriorated so dramatically in such a short
time. Urmaneta and Major López Ibañez were sympathetic when I
asked for compassionate leave; but permission must come from
Colonel Rada and so Urmaneta took me at once to see him. The
Colonel doubted if even he had authority to let me leave the country.
However, when I gave him my word to return to his command as
soon as possible, he gave me a *salvoconducto* as far as the French
frontier. Within hours of reading that telegram I was sitting in the
back of an open lorry bound for Toledo.

Today, of course, I could have reached home in a few hours. But
there was no available air travel then and road travel was painfully
slow in Spain. From Talavera I hitched a lift in a very old small car
with three men who warned me we might not make it to Avila over
the six-thousand-foot, snow-covered Gredos mountains; we broke
down twice on the famous Puerto del Pico pass but eventually
reached Avila at about 9 pm. There I caught a train, and after a
freezing and uncomfortable journey reached San Sebastian the next
afternoon; I found a friend there who not only changed my money
for me, but drove me to the frontier at Irun. I had some anxious
moments passing through the French controls because I had had
no time to find civilian clothes in my hurried journey from Getafe,
and was still wearing my *Requeté* uniform, hidden only by my

teddybear overcoat and a scarf. But nobody searched me, and I caught the midnight train to Paris and arrived home the following afternoon – just twenty-four hours after my father's funeral.

I remained only two weeks in England. It was hard to explain to my mother that, having given my word to Colonel Rada, I must go back to Spain so soon. As usual, she never complained, at least not to me, and tried to hide the distress she must have felt – for she would be very much alone since my brother, who had been given only twenty-four hours' leave for the funeral, had already rejoined his ship.

Two days before I left, the local police superintendent telephoned. He had heard of my activities in Spain and although he didn't try to stop me, he warned me that I might be liable to prosecution under the Foreign Enlistment Act; I answered that I didn't think the Act applied to civil wars, and that soldiers of the International Brigades were having no trouble and so I would risk it. He wished me luck.

My problems began when I tried to get back into Spain and rejoin Colonel Rada. In Biarritz friends warned me that in view of the stricter application of non-intervention provisions I would need a visa from the British vice-consul at Bayonne to pass the French frontier control. The vice-consul proved to be an ill-tempered, ill-mannered Swede who jerked his white beard aggressively at me as he accused me of being a volunteer for the Nationalists (which of course I was); I'm sure that if he had thought I was fighting for the other side he would have been all smiles. Only partially satisfied by Collin Brooks's letter, he reluctantly gave me a visa. Still wearing my *Requeté* uniform, concealed beneath my overcoat and scarf, I crossed the frontier in one of the courier cars and reached Salamanca, now Franco's headquarters, late at night on 7 February 1937.

The following day the Nationalists occupied Malaga. In this offensive, for the first time in the war, Italian troops took part – a political gesture by Franco to Mussolini which didn't increase the Italians' popularity among the Spaniards, who had also fought hard there and received no recognition for it. To rub salt into the wound, the Italians had their visiting cards inscribed with the legend *'Vincitore di Malaga'* under their names.

Nevertheless this victory caused great rejoicing throughout Nationalist Spain. Malaga had been a centre of extreme-left Republicanism, as well as the scene of its worst excesses – notably the dreaded 'Dawn Brigade', directed by the infamous García Atadell, whose members used to drag suspects from their houses in the small hours to shoot them; the Nationalists captured García Atadell in Malaga and executed him. Another of their prisoners was the journalist Arthur Koestler, at that time an agent of the Comintern, although he didn't reveal it until after he had published *Spanish Testament.**

From Salamanca I took a bus to Avila, where I had to get another *salvoconducto* to take me to the Madrid front and Colonel Rada. I found on duty in the *comandancia militar* a sour and fussy old major, obviously a dugout from some distant Moroccan war, who looked with disfavour on me and my original *salvoconducto* from Colonel Rada. It was well known, he told me, that all Englishmen were Reds and I couldn't possibly be a *Requeté*. I was most probably a spy and I wasn't going to fool him into giving me a pass, even if I had fooled Colonel Rada.

'If you present yourself again in this office,' he shouted through ill-fitting false teeth, 'I will put you under arrest. Do me the favour of removing yourself.'

Swallowing my indignation, I tried my luck again at General Mola's headquarters in the town. Within twenty minutes I had my *salvoconducto* and a place reserved for me in the official postal car leaving next morning.

In Talavera I lunched with Pablo Merry del Val, a very senior official of the Ministry of Press and Propaganda and the younger son of a distinguished ambassador to Germany. A most intelligent man who had been educated at Stoneyhurst, he still retained the athletic appearance and austere manner of a sixth-form prefect. His help and influence were to prove invaluable to me. But in his presence I always had an uncomfortable feeling I was a delinquent from the lower fourth, and was about to be told to bend over and take six of the best.

I had some difficulty in finding Colonel Rada, who had moved from Getafe, but after forty-eight hours of hitch-hiking around the outer suburbs of Madrid I arrived at last, on 9 February, in the back of a lorry, at his new headquarters at La Marañosa, a tiny hamlet of a few battle-scarred houses about twelve miles south-east of Madrid, close to the confluence of the rivers Manzanares and Jarama.

Three days earlier the battle of Jarama had begun, with a Nationalist offensive under General Varela. Its objective was to cut the Madrid-Valencia road and capture the town of Arganda on the

* Brian Crozier quotes from Koestler's autobiography in his foreword to *Franco: a Biographical History* (Eyre and Spottiswoode, 1967).

road; if successful it would cut the last direct supply route connecting the defenders of Madrid with their bases in La Mancha and on the Mediterranean. That it was not successful was very largely due to the courage and tenacity of British elements in the International Brigades; I am told it was there they suffered their worst casualties of the war – including several I had known either at Cambridge or in London. Colonel Rada, who was commanding one of Varela's formations, had launched his attack from Pinto, near Getafe, on the first day.

The country over which the battle – or rather, series of battles – took place was an undulating plain covered with scrub, which sloped gradually eastwards to the valley of the Jarama. The most important tactical features were the heights of La Marañosa, above the village, overlooking the Manzanares some six hundred feet below them, and a spur dominating the valley where the Manzanares joined the Jarama, known as the Espolon de Vaciamadrid. Olive groves and farmland covered the Jarama valley on both sides of the river; olive groves also covered the hills on its eastern side.

By the time I reached La Marañosa the Nationalists had overrun the country to the west of the Jarama, and occupied the hills above La Marañosa and the Espolon de Vaciamadrid; from the latter their guns could shell the Madrid-Valencia road. The following day they forced the Jarama crossing and occupied the hills on the eastern side to a distance of four kilometres beyond the river, where they were held by the determined resistance of the International Brigades. There followed two weeks of heavy fighting, in which the Nationalists beat off Republican counter-attacks but were unable to make further progress towards Arganda and the Valencia road. By 24 February the battle was over. Although the Nationalists had failed to secure their main objective, Arganda, their artillery could now deny the use of the road, at least by day, to the Republicans; henceforward the only safe route between Valencia and Madrid was by the Aragon road and across country. During the battle I was for most of the time a mere spectator, but I was able to observe its progress from the Espolon de Vaciamadrid and, later, from the Jarama valley.

The morning of my arrival at La Marañosa was bright and crisp. I found Rada at his headquarters in a small house with a garden and a low wall, standing in the lee of the hills north of the road on top of which were located our defences. He seemed surprised to see me back. He couldn't return me to my old infantry battalion, he told me, because it was no longer under his command, but he would send me to a newly raised unit of *Requetés*, the Tercio del Alcazar, which would arrive the next day at La Marañosa. Meanwhile, I could stay the night at his headquarters.

While we were talking there was a small air raid, which Rada took us outside to watch. Six enemy Ratas – Russian fighters – were machinegunning the positions above us; they also dropped a few small bombs, but not very near to our house. Later on, at dinner, an enemy battery opened fire, trying to hit Rada's headquarters; the shells landed quite close, damaging one or two buildings in the village and causing some casualties. A feeling of tension among my companions indicated something important was to happen on the morrow – the evening of the Jarama, it turned out. As darkness was falling a *bandera* of the Foreign Legion formed up outside; lean, dark and grim, with tremendous pride in their bearing, they were singing the two great Legion songs, '*El Himno del Legionario*', 'The Hymn of the Legionnaire', and '*El Novio de la Muerte*', 'The Sweetheart of Death'. These were stirring tunes, which I was to know by heart within the year, and they moved us all now as we heard them sung by men who were about to die. Within hours many were indeed dead. They attacked at dawn, five or six hundred strong, to force the Jarama crossing; by evening there were barely two hundred left.

I reported next morning to the CO of the new *Requeté tercio* in his office opposite Rada's headquarters. Major Emilio Alamán was a fine soldier, a regular Army officer who had distinguished himself, and been severely wounded, in the siege of the Alcazar at Toledo; tall and rather stout, with a loud voice, he was by nature a jovial and good-hearted person, but obviously still suffered from the strain of that terrible siege and so was liable to sudden and terrifying outbursts of temper. He spoke no English and I found his Spanish especially hard to follow because a wound in the mouth had impaired his speech. His *tercio* had already seen action in the Casa del Campo, where he had shown himself to be a courageous and skilful commander.

He seemed none too pleased to have a strange Englishman thrust upon him, but he received me courteously and told me to remain at his headquarters for the time being. His adjutant allotted me a batman and a mattress to sleep on in the corner of a first-floor room in an adjoining house. I shared the room with five other officers, among them a middle-aged French ensign, a tubby, jolly and voluble fellow with a connoisseur's passion for food; he used to spend a good deal of time in the kitchen, before and after meals, giving detailed instructions and general hell to the cooks.

Another who shared our bedroom was a little mongrel dog, who spent the day in the kitchen and at night used to sleep on one of our beds; we were all fond of him, but he would have been more welcome if he didn't usually make a mess on the bed he chose. We were very short of water, which had to come to us from Pinto in lorries, and so we had barely enough to drink and none to spare for washing. Although there was plenty of wine, it was almost undrinkable.

For the first two days we were shelled intermittently from across the Manzanares and for much longer there were air raids in the early hours of the morning. They didn't disturb our sleep very much, but on one occasion I was woken in the middle of a raid by furious shouts from the French *alférez: 'Merde! Merde! C'est le chien qui chie!'* The little dog had chosen his bed that night. The Ratas never came by day, because by now the Nationalists were beginning to win command of the air, hitherto held by the Republicans. Their success was largely the work of the fighter ace, García Morato; commanding a squadron of Fiat CR42 biplanes, he trained his pilots to a pitch of excellence for which the enemy were no match. In dogfights over the Jarama they chased the Republicans from the sky.*

Soon after my arrival a young German officer joined us, Lieutenant von Gaza, a fresh-complexioned young man with reddish hair, freckles, blue eyes and a smart, plainly military bearing. There was a mystery about him because, while he claimed to be a machine-gun lieutenant in the Reichswehr and wore German Army uniform, we couldn't understand why he had come to us by himself. He spoke no Spanish, but soon learned it, and he spoke fluent English in a clipped, precise manner; he was polite but formal and he seldom smiled. He came from East Prussia, he told me, of a Junker family, and he was an orphan; the Bolsheviks had murdered both his parents in Riga after the First World War. He would have nothing to do with the two German *Requetés* in our unit, which gave them great offence.

He transferred quite soon from us to the Foreign Legion, where he served under Captain Cancela, who later became my own company commander and who told me more about him. He was, as he claimed, an officer of the Wehrmacht, but had committed some misdemeanour which incurred the displeasure of his superiors, and so was given the choice of a court martial or service in Spain – but with the condition that he must not serve in any German military unit there. Cancela told me von Gaza was a true professional soldier and the best officer he ever had. He was killed, along with three other officers of his *bandera*, when a shell struck the bungalow where they were playing cards.

* Among García Morato's pilots was a young man, Pepito Larios, educated in England, who wrote in English his personal account of life in that squadron.

Another German was an Associated Press photographer, Franz Roth, who had taken over a house in La Marañosa; he had already reported one war, the Italian attack on Ethiopia, from Addis Ababa. We used to climb one of the hills above the Jarama to watch the fighting beyond; we could see through our binoculars the white puffs of bursting shrapnel above the olive groves and the black smoke of shells exploding among the trees, while the sound of incessant machine-gun fire came to us faintly across the valley.

One day he asked me to go with him down to the Jarama. There was a report that a French company of the International Brigades, crossing a bridge over the river, had been almost annihilated by a *tabor* of *Regulares* and that the Moors had castrated the victims. I agreed to go, because there had been a flood of stories about Moorish atrocities and I felt I should check this one for myself; I couldn't imagine the Spanish officers of *Regulares* ever permitting such behaviour. Anyway I wanted a closer look at the Jarama. In the early afternoon we walked down into the *vega*, the cultivated plain, of the Jarama. By a ruined farmhouse we saw a German anti-tank gun with its crew and their officer; we tried to approach and Roth called in German to the officer, but he shook his head and wouldn't let us come nearer.*

The bright sunshine lit up the golden fields and the olive trees; it shone, too, on the huddled corpses of the Frenchmen heaped around the bridge where the Moorish machine guns had caught them in a crossfire. Most had been stripped of their uniforms and boots, and lay in their underclothes in grotesque attitudes, stinking and shrivelled by two days exposure to a hot sun. With a ghoulish intensity Roth probed the bodies, urging me to do the same. We found no trace of mutilation and Roth seemed disappointed. After ten minutes of this grisly activity I was horribly sick and told Roth I couldn't go on; I was shaking all over and my legs would scarcely carry me back to La Marañosa, where it required half a bottle of Roth's brandy to pull me together. If this is what I must do to prove myself a man, I thought, I'll stay a mouse. Roth appeared quite unmoved.

Having nothing to do at Major Alamán's headquarters except get in his way, von Gaza and I were delighted when he sent us, on 15 February, to one of the positions on the heights of La Marañosa. Taking a rifle and pack each, we climbed for twenty minutes, past Rada's headquarters, to our position on the top of a ridge, overlooking the Manzanares plain, on our extreme right flank. Below

---

* This was the first and last time I saw Germans manning anti-tank guns; soon afterwards they handed them over to Spaniards they had trained.

us, less than a mile away, was a broad belt of olive trees that stretched away to our left; to our front lay a deserted village with a track connecting it to the groves. Beyond this village flowed the Manzanares; the country between the river and the trenches was no-man's-land. Von Gaza, brought up on the lessons of the First World War, was amazed that we never sent out patrols at night to reconnoitre it. We offered to go ourselves but were told it was unnecessary. Perhaps if the Nationalists had done a little night patrolling, they might not have lost Brunete and Teruel so easily later on that year. Both towns fell to the Republicans without loss, in surprise night attacks mounted by one of the ablest of the Republican officers, Colonel Enrique Lister, who, almost alone among Spanish commanders on either side, specialised in night operations. In both those actions the Nationalist garrisons were overwhelmed almost before they had woken up and on both occasions the garrison commanders were taken in their beds.*

Lister, born into a peasant family in Galicia, was a military genius who commanded the most formidable Spanish division in the Republican Army and went on to command a Red Army division at Stalingrad. He hated the executions of Nationalists which were forced on him by the Republican political leaders and quarrelled bitterly with Stalin later on over the purges. He was very lucky to survive. He still calls himself a communist, although he is not on speaking terms with Santiago Carillo, the leader of the Spanish Communist Party.

Our defences in this position consisted of rough earthworks with shallow – much too shallow – trenches and parapets of earth and stones, bolstered with a few sandbags; sited on the crest of the ridge, they would have been a death trap for the defenders in the face of any heavy concentration of artillery. We also had a Hotchkiss machine gun and a light automatic, like a Lewis gun. Down below the crest, about a hundred yards to the rear, stood a small, empty house in a little grove of trees; this was platoon headquarters where we slept.

On the morning of 17 February we awoke at dawn to the sound of heavy firing away on our left. Running to our trenches, we took up firing positions, but at first we could see nothing, for the valley below was still hidden in mist. Soon, however, the rising sun began to disperse the haze, and we made out groups of little dark figures moving towards us across the fields and along the track from the

* I had this information from Lister himself, in a two-hour talk with him in June 1986 – he said he was always happy to talk with anyone who had actually fought in the war, no matter on which side.

village. We let them reach the olive grove undisturbed by our fire at such long range. Surely, I thought, they don't intend to attack now, across those open fields in front, without any artillery cover? Even if they do outnumber us heavily, it will be sheer suicide.

But a moment later we saw them leave the trees and advance towards us at a trot. Now they were within easy range, but we waited until they were well out in the open, away from any cover; then, at a sharp order from our platoon commander, our machine guns opened fire, joined by our rifles. The trotting little figures halted and toppled to the ground in heaps. A machine gun in the olive grove started to reply but its bullets were flying high over our heads; some of the enemy lying in the open tried to cover their comrades' advance with light automatic weapons, but with no cover in those open fields they stood no chance in the face of our fire and soon they were bolting back to the shelter of the olive trees, leaving their fallen companions strewn among the stubble; many more fell as they ran.

It is sheer bloody murder, I muttered to myself. What criminally incompetent and callous staff officer could be sending them into battle like this, against a strong natural position, well defended? Well-trained, experienced troops might perhaps have found some dead ground for concealment, but it seemed unlikely; no experienced commander should have ordered them to do it, except in the direst emergency. Maybe they had counted on surprise, but if so they had planned it badly.

Judging by the renewed sounds of firing I imagined the enemy was now pressing their attack on both our flanks and I was disturbed that we seemed to have no artillery to support us. The enemy certainly had. There was a whistle as a shell passed overhead, followed by several more, each landing a little closer. Our earthworks were flimsy and our shallow trenches gave us small protection even from field guns. It was obvious they were aiming at the house with our platoon headquarters and so our platoon commander ordered it to be evacuated – none too soon, for a salvo of shells hit it immediately afterwards, reducing it to rubble. Thereupon they concentrated on our position and shells started falling unpleasantly close, causing a few casualties.

Now the enemy infantry were advancing again, picking their way among the bodies that had fallen in their previous attempt. Once again we opened fire and again the attackers were thrown back, leaving more of their comrades on the ground. A third time they advanced, fewer of them now and flagging in their pace.

'Hold your fire!' called our platoon commander. 'Let them get closer this time. And stay under cover yourselves!'

They came on in bounds, one group giving covering fire while another advanced. When the nearest were within four hundred yards and well out in the open we had the order, 'Fire!'

It *was* murder. The poor creatures fell in heaps. The survivors turned and ran for cover, dropping their weapons in their mad haste. When the last few had vanished into the olive groves the entire plain in front of us was littered with bodies. Von Gaza told me later that he saw two officers shot by their own men while trying to stem the rout. We ourselves had suffered a mere half dozen casualties.

For a while there was no sign of movement in front of us and silence fell over the battlefield. It was broken by the sound of heavy engines and there emerged from our right front six Russian tanks, each with a 37-millimetre gun in its turret. In line ahead they crossed in front of the olive groves, turned towards us and lumbered forward in line abreast. They looked like trouble and certainly would have been if any infantry had followed them; but there was no fight left in their infantry. If the tanks had supported the earlier attacks the result might have been very different; but even now we were expecting a rough time. At that moment our own artillery, hitherto silent, opened fire. It soon found the range, and we watched the black smoke puffs exploding all round the tanks and very close. The tanks seemed to waver, then came to a halt. Seconds later one of them was enveloped in black smoke as a shell struck it and it began to burn. Another tank took a direct hit at the base of its turret. The remaining four turned round, spread out and made for their own positions.

We had no idea how things had been going in the centre and on the left of our line; but at noon, when fighting had died down, a runner arrived from battalion headquarters with news that the two companies on our left flank had suffered heavy casualties and needed reinforcements; our platoon commander was asked to send there any men he could spare. Von Gaza and I were among them. At battalion headquarters we met a young Catalan, Felipe Palleją, who spoke good English – I had already met his very pretty sister in San Sebastian.

'Our positions in the centre and on our left have been under heavy fire all morning from artillery and mortars,' he told us. 'Comandante Alamán is up there now and I will take you to him.'

Everything seemed quiet when we arrived there; the enemy was obviously respecting the hour of the siesta. Alamán was in excellent spirits; but he expected the attacks to be renewed later that afternoon and next day. Most of our heavy machine guns were in the centre and so he sent von Gaza there, to make use of his special knowledge. For the moment I was to stay with Alamán.

During the afternoon we suffered intermittent shelling, but there was no new attack. It looked as if the enemy were regrouping for another assault the next day. They had already taken up positions in the olive groves. I visited our centre and left flank positions with Alamán; they followed the crests of the heights, the centre facing north over the Manzanares and the left curving away and facing more to the north-west, towards Madrid. The Major expected the main attack on the left, to turn our flank and cut the road to Pinto. Pallejá and I would move up there at dusk.

When we arrived the defences turned out to be in a better state than I had expected; the enemy artillery must have been of a light calibre. Where the parapets had collapsed, men were at work repairing the damage with earth and sandbags. It struck me that the trenches were very poorly constructed – not only too shallow to give decent protection but dug almost in a straight line instead of traversed. Indeed, throughout the Civil War it was my experience that Spanish troops – even the Foreign Legion – were most reluctant to dig proper trenches. 'We won't win this war by hiding ourselves in trenches,' I was told, 'but with our *cojones*.'

We returned to battalion headquarters to snatch a meal. I found the tubby French lieutenant there; he had found time during the lull to slip away from his post and give more hell to the cooks about some soup they had sent up.

Just after dark Pallejá and I went up to our new station. We found a dugout to sleep in, which we shared with eight others; it was a bit cramped, but would do well enough for the scanty sleep we could expect. Next, we reported to the company commander, Captain Santo Domingo, and found him with another captain, Frejo, and the company chaplain, Father Vicente, a lean, stern-faced Navarrese with the eyes of a fanatic gleaming behind his glasses. Santo Domingo had a great reputation in this *tercio* as a soldier and was greatly loved by his men, whom he inspired by the sheer force of his own example; he was about forty-five with a strong but gentle face, full of character. Father Vicente was in great spirits and dominated the gathering. He was at once the most fearless and the most bloodthirsty man I ever met in Spain; I thought he would have made a better soldier than priest.

'*Holá*, Don Pedro!' he shouted to me. 'So you've come to kill some Reds! Congratulations! Be sure you kill plenty!' The purple tassel of his scarlet beret swung in the candlelight. Santo Domingo frowned.

'Father Vicente, you are always talking of killing. Such sentiments do not come well from a priest. The Reds may be our enemies, but remember they are Spaniards and Spain will have need of men after the war.'

'Of good men, yes. But not of evil.'

'Of good men,' repeated Santo Domingo, 'and of evil men converted.'

As the argument became heated, the roles of priest and soldier fascinatingly reversed; but I noticed that Father Vicente was alone among the party in his condemnation of all 'Reds' as traitors who must be killed. He needn't worry, I thought, we'll have to kill all we can tomorrow, if only to save our own skins.

Captain Frejo spoke: 'It will be a hard battle tomorrow; they must outnumber us by at least ten to one. We have no other defences to fall back on and if we break the whole Jarama front will fold up.'

'God will not desert us,' pronounced Father Vicente.

None of us felt like sleep; it was long after midnight before Pallejá and I returned to our dugout, to throw ourselves fully dressed on the ground. The imminent prospect of a violent if glorious death tends to concentrate the mind wonderfully on past misdeeds and future hopes of salvation. I admit that I said a few prayers that night and even made some resolutions.

I was not the only one who found it difficult to sleep. I must have dozed, for the next thing I knew was that someone had lit a candle and my companions were stirring themselves. I put on my belt, pouches and steel helmet, took my rifle and crawled out into the open. I stood up on the hillside, taking deep breaths of the clear, cool air, which revived me perfectly after the fusty atmosphere of the dugout.

It was beginning to get light. I could make out dimly the shape of our own trenches and the position on our right, lined with tense, waiting figures. As the light grew I stood looking down into a mist-draped valley where the enemy lay hidden in the gloom. Not a sound came from it. I could see the tops of the olive trees beginning to appear through the grey blanket. From the right a single shot broke the stillness.

The next moment the whole valley exploded into countless flashes and the thunderous noise of firing; the air around me was humming with bullets. I ran a few yards to the trench and flung myself against the parapet, with my rifle to my shoulder, as our own line burst out in reply.

All around us the earth was thrown up by shells and mortar bombs, the air torn by bullets. Once again the enemy machine guns were firing high, but their artillery already had our range, while mortar bombs were landing on the parapets and in the trenches. As the mist parted we saw that under their cover the enemy had been moving towards us. The plain in front of the olive groves was full of them and more could be seen coming up from the river. As Major Alamán had forecast, they were working round on our left flank.

My throat was dry, my face hot and my hands shaking as I feverishly loaded and fired my rifle. With a great effort I pulled myself together and began to fire more slowly, checking my sights, resting my elbows on the parapet and taking careful, aimed shots. This had a steadying effect on me and I began to feel much better. I began, too, to feel a kind of pity for my enemies, exposed in the open to this murderous fire; so that, as I aligned my sights on one of them and pressed the trigger with a slow steady pressure as I had been taught, I found myself praying that my bullet might put him out of action, but not maim him grievously for life.

Once again the enemy's planning had let them down. Their troops were indeed nearer to their objective than on the previous day; so also were they further from cover. Their only chance seemed to be a rapid advance, regardless of casualties. About three or four hundred yards in front of our trenches was a line of low hillocks extending to our left; these, if they could reach them, would afford some protection, enabling them to concentrate for a final assault. At first they made no progress against our fire. Many fell; some lay down where they were and fired back at us, others turned and ran in all directions looking for cover, not realising that this was the most certain way of being killed.

The morning drew on with occasional brief lulls in the fighting, which gave us time to evacuate the dead and badly wounded, dress lesser wounds, repair defences where possible, replenish our ammunition and take a drink from our water bottles. But the mortars in the olive groves gave us no rest.

The bombardment intensified as a new wave of attackers surged forward in much greater strength than the first. They had learned by now to use what little cover there was, and to combine fire and movement more skilfully than before. In spite of their losses, numbers of them reached the shelter of the hillocks, where with rifles and light machine guns they opened fire on us to cover the advance of their comrades.

The bombardment was reaching a climax. Our ears were throbbing with the explosions, our eyes almost blinded with dust; not so blinded, however, that we could not see that the enemy was getting closer, finding their way surely round to our left flank. Bullets from their machine guns were slapping against the parapets and whistling by our heads. Sometimes a *Requeté*, carried away by excitement, would clamber up on the parapet, half out of the trench, to get a better shot; in a moment he would slump back, torn with bullets, or fall forward over the parapet to roll a few yards down the slope in front. Whenever the latter happened – and I personally saw it happen several times – Father Vicente would leap from the trench and run down the hill to where the body lay, the purple tassel of his beret flying in the wind; there he would kneel, oblivious to the bullets churning the earth around them, while he prayed over the dead or dying man.

Major Alamán was moving along the line between us and the position on our right, limping on his heavy stick, now quite imperturbable in the heat of battle, his harsh, guttural voice croaking encouragement at us all. Looking over my shoulder I saw Frejo and Santo Domingo on top of the *parados* (the rear parapet of the trench), each standing behind his men, each wearing his red beret and wrapped in a *capote*, unmoved by the bullets flying around them, calmly directing the fire and encouraging the defence. This was the true *Requeté* tradition. Even when Frejo collapsed with a shattered shoulder and was carried away unconscious with pain, his inspiration remained with us.

My ammunition pouches were empty, the barrel of my rifle too hot to touch. Near me lay a dead *Requeté*; I stooped over him to replenish my pouches from his and take his rifle. As I straightened up to return to my firing position there was an explosion almost on top of me, which threw me to the ground, where I lay for a moment with my ears singing. Realising that I was not hurt I got up, adjusting my steel helmet. A bit of it seemed to be pressing against my forehead and so I took it off; I found a large dent in the front, where a piece of metal had hit it. Hitherto I had been inclined to laugh at tin hats.

It was nearly noon. There seemed no prospect of reinforcements for us; our ammunition was running low and the enemy, now within three hundred yards of us, were preparing for the final assault. We were so heavily outnumbered that there could be only one outcome if they reached our trenches. The firing died away and a lull descended, while the enemy collected their forces for the attack and we made ready to meet them.

Then we heard a new sound from the left flank beyond the enemy – the sound of tank engines. In a few moments a column of our own light tanks swept into view – about sixteen of them, each with two machine guns. They came on fast, fanning out into line abreast, then opening fire together on the enemy's unprotected flank and rear. The battle was decided. The Republicans had no chance. Caught between our fire and the guns of the tanks, they were shot down in swathes as they ran for the shelter of the olive groves. Few of them reached it; those who did continued their flight to the Manzanares and beyond. Their mortars fell silent; even their artillery ceased fire.

I was conscious of Father Vicente beside me; his spiritual duties finished, he was bent on seeing that we did not allow the fleeing enemy to escape unpunished. He kept on pointing out targets to me, urging me shrilly to shoot them down and effectively putting me off my aim. It seemed to me that he could barely restrain himself from snatching my rifle and loosing off. Possibly recollecting that I was a heretic and therefore little better than a Red, he soon left me to concentrate on my neighbours. Whenever some wretched militiaman bolted from cover to run madly for safety, I would hear the good Father's voice raised in a frenzy of excitement:

'Don't let him get away! Ah! *don't* let him get away! Shoot, man, shoot! A bit to the left! Ah! *that's* got him,' he screamed, as the miserable fellow fell and lay twitching.

It had been a very near thing. If our tanks had not arrived, or if they had arrived even a little later, we should almost certainly have been overrun. I do not know where they came from; they were obsolete German tanks, though the crews were Spanish. As we had been told to expect no reinforcements we were as surprised to see them as the enemy must have been. I have reason to believe that these tanks constituted nearly the whole of General Varela's mobile reserve; if so, he used them brilliantly to strike at exactly the crucial moment to turn impending defeat into total victory.

Thus ended the two-day battle of La Marañosa. Although we were shelled heavily that afternoon and frequently during the next few days, we were not attacked again. This had been part of the Republican General Miaja's counter-offensive, which he now switched to other points on the Jarama front. The formation that had carried the brunt of the attack against us was a Spanish brigade with the inspiring title of 'The Grey Wolves of La Pasionaria', named after the Communist deputy, Dolores Ibarruri. Certainly their fiasco was due to no lack of courage – indeed they showed remarkable bravery in such hopeless circumstances.

Our own losses were considerable. At the beginning of the battle our fighting strength was about three hundred; of these we lost more than a hundred in killed and seriously wounded; I think we were lucky to get off so lightly. Major Alamán, who had contributed notably to it, expressed himself as well satisfied with our performance, and both Colonel Rada and General Varela sent us personal messages of commendation.

By 24 February the Republican counter-offensive was exhausted. Conducted as it was, it is not surprising that it achieved no success.

The battle of the Jarama might have been a decisive victory for the Nationalists if they had had more troops; but at the time of General Varela's original offensive, at the beginning of February, a large part of the Nationalist effort was directed against Malaga.

After the Jarama the southern and western sectors of the Madrid front remained more or less static until the Republican attack on Brunete in July. The Nationalists made one last attempt to capture Madrid – the disastrous Guadalajara offensive mounted from the north-east, largely with Italian troops, in March 1937. After its failure the fighting switched to the Basque Republican provinces and Santander.

But at the beginning of March I received a letter from my mother, asking me if I could get a few weeks' leave to deal with various matters arising from my father's death. At the same time I heard from my brother, who was in the cruiser *Neptune* at Gibraltar, offering me a passage home in his ship if I could get there by the middle of the month. Alamán and Rada agreed, and I left the next day for Salamanca, where I had to have my leave pass confirmed at General Franco's headquarters.

Chapter 5

THANKS TO PABLO MERRY DEL VAL whom I met in Salamanca, I had no difficulty in getting my leave confirmed. He also introduced me to a tall, well-dressed Spaniard, whose distinguished appearance suggested some ambassador of the old school; the Marqués de Manzanedo was in fact serving in the Nationalist deplomatic service. A great anglophile who spent much of his time in Britain, he was always very kind and helpful to me; on this occasion he gave me a lift in his car to Seville, where I took a bus to La Linea.

In the bar of the Rock Hotel my brother joined me with the news that his ship was sailing in two days' time and he had the Captain's permission for me to sail in her.

'I'm afraid there won't be a cabin for you,' he added, 'and I'm damned if I'll give up mine. We'll sling you a hammock instead. As a matter of fact, I think you'll find it very comfortable.'

He was quite right. Although at first it was difficult for me to climb into the hammock, which was slung at shoulder height, once I had mastered the process I slept in it beautifully; it was much more soothing, too, than a bunk because it swung with the motion of the ship and I almost felt I was being rocked in a cradle. There was only one drawback; it was slung over an open hatch leading down to the boiler room; it didn't worry me when I turned in, well loaded with ward-room whisky, but it gave me a nasty shock, on waking with a thick head next morning, to look straight down into a gaping pit.

I shall never forget the hospitality I enjoyed in HMS *Neptune* from Captain Benson and his officers on that journey. She was a very happy ship. Neil, who was in the Fleet Air Arm, was pilot of the seaplane she carried. His brother-officers called him 'Three-plank' because, they said, each of his feet covered three planks of the deck; they immediately christened me 'Two-plank'.

It was Neil's last voyage in HMS *Neptune*. She was to pay off in England before sailing for South Africa with a new complement. I was deeply distressed by the news, in 1942, that she had struck a mine in the Mediterranean while chasing three Italian cruisers and capsized with the loss of every man on board.

It was the same bad-tempered Swede who received me in the British Consulate at Bayonne when I applied again for a visa to re-enter Spain; he was nearly incoherent with rage as he stamped my passport. The next time I have to cross this frontier, I thought, I'll have to find another way.

By now it was mid-April. After their disaster at Guadalajara the previous month the Nationalists switched their offensive to the North and were now advancing slowly, painfully, and with severe casualties, towards Bilbao. Although they enjoyed undisputed command of the air and enormous superiority in artillery, they were up against an enemy as brave and resolute as themselves, entrenched in strong natural defensive positions in some of the most mountainous and difficult country in all Spain; the weather, too, was atrocious, hindering movement and often preventing air operations. It looked as if Bilbao was going to be an unconscionable long time falling.

My return to Spain coincided with a major political crisis in the Nationalist government: no less than a Falange plot, allegedly with German encouragement, to remove Franco from the leadership. The only public announcements on the subject were first an official statement that Señor Hedilla, the head of the Falange, was under arrest and secondly a decree amalgamating the Falange and the *Requetés*, and abolishing all other political parties. The new organisation bore the title *Falange Española, Tradicionalista y de las Juntas de Ofensiva Nacional-Sindicalista* – and, added Spaniards with their gift of ridicule, *de los Grandes Expresos Europeos*. It would be hard to think of two parties more hostile to each other than the *Requetés* and the Falange. To unite them seemed grotesque. Writing of the resulting 'magnificent harlequin', Salvador de Madariaga said it was 'as if the President of the United States had organised the Republican-Democratic-Socialist-Communist-League-of-the-Daughters-of-the American Revolution, in the hope of unifying American politics'. Either the Falange or the *Requetés* would inevitably dominate this unnatural coalition; and the skill of the former at intrigue and the political ineptitude of the latter determined the outcome: the *Requetés* ceased to have any influence on Spanish politics; for the moment the Falange seemed to be in the ascendant – but only for the moment. The official uniform of the new party was the blue shirt of the Falange and the scarlet *Requeté* beret. But at least the *Requeté* fighting formations retained their old military uniforms as before.

The controlled press naturally greeted the amalgamation as an act of statesmanship and thereafter ignored the whole business. But unease persisted and increased when General Faupel, the Nazi Ambassador, was sent back to Germany in disgrace. At the time I knew nothing about the plot except for the scanty information released in the Nationalist press; nor was I greatly concerned to know more. Having taken so much trouble to return to Spain I was only interested in getting back into the war. But it seems that there was indeed a Falange conspiracy, instigated by the Germans through their Ambassador, to get rid of Franco. The Germans had become impatient at the slow progress of the war under Franco's direction; they considered his tactics and strategy archaic, and tried to persuade him to change them into something more like *Blitzkrieg*. Franco had no wish to see his country devastated by a storm of high explosive; moreover he was a *gallego* (from Galicia), with all the obstinacy and cunning of that talented race, and he was not going to submit to foreign dictation. The Germans therefore decided to replace him with a creature of their own and selected Hedilla as the leader of the most pro-German party. Faupel persuaded Hedilla to stage a *coup d'état*, which nearly succeeded. But Franco suppressed the conspiracy, sent Hedilla to prison for thirty years and demanded the recall of Faupel. He then consolidated his own position by appointing himself leader of the new and only party. It wasn't until March 1938 that he launched an offensive on *Blitzkrieg* lines.

I had decided to try for a posting to a *Requeté* unit on the Bilbao front, which was the only front where there was any action, but it was nearly two months before I succeeded. I had to spend much of this time travelling from one headquarters to another, or waiting in Salamanca, where by now I had friends in Franco's HQ who might help me and who did indeed try, but with little success; I also had to go to Avila to see Colonel Rada and get his written permission to transfer to the northern front.

There were certainly consolations in having to wait in Salamanca, chief among them the city itself – surely one of the most beautiful in Europe. For a time I could forget my impatience as I sauntered through the colonnades in the architectural miracle of the Plaza Mayor, 'the drawing room of Salamanca', as Jan Morris calls it in her superb evocation of the landscape and the spirit of the country.*

* *Spain* (Penguin, 1982)

Salamanca was always pre-eminently a university and its university, founded in the thirteenth century, was once rated the third most distinguished centre of learning in all Europe. But there were few students or scholars to be seen when I was there; instead the city was full of military uniforms. Prominent among them was the portly figure of General O'Duffy, commander of the 'Irish Brigade', with a petulant, self-indulgent face and conceited strut.

A former chief of police in the Irish Free State – hence his rank of general – O'Duffy entered Irish politics in the 1930s as leader of his own party, the United Party or 'Blueshirts'. When the Spanish Civil War broke out he saw in it a chance to increase his political prestige in Ireland, where support for the Nationalists was strong among the Catholic population. He therefore raised a 'brigade' of Irishmen to fight for Franco and although the 'brigade' was barely of battalion strength Franco granted him the honorary rank of general. Few generals can have had so little responsibility in proportion to their rank – or so little sense of it.

Having installed himself in comfort at the Gran Hotel, and bought up every available bottle of whisky between the Gredos mountains and the Portuguese frontier, he used to hold court every evening in the main lounge of the hotel to journalists, politicans and an occasional high-ranking soldier. There I was introduced to him – a brief audience which concluded with mutual expressions of courteous esteem and mutual feelings of intense antipathy. Hearing that I was British he told me how much he loathed my fellow countrymen and offered me a glass of whisky, which I declined – something I very seldom did in those days.

O'Duffy never lost sight of the real purpose of his Irish 'brigade' – to strengthen his own political position at home. He therefore gave the most responsible commands in the 'brigade' to his own political supporters, regardless of their military qualifications, or lack of them – one company commander's previous experience had been confined to operating a lift in Jury's Hotel in Dublin – and rejected applications from former officers of proven experience and ability. The tragedy was that the rank and file of the 'brigade' were good men who had followed O'Duffy to Spain to fight for their faith against communism; properly led they could have made first-class soldiers. O'Duffy cared little or nothing for them and rarely visited them at the front; for their part, they would refer to him as 'General O'Scruffy' or 'Old John Bollocks'.

Some of the history of this unhappy unit came to me from Lieutenants Fitzpatrick and Nangle, who had served in the 5th Bandera of the Foreign Legion in the advance on Toledo the previous September and, to their indignation, were transferred afterwards to O'Duffy's 'brigade'; and from Lieutenant Lawler, who had come out with it from Ireland. The men were crammed like cattle, said Lawler, in the stinking holds of an ancient, unseaworthy ship, with bad food and little of it, and barely enough drinking water. Disembarking at La Coruña in Galicia they entrained for Caceres, which was to be their depot. Their route ran through Salamanca, where they arrived at about ten in the morning, having had no breakfast; they were received on the station by a delegation of the Nationalist authorities, who gave them a *vin d'honneur* attended by senior Army officers. Lawler said to me: 'I knew it was going to be sheer bloody murder with the boys drinking all that wine on empty stomachs. I tried to see if we couldn't get them some food, but it was no use. Sure enough, when the time came to get back into the train the boys were so drunk it was all we could do to push them into it. And even that wasn't the end of our troubles. When we'd got them all in and the train was ready to start, the band struck up the Spanish National Anthem, and all the officers and generals came to attention and stood at the salute. And all the time the band was playing, there was one of our lads – as drunk as a coot he was – leaning out of the carriage window being sick all down the neck of an old general. And the old boy – I was watching him – stood there like a rock at the salute through it all.'

Misfortune followed them even to the front; their first casualties were at the hands of their allies. One of their companies, marching in column to take up positions on the Jarama, was fired on by a unit of the Falange, who unaccountably mistook them for a unit of the International Brigades. The first shots did no harm, but the Irish company commander lost his head and allowed a minor battle to develop.

It is only fair to mention that when the 'brigade' at last went into action, near the Jarama, the Spaniards themselves paid tribute to the courage and bearing of its troops. There is no doubt that, with good leaders, men of such quality, inspired as they were by their faith, could have been worthy successors of the famous Irish Brigade that fought for King Louis in the eighteenth century. But with O'Duffy's leadership they stood no chance. Quarrels with the Spanish authorities became more frequent and more bitter; in the summer of 1937 this ill-fated troupe went home.

Hoping to hurry up my posting to a *Requeté* unit in the North, I moved to Vitoria. I found the city full of foreign journalists, for the Nationalists had at last relaxed some of their restrictions on visits by correspondents to the front. Among the British I found Harold Cardozo of the *Daily Mail*; he was sharing a flat with a Frenchman, Botteau, of Agence Havas, a good-hearted but highly excitable little man – also a Great War veteran – who would sometimes dissolve into tears of fury and frustration at his treatment by Spanish press officers. The two of them generously invited me to stay with them while I was waiting.

At this time the story of Guernica was occupying the headlines in the international press – and causing a good deal of damage as well as embarrassment to the Nationalists. It was a perfect example of the success of Republican propaganda and the futility of Nationalist efforts to counteract it. Its success was due partly to the superior skill and experience of those who directed Republican propaganda within Spain and abroad, partly to the vast sums of money spent on its promotion – Botteau heard from his Paris office that it approached a figure of half a million pounds.

The story circulated at the time, and widely believed all over the world, was that Guernica, an open town and sacred in Basque history and culture, was heavily bombed by Nationalist and German aircraft using high explosive and incendiaries, and virtually destroyed, with heavy loss of life. Cardozo was indignant at the success it was having in Britain. He himself had entered the town with the first Nationalist troops and was able to investigate the damage for himself; he had also talked with some of the inhabitants who had been there during the bombing. He was convinced the Republicans, particularly the Asturian miners, who of course had nothing in common with Basque sentiments, had done most of the destruction themselves before retreating. In particular, Cardozo claimed he had scraped thick deposits of carbon off the walls of houses, which clearly indicated the use of petrol to set fire to them; since he had considerable experience of warfare, and since I knew he was an honest and meticulous reporter, I paid attention to his views. It is certainly true and widely attested that when the Republicans retreated from Irun, Eibar, Amorbieta and other Basque towns earlier on, they set fire to them and dynamited houses before leaving. The Nationalists did of course bomb Guernica; however, it was by no means an open town, but a divisional headquarters and an important communications centre.

I know of no published accounts of the Guernica bombing by an eyewitness; all have come to us second hand. Personally I find it hard to accept that Franco, who had only just survived a quarrel with the Germans on this very issue of blasting his country into rubble, would have easily consented to the kind of air attack alleged by the Republicans. Whatever the facts, the Republican version, sedulously cultivated by the Comintern and, at the time, by one or two less than scrupulous journalists, and perpetuated in the painting by Picasso, is the story now accepted as history.

I was beginning to lose hope of getting myself posted to the northern front – bureaucracy up here seemed much more entrenched than earlier in the war around Madrid – when in the second week of June a friend in Vitoria introduced me to a large, middle-aged Englishman, Edward Earle, whose florid complexion and expansive face showed the signs of amiability and good living; he had lived for many years in Bilbao, where he was a leading industrialist, and now he had himself financed the raising of a new *tercio* of *Requetés*, that of Nuestra Señora de Begoña, named after the patron saint of Bilbao. They were already engaged in the fighting for the city and he would arrange for me to join them at once. But first I must return to Salamanca to get the necessary *salvoconducto* and other papers from HQ. Next morning I hitch-hiked to Salamanca in the best of spirits and within two days I was on my way back to join this new unit.

The two days I spent in Salamanca are memorable for my first meeting with a highly eccentric British officer. I was lunching there at a famous restaurant with the charming name of 'The Friar's Widow', when a tall, lanky lieutenant of the Foreign Legion uncoiled himself from a neighbouring table and came over.

'Excuse me,' he began. 'You've been pointed out to me as the English *Requeté*. I'm English too – or rather Irish,' he corrected himself. 'I've just done a stint with that shit O'Duffy and now I'm here trying to arrange a posting back to my old *bandera*, the 5th.' Over lunch, and on frequent occasions later, I learned something of his story and background. He spoke with an engaging, self-deprecating frankness, with frequent wiggling of a comic moustache, which seemed to move quite independently of his facial muscles – he would raise one side of it while simultaneously depressing the other. After Eton he had gone to Sandhurst and from there had been commissioned into the Royal Norfolk Regiment – 'from which I transferred a year or two later,' he told me, 'with the enthusiastic cooperation of my commanding officer. After a few years in another line regiment,' he went on, 'I decided that the career of a regular officer was not for me – an opinion which I believe my new CO also shared. In his confidential report on me, which I had to sign, he stated, "No troops would ever follow this officer, except out of idle curiosity."'

Born Noel Skeffington-Smith, he had recently changed his name to Fitzpatrick when an uncle left him a property in Ireland. He was known to his many and devoted friends as 'Skeffie' or 'Fitzie'. When the Civil War broke out he was in his early thirties and running a motor business of his own in London.

'But then I found that my secretary, whom I greatly fancied, was sleeping with my manager and both were having a good laugh at me. So I packed it in and came out here. That was last August.'

When he arrived in Spain he was attached in his British Army rank of lieutenant, to the 5th Bandera of the Foreign Legion, under Major Castejón, during its eastward advance from Estremadura to Toledo; with Fitzpatrick was an old friend, Bill Nangle, a former officer in the Indian Army. Both of them were mentioned in dispatches during the battles for Toledo and were among the first dozen troops to enter the Alcazar. Both were transferred afterwards to O'Duffy's Irish 'brigade' as liaison officers. Nangle had already preceded Fitzpatrick in getting back to the 5th Bandera.

Spaniards did not easily give praise to foreigners in their Army; but they spoke in glowing terms of both those British officers. I gathered that Fitzpatrick occasionally created a problem for his companions; in the heat of battle he would sometimes lose his sense of direction and, believing he was shooting at the enemy, might loose off a potentially murderous swathe of fire towards his own troops. But because of his obvious courage and enthusiasm these occasional lapses were overlooked.

On 3 June General Mola was killed in an air crash – a severe blow to the Nationalists and, in particular, to the *Requetés*, whose respect and loyalty, almost veneration, he had won in their desperate early months of fighting. I was personally sad too, because when I had met him recently in Vitoria he had impressed me particularly with his courtesy and attention to such a junior officer as myself, and with his complete lack of pomposity.

On 11 June the Nationalists began the last phase of their offensive against Bilbao, the assault on the 'Iron Belt', the last and strongest line of fortifications on the hills above the city. After intense air and artillery bombardment the forward positions fell on the first day, but the main defences, though breached, held for another eight days.

On the morning of the 19th I set out from Vitoria, with all my papers in order, to join my new unit, but it was evening before I found it. Nobody seemed to know precisely where the Tercio de Nuestra Señora de Begoña was in action, only that it formed part of the 5th Navarre Brigade; and so I spent the afternoon wandering over the battle area in pursuit of well-meaning but inaccurate directions. At one point I found myself in Las Arenas, a pleasant summer resort on the right bank of the estuary of the Nervion river, which bisects Bilbao a few miles upstream. It was clear of the enemy but in the brilliant sunshine I could see the estuary was crowded with boats, from dinghies to small steamers, all trying to escape from the doomed city. They stood little chance, since the waters outside were closely patrolled by the Nationalist Navy, and the entire estuary was within range of Nationalist artillery and machine guns. I felt very sorry for the desperate people in those boats. Most were forced to turn back, but one lone steamer tried to struggle on through the ploughed up, shell-torn river. I admired the courage of her captain, but it was wasted. Through my binoculars I saw spouts of water leaping up all round her as Nationalist batteries found her range. Suddenly there was a flash on board, at the base of her funnel, followed by several others as more shells struck her. Smoke and steam poured out of her, and then she heeled over and sank in a vortex of foam.

At last, in the late evening, I came upon the *tercio* I was to join; they were resting in woods on the heights of Archanda, which they had taken by storm that afternoon. This ridge was the last Republican line of defence before Bilbao and now the city lay below us, totally undefended. The *Requetés* looked happy but very tired; they had fought a bloody battle all day, struggling through the trees up the nearly vertical hillside in the face of a murderous fire from machine guns and mortars sited on the defences above, and from showers of grenades hurled on them by the Republicans – the fiercely brave Asturian miners and *dinamiteros* who would neither surrender nor run away, but stood and fought it out to the last man. The *tercio*, still well under strength, had begun the assault with about a hundred and seventy men; now scarcely forty of them remained.

However, among those forty I found my old friend Father Vicente from the La Marañosa battle, who had joined the *tercio* at the start of this last offensive. Today, I heard, he had led one wing of the assault, mounted on a white horse and flaunting, as usual, his scarlet, purple-tasselled beret; he made a perfect target. Needless to say he had only been lightly wounded, in the hand, while his poor horse had been killed under him and the *Requetés* behind him fell in swathes. He was in excellent spirits, of course, as he greeted me warmly and commiserated with me for having missed such a first-class fight. Then he took me to the commanding officer, Major Ricardo Uhagón, who was sitting against a tree, sad and silent. A regular cavalry officer and a fine soldier, Uhagón was a humane man who hated losing men.

'You had better stay here for the moment,' he told me. 'Tomorrow at dawn we march down into Bilbao. I suggest you find yourself somewhere to sleep,' and he told his batman to fetch me a blanket.

I walked up the hill, carrying my blanket, to a meadow at the top where a few *Requetés* were sitting or lying on the grass in the dusk. They gave me a hunk of bread and a tin of sardines. Although hungry, for I had eaten nothing all day, I was also very thirsty after so much walking in the heat; but so was everyone else and there was no water to be had – or wine either. A grinning *Requeté* proffered a canteen full of brandy and I was fool enough to drink some, which only made me thirstier. The *Requeté*, however, tilted the canteen to his mouth and swallowed most of the contents in a few gulps.

'Why drink it like that?' I asked. 'It all goes down at once and you get no pleasure from it.'

'Certainly I do,' he laughed. 'Now it is all inside me and I get the pleasure from here,' and he tapped his stomach. I was to discover that most Spanish troops drank liquor like this when they had a bottle.

I was very cold that night, even under the blanket; and after months of sleeping in a bed the hard ground pressed painfully against my hips and shoulders. In the long wakeful hours I felt ashamed of my softness, as well as lonely among these strangers.

We were roused before daylight, and I was glad to stand up and stretch my cold, aching limbs. My *Requeté* friend handed me his canteen and this time I was really glad of the brandy. As day broke we mustered and formed up on the road to await orders to move. The sky was clear and promised a hot day.

At six o'clock we set off in column down the steep, winding road that led to Bilbao; Major Uhagón marched at the head of the column, with me beside him. There was no sign of Father Vicente, which surprised me because this was a Sunday. Our *tercio* was leading the line of march and we had thought we would be the first troops to enter the city; but it turned out that the enemy had evacuated it the previous afternoon and our tanks had moved in the previous night. On our way down we passed a few groups of civilians, looking thin and haggard, who watched us in apathetic silence.

Lying in the valley of the Nervión, almost hemmed in by steep hills, Bilbao on a warm day has a steamy, relaxing atmosphere, so that by the time we reached the outskirts I was already tired and sweaty. In the town we turned left and entered the main square, the Arenal, where we halted at some field kitchens, and gratefully swallowed a mug of black coffee and a hunk of bread. Afterwards we formed up in the square for Mass.

There must have been over five thousand troops gathered there, facing the church on the east side of it. Our *tercio* was in the front. Mass was attended by senior officers of the three armed services, including Franco himself. And who should deliver the sermon but Father Vicente. He stood before us, his wounded arm in a sling, his ascetic face raised to heaven, and his strident voice thrilling with emotion as he poured out in stately, measured periods his paean of faith and triumph, and thundered repeatedly the refrain of his text:

'*¡Contra Dios No Se Puede Luchar!* [Against God no one can fight!]'

Chapter 6

BILBAO IS NO stranger to sieges, having endured several during the Carlist Wars of the last century. But this siege seemed to have caused little serious physical damage, although the city presented a sad and neglected appearance. The streets were littered with debris and broken glass, some windows were smashed, and others bricked up and loopholed for defence; but the houses and shops seemed intact, and there were few signs of looting – although I heard there had been more of it in the early days of the war. Industries and factories appeared undamaged, even if they were without power. Most serious was an acute shortage of drinking water, since the Republicans, who still controlled it, had cut off the water supply and it wasn't restored for another month.

The condition of the inhabitants, however, was tragic. On the first day pitiful, emaciated figures constantly approached us, begging tearfully for a piece of bread. We did our best for them with our own limited rations, but happily the Nationalists tackled the problem at once, rushing in bread, meat, rice and potatoes, and opening restaurants which would serve any civilian with a free meal. The city recovered quickly. By mid-week there was power and light, and trams were running; the shops opened too, although they had very little to sell.

We spent a fortnight in Bilbao, bringing our ranks up to strength with recruits from sympathisers who had been in hiding under the Republican regime. We had more applications from them than our shortage of instructors and equipment allowed us to accept; and soon the Tercio de Nuestra Señora de Begoña was up to four hundred strong. I had a platoon to train with, luckily for me, two most efficient sergeants. Early in July we all moved to Las Arenas, which was a pleasant change from the heat, humidity and dirt of Bilbao.

As an Englishman I found my prestige in Las Arenas was remarkably high. This was reflected glory from the outstanding courage of an English governess, Miss Boland, who lost her life during the last days of the Republican regime, trying to save her employer's family from execution. The Zuburría family, who lived in Las Arenas, had four sons, the youngest still at school, the oldest just married, and Miss Boland had continued to live with them after the sons grew up. The day before Bilbao fell some *milicianos* came to arrest the four boys and the wife of the eldest. Knowing they intended to shoot them Miss Boland insisted on accompanying them, and made such a nuisance of herself in her attempt to save the victims that the *milicianos* shot her before the others.

In London the summer of 1937 saw the Coronation of King George VI with nationwide celebrations. For me it was a frustrating period of inactivity on a front that had become stabilised. Moreover I was receiving letters from home from well-meaning friends and relatives, urging me to waste no more time in Spain, but come home and find some lucrative employment. I saw their point, but having continued for so long in this war, about which I felt even more strongly now than when I first joined it, I could not bring myself to walk out before its end.

Nevertheless I found my present inactivity particularly galling. In spite of all my efforts to join a fighting unit in the North, I had arrived just too late for the last battle and I now seemed condemned to idleness on the Vizcaya-Santander border – admittedly in some of the most beautiful country in Spain and at the height of a glorious summer, but I wasn't much thrilled by the tourist attractions.

The reason why operations in the North had come to a halt was the great Republican offensive of Brunete, which began on 6 July. Brunete, some fifteen miles west of Madrid, fell to the Republicans on the first day in a surprise dawn attack under Colonel Enrique Lister. But the Republicans failed to follow up their initial success, which consequently ended in disaster for them and very heavy losses. By the end of July the Madrid sector was once more stable and the Nationalists free to pursue their advance on Santander. My own hopes for action there were quickly disappointed. The main Nationalist attack came on 20 August, but from the south, where two Italian divisions, supported by Spanish and Italian 'Mixed Brigades', broke through the Republican defences after very heavy fighting. We ourselves slogged painfully but unopposed westwards for two or three days, clambering up and down the beautiful but arduous slopes of the Biscay mountains – which at least restored my physique if not my temper. There we were halted to await the city's fall. Uhagón sent most of his officers, including me, on a fortnight's leave.

In the end I did witness the fall of Santander, but only as a spectator. I hitch-hiked my way by lorry to Bilbao, where I found two journalist friends, Reynolds Packard of UP (United Press) and Dick Sheepshanks of Reuters; they were leaving that evening by car for Santander, which they hoped to enter with our leading troops next morning and they invited me to go with them. We drove all night and at about 9 am reached a hill looking across the marshes to Santander.

A column of Italian infantry was formed up on the road leading to the city, with a squadron of their little two-man tanks at its head. After a while we saw two men approaching slowly and wearily along the road from Santander; they were the Republican commander and the chief of police, come to parley with the Nationalist commander, General Dávila, who was standing apart in a field beside the road. Both delegates looked very white, but whereas the policeman retained his dignity throughout the discussion, the soldier seemed close to collapse. The proceedings ended abruptly when one of them expressed a hope that the victors would spare the women and children – a gratuitous insult to which General Dávila promptly replied by ordering the two Republicans to withdraw.

After a couple of hours the column of Italian infantry began to march towards the city and we left our car to join the leaders; at the same time Spanish troops were entering from the west. On our way we met groups of Republican *milicianos*, still in their blue overalls, hurrying from the town in a last pathetic effort to escape; they were quickly rounded up by the Guardia Civil who accompanied us and taken for screening to the bullring.

I was walking with a *Requeté* friend from the press office and we were well ahead of the rest of the column when we saw a car approaching, painted in camouflage colours and containing four militiamen. We held them up with our pistols, disarmed them – they were too demoralised to put up a fight – and handed them over to the Guardia Civil. My friend, who had his own car at hand, suggested I should take possession of this brand new Citroën coupé, which I did; it would be welcome to my *tercio*, who were short of transport. I left it near the road, locked it and rejoined the column on foot.

Nearing the centre of the town we found the road lined deep on both sides with civilians, who waved, pelted us with flowers and cheered as if they had gone mad. I saw women and girls dressed in their best clothes, pathetically shoddy as those were; their faces were radiant, yet showing the signs of months of famine and fear that no make-up could hide. Republican rule had been particularly savage in Santander, the former home of Dolores Ibarruri, 'La Pasionaria'. Hundreds of Nationalist sympathisers, or suspects, were thrown from the cliffs above Cabo Mayor to their deaths on the rocks below.

Leaving the column I wandered through the streets on my own and immediately noticed the sidestreets were crowded with *milicianos*, some still carrying arms but all looking utterly dejected, apparently overcome by the suddenness and extent of their defeat; they ignored me, showing neither hatred nor fear at the sight of my uniform. The civilians, however, showed heart-warming enthusiasm when they saw my red *boina*: men would run up to shake my hand, pumping it up and down in their excitement; women would embrace me, kissing me on both cheeks – more the older women, I reflected sadly, than the young, who still retained a deplorable maidenly modesty. Quickly realising from my height of over six feet, my ruddy complexion and fair hair that I was unlikely to be Spanish, they asked me my nationality; when I said I was British, their welcome almost overwhelmed me. Some of our soldiers were from Santander and there were some deeply moving scenes as they sought out their own families or questioned friends for news of them.

At about half-past three I decided to return to Bilbao; my new car was full of petrol, obviously prepared for a long journey. I wasn't altogether happy about using the more direct coastal road, because I thought there might be a large pocket of Republican troops trapped on it between Santander and the Navarre brigades to the east. However, a sentry on the outskirts of the town assured me it was clear and so I drove on, the car running beautifully – it must have been tuned to perfection.

For the first twenty-five miles I saw nobody, not even an animal. But as I approached the little fishing port of Laredo I saw the narrow streets were thronged with figures in blue overalls and black berets; they carried rifles slung from their shoulders, and pistols and grenades hung from their belts. It was too late to go back and impossible in any case to turn; I could only drive on, very slowly because of the press, into the remnants of the Basque Republican Army. That sentry had been wrong and now I was in a fine mess. These men were heavily armed and showed none of the dejection of their comrades in Bilbao. If they were to arrest me I could hope for, and probably deserved, very little mercy. However, they did seem a bit bewildered and so my best, indeed only, hope was bluff; I must pretend to be the advanced guard of the victorious Nationalists.

Looking as unconcerned as I could, I drove on through the main street, flaunting my scarlet beret with its one silver fleur-de-lys as though I was expecting surrender and praying the *milicianos* would bow to this apparently inevitable defeat, but I was feeling a sneaking sympathy for the four previous occupants of my Citroën. Forcing a confident smile on my face and sounding my horn repeatedly to clear the way, I drove on through the throng; whenever anyone looked in at my window, I called out the name of my unit in my most peremptory tone until at last I was almost clear of the town. Here a pair of *milicianos* with white armbands signalled me to stop, but although they barred my way, they didn't point their rifles at me. I put my head out of the window and shouted at them: *'¡Tercio de Nuestra Señora de Begoña!'* They stepped aside and as I drove on out of the town, breathing several deep sighs of relief, I glanced back to see their faces gaping after me in blank astonishment. Maybe, I thought, the devil really does look after his own. Soon afterwards I came upon the advanced units of our 'Mixed Brigades', who seemed as astonished to see me approaching from Santander as had the *milicianos*.

By this time my experience with the *Requetés* had forced me to conclude that despite their superb courage, enthusiasm and self-sacrificing patriotism, they had neither the strict discipline nor technical expertise, let alone training, to fit them for a major role in modern warfare; and this was now becoming a modern war, radically different from the early days when courage and enthusiasm alone might bring victory. Although not gifted with exceptional foresight, even I could see that the Second World War was looming over the horizon and I felt it was high time I began to prepare myself for it. Besides, I thought, if I was going to fight this war I might as well do it properly. I therefore decided I must join the Foreign Legion. This was the *corps d'élite* of the Nationalist forces, the shock troops on whom they depended for their most arduous and difficult operations; they were also by far the best trained and equipped force in the Army.

My problem was how to arrange a transfer to the Legion in my present rank, which I was most reluctant to abandon after all this time and effort, simply to revert to the ranks. I gave it a lot of thought during my leave, which I spent in San Sebastian, where I hoped to find many friends to brighten the days and enliven the nights.

I put up there at the Hotel Continental, to be greeted like a son by the manageress, a warm-hearted and courageous Frenchwoman, who had protected many Nationalist supporters at the risk of her life during the period of Republican rule. Now in this glorious weather it was an attractive, bright and cheerful city, full of soldiers on leave and the families of others at the front. I found many friends there, including Noel Fitzpatrick, now on his way home to deal with family affairs, and Miguel de Larrinaga, a Spaniard who lived in Liverpool, where his family owned a shipping line; in his mid-thirties, Larrinaga had come to Spain in response to a military call-up, but being considered too old for active service he had been posted to garrison duty, in the rank of corporal. I was to see a great deal of him over the next thirty years.

Among the outstanding attractions of San Sebastian was Chicote's bar, already famous in Madrid before the Civil War; during the war it became a favourite haunt of journalists like Hemingway. When the war broke out Chicote wisely removed himself to Nationalist territory and soon opened the new Chicote's in San Sebastian. If there is a world hierarchy of barmen, as there should be, Perico Chicote must rank – or have ranked, for alas he is now dead – among its most eminent cardinals. Known on two continents as much for the warmth of his heart as the skill of his hand, he radiated through this bar an atmosphere of well-being and *simpatía* in which past and future problems and perils ceased to trouble. The 'Chicote Special' was considered by many serious drinkers to be one of the masterpieces of modern art. When, the following summer, I found myself in hospital in San Sebastian, the heart-warming welcome and kindness I used to enjoy from Don Perico did more than anything else to alleviate my incarceration there.

After a week of relaxation in this pleasant resort I decided to go to Salamanca; as the Generalisimo's headquarters, it seemed much the best place to try and arrange my transfer to the Legion. I was lucky. On the way I spent a night in Burgos, where I ran into Pablo Merry del Val. When I told him of my wish to join the Legion, he smiled.

'You are indeed in luck. General Millán Astray is here in this hotel; I'll have a word with him and see what can be done.'

Millán Astray, the 'Father of the Legion' and its cofounder with Franco, was a legendary figure throughout Nationalist Spain, famed for the number and severity of his wounds, and his eccentric, ferocious manner. A most flamboyant personality, with a severe limp, only one arm and one eye – and a daunting glint in the other one – he attracted immediate attention in any gathering. In Legion affairs his power was absolute.

Merry del Val spoke with him briefly, then called me over. The general fired questions at me like a machine gun, asking me about my service while concentrating that fierce, unblinking eye on me as I answered. At the end he said tersely, 'I will speak personally to the Generalisimo and recommend you be admitted to the Legion as *alférez*. Return to your *Requeté tercio* for your discharge, then wait in Salamanca for your orders from the Legion. Good luck to you!'

Riaño, in Asturias on the border with Leon, was a delightful little village beside a swift-flowing river which would have sorely tempted me if I had been a fisherman; on the other side of the valley rose steep and rocky mountains running north as far as the Picos de Europa. On the bank of the river was encamped the Tercio de Nuestra Señora de Begoña, taking advantage of the bright autumn weather; and here I found Major Uhagón. He congratulated me on my posting to the Legion and fully sympathised with my reasons for seeking it. I should have liked to linger in that lovely valley, where the yellowing birches by the riverbanks made a warm and mellow contrast in the sunlight with the grey and sombre grandeur of the towering cliffs; but my orders from Millán Astray were to report as soon as possible in Salamanca.

However, when I arrived there and reported to HQ, I was told that my posting was in hand, but it would take at least a month to come through. And so I accepted an invitation from Pablo Merry del Val to accompany him and the British MP Sir Arnold Wilson on a quick tour of Castile and the Basque provinces; Merry del Val arranged I should be notified immediately if my posting came through.

I had already met Sir Arnold when he had come to Cambridge to address the University Conservative Association, of which I was secretary, and had found his forceful and outspoken manner rather frightening. He had previously had a distinguished and unusual career in the Middle East, where he had been High Commissioner in Mesopotamia and, finally, general manager of the former Anglo-Persian Oil Company; he was a leading authority on Persia and Iraq. He also possessed extraordinary physical and mental powers; he could, for instance, memorise a book after reading it only once and for a pleasant summer holiday he would sign on for three months as a stoker in a cargo boat in the Persian Gulf. But in politics he was a highly controversial as well as colourful character, for he had decided views on most matters and would tolerate no opposition, however sincere. His abhorrence of communism and fear of Soviet Russia led him to an openly expressed admiration for the Nazis, apparently in ignorance – like many others at that time – of their nature. But he was a sincere patriot, as he showed when war broke out with Germany. At the age of fifty-five he became a pilot officer and rear gunner in the RAF, having passed every medical test the authorities could devise to stop him.

'I will not,' he declared, 'shelter behind a rampart of young bodies.'

Christened by his colleagues, 'Sir Gunner', he was killed in 1940, shot down in flames over Holland.

On our journey through Castile we naturally visited Toledo. Sitting in a café opposite the ruins of the Alcazar I noticed a party of Legion officers across the room; their yellow flashes indicated they were from the 5th Bandera, where I knew Fitzpatrick's friend Bill Nangle was serving. Luckily he was there with the other officers and so I made myself known to him. He was dark and thin, reserved in manner, but very friendly to me, thanks to Fitzpatrick. He looked what he was, a thoroughly competent professional soldier. After passing through Sandhurst he was commissioned into the Indian Army, where he found the life too monotonous for his restless temperament; moreover, his failure to show proper respect for senior officers, particularly staff officers, hardly endeared him to the authorities. His career as a regular soldier ended when, after a tour of duty in command of Fort Alexander on the Northwest Frontier, he was required to write a report for the staff at Simla; written in the correct military phraseology, it concluded with his own postscript: 'How much string does it take to go round St Paul's?'*

By the time his report was in the hands of the staff Nangle had returned to England on leave. He sent in his papers at once, but without waiting for them to be accepted he enlisted in the French Foreign Legion. He was thoroughly enjoying his new life in the desert when the then Prince of Wales, a friend of his parents, was persuaded to intervene with the French authorities and, to his disgust and indignation, he was discharged. When I met him he had been serving for just over a year as an officer in the 5th Bandera, where, as I have said, he was both popular and respected – despite recurrent attacks of *le cafard* (desert madness), acquired in the Sahara, which could make him an awkward companion. Family reasons obliged him to return home in December of that year. I saw him briefly in the summer of 1943 in Cairo where, back in the Indian Army, he was still looking for action. He found it with the Long Range Desert Group and was killed in battle with them in Italy.

Back in Salamanca I was lucky to get a room in the Gran Hotel.

---

* The answer is 'balls and balls and balls'.

It had a pronounced cosmopolitan atmosphere now, partly due to the presence of some senior German staff officers, most of them signals or aviation specialists who kept to themselves and regularly ate at a large table in the dining room; also partly owing to the presence at a table next to them of several British and American journalists, including Randolph Churchill, reporting for the *Sunday Dispatch*, and Kim Philby of *The Times*. Philby was very quiet and courteous, apart from the slightly supercilious tone he adopted when addressing creatures whose intelligence he despised, like, for instance, me. Churchill would entertain his fellow journalists and considerably embarrass their Spanish conducting officer by airing, in a voice that carried clear across the room, his views on the beastliness of all Germans, especially Nazis.

'Is there not one Jew left in Germany,' he would shout, 'capable of shooting that bastard Hitler?'

O'Duffy's Irish 'brigade' had gone home, except for a few stragglers, among them my old friend Peter Lawler, a tough little Irish Australian who had served with the Australian Army in the First World War and as a subaltern under O'Duffy in this war. During the Irish troubles of the early 1920s he had been a trusted lieutenant of Michael Collins and was still known in his own part of Ireland as 'The Commandant'. Now he was hanging around Salamanca, waiting to collect six months' back pay from the Spaniards, who were responsible for paying the Irish. When he finally collected it, a month later, he returned home, very bitter about O'Duffy.

I was standing one morning in the hotel lobby when a bulky, Falstaffian figure shambled up and stood beside me.

'Morning,' he said. 'I see you're English too. May I introduce myself? Archie Lyall.'

He extended a large hand. I studied him closely. He was tall and corpulent, with a florid complexion, a high, broad forehead and a large head from which the hair was beginning to recede; he had heavy jowls and marked pouches under his eyes, as well as a small blond moustache and eyebrows that turned up sharply at the ends like those of Kaiser Wilhelm. His expression, half-innocent, half-sensual, gave him the look of a dissipated baby. He was now in his mid-thirties, and described himself as an author and freelance journalist. He had just returned from a visit to Santander, reporting on the Nationalist trials there of war criminals,* which, as a qualified barrister, he thought had been fairly conducted. Previously he had founded and run a donkey hospital in Fez, Morocco, which he

---

* One Republican crime had been driving a group of Nationalist sympathisers over the cliffs by the lighthouse on to the rocks below.

supported, along with himself, quite handsomely on subscriptions from charitable old ladies in the United States. He had also written several travel books, chiefly about the Balkans; but his most enduring work was a detailed phrasebook covering all the European languages, entitled *Lyall's Twenty-Five Languages of Europe*. It was still exhibited on most railway bookstalls twenty-five years later; and a friend of his assured me he had once completed the seduction of a Lithuanian chambermaid in fifteen minutes flat with no other help than *Lyall's Languages*. An entry under his name in *Who's Who* described his hobbies as 'Reading, travelling and collecting matchbox labels'.

I found him an entertaining and stimulating companion; along with a pungent wit he had the gift of spotting the absurdities in every situation that arose. We remained close friends for nearly thirty years until his early death in 1964.

On this occasion we dined together and continued drinking into the small hours – not too easy in Salamanca at that time because some military clown had decreed that all bars should close at midnight. But Lyall knew better.

'Come with me,' he commanded. 'We'll go to the *barrio chino* [the red light district] and find a nightclub there. All we have to do is order a bottle or two from *madame* and split them with her and her girls, and they'll let us stay drinking till morning.' He proved to be right. We even found a cabaret where we could drink and listen to a *guitarrista* who accompanied himself in a beautiful, deeply moving interpretation of García Lorca's lament for the bullfighter Sanchez Mejías.

On 26 October I received orders posting me to the Legion in the rank of *alférez*. I was to report first to Talavera, to sign on and draw my uniform, and then present myself at the headquarters of General Yagüe, GOC the Legion, at Illescas, near Madrid.

Chapter 7

AT THE DEPOT in Talavera I reported to a sour-faced captain quartermaster, who made me sign a document undertaking to serve in the Legion for the 'duration of the campaign' and issued me with my uniform. Very pleased with myself in my new green battledress and Legion officer's forage cap with its red and gold tassel, I hitch-hiked to Illescas, where I reported to Major Merino, General Yagüe's adjutant, a broad-shouldered officer with a domed forehead and quiet, sympathetic manner. He told me I was posted to the 14th Bandera, 2nd Tercio of the Legion.* The Bandera was at present in barracks at Getafe, where I reported late that night, very tired and short of sleep.

Don Alfonso de Mora, *comandante* of the 14th Bandera, greeted me coldly when I presented myself the following morning.

'We require discipline in this unit,' he observed. 'You were ordered to report to me at nine. It is now nearly ten.'

The previous night I had found him on his way to bed and he had told me to come back in the morning. I had asked my landlady to be sure and wake me early, but she had simply ignored my request and left me to sleep on. In halting Spanish I stammered my excuses. De Mora ignored them.

'I have assigned you to the 56th Company, which is the machine-gun company. Do you know anything about machine guns?'

---

* The official title of the Spanish Foreign Legion was 'La Legión', but it was generally known, incorrectly, as 'El Tercio'. It was now divided into two *tercios*, each of nine infantry *banderas* and one of tanks. The original *tercios* were the military formations of the Spanish infantry in the sixteenth century, at that time the finest infantry in all Europe. A *bandera* now contained three rifle companies and one of machine guns, and constituted some five hundred men. The CO was a major, always known as '*el comandante*'.

71

'No, sir, but I will learn.'

'You'd better. Now report to Captain Almajach.' He ordered a legionnaire to take me there. A fine start, I said to myself.

Captain Gutierrez Almajach was one of the most efficient company commanders in the Legion. Of medium height and build, he wore a perpetual half-smile on his thin lips, giving at first an impression of humour, even amiability, but his eyes behind their thick glasses were hard and his smile turned quickly into a sneer. Painstaking, very competent and undismayed by danger, he was also bloody-minded. His men feared him for his cruelty, but respected him for his steadiness in action. He chased me without mercy, never letting me get away with the smallest mistake or oversight; in consequence I learned a lot more, and more quickly, than I might have done under some more tolerant commander.

The look he gave me when I reported to him made me think he was about to summon the sanitary squad. He asked my nationality and I was sure of it.

'I shit on Englishmen,' he assured me.

I encountered this attitude, albeit less brutally expressed, throughout my service with the Nationalists; in the eyes of most of them the British were on the side of the 'Reds' and rapidly drifting towards communism. My nationality was the main reason for the suspicious, almost hostile reception I received in the 14th Bandera. Another reason for it was that most Legion officers had to achieve their commissions either through selection from regular officers of the Spanish Army, or by long service in the ranks of the Legion, whereas I had achieved mine through influence. There were hardly any foreign officers in the Legion – a mere two or three if you except such units as O'Duffy's – and now the 14th Bandera had to accept me as an officer – not only a foreigner, but an Englishman to boot! After the war de Mora told me candidly of his disgust when he heard officially of my posting; he was kind enough to assure me it hadn't lasted. However, I must say that after I had been in action once or twice with the Bandera, and they had accepted I was seriously committed to the war and not a mere *turista de guerra*, my brother officers reversed their attitude, and became more sympathetic and more indulgent towards me than if I had been a Spaniard.

The 14th Bandera was a newly formed unit, consisting partly of veterans from older *banderas*, partly of officers and other ranks fresh to the Legion. But it had already been blooded in action, near Toledo about a fortnight before and had done well in the battle, so morale was high. The *comandante*, de Mora, now in his early thirties, was a small, lightly-built man with finely chiselled features, a strong jaw, clear grey eyes and dark, curly hair receding from a high forehead. His quiet, reserved manner concealed a strict disciplinarian who demanded instant, unquestioning obedience – and got it, for he was greatly respected in the *bandera*. He was an inspiring commander whom I never saw ruffled in action, however frightening the prospects, and who never lost control of the situation for one moment. His mere presence in battle filled us with confidence.

When the Civil War started, de Mora was a lieutenant in the 7th Bandera; he took part in the bloody battle for Badajoz in August 1936 and won the *Medalla Militar* – a rare honour for such a junior officer – for conspicuous gallantry in the attack. His company had led the assault – on those same walls that had caused Wellington's army such terrible losses – in the face of intense fire from rifles and automatic weapons; de Mora and fifteen legionnaires were all that survived out of the entire company to enter the city. Standing on the ramparts, a clear target for the enemy, and waving the Nationalist flag to encourage his men, he was struck by a bullet which exploded the magazine of the pistol he carried on his hip. Two years later he had to receive daily treatment from the doctor for the still open wound, which caused him constant pain; yet I, who saw him almost every day, knew nothing of his injury until told of it by another officer at the end of the war.

The four company commanders were all veterans. Captain Eduardo Cancela commanded the leading company, the 53rd – in the Legion the companies were numbered consecutively throughout the corps. He was a slender, good-looking *gallego* with a rich, hearty laugh, a warm and friendly manner, and a rakish, confident bearing, which he maintained even in battle. He it was who told me of von Gaza's death near La Marañosa. He was the one officer in the *bandera* who from the first accepted me as a friend and comrade – he spoke a few words of English, learned in Cuba, and was very proud of them. The 53rd was the happiest company in the *bandera* and one of the most efficient; when I transferred to it from machine guns some six months later, I began my most enjoyable period of service in the whole war.

A small squat, dark officer, Captain Rodríguez, commanded the 54th Company; I remember he was quiet and courteous, with a likeable, ugly face, but I never saw much of him or his company.

The 55th Company at this time was under the command of Captain José Luengo, a strange, erratic creature with sandy hair and pale blue eyes who spoke very little, but had more disturbing ways of drawing attention to himself. He was an officer of many years' seniority in the Legion, and would certainly have achieved higher rank had not a series of distressing incidents convinced his superiors that he would never be amenable to the principles of good order and military discipline; indeed, his eccentricities were a byword in the corps long before this war began. For example, on one occasion when he should have been commanding a post up-country in Morocco his general saw him fighting a bull in the ring at Malaga. Fearless in battle, he was unfortunately inclined to bring the atmosphere of the battlefield into the bar; after a few drinks he would draw his pistol and, slowly and with great dignity, shoot out all the lights, one by one. He was universally loved in the *bandera* and even de Mora had a soft spot for him; but eventually he went too far and a court martial dismissed him from the service.

These three rifle companies each had its own mess, while the officers of Captain Almajach's 56th Company of machine guns messed at *bandera* headquarters with the *comandante* and his staff, consisting of the chaplain and the two medical officers; when I joined we had no second-in-command and no adjutant.

The chaplain, always addressed as '*Pater*', was a regular Army *padre*, a podgy, very serious-minded man in his late thirties. Conscientious, kind-hearted and very devout, he had to put up with a good deal of provocation from some of the more irreverent officers, notably the senior MO, whose flow of obscene and blasphemous language would have shocked most laymen. The *padre* endured it with Christian stoicism. His only relaxation appeared to be *julepe*, a card game at which most of the officers used to gamble – often for higher stakes than they could afford; I saw this game engender so much ill feeling that I resolved never to learn it. Although he deplored my Protestantism and was deeply shocked when I once told him clergymen of the Church of England were permitted to marry, the *padre* was always courteous to me, showed me many small kindnesses, and even took my side in the frequent arguments I had to endure from my brother officers about Britain and British policy. He was visibly relieved when I was able to assure him I was not a Freemason; in the eyes of almost all Nationalist supporters Freemasons the world over were in league with the communists.

The senior doctor, Lieutenant Larrea, was also from the regular Army. A large, portly figure with a loud, hectoring voice, he irritated me at first by his constant attacks on Britain and the British – he knew nothing of either – and by his witty sallies or outbursts of temper at my expense. Although he seemed a bully, once I had served with the *bandera* in action, his attitude changed and he soon became a good friend, for he was in fact fundamentally a good-hearted man. But I thought he was unduly severe on the legionnaires; he once sent a man to the punishment squad for asking to be sent to hospital for gonorrhoea:

'Damned shirker!' he growled. 'Whoever heard of a man going to hospital for a dose of clap?'

The other doctor, Ensign Ruiz, was a cheerful little man with a small toothbrush moustache, very good at his job, hard-working, uncomplaining and very popular with all ranks.

In my company of machine guns the senior officer after Almajach was Lieutenant Noriega, a small, wiry, grey-haired veteran of many years' service who had risen from the ranks. Although legionnaires were not always fond of ranker officers, they made an exception of Noriega, who treated them with exactly the right blend of severity and kindness; for their part they knew he would never call on them to do anything he wasn't able and willing to do himself. He had a quiet, almost taciturn manner but an admirably dry sense of humour and a remarkable knowledge of the world. In his younger days he had been a seaman and had travelled widely; later he had been in South America, smuggling arms to one or both of the belligerents in the Gran Chaco war.* Ensign Colomer, the other officer, was a Catalan, about my own age. He was a harsh-voiced, rancorous little man, forever quarrelling with his brother officers, usually over cards, and bullying his men.

The men of the 14th Bandera, like the rest of the Legion, were almost all Spanish; the remainder were mostly Portuguese – good soldiers but hard to understand, even for Spaniards. There were a few Germans, not of the best type – quite different from von Gaza – and poor fighters; also a White Russian and a Turk – the latter was almost impossible to understand, but as he hardly ever spoke it didn't matter. I soon realised my own command of Spanish wasn't nearly as good as I had thought, or as it needed to be when it came to giving orders with the flow of obscene abuse that a legionnaire expected as the proper accompaniment to any order; I found that without it my orders were either ignored or slowly and lazily executed. I quickly set about putting the matter right.

The legionnaires, like their officers, had all volunteered for this élite corps. Some were attracted by the prospects of adventure provided by service in its ranks, some by the better pay and food, and others by the prestige of belonging to it with its superb *esprit de corps* and the wide latitude allowed to legionnaires when off duty. A few had signed on for five years or three, but most, like me, for the duration of the war. Pay for all ranks was about double that of

* Fought between Bolivia and Paraguay in the 1930s over a piece of border territory; the Paraguayans won.

the regular Army conscripts, and the food was incomparably better and, except on operations, very well cooked. The officers had the same rations as the men, supplemented by a few luxuries bought out of their own pay.

Spanish troops, with good leadership and discipline, show superb qualities of courage and endurance. It was the pride of the Legion that it developed these qualities to their fullest height. From the moment he enlisted, it was impressed on the recruit that he now belonged to an élite brotherhood – the finest fighting force in the world, he was taught; it was up to him to prove himself worthy of the privilege. Battle was to be the purpose of his life, death in action his greatest honour, cowardice the ultimate disgrace. The Legion's motto was '*¡Viva la Muerte!*' This 'cult of death' has attracted much ridicule from intellectuals of the opposition, but it is essentially in keeping with the Spanish character and it produced the best soldiers of the Civil War – men almost impervious to danger and fatigue, hunger and cold. As an Englishman I have to say that the thrill of serving with and commanding such troops in action was one of the greatest experiences of my life. I also believe that a very similar spirit existed in the best units of the Republican Army like the Lister Division and, of course, the International Brigades.

The turnout and bearing of the legionnaire, whether in his *bandera* or on leave, was expected to be exemplary – 'Pride in his port, defiance in his eye –' and far superior to that of other units. Off duty he was allowed the widest freedom; he was taught to be proud of his individuality and his official designation was *caballero legionario* or gentleman legionnaire. By contrast, discipline on duty and in the field was harsh, even savage by British Army standards. Orders had to be carried out at the double, and always came reinforced by a flow of imprecation and threat; any hesitation, laxity or inefficiency was punished on the spot by a series of blows across the face and shoulders from the *fusta*, a pliant switch carried by all officers and sergeants. Serious or persistent offenders were consigned to the *pelotón de castigo* or punishment squad, to labour at the most exhausting or disagreeable tasks from before dawn until well after dark under the command of a corporal chosen for his ferocity; food in this mobile glasshouse was meagre, beatings frequent and severe. Any officer could send a man to the *pelotón*. Death was the penalty for insubordination.

From such discipline a legionnaire was apt to emerge with blunted sensibility and a callous indifference to suffering, his own or other people's, as well as near total disregard of the most horrible and squalid aspects of war. One of my machine-gun sergeants took great pleasure in telling me how he and his comrades had managed to spend a comfortable night lying out in pouring rain after a battle near Madrid.

'The ground was waterlogged of course, but fortunately it was littered with corpses. And so we collected these, arranged them in rows and used them as mattresses, covering ourselves with our greatcoats from the rain.'

After the 5th Bandera captured Talavera, my friend Fitzpatrick found a legionnaire hammering with his rifle butt at the face of a dead *miliciano*; when he protested that the man was dead, the legionnaire serenely answered, 'Yes, sir, but see! He has several gold teeth.'

I had four machine guns in my platoon, divided into two sections, each under a sergeant. The guns were Maxims that had seen service in the First World War and that we had captured from the Republicans. They were unsatisfactory weapons, already worn out and very liable to jam or suffer breakage of the firing pin; in all there were twelve machine guns in the company and two 81 mm mortars. I spent the week after I joined the Bandera in routine training, getting to know my men and trying to learn about the guns under the instruction of my two sergeants. I soon came to wish I had been sent to a rifle company, for I knew nothing of the tactical deployment of machine guns and, having no technical bent at all, could never really understand their mechanism. Almajach drove me relentlessly, with no sympathy for my ignorance, constantly exhorting me to abandon my slovenly *Requeté* habits and to improve my fluency in Spanish.

I had a batman, or *asistiente*, assigned to me, one Paulino Albarrán, a legionnaire of about my own age. He was a peasant from a village near Salamanca, of sturdy build with a podgy, fresh-complexioned face, slightly protuberant eyes and the expression of a puzzled but friendly little pig, which earned him the nickname of 'Tocinito' (*tocino* is fat bacon). He had been a first-class machinegunner and was one of the best-natured fellows I ever met; but he was a better soldier than servant – at least when he first came to me.

On 7 November the *bandera* received orders to move. After a brief march we all piled into a train – first-class carriages for the officers, five to each compartment, second class for the sergeants and cattle trucks for the men, who must have frozen in them at night; and so began a slow journey of several days and nights, via Talavera, Salamanca and Burgos, to the North East.

Chapter 8

RUMOUR HELD THAT we were bound for the Guadalajara front, to take part in a new offensive on Madrid; so indeed we were, but it was a month before we got there. We passed the interval in Aragon, billeted in various small towns and villages south of Saragossa, along the main Saragossa-Teruel road. Among the most attractive was Calamocha, where we spent a comfortable fortnight, the officers staying in private houses; there was an ancient church with a moat, in which mules would paddle, and a stone, humped bridge across a swift-running stream.

The Aragonese, or *maños*, are blunt, hard-headed, plain-speaking and obstinate; but they are among the most hospitable people in Spain. I spent the greater part of a year in various parts of Aragon, and noticed that however harsh and uninviting the countryside, the people fared remarkably well for food and drink. They had a great hatred for the Republicans, from whom they had suffered much in the early days of the war – which made them particularly friendly towards us.

We had few duties at this time and so I often went walking outside Calamocha, where the bare contours and harsh colours of the countryside gleamed soft and mellow in the bright sunlight and clear air of late autumn. The grape harvest was in and the peasants were busy preparing the new wine. One afternoon I came upon a whitewashed farmhouse with a wine press in the vineyard beside it; an old man with a pointed white beard was working there, with his family round him. When he saw me he called out in a hearty, raucous voice.

'Come here, young man!' With some curiosity I approached. 'I'm Satan,' he roared. 'You know they call me Satan because of my beard. Also, I think, because of the good wine I make. You and I are going to drink some of it together.'

He handed me a great beaker of purple, bubbling liquid. When I had praised it and thanked him while his family stood by, the men with broad, friendly grins, the girls giggling happily, he went indoors and came back with a dusty bottle. He made me drink half of it, sharing the rest between his two sons and himself. Then he fetched another bottle, which he split with me, muttering the while, 'Oh, I'm Satan alright,' wagging his beard, now flecked with purple. At last I managed to take my leave and make my way unsteadily back to Calamocha, with several halts on the way to rest. At the entrance to the *plaza* I met the *padre*.

'*¡Hola!*' he greeted me. 'Where have you been?'

'Drinking with Satan,' I gasped, and left him standing agog.

After two weeks in Calamocha we moved by lorry to a small village in the bleak uplands east of the Saragossa-Teruel road, about three miles from the front; this was Torrecilla and we were to see much more of it in the following February. We spent the first ten days of December there, prepared to go into action at a moment's notice – which, however, didn't prevent us from celebrating the feast of the Virgin of the Immaculate Conception, patroness of the Spanish infantry, with an enormous lunch on 8 December; it was as well we weren't called into action that day or the next. However, two days later the fleet of lorries arrived again, at five in the morning, to take us on an eleven-hour journey right across Aragon into Castile, until we reached the village of Berlanga del Duero, with its square castle standing by itself on a mound above it. Here we disembarked and moved into billets.

Now at last, it seemed we were about to take part in the great Guadalajara offensive, which we believed was to settle finally the fate of Madrid and finish the war. On 13 December de Mora summoned all officers for a briefing.

'The operations against Guadalajara and Madrid,' he began, 'are about to start and I expect the order to move off at any time now. There will be three Army corps taking part, and we shall be with the Marroqui Army corps, on the right flank. We constitute the *brigada móvil* of the corps, along with the 16th Bandera and cavalry, artillery and tanks; our two *banderas* will form the brigade's motorised infantry group, transported in lorries, under the command of Lieutenant-Colonel Peñaredonda. I will brief you in detail before we go into action,' continued de Mora. 'Meanwhile, here are some points for you to remember. There appears to be an idea that in an advance officers should always be at the head of their platoons or companies; also that it is an officer's duty to expose himself all the time to enemy fire, to encourage his men. Both these ideas are nonsense and I'll have none of them in my *bandera*. The only time when an officer's place *is* at the head of his men is in the final assault; otherwise it is in the *middle* of his company or platoon, where he can exercise proper control. I want this rule observed and I also warn you all that I will deal most severely with any officer exposing himself needlessly to fire or allowing his men to do so. I've no doubt there will be plenty of opportunities to display your courage; but otherwise officers must keep their vanity and exhibitionism under proper restraint.'

He went on to deal with technical and tactical details for the forthcoming operations, and concluded:

'One final point: you will make certain the rights of civilians are scrupulously respected. There will be no looting. If there is any instance of an attempt on the virtue of a woman it will be punished on the spot – with death. Remember, the orders I've given you now will be observed in any future operations under my command.'

Two days later the Republicans struck at Teruel.

They mounted a night attack – once again the architect was Colonel Enrique Lister – and entered the town almost without loss after surprising the Nationalist garrison in their sleep. In truth the position of Teruel was always precarious. It formed a small salient running into Republican territory and was dominated on three sides by the enemy; its only communication and supply line was a single road and railway leading north through Calamocha to Saragossa, which the Republicans overlooked from their positions in the Sierra Palomera to the east and which they frequently shelled. Only in a civil war would it have been defended, but because it contained twenty thousand inhabitants the Nationalists had to hold on to it.

Busy with their preparations for the Guadalajara offensive, they were taken completely by surprise. Franco immediately abandoned his plans for Guadalajara and hastened to regroup his forces for the recapture of Teruel. We thought it strange at the time that he should leave his principal objective for a secondary one; possibly he felt this was an opportunity to destroy the Republican Army around Teruel and open the way for an advance towards the Mediterranean. I don't suppose he knew what suffering he was going to cause us all; for no one, even in Spain, could have foreseen the full ferocity of that approaching winter.

The Nationalist counter-offensive began on 22 December; Teruel was not yet wholly in the Republicans' hands, but they had surrounded it and cut it off from all sides. Two Nationalist Army corps attacked, one from the north, the other from the south west, and slowly pushed back the Republicans until, on the last day of 1937, they were poised to break through and relieve the remnants of the Teruel garrison. That night the winter set in with a pitiless, numbing cold not experienced in living memory. Spaniards have told me, only recently, that their country has not known so severe a winter since then; and some, who fought with the 'Blue Division' in Russia, assured me they never had to face such cold there as they did at Teruel. It was bad enough on the plains of the *meseta*, but nothing compared to conditions here at well over three thousand feet – as I was to find out for myself.

It began to snow. The temperature dropped to −20°C. The advance came to a halt. Caught in the open by the blizzard, without shelter or adequate clothing – neither of the opposing armies had proper clothing for such weather – and unable even to light fires for warmth because they were in sight of the enemy, the Nationalists lost more men from cold and exposure in the next few days than from enemy action. The general commanding one of the Navarre divisions – they had been expanded from the original brigades – told me later that over the next three or four days his division suffered 3,500 cases of mild or severe frostbite. Meanwhile, the Republicans, better protected from the weather with the cruel east wind at their backs, pressed home their assault on the city; it fell to them on 8 January.

Only the scantiest news of these events reached us in Berlanga del Duero, through the official communiqués, which did, however, announce the fall of Teruel. It was clear that the operations discussed in de Mora's briefing would not take place, at least for some time. We settled into an unexciting routine of training, parades and long route marches in the snow. We saw a lot of Colonel Peñaredonda and the more we saw of him the less we liked him. A tall, well-built officer of about fifty, with a fleshy face and sullen, discontented expression, he spoke very little and almost always to complain; he found fault with everyone from de Mora downwards and soon managed to dissipate the old happy atmosphere in the *bandera*. But it wasn't until we had to fight under him that we realised what an incompetent and evil man he was. Just before Christmas Captain Luengo left us, to the great relief of the café proprietors of Berlanga; in his place came another veteran of the pre-war Legion, Captain Alonso de Castañeda, a tall, slim, fair-haired officer with a handsome face and dashing manner. He was an old friend of de Mora's, intelligent, independent-minded and unorthodox in his opinions, which he never hesitated to express, for he loved an argument. He would poke fun at the Church when the *padre* was there, or cast doubts on the so-called universal depravity of the Republicans to provoke de Mora or Cancela; but he was much too good-hearted a fellow to arouse serious anger and nobody could question his fine martial qualities. He always took my side in disputes about British policy or conduct – probably for contrariness rather than conviction, but it was a comfort to have him on my side. A truly dedicated soldier, he also had a sincere love of literature, especially poetry.

Any lingering hopes that we might take part in a motorised offensive disappeared with the arrival of mules, thirty-one of them in our company, to carry our machine guns and ammunition. I had eight in my platoon. At first they caused a good deal of grumbling and some pretty purple language among our legionnaires, who hadn't had dealings with mules before, and had no idea how to attach and secure their leads; while the mules themselves showed an obstinate if understandable reluctance to keep formation in the ranks. But in time and with patience and good treatment they became quite tractable, and the men became fond of them. We found they would carry heavy loads all day over the roughest mountain country with hardly any food or even water and they were much more sure-footed than a horse would have been; moreover they hardly ever panicked under fire.

During these two months while 1937 drew to its cold and bleak conclusion, only one incident stands out in my memory: the great fire of Berlanga. It happened in the week before Christmas, one night when I had the bad luck to be officer of the *vigilancia* – a kind of military policeman for the *bandera*. My billet was in a small house by the Plaza Mayor owned by a middle-aged working couple, who treated me as one of their own family; they had two pretty daughters of sixteen and nineteen – who engaged most of my batman Paulino's attention. I had returned there for a drink and a chat between patrols when an agitated legionnaire reported that a fire had broken out in the seventeenth-century *palacio* in the *plaza*, and was rapidly taking hold. The owners of the *palacio* had long ago left Berlanga and the old building was now a billet for troops – legionnaires from the 16th Bandera and *Requetés*; it was as well they were there, for if the townspeople had been left to put out the fire I think not only the *palacio* but a large part of the town would have burnt. When I arrived there I found the *palacio* a mass of flames, which lit up the sky and the whole *plaza*, and silhouetted the castle on its bare mound in macabre floodlight. The *Requetés* and legionnaires were working with a will, climbing up the walls and scrambling over rooftops with hoses and axes, or passing buckets of water from the fountain in the *plaza* and from the river to the two ancient, hand-pumped fire engines that were Berlanga's sole equipment, each with its crew of four puffing, laughing peasants. The townspeople stood around the *plaza* in little groups, smoking and pointing happily to the blazing building.

'Look how it burns!' they shouted. 'We haven't had as good a fire as this for fifty years!'

They seemed deeply pained, even shocked, by my suggestion that they should help in the work.

There was no hope of saving the *palacio*, but we had to stop the flames spreading to the rest of the town; luckily it was a calm, windless night. I was on my feet till daylight, directing and helping in the firefighting; but the fire was still blazing and threatening to spread at seven the next morning. The townspeople, having enjoyed the spectacle for a few hours, had gone home to sleep, but now they began to emerge again to have another look; the firemen had abandoned their engines and turned in, and so I put some of our legionnaires to pump them. I found two fresh engines standing idle in a street; when I expressed my indignation to the *alguacil* or town clerk, he said in surprise, 'You mean that they should work?' It seems they had come from a town fifteen miles away. I found the crews eventually and asked them sharply to get a move on.

'We're going to do just that, lieutenant,' they answered cheerfully as they swigged from bottles of *aguardiente*,* 'as soon as we've had a little drink to warm up.'

I was truly thankful to come off duty half an hour later, just in time to have coffee and a shave before going on parade. The fire burnt on until late afternoon.

The New Year of 1938 opened sadly for me with the death of a good friend, Dick Sheepshanks, the *Daily Telegraph* correspondent. He was killed near Teruel, travelling in a car with three other journalists, two of them American and the other Kim Philby. A Republican artillery shell burst beside the car, killing Sheepshanks and the two Americans; Philby alone survived, with a spectacular but not very severe head wound. God is not always on the side of the angels.

A new ensign, senior to me, was posted to our company and took over my machine-gun section while I was relegated to command the mortar platoon. I was sorry because I was getting to know and like my men and NCOs – if not their guns. I was deeply troubled when a group of them under a corporal formed up and begged me to ask the captain to let me stay with them – until I was fool enough to pass on their request to Almajach.

'Of course they want you to stay. They get away with much more under you than under any Spaniard.'

* A rough, aniseed-based spirit drunk all over Spain.

At about this time we in the 56th Company had to suffer a new burden in the form of a *subteniente* who appeared on our strength; this rank, corresponding very roughly to warrant-officer class-one in the British Army, no longer existed in the Spanish Army but persisted in the Legion. This creature was a cocky, officious little man with a shiny red face, a pert manner verging on downright impertinence towards us ensigns, a squeaky, querulous voice, and the appearance and manners of a monkey. He started to throw his weight about from the very first moment, abusing the NCOs and laying into the men with his *fusta* on the slightest pretext, or with none. We couldn't hope to control him, because Almajach strongly approved if not of him then at least of his methods; in turn the *subteniente* behaved towards his captain with a sickening obsequiousness. Day and night thereafter we had to listen to his hideous brays of criticism and complaint.

On 10 January the *bandera* left Berlanga to spend the rest of the month travelling around the province by lorry or on foot. My mortar platoon was out on detachment part of the time, in support of one or other of the rifle companies, especially Cancela's 53rd; I enjoyed the week I spent with them, for under Cancela's leadership the men were the most cheerful in the *bandera*, the officers the most hospitable and friendly. Our work was not dangerous in this stable section of the front, but we had to watch out for snipers since we were in full view of the enemy and I lost one of my runners from a machine-gun burst. The work, though, was dull and arduous, fortifying hilltop positions by night – it was impossible in daylight. The ground was almost solid rock and the legionnaires' hands, as they hewed into it with their picks, were soon covered in blisters. But their spirits remained high and neither the pain of their sores nor the bitter cold of the nights could depress them.

It was clear we were facing a demoralised enemy here, conscripts of poor quality. We had a constant trickle of deserters crawling through their wire at night to hand themselves over to us – frozen, starved, miserable and frightened. Having been told by their political commissars that we shot all prisoners, they soon cheered up when we gave them soup and cigarettes, and they chattered freely; they complained of well-fed political commissars from Madrid who came for a few hours to give them lectures on the 'fighting spirit' or the 'meaning of democracy'.

We spent most of the daytime in one or other of the villages nearby, after setting outposts on the hills. Bleak and gloomy as was this bare landscape, the condition of the inhabitants was even sadder. Their houses were little better than hovels, the village streets were piled with refuse, and dangerously pitted with holes and shell craters; there had been heavy fighting in this area during the Italian offensive of March 1937. Each morning and evening when the troops assembled for *rancho* – food – the village children would gather round our field kitchens with little bowls or jars, which our cooks would fill with meat, fish, bread and vegetables; but after two or three days their parents asked us to cease giving them meat and fish because they had never eaten them before and they upset their stomachs. Bread, too, was an unknown luxury, for their regular diet was a mess of beans or *garbanzos* (chickpeas). But for all their wretchedness and starving condition, these people were a kind and warm-hearted breed who spared no effort to make us as comfortable as they could.

On 1 February we left the Guadalajara area and embarked in lorries for another long journey, back to Aragon. We disembarked in a large village near Calamocha, where we spent the next few days preparing ourselves for action, at last, in the battle for Teruel. We were issued with new uniforms, similar to the British Army battledress of the Second World War; they included, most welcome of all, thick, wide-skirted, green greatcoats to replace our worn out old *capotes*. But I remember that day particularly for a most unpleasant incident. I was supervising the company's midday *rancho* and was watching the distribution of it, while the men stood in line and the *subteniente* and CQMS observed from a distance. Suddenly I heard the *subteniente* burst into a scream of anger and saw him advance on one of the men at the end of the line; in a moment he was laying into the legionnaire with his *fusta*, almost incoherent with rage. To this day I don't know the cause of it; but when I hastened over to them the *subteniente*, flushed and quivering, was standing in front of the man, whose face wore an expression of angry defiance and whose cap was lying on the ground where the *subteniente* had knocked it.

'Now pick it up!' he yelled.

'I will not,' growled the legionnaire.

'You're under arrest!' I snapped at him. 'Escort him to the *vigilancia*,' I ordered two of the others. '*Subteniente*, please make a written report on this affair.'

Almajach was indignant when I told him and I could see the *comandante* was not pleased either.

'Did you not have a pistol?' snarled the Captain. 'Well then, why didn't you shoot the fellow on the spot? That is how we deal with mutiny in the Legion. Now we'll have a court martial on our hands.'

As it happened, we had more important things to occupy us for the rest of that month; but I was left wondering if I should ever make a Legion officer.

Chapter 9

ON THE MORNING of 5 February the harsh contours of the Sierra Palomera gleamed in bright sunlight beneath a clear blue sky; mist still hung in wisps down in the plain behind us, where the road we had crossed the previous day ran north from Teruel towards Saragossa, but up here on the slopes the jagged outcrops of rock and deep narrow ravines stood out in a stark contrast of light and shade. I was standing on the steep side of a mountain, some two hundred yards below the crest of a stony ridge between two great shoulders of rock that sloped back towards the plain; they formed a wide amphitheatre a half mile in circumference. Its craggy sides, bare of vegetation, were swarming with troops – legionnaires in olive-green battledress, *Requetés* in scarlet berets, khaki-clad infantry and gunners; the whole amphitheatre appeared covered in men, horses, mules, artillery and equipment. The 5th Navarre Division, with the 14th and 16th Banderas, was massed below the crest waiting to launch a great assault.

We had left our billet near Calamocha the morning before and marched most of the day; crossing the Saragossa-Teruel road at the village of Caminreal, we had climbed east-south-east into the hills and spent the night in the open. Despite the cold and the hard ground we slept well and awoke refreshed, everyone in high spirits with the prospect of imminent action after months of inactivity and boredom.

Before moving up to our assembly point this morning we were told to leave our blankets and greatcoats for the *bandera* pack train to collect and deliver to us in the evening, along with the rations; they would only impede our mobility in action. As we wound up the steep track in a narrow column I saw Colonel Peñaredonda watching us; he was in a genial mood.

'*Hola*, Mr Peter,' he called to me. 'Are you looking forward to this?'

'We're really going into action, sir?'

'Certainly we are. There are five divisions taking part in these operations.'

We were now standing on the mountainside, waiting for the artillery and air bombardment to begin. I could sense the tension spreading among the troops all round me; a hush seemed to fall over the whole area. Men talked only in undertones; the clink of weapons and harness sounded unnaturally loud, and the bray of a mule from far off might have been a trumpet call. I heard a strident female voice and saw a girl in Legion uniform talking to a sergeant in Cancela's company; she was aged about thirty, but looked older, with a brown, leathery face and short black hair. She was a *legionaria*, one of a breed familiar to all *banderas*; they were licensed camp-followers, cooking, washing and mending for the men generally, and making themselves useful in various ways. However it was not often they followed their *bandera* into action. This girl had been with the Legion a long time, she had a good training in first aid and acted as assistant to the *practicante*, or medical orderly, of the 53rd Company. She was as tough and brave as any of the men, as she was soon to show.

'Excuse me,' a voice said in English beside me, 'but didn't we meet at Cambridge?' I turned to find a gunner lieutenant of about my own age studying me closely. He was tall and slightly built, with a pleasant, clean-shaven face and sallow complexion. He put out his hand. 'I'm Guy Spaey – known as Guido here. You're Kemp, yes? I was at King's and you, I think, were at Trinity.'

I nodded and shook hands. He went on to tell me he was of mixed Belgian, Dutch and German extraction, but he spoke flawless English. He had arrived in Spain a month before me and had joined the Nationalist Army immediately. At present he was gun position officer of a mountain battery of 105 mm artillery attached to Peñaredonda's command.

It was about 10.30 when we heard a droning in the sky and saw a formation of silver twin-engine bombers approaching from the west with an escort of biplane fighters. They flew over our heads towards the enemy positions and a minute afterwards we heard the deep thunder of their bombs. At the same time, from all around us our batteries opened fire, from the mountains on either side, from the foothills and from the plain behind us; the air was alive with the hiss of their shells passing over us. The aircraft returned to circle above us for a second run and we heard again the roll of exploding bombs.

The bombardment lasted two hours, with a continuous barrage from our guns, while successive waves of bombers flew over to unload on the enemy fortifications. Not a shell came back in reply, nor was there a sign of enemy air activity. Surprise must have been complete. When it became clear that this was going to be a protracted bombardment we all relaxed and tried to make ourselves comfortable. None of us had the faintest idea of our plan of battle, but I supposed de Mora would brief us when the time came to advance. I watched another formation of our bombers approaching. From where I sat they looked almost beautiful as they came on in perfect formation, steady and unhurried, silver against the deep blue sky, with the sun flashing on their metal fuselages and wings – flashing, too, on a tiny object that dropped from the leader, to be followed immediately by more from the entire formation. It took me a moment to understand our appalling predicament. Then, as I heard Almajach's urgent shouts, I roared at my platoon:

'Down where you are! Flat on the ground! Hold on to your mule ropes! Keep your faces down!'

Seconds later the ground exploded in a great orange flash, and a fountain of earth and stones erupted from the slope a hundred yards away. I threw myself down, pressing my face against my arms into the rock. Then the entire mountain was torn apart in a convulsion of flame, the ground shook as in an earthquake, and the air was full of flying metal and boulders; the explosions hammered against my eardrums and tore at my clothes. There followed a horrible silence. I staggered to my feet, deaf and battered by blast, and blinded by the dust that hung in a thick cloud over the whole area. Slowly the singing in my ears subsided, and I began to hear the groans and whimpers of wounded and dying men, the screams of injured and frightened animals, and a swelling roar of fury and indignation from the troops. As visibility returned I saw that most of the bombs had landed among us – an entire division massed together on that mountainside in the open with no cover; and the rocky ground with all the loose stones had increased the destruction wrought by the explosions. I called to my men; although badly shaken they were unhurt, apart from cuts and bruises. I was examining the mules when I heard fresh shouting. Looking up I saw the bombers had circled and were coming back, still in perfect formation, to pass right above us. Oh my God, I thought, they can't be going to do it again! Please, dear God, *don't* let them! But as I focussed my glasses on them I saw, with horror, the leader unload his second cargo of bombs, followed by the others. Yells of fury rose from the troops.

'*¡Cabrones! ¡Cabrones! ¡Hijos de la gran puta!*'

Men were running in all directions up the flanks of the mountain, in a mad, useless and crazy rush to escape. Once again I shouted to my platoon.

'Stay where you are and get *down*! Hold on to the mules!'

The bombs seemed to take forever falling. I was praying feverishly I shouldn't be hit, or at least not maimed – and I'm quite sure I wasn't the only one praying. Then the ground was shaking once again, the detonations hammering at my ears, flying fragments screaming close overhead, then the choking dust and the grisly silence. A minute later came the cries and groaning of the wounded.

When I dragged myself to my feet my legs were shaking so that I could scarcely stand; I had to get my voice under control before I could call to my platoon. But I was uninjured and so, I was thankful to learn once more, were my men. One had a narrow escape when a bomb burst within a few feet of him; he had a small cut in the forehead from a splinter of rock and was so shaken by the blast that he was vomiting all day. Two of my mules were dead; one had bolted but was soon recaptured. These animals had shown astonishing docility both during the bombing and afterwards; one even had a bomb fragment in the shoulder, but continued to carry his load throughout the next two days' operations with no sign of pain or fatigue. The *bandera* had been very lucky, with only two legionnaires dead and three wounded badly enough to go to hospital. But elsewhere the carnage was terrible: over five hundred casualties, including 156 killed, in under five minutes. Our sister *bandera*, the 16th, had suffered heavily, losing one of its best company commanders, whose foot was taken off at the ankle by a splinter. The entire amphitheatre resembled a monstrous *abattoir*, with disembowelled horses, shreds of human flesh and clothing, and severed limbs strewn around among the broken wreckage of guns and equipment. I noticed the *legionaria* I had seen earlier moving among the wounded, calmly and competently tying bandages, applying tourniquets, giving morphia pills and exchanging jokes in her hoarse chuckle with the less serious cases.

We saw – and wanted to see – no more of our aircraft that day. At the time we couldn't imagine how the mistake had occurred; we had spread white identification panels in front of our position to show the aircraft where we were, but they had evidently failed to see them. After the war, however, a Spanish friend of mine, who was navigator of the leading aircraft, confessed to me that it was a plain error on his part. It was a costly and unforgivable one.

And so began the Battle of the Alfambra or Battle of the Sierra Palomera. The Nationalist objective, we now learned, was to clear the Republicans from their positions in the Sierra, from which they had harassed the road and railway running north from Teruel, and to occupy all the territory eastwards as far as the River Alfambra. Their plan was simple. The Republican positions on the Sierra were considered too strong for a frontal assault; but behind them, between the mountains and the Alfambra, the ground opened out into a wide, undulating plateau, broken by a few hills and ridges, which sloped gently down to the river valley. This area was to be the battleground.

The operation, a great enveloping movement, was to involve not merely the five divisions mentioned to me by Peñaredonda but three Army corps, one attacking from the south-west, another from the north-east and the third from the north-west. Once the bombardment had destroyed the Republican positions on the Sierra, a cavalry division was to sweep across the open country behind to the banks of the Alfambra, while the infantry followed on. In the end, the fighting lasted only three days, in which the Nationalists inflicted some fifteen thousand casualties on the enemy and took another seven thousand prisoners, at very little cost to themselves. It sealed the fate of Teruel.

We junior officers in the 14th Bandera were aware of only the bare outline of this plan as it affected our own areas; we found we had no serious fighting to do – but plenty of walking. We envied the cavalry as we saw them galloping across the plain in extended order while we plodded on wearily in what soon became very trying heat. We were thankful we had left our greatcoats and blankets behind – we were to change our minds when night fell. We soon realised the Republicans had abandoned their defences as far as the Alfambra after that storm of shelling and air bombardment; after our own experience of that morning I, for one, couldn't blame them. I was still feeling its effects and it was a while before I was able to watch without apprehension our own aircraft flying over us. The truth was I had been badly frightened – as, I discovered, had most of us. I overheard Cancela talking to Almajach.

'That *practicante* in my company,' he was saying, 'certainly has guts. She is still with us and for any woman to want to go on after what happened this morning – well, I can only tell you I feel like lying down the moment I hear an aeroplane!'

Towards dusk we halted for the night on a bare, snow-covered ridge overlooking another broad plain and two villages where the Republicans had retreated after abandoning the ridge. The darkness brought a sharp fall in temperature and now at over four thousand feet above sea level it was bitterly cold, with a faint wind from the East like a caress of ice. It was clear that our pack train, with our overcoats and blankets, would never find us in the darkness; moreover, we received strict orders that because we were in full view of the enemy we must, as before, light no fires. When we had opened the tins of sardines and tunny we had brought along as emergency rations, and eaten them in our numbed fingers (since Teruel I've never been able to face tunny), we lay down in the snow in our battledress, but with little hope of sleep. We warned those men who had flasks of *aguardiente* not to drink from them because it would make them feel the cold even more. The temperature dropped to well below freezing. Lying on my back in the space I had cleared of snow, I looked up at the bright stars twinkling overhead in the clear sky; they seemed to be mocking my vain efforts to sleep. It was indeed a beautiful night, but I was in no mood to rhapsodise over it. When the cold became unbearable I would get up and pace around to get some warmth and circulation back into my body, before trying again to sleep before the glow passed off.

I must have succeeded because I awoke without even knowing I had slept, to find the sky a pale rose above the valley of the Alfambra. When I tried to stand up I found the front of my jacket and breeches were stiff and white with frost; it was thick in my eyebrows and my hair, and had indeed formed icicles in my nostrils, as that old colonel back in London had warned me. I smiled at the memory, but the smile left my face almost at once when I saw a group of legionnaires bending over a row of stiff figures on the ground. Some of our men had not survived the cold.

The daylight brought the pack train – better late than never – and welcome news that we might light fires. Gratefully we swallowed mugs of hot coffee, liberally laced with the *aguardiente* we had avoided hitherto, surely the best pick-me-up after such a cold and sleepless night. As we advanced, the warmth of the sun and the movement of our stiff limbs put new life into us and we forgot our miseries. There was no sign of the enemy, but the sound of firing from the Alfambra told of their continuing retreat. In the late afternoon we came to Visiedo, the last village before the river, and received orders to camp there for the night. A few houses had survived the fighting and some were still inhabited; but best of all we came upon the abandoned supply depot of a Republican division. We placed a guard on it, but not until we had distributed crates of tinned food among the companies.

In Visiedo we encountered our only serious opposition of the day – in the form of a furious old woman, who stormed into de Mora's headquarters about an hour after our arrival to complain that our men had stolen one of her chickens.

'Villains!' she screamed, shaking her fist at all of us. 'Bandits! They thought I didn't see them, but I saw them all right! Liberators you call yourselves? Why, you're worse than the Reds!'

De Mora let her finish – I believe she would have scratched out his eyes if he'd tried to interrupt. Then he asked her what she thought her loss was worth, paid her the sum she demanded and sent the officer of the *vigilancia* to find the culprits. They did a month in the *pelotón*. The Iron Duke, who hanged or flogged his troops for looting, would have approved of de Mora.

The only houses fit to sleep in were occupied by their owners and so we spent another night in the open; but at least it wasn't as cold on the plain as it had been on top of the Sierra, and moreover we had our greatcoats and blankets. The following day we retraced our steps westwards to the Sierra Palomera; the Nationalists had no intention of pursuing the enemy beyond the Alfambra. We spent the next three nights camped on the Sierra and the intervening days rounding up the broken remains of the Republican forces trapped in those mountains. They offered scarcely any resistance and only wished to surrender as quickly as they could; these were no hardy fighters of the International Brigades, but reluctant Spanish conscripts, whom we disarmed and, after giving them a few cigarettes, sent back to prisoner-of-war camps. The days involved us in hard climbing among the stony ridges of the Sierra and the nights in acute discomfort, lying on the rocky ground in an icy wind that cut clean through our blankets and greatcoats. We completed our sweeps on the fourth day, made our way by steep, winding tracks down to the plain and limped wearily into Torremocha in the evening, to enjoy a few days of comfortable billets and good food. The battle of the Sierra Palomera had cost the *bandera* a bare half dozen casualties from enemy fire. But the cold had killed an equal number of us.

From the rocks of the Sierra Palomera to a comfortable bed in the Gran Hotel at Saragossa was the kind of abrupt change one regarded as normal in the Civil War. Torremocha was a bare three hours by road from Saragossa, where Spaey and I arrived on forty-eight hours' leave a couple of days after our descent from the Sierra. After a hot bath and change of clothes I went downstairs to meet Spaey for a drink, but we had been only a few moments standing in the great marble lounge of the hotel when we heard our names shouted from across the room. Seated at a table with three whiskies and sodas in front of him was Captain von Hartmann, a Finnish cavalry officer I had already met in San Sebastian. He had a knowledge of almost every European language, and spoke English with a strong American intonation and a curious use of idiom.

'Goddamnit!' he cried. 'I see you two bastards crossing the foyer half an hour ago, so I order these whiskies. It's a local whisky and it's terrible! See if you can drink it.' I couldn't, nor could Spaey.

'Neither can I,' said von Hartmann. 'I'm a cavalryman and I know what that stuff's made of. We'll settle for brandy.'

Goggi von Hartmann was short and wiry, with impressive good looks; otherwise he resembled a typical Prussian officer of stage and screen, with close-cropped hair, a scarred face and a monocle. But he had an enthusiastic and volatile temperament, a generous nature and a keen sense of humour. There was scarcely a place on the world map that he didn't know. 'Sure, I've been there,' he would say. 'They put me in the can.' A nephew of the great Finnish national hero, Marshal Mannerheim, he had gone to war at an early age, serving in the German Army on the Eastern Front in the Great War, first as a cavalry officer, later as a pilot. Afterwards he had fought under his famous uncle in the First Finnish War of Independence, when Finland defeated the Bolsheviks. In the early months of the Spanish Civil War he commanded a squadron of mounted Falange, but later became involved in the Hedilla plot against Franco, was put under house arrest and lost his command. Now he had just been released and was about to take over an infantry battalion. He must have owed this leniency to his universal popularity and the Nationalists' respect for a fine fighting soldier. He had more wounds than General Millán Astray, some of which showed on his face; he was to suffer yet more, one in the Civil War and others in the Second Finnish War of Independence, including the loss of an eye at Petsamo.

Our forty-eight hours' leave passed all too quickly and on the afternoon of 15 February we left Saragossa to rejoin our units. We found Spaey's battery in a village about fifteen miles north of Torremocha; they told me my *bandera* had moved east to Torrecilla del Rebollar, where we had been in December. The battery was going that way at dawn and would give me a lift. After a few hours' broken sleep on the floor of a chilly, unheated room I climbed into a lorry in the freezing darkness of early morning and reached Torrecilla in the first hour of daylight. It was deserted, but a little further on I came upon the *bandera* commissariat, where I learned that the *bandera* was in action about a mile to the north-east. Already I could hear the explosions of shells and mortar bombs. I found a legionnaire to guide me and hastened on foot in the direction of the fighting.

The road ran eastwards for a few hundred yards before dropping into a rocky valley studded with shrubs and pine trees. It was hard and very slow going, but the sound of firing gradually drew nearer and intensified, bullets started to whistle through the branches overhead and a few shells landed on the hillside nearby. As we were crossing the valley I saw a young Catalan ensign from the 53rd

Company walking slowly down the hill towards us from the direction of the fighting; he was very pale and had his arm in a sling. Although obviously in great pain he managed to smile a greeting.

'Take care up there, Peter,' he gasped. 'Things are pretty bad and we've taken a lot of casualties. I've got a bullet in my wrist and it hurts like hell.'

He continued on his way back and I started to climb the ridge ahead. About a hundred yards below the crest I found de Mora with Noriega, the *padre* and the two doctors; the *subteniente* was there too, looking thoroughly miserable and taking surreptitious swigs from a bottle of brandy. The next twenty-four hours saw my first experience of the International Brigades.

The previous day the Republicans had launched a surprise attack on this sector with two International Brigades, one Canadian and one Anglo-American, so I was told, with two Spanish brigades in support. In their first onslaught they had overrun the Nationalists' forward positions, capturing the road and rail junction at the village of Segura. But their further advance was blocked by a second line of defence, on this ridge where we were now sitting near the hamlet of Villanueva del Rebollar, four miles east of Torrecilla. The two 'mobile *banderas*', the 14th and 16th under Colonel Peñaredonda, were rushed to the scene with orders to counter-attack and retake Segura and the lost positions; in support were an infantry battalion and one or two batteries of field guns. It was a thoroughly ill-conceived operation. The Nationalist command, General Camilo Alonso's 4th Navarre Division, seemed quite ignorant of the enemy's strength and of the distance our own troops must cover between their assault positions and their objectives – about a mile of difficult country, much of it brutally exposed to the defenders' fire. And so a force of under two thousand men, with scarcely any artillery and no air support, was sent into a daylight attack against an enemy greatly superior in numbers, well dug in on a high ridge, well supplied with automatic weapons and supported by at least the same weight of artillery as the attackers; this enemy, more-over, consisted of the Republicans' crack troops, the International Brigades.

Between the opposing lines ran two valleys separated by a low, pine-covered ridge; scrub and small bushes grew in the valleys and on the lower slopes. At first light that morning de Mora, with his company commanders, had made a personal reconnaissance of the nearer valley – the one I had just crossed – to select a route for his advance. They came under fire immediately. Captain Almajach received a bullet in the foot, which shattered the bone and crippled him for life. Noriega took over the company. Taking advantage of such cover as the undergrowth afforded, the *bandera* advanced down the forward slope against a lethal volume of fire from almost a hundred heavy and light machine guns. In spite of casualties it crossed the first valley and reached the low ridge of hills about six hundred yards from the enemy. Here de Mora halted and placed his machine guns. When I arrived he was about to continue the attack.

I was put in command of a machine-gun platoon on top of the ridge, on the right flank; two of its four guns had already been destroyed by shell or mortar fire. I hurried off to supervise the distribution of ammunition, and arrange for the provision and carriage of fresh supplies during the ensuing engagement; then I prepared to bring my two remaining guns into action, to cover the rifle companies' advance. Across the valley I could make out where the enemy positions were located, well concealed among the pines and dominating our own; my orders were simply to maintain as high and accurate a volume of fire upon them as possible. My left-hand gun was emplaced behind a low, broken-down brick wall which had once formed part of a pigsty; it gave cover rather than protection; the other gun was shielded, inadequately, by a rough, shallow earthwork constructed by the crew.

As soon as the rifle companies began to move down through the trees in front, the enemy opened fire all along their line, sweeping the forward slope and the crest of our ridge with a steady rain of bullets, mortar bombs and shells. As I ran from gun to gun, crouching low and taking what cover I could from the formation of the ground, I wondered how anyone could survive in the open against such a devastating weight of fire. I flung myself to the ground beside each gun in turn, straining to mark through my glasses the impact of its bursts on the enemy positions, and passing corrections in elevation and direction to the sergeant in command, shouting my orders to make myself heard above the stammer of the gun. I tried to hold the glasses steady, to give my orders without a tremor in my voice and to ignore the vicious spatter of the enemy's bullets. The legionnaires needed no encouragement from me; quietly, efficiently and with occasional jokes they worked the two guns, maintaining a steady rate of fire as if they were on range practice.

It was difficult at that distance to be certain just where our shots were falling, but when I had satisfied myself as best I could that we were firing on target I stationed myself and my two runners in between the guns where I could control them both. The enemy artillery and mortars were searching for us, their shells throwing up earth and stones around us. Shells from our own guns on the ridge behind us whirred close overhead, some of them landing short, uncomfortably near. We had been in action for twenty minutes or half an hour when a mortar bomb landed on my right gun, dismounting it and scattering the crew. I hastened to the spot, to find the gunner dead and the sergeant severely wounded in the face and chest; there were no other casualties, but the gun was wrecked beyond repair. I withdrew the survivors of the section behind the shelter of the crest and returned to place myself beside my remaining gun. It seemed only a matter of time before it, too, must be destroyed.

Some fifteen minutes later a runner arrived from *bandera* headquarters with the order for me to cease fire and report to de Mora. On my way down the hill I met the *subteniente*, red-faced and puffing, on his way to take command in my absence. I found the Major with his company commanders and the other machine-gun officers. It was a grim and gloomy gathering; even Cancela had lost his usual ebullient good humour. The rifle companies had suffered heavily and made little progress; even if they were to reach their objective it seemed impossible that they should capture it against such superior numbers. De Mora, who valued the lives of the men he had trained and formed into this fine fighting unit, was unwilling to sacrifice them uselessly in such an ill-planned operation. On his own responsibility, therefore, he halted the advance, having ascertained that the 16th Bandera, too, could make no headway; then he sent back a report to Colonel Peñaredonda and division, requesting at least some air support or more artillery. It must have taken a great deal of moral courage for him to make this decision in the face of his orders. In the event it nearly cost him a court martial; but it saved the 15th Bandera, and probably the 16th as well, from annihilation.

It began to snow. With numbed fingers we opened tins of sardines and tunny, spreading the frozen contents on lumps of hard bread. The enemy had ceased firing; a dispiriting silence pervaded the dismal landscape of the Sierra under the murky yellow sky. In all my life I had seldom, if ever, felt so disheartened. The other officers shared my gloom, but the men, whether from ignorance of our situation or from natural good spirits, seemed in excellent humour. I noticed, with gratitude and almost a feeling of shame, one of the survivors from the crew of the gun I had just seen destroyed: an energetic little man with a flair for buffoonery, he darted from post to post cracking jokes with his comrades in a high, squeaky voice that brought shouts of laughter and applause.

In the afternoon orders came to continue the attack. Indignant that neither Colonel Peñaredonda nor anyone from division had thought it necessary to come forward and see the position for himself, we dispersed to our battle stations. I grieved for the men of the rifle companies, sent to futile execution by this heartless lunacy; I could not bring myself to look at de Mora. Strutting in front of my only machine gun was the *subteniente*, a bottle of brandy in one hand; he offered me a swig, which I refused, though unwillingly.

'Come, Mr Peter!' he shouted. 'Let's see if those *cabrones* in front can kill us!' Taking me by the arm he swaggered forward about twenty yards down the slope; there he stood and spread his arms, shouting insults towards the Republican lines amid a chorus of titters from the men. Of all silly ways to get killed, I thought, and cursed myself for not checking the exhibitionism of this drunken mountebank. Yet I felt I must put a good face on it in front of the troops – though I wonder if they would not have respected me more had I bawled him out on the spot. To my relief the enemy chose to ignore us – if they even saw us – and after a minute I said: 'The battle is about to start again, *subteniente*. I think you had better go back to Lieutenant Noriega.' He scuttled off down the hill like a flushed rabbit.

As the guns on my left opened fire I threw myself down beside my sergeant and gave the order to engage the enemy, checking our bursts through my glasses. The enemy replied vigorously, their bullets coming from the front and both flanks; they seemed to come at us like hail, with all the hiss and spatter of a heavy storm. Soon his mortars and his artillery joined in, repeating the pattern of the morning's battle. I tried to look as though this were the one thing in life I enjoyed, but with dry throat and thumping heart I doubt if I succeeded. I am inclined to turn red in the face when scared and I couldn't help laughing when one of the ammunition leaders cried out, 'Look at the colour of the *alférez*'s face! It's giving away our position.'

It had stopped snowing, but the light was beginning to fade; it was becoming increasingly hard to make out the enemy parapets among the dark pine woods. The Republicans must have found the same difficulty, for I noticed that they were beginning to fire high. Suddenly to my horror, our gun stopped firing; as the crew wrestled with it I heard the sergeant mutter savagely, '*¡Percutor!*' (firing pin) with tears of vexation in his eyes – it had broken, as too often happened with these old weapons. There was no way of repairing it, nor any means of replacement. I had no alternative but to withdraw the gun and crew into cover behind the ridge. When I reported the mishap to Noriega all he said was, 'It doesn't matter, Peter. The *comandante* is breaking off the action.' De Mora had just returned from the rifle companies in front and from a conference with the commanding officer of the 16th Bandera on our left.

At nightfall we received orders to withdraw; a dejected and depleted *bandera* dragged itself wearily back to the ridge it had left that same morning. There, after posting guards, we lay down to sleep in the snow, too weary to eat, too sad even to talk of the day's misfortune.

Thanks to de Mora our casualties had been remarkably light in the circumstances – four officers and about a hundred men killed or seriously wounded; the 16th Bandera had fared worse, losing a large percentage of officers. During the next two or three days I accompanied de Mora on reconnaissance to try and find a safer approach route, for we expected to renew our attack soon. On the second afternoon de Mora summoned all officers to a conference, to give his operation orders for an attack at dawn the next day, supported this time by air bombardment and a much heavier artillery concentration. That same night, however, division called off the operation. We were favoured, at last, with visits from senior officers, including the divisional commander and even General Yagüe, the Legion commander. De Mora's arguments must have impressed them, for we received orders soon afterwards to dig in on our ridge and hold.

This ridge was high and steep, its reverse slope thickly wooded. With the help of a few sappers we strengthened the existing trenches along the crest and added new strongpoints. De Mora put two companies into the line, keeping the other in reserve; all our machine guns went into the line, but we rotated the crews to give everyone a rest. Those of us who were in reserve set about making ourselves as comfortable as possible, building dugouts in the side of the hill, where we slept warm at night and entertained each other with lavish supplies of drink brought from Saragossa. My batman Paulino built me a roomy dugout with an ingeniously constructed fireplace and chimney. In the wall he levelled out a wide ledge of earth, spreading it lavishly with dried grass and covering it with a blanket to make a comfortable bed; he hollowed out smaller recesses for seats all around and put a rough table of packing-cases in the middle of the floor. To me it seemed like a palace.

Each day we saw large formations of enemy bombers, escorted by fighters, flying over us in the direction of Teruel but they never bothered us. After the recapture of Teruel by the Nationalists on 22 February the enemy abandoned the offensive on our sector, only troubling us occasionally with artillery bombardments by 75s (infantry support guns) and heavier field guns; they caused very few casualties but were alarming because our dugouts were only thinly covered with earth. One morning a shell from a 75 struck a tree where four or five of my mules were tethered. I ran to the spot, expecting to find a shambles; instead, I found all the mules unhurt, apparently not even frightened.

About this time I had a letter from my brother Neil, now stationed at Gibraltar in an aircraft carrier; he was flying one of her Swordfish torpedo-bombers and he had written to tell me that his observer, Charles Owen, had a brother serving as an officer in the 16th Bandera of the Legion; the family were half Spanish and had lived in Vigo before the war. Charles's brother, Cecil, had joined the *Requetés* on the outbreak of the Civil War and transferred later to the Legion. Now that Fitzpatrick had gone home, Cecil Owen and I must have been the only British officers in the Legion; it was curious that our brothers should be flying together in the same aircraft. I met Cecil Owen once on leave in San Sebastian, and found him a quiet but sociable fellow. He was killed soon afterwards in the Battle of the Ebro, having won an individual citation for the *medalla militar*.

During these days I saw a great deal of Cancela and his officers of the 53rd Company; we would spend nearly every evening talking and drinking together in one or other of our dugouts, and the more I saw of them the better I liked them. Cancela's second-in-command, Lieutenant Torres, was a dark, well-built officer of about twenty-five, a quiet, grave young man who intended to go into the family business after the war – they owned a fruit-canning plant in Logroño, capital of La Rioja. Although a serious-minded officer now, he had been a wild youth in the turbulent days of the Popular Front government of 1936, earning a living as a *pistolero* for his political party, the *Requetés*. All the political parties, he told me, employed professional gunmen in those times, to act as bodyguards for the leaders and occasionally get rid of enemies. When the war broke out Torres joined the *Requeté* militia and was severely wounded in a lung. He was conscientious and competent, and much respected by the legionnaires. The other officer was Ensign Antonio Marchán, an *andaluz* of my own age who had been a chemist's assistant in Seville. He had all the proverbial *sevillano* humour and *gracia*, and with it a passionate devotion to the Legion and a fierce loyalty to Cancela as the personification of its spirit.

The company was short of an officer now, after the loss of the Catalan ensign wounded in the last battle. I had never been very happy, and certainly not very efficient, as a machine-gun officer and had already resolved to ask for a transfer to a rifle company – where, after all, I could hope for some close action. I longed to join Cancela's happy and devoted unit, and at last summoned the courage

99

to ask him if he would accept me in the wounded officer's place. He said he would be delighted and promised to arrange it with de Mora.

After a week of this happy existence I was ordered up to the ridge to take over one of the machine-gun sections. My command post was a strongpoint on a hillock that dominated the position; it was comfortable enough to live in, and protected from bullets and mortar bombs by walls and a low, domed roof of wooden beams and sandbags; but a single shell could wreck it. I had to be careful when walking through the trenches, for they were not deep enough to hide me, and we were under continual fire from snipers and machine guns. I soon became used to keeping my head down but I hated the shelling. We did most of our sleeping during the day, standing to an hour before dawn and dusk, and keeping alert at night in case of attack. In the early hours of one morning, two days after I took over, my sentries heard noises close to our wire, about twenty yards down the slope in front; we fired a few bursts and the noises ceased. In the morning we saw two khaki-clad bodies entangled in the wire. When we retrieved them that evening we found them to be Canadians from the Mackenzie-Papenac Battalion of the International Brigades. Whether they had come to desert or to probe our defences we never discovered. At 9 am on 28 February I was ordered to withdraw my guns and rejoin the *bandera* below; by ten I had completed the withdrawal. Around noon a 75 shell landed squarely on top of my recent command post, blowing it inside out.

Chapter 10

THAT SAME EVENING at dusk we left the ridge and pine woods of Villanueva del Rebollar for the last time, and marched north-westwards for eight hours to a small village on the other side of the Sierra de Cucalon. There was a rumour that our high command was to mount a great offensive in Aragon and our *bandera* was to take part. Replacements arrived to bring us up to strength, including a new captain to take over the machine-gun company; he was a podgy, middle-aged officer, quiet and soft-spoken, very unlike Almajach.

A day or two later we moved, this time in lorries, to a pretty little village in the mountains east of Calatayud. This is one of the richest parts of Aragon, with an abundance of wine and olives. Bright, warm sunshine and almond blossom heralded an early spring; as we drilled or practised the guns in our shirtsleeves the scented air drove away our bitter memories of winter. Perhaps the end of the war, too, was in sight, or so we began to delude ourselves.

My billet was in the house of an old peasant farmer and his wife, who gave me an enormous feather bed and cooked me some of the best meals I had in Spain; they treated me like a son, especially delighted, it appeared, to have an Englishman in their house. Every evening after supper we sat over a huge fire, talking and drinking the old man's smooth but powerful *anis*, which he had made and matured himself. When the *bandera* had to leave, the old lady was in tears and they firmly, almost indignantly, refused to accept any payment from me.

The lotus-eating ended abruptly on 6 March, when our lorries arrived to take us to the front. We passed through Cariñena, famous throughout Aragon for its wine, and continued east towards Belchite, which the Republicans had captured the previous year. At dusk we halted, clambered from our lorries and moved swiftly off the road into the shelter of thick pine woods. This was to be our bivouac for the next two days and nights. The enemy was entrenched only a mile or two away, in fortifications that dominated the entire area; and so not only could we light no fires but we had to keep under cover all day. We reverted to the old regime of cold tunny, sardines and bread, and lay down to sleep under the trees.

Next day de Mora sent for me to say he had approved my transfer to Cancela's company, and Cancela assigned me to command his Number 3 platoon; Marchán commanded Number 2 and a new officer, Lieutenant Martín, Number 1. Torres remained as second-in-command. I was very busy all day getting to know my new NCOs and legionnaires, and familiarising myself with their weapons. Very soon we were going into action and it was vital that we should have confidence in each other. I had thirty men in my platoon – two *pelatones* (or sections), each under a very capable and experienced sergeant. They seemed a merry, self-confident lot who knew their job and were looking forward to the coming battles; I also had two *enlaces*, or platoon runners.

At nine o'clock the next morning de Mora held a conference for all officers, to brief us on the impending operations. So far we knew nothing about them, save that we should have plenty of air and artillery support and, for once, superiority in numbers. But we also knew the enemy positions were truly formidable, considered by the Republicans to be virtually impregnable.

This, it turned out, was to be the greatest Nationalist offensive of the war and it decided the outcome. It was to be conducted on the *Blitzkrieg* pattern so long advocated by the Germans. General Franco gave the Republicans no time to recover from their reverses at Teruel. Within a fortnight of the recapture of the town he had regrouped his Army of the North, under General Dávila, in seven Army corps along a line running from the Pyrenees to Teruel. Concentrating an overwhelming superiority of troops, artillery and aircraft, supported by the few tanks they possessed, the Nationalists smashed through the Republican defences, and in less than six weeks swept across Aragon to the borders of Catalonia and to the Mediterranean, cutting Republican Spain in two. There were three phases in this offensive, of which I only took part in the first, lasting from 9-17 March; it involved the breaking of the Republican front south of the Ebro river, and the Nationalist advance to Caspe and Alcañiz. The 14th and 16th Banderas, under Colonel Peñaredonda, operated as the mobile striking force of General Yagüe's Marroqui Army corps, on the left of the advance with its left flank on the Ebro, and we were attached temporarily to the 5th Navarre Division.

At his briefing conference de Mora gave us an outline of our part in this plan. At dusk that day we were to move forward into our assault positions, east of the village of Villanueva del Huerva; we would attack the next day, 9 March, at daybreak. Our advance would follow the line of the Cariñena-Belchite road to Belchite, our first major objective. After capturing Belchite we would continue eastward to the town of Azaila, where we would join up with 15th Division on our left, who were advancing along the south bank of the Ebro. Then on to Escatron, and from there to the important road and rail junction of Caspe, on the borders of Aragon and Catalonia, which was also a Republican headquarters. We would be operating as motorised infantry for much of the time, in conjunction with tanks. The three rifle companies would take turns to lead the *bandera*. There it was, the operational plan, all nice and pat and plain sailing as we heard it. We would see whether its execution would prove as simple.

The attack would begin with an intensive air and artillery bombardment. Our first objective that morning would be a hill, known as El Fronton, a heavily fortified position of formidable natural strength. A *frontón* is a *pelota* court and the face of this hill resembled just that, the back of a fives court, rising perpendicular from and completely dominating the plain across which we must advance to attack it. If we met any serious resistance from its defenders after the bombardment we would have a hard time.

The sun had dropped below the western hills when I led my platoon out of the pine woods and down a winding track into a shadowy ravine. The company were all in high spirits because we were on the offensive at last, under commanders we trusted, and we were taking the enemy by surprise. I was thrilled to know that I was going into battle, under a company commander I liked and in whom I had such confidence, as I also had in my new platoon. Both Cancela and de Mora had the precious gift of leadership, their very presence inspiring their subordinates to feel capable of endurance and achievements beyond their normal limits. My platoon were singing, though softly, the popular song, '*Mi Barco Velero*'; its cheerful, lilting rhythm fitted well the quick-marching step of the Legion. A bright, full moon was rising, washing the sides of the valley in silver light and casting darker shadows in the fissures among the rocks. Suddenly we heard the drone of an approaching aircraft; an order passed down the line to halt and get under the steep cliffs that rose above the road. We heard the plane circling overhead for several minutes, before it straightened into a bombing run; seconds later we saw flashes, and heard explosions in front and to the left of us as a stick landed on Villanueva del Huerva. Soon afterwards we crossed the valley and emerged on to open pasture with hills on three sides, intersected by ravines; in one of the ravines we halted for the night.

I slept well, wrapped in my greatcoat and the blankets, and awoke before sunrise with the first paling of the sky. The ground, white with hoar-frost, was also thick with troops; some were still sleeping, others bustling about or just stamping their feet for warmth. Paulino brought me bread and a few slices of smoked ham, which we ate together, washing them down with rough red wine from my leather *bota*. The sun came up warm in a clear sky, promise of a perfect day of spring. I was feeling both excited and content. A runner came from company headquarters with orders for me to report to Cancela. With him I found Torres and his other officers.

'The bombardment will be starting soon,' Cancela told us, 'and so I'll give you my orders now. Today we are the left flank company of the *bandera*. The *comandante* is deploying the *bandera* in inverted arrowhead for the attack and I'm going to use the same formation for our company. Marchán's platoon will be on the right, Martín's on the left, Peter's in reserve [I was always called Peter in the *bandera* because the double consonant at the end of my surname is difficult for Spaniards to pronounce]. Company headquarters will be between the two leading platoons, so watch me carefully for signals; above all, when you see me stop, halt your platoons at once and get down on the ground. Keep your men well spread out, and see they keep formation and distance all the time. Don't hesitate to check them whenever necessary – it will keep their minds off the bullets.'

Soon after nine o'clock the first squadron of bombers flew over towards the enemy and our batteries opened fire with a barrage far more powerful than any we had witnessed in the Sierra Palomera. The bombardment went on for more than two hours with constant relays of aircraft and incessant fire from our guns; the enemy artillery, if there was any, kept silent. Beyond the low ridge of hills in front of us, which hid the enemy from view, columns of smoke and dust drifted skywards.

Shortly before noon we heard the rumble of engines as our tanks moved into position. We were to have a screen of armour ahead of us, about two hundred yards in front, with one section of tanks to cover each company. A section consisted of six old German light tanks, each mounting two machine guns, and two of the bigger captured Russian tanks, each carrying a 37 mm gun; the crews were all legionnaires from one of the two tank *banderas*. We left the shelter of the hills and began to cross a flat, open plain covered with coarse grass. Less than a mile in front of us I saw, for the first time, the bulk of El Fronton – a great black mass of rock rising sheer above the plain; a grey pall of smoke hung over and around it; clouds of earth and stones erupted from it as our guns continued their pounding. I deployed my platoon in open order, with one *pelotón* in advance and to the left of the other, myself and the two runners in the middle. I had plenty to occupy my attention, watching Cancela and seeing that my platoon kept station; it was a while, therefore, before I noticed how meagre the enemy's fire was. Our bombs and shells were no longer falling on El Fronton, but small units of our fighters were diving on the position, raking the trenches with machine-gun fire. About two hundred yards ahead our tanks halted; at the same moment a burst of machine-gun fire passed uncomfortably close. As I saw Cancela halt I ordered my platoon to get down. One of our captured Russian tanks fired three shots from its gun, then moved forward; Cancela stood up and waved us on. A few bullets whistled past us and I shouted to my sergeants to keep the men well spread out; someone was hit to the right and the stretcher-bearers ran to him. Next moment I was treading on flattened barbed wire and a line of trenches was gaping a few yards ahead of me; huddled in the bottom and slumped across the further parapet were a few dead bodies; the surviving defenders had fled. For the last part of our advance we had been slowly climbing; this was the first line of El Fronton's defences. In a few minutes our two leading companies had occupied the whole of the position.

We could not believe that it had been so easy. The 53rd and 54th Companies had less than a dozen casualties between them, of which my company had two, neither of them serious. But when we looked around at the effects of the bombardment we began to understand why we had escaped so lightly; the whole mountainside was blasted into craters; parapets had caved in, trenches were filled with earth and rubble, pillboxes had collapsed. A few nerve-shattered and tearful prisoners were being given cigarettes by our men before being sent to the rear; they belonged to one of the Republican second-line divisions.

'If those had been first-class troops,' commented Cancela, 'we would have suffered heavily.'

Half an hour later we formed in column on the Belchite road and continued our advance eastwards. Having entered the deserted village of Fuendetodos without opposition we halted there for food and rest. This village is the birthplace of Goya; the museum in his house had been gutted by the enemy, but a few of us left our ranks to gaze respectfully at his monument. In our immediate neighbourhood the fighting seemed to have subsided; but the sky was full of aircraft, and from a mile or two away to the south came the sound of intense machine-gun fire and the roll of bursting bombs. We met no more resistance that day. Other troops, who had taken our place in the van of the division, were sweeping aside such hastily organised opposition as the enemy could muster. As we marched along the road we saw ahead of us 'circuses' of our fighters diving in rotation to machinegun the fleeing Republicans, harrying them incessantly with hand grenades tossed from the cockpits as well as with their guns. Later we heard from prisoners that these grenades, although they caused few casualties, were very demoralising. In this manner we continued until dark, when we encamped for the night on some high ground beside the road.

Cancela seemed satisfied with our performance that day.

'Of course,' he said, 'you had no chance to prove yourselves in action; but I could see you had your platoons well in hand.'

I awoke with the dawn of another fine, clear day. Before the sun was up we had started our advance along the road. After an hour of marching in column we bore to the right off the road into open country and deployed in order of battle. Ahead of us lurched a section of our tanks, keeping a constant distance of about a hundred yards between themselves and our foremost files. The other two companies were leading the attack this morning; from our place at the rear it was difficult to see what was going on. Although the country seemed to be as flat as a billiard table, no enemy fortifications were visible; however, our artillery was firing in support, using high-explosive shells that burst overhead as well as percussion fuses, so that we could mark roughly where they were; moreover, our fighter 'circuses' were at work above them. As we approached we ran into small-arms fire; we halted and lay down while our heavier tanks blasted individual strongpoints and the light tanks swept the positions with their machine guns. A few of our casualties came through to the rear, one or two on stretchers, others walking; among the latter I noticed the *bandera* standard bearer, a tall, fine-looking corporal with long black side-whiskers; he had a bullet in the thigh, but was limping along cheerfully enough, supported on the arm of a comrade, exchanging jokes with his friends in our company.

We remained on the ground for a little more than ten minutes, while the firing in front increased in volume and then subsided. Cancela rose and waved us on at a run. Once again I found myself tripping and stumbling over wire, but the fighting was finished before we reached the trenches. Beyond were several half-ruined shepherds' huts; against their walls about a dozen prisoners were huddled together, while some of our tank crews stood in front of them loading rifles. As I approached there was a series of shots and the prisoners slumped to the ground.

'My God!' I said to Cancela, feeling sick. 'What do they think they're doing?'

Cancela gave me a grim look.

'They're International Brigades.'

We were given no time to rest. Reforming in columns of platoons we struck left to rejoin the Belchite road further east, crossed it and climbed on to a ridge of the Sierra Carbonera. We had eaten nothing all day and so when a halt was called to allow the artillery to come into position we were glad of the chance to swallow some food. Some of us were inhibited from eating by the old theory that if a man were hit in the stomach he would have a better chance of survival if he had eaten nothing; the drawback to this theory is that you cannot fight indefinitely on an empty stomach. My trouble, I found, was rather that as soon as I sat down to eat the order would be given for us to move on and I would have to jettison my food in a scramble to join my platoon.

The spur on which we halted overlooked the road where it ran through a ravine towards Belchite. Beyond the road rose a steep hill, on the top of which stood an imposing monastery, the sanctuary of the Virgen del Pueyo. This was one of the enemy's strong points for the defence of Belchite. The upper slope of the hill was honeycombed with trenches – no hurriedly improvised defences such as we had stormed earlier in the morning, but a well-planned system of fortifications cut deeply into the rock, with a clear field of fire in all directions. The view through my field glasses was not reassuring.

A mountain battery was climbing the slope behind us to take up position on our left; I caught sight of Spaey, whom I had not seen since the morning of the battle of Villanueva del Rebollar, three weeks ago. After a while he walked over to join us.

'We shall be opening fire on that monastery soon.'

'Well, let's hope you make good shooting,' we answered, 'we've got to take it.'

'I don't think you need worry. By the time the guns and aeroplanes have finished there won't be much resistance left.'

Behind us, from the west, we heard the drone of aircraft. Following the line of the road from Cariñena appeared a squadron of silver twin-engined Junkers. In three flights they turned towards the monastery; when they were almost over it we glimpsed the flashes of sunlight on the falling bombs. Staring through my glasses I saw the whole hilltop erupt in reddish brown smoke, which blanketed the monastery for nearly a minute. The echoes of the explosions had barely ceased reverberating round the hills when we heard another squadron approaching; at the same time, from our ridge and from other heights across the road on our right, battery after battery of medium and field artillery opened fire. For the next ninety minutes our view of the monastery was obscured in a pall of smoke and dust; no sooner had one bomber squadron dropped its load than another would approach the target, while all the time the guns kept up their fire. At the end it seemed impossible that anyone could be left alive on that hill or, if they were, that they could still be capable of fighting. When the last bomber had turned away to the south and the shells had ceased to fall on the hill, all we could see of the monastery through the thinning cloud of smoke and dust was a ruin with rubble spilled all round.

From the hills on the right descended a column of infantry, a khaki snake winding across the slopes towards the ravine. A few minutes later we were on our feet, making our way across broken country towards the foot of the monastery hill. Not a shot came from the top as we panted slowly upwards and picked our way through the torn barbed wire. Only the dead remained to greet us, sprawled in the trenches or mangled under mountains of brick and stone.

Two of our companies, including the 53rd, were ordered to occupy the ruins for the night; the rest of the *bandera* encamped at the foot of the hill. At about five o'clock that evening we heard that the town of Belchite was in our hands.

Belchite had fallen to the Republicans in an offensive the previous summer and the fate of its defenders may have had something to do with the ugly treatment I saw being handed out now to our prisoners from the International Brigades. It had fallen to units of the International Brigades, under the overall command of a 'General Walter', a Hungarian Communist whose real name was Gerö.* On his specific orders, every Nationalist officer among the prisoners was shot out of hand and some NCOs as well. Although some of those International Brigade soldiers were very unhappy about this order, they had no choice but to carry it out.

When we entered the monastery we found its defenders had included, along with Spanish units, our old adversaries from Villa-nueva del Rebollar – American and Canadian contingents of the International Brigades. In their flight they had abandoned their personal belongings, including a large quantity of mail from home, some of it unopened. Cancela asked me to look through the letters in English while he and the other officers examined the Spanish. I

* It was this man who in 1956 succeeded the infamous Rákosi as ruler of Hungary and by his harsh and inflexible behaviour ignited the spark that set off the Hungarian Revolution.

had barely started to read when he called me back; I found him convulsed with laughter over a letter from a girl in Valencia to her boyfriend, which he insisted on my reading. It was a funny and salacious letter, every sentence alive with a bawdy wit that was strangely moving in its cheerful allusions to the squalor and discomforts of that suffering city.

'You tell me you haven't enough to eat at the front,' she had written. 'So hurry back here as soon as you get leave. Here I promise you *no te faltará conejo* [you won't lack for crumpet].'

Some of the letters I had to examine were more tragic; letters from sweethearts, wives and even, in one or two cases, children. Many of these men, who spoke my own language and who had come even further from home to fight for a cause in which they believed as deeply as I believed in ours, would never return to the people who had written these pages.

'The radio is on,' a girl from Brooklyn had written, 'and I'm writing letters. Yours comes first, of course. They are playing the Seventh Symphony. You know how that music brings us together. Please, oh please, come back to me soon.'

The next day, 11 March, was marked by some ugly fighting in which my own carelessness nearly cost me my life. We had been advancing since dawn, after bypassing Belchite; at about midday we went into action against a line of trenches and barbed wire similar to those we had stormed the previous morning. The enemy resisted tenaciously and the bare plain across which we were advancing hummed with bullets – most of them, fortunately, above our heads. We were one of the leading companies and my platoon was on the left. About a hundred yards short of the wire the enemy machine guns pinned us to the ground. As we lay there, gathering ourselves for the final assault while our tanks blasted the position, a shell burst in the air almost directly over my head; the blast seemed to tear at my breeches and I felt a slight pain in my right thigh, like the slightest touch of a hot iron. I looked down at a jagged rent where a piece of shrapnel had ripped through the cloth, leaving a faint graze on the skin. I had time only to note that there were no casualties in the platoon, before I saw that the tanks were moving forward and Cancela was waving me on to the charge. I shouted to my men and, drawing my pistol, leaped over the remains of the enemy wire, closely followed by my two runners. A figure rose up at me out of the trench in front, levelling his rifle and slamming home the bolt. I aimed my pistol and tried to press the trigger; but nothing happened – I had forgotten to release the safety catch. Even in that second of hypnotised terror as I watched the rifle come to his shoulder there flashed through my mind the bitter message: 'If ever a man deserved to die, you do now! You're no more use in a rifle company than you were in the machine guns.' At that moment there came two rifle shots, almost simultaneous, from behind me; the man fell back into the trench. My two runners had been wider awake than I.

By now the *bandera* had overrun the whole position; legionnaires were moving among the trenches, dispatching with rifle butt and bayonet the few remaining defenders. The enemy were Germans from the Thälmann Brigade, good soldiers and desperate fighters, since even their homeland was barred to them. They expected no mercy and received none; I felt disgust as I watched the legionnaires probe among the fallen, shooting the wounded as they lay gasping for water. I resolved to speak to Cancela at the first opportunity; I had not come to Spain for this.

We slept that night on the bare, rocky side of a mountain so precipitous that no one could find a level place to lie down. Torres was suffering from acute tonsilitis, the rest of us from blistered feet and frayed tempers, inflamed now by a biting wind from which there was no cover. I decided to postpone any discussion with Cancela about the shooting of prisoners until a more favourable opportunity arose.

It didn't arise the next day, which proved the most strenuous of the whole offensive, because on that day the Marroqui Army corps made a spectacular advance on foot of thirty-eight kilometres. Starting from a few miles east of Belchite, the 5th Navarre Division swept through the road junction of Azaila in the early afternoon and reached the south bank of the Ebro at the town of Escatron late in the evening: by this rapid advance large enemy forces were cut off with the Ebro at their back, in a pocket between Escatron and Quinto to the north-west; there they were destroyed at leisure. As the spearhead of the division, the *bandera* covered a full twenty-five miles on foot during the day, marching and fighting from daylight until long after dark with scarcely a pause for rest.

Our manœuvres followed a familiar pattern: preceded by an advanced guard of tanks we marched at a forced pace along the main road; ahead of us flew fighters for reconnaissance and protection. At the first sign of resistance we would deploy across country in battle order, the tanks extending in line abreast in front of us; if the position was strongly defended there would be a brief artillery preparation before we went into the assault, in the same manner as on previous days. Although we repeated this performance several times that morning and afternoon, our casualties were remarkably light; the speed of our advance had disorganised the enemy, who were throwing in their forces piecemeal in a vain effort to gain time for a stand further east. Only on one occasion did we meet serious opposition – in the morning, at a place between Belchite and Azaila, where the old front line used to run before the Republican offensive against Belchite in August 1937. Here the enemy trenches were deep and well traversed, stoutly reinforced with concrete, well concealed from observation yet commanding an excellent field of fire. They held us up for an hour before we overran them and their garrison of International Brigades.

At about five o'clock we were enjoying a brief rest on the top of a broad escarpment that overlooked the valley of the Ebro. I had taken off my boots and socks and was rubbing my swollen feet with surgical spirit, revelling in its refreshing coolness, when Spaey walked over from his battery.

'Hello!' I greeted him. 'Your bloody battery dropped some shells pretty close to us this morning.'

'Nonsense! You infantrymen always think it's us when it's really the enemy shelling you.'

'Their artillery has been pretty active today for a change,' I observed.

'But not very accurate. You can think yourselves lucky they've got no officers. I'm prepared to bet those are sergeants in command of batteries.'

At that moment Peñaredonda approached with de Mora and two legionnaires, escorting a prisoner, a lieutenant who had surrendered after the last engagement; he was a stocky little man with dark, curly hair, whom fear and exhaustion had made into a pitiful figure. He was from the *Carabineros* who, like the Guardia de Asalto, were especially detested by the Nationalists; few of their officers who were taken prisoner survived. Addressing Cancela, de Mora said:

'The colonel wants some men to shoot this prisoner.'

There was a wild scramble around me as a dozen legionnaires leaped to their feet, clamouring for the job with an eagerness surprising in men who a moment earlier had seemed exhausted. Even Peñaredonda was startled.

'Quiet, my children, quiet!' he urged in a pained voice. 'There's nothing to get excited about. This is simply a creature who is about to pass over to the other side.' His unctuous tone barely veiled his satisfaction. He turned to de Mora.

'I think we'd better have an officer.' De Mora caught sight of Torres.

'Will you undertake it?' he asked. Poor Torres, still suffering from his tonsils, turned a shade paler.

When the prisoner had made his confession to our *padre*, Torres pulled himself together and, with obvious reluctance, approached the man; they spoke together for a moment; then they walked slowly towards the edge of the escarpment, the escort following. The prisoner stood with his back to us on the top of the bluff, gazing across the shadowed valley to the further side where the slanting sunlight touched the hills with gold. Torres stepped back, drew his pistol and shot him once through the back of the head.

It was after midnight when we halted beyond Escatron, turned off the road and encamped for the night on a clifftop overlooking a small tributary of the Ebro. After a while Cancela returned from a visit to *bandera* headquarters with the news that we were to rest all the next day.

'I'll split the liver of the man who tries to wake me before eight o'clock!' he announced as he sank to the ground.

It was over lunch next day that I nerved myself to ask Cancela: 'Where do the orders come from that we must shoot all prisoners of the International Brigades?'

'As far as we're concerned, from Colonel Peñaredonda. But we all think the same way ourselves. Look here, Peter,' he went on with sudden vehemence, before I'd had a chance to put my case, 'it's all very well for you to talk about International Law and the rights of prisoners. You're not a Spaniard. You haven't seen your country devastated, your family and friends murdered in a civil war that would have ended eighteen months ago but for the intervention of these foreigners. I know we have help now from Germans and Italians. But you know as well as I do that this war would have been over by the end of 1936, when we were at the gates of Madrid, but for the International Brigades. At that time we had no foreign help. What is it to us if they do have their ideals? Whether they know it or not they are simply the tools of the communists and they have come to Spain to destroy our country! What do they care about the ruin they have made here? Why then should we bother about their lives when we catch them? It will take years to put right the harm they have done in Spain!'

He paused for breath, then went on: 'Another thing; I mean no offence to you personally, Peter, but I believe that all Spaniards – even those fighting against us – wish that this war could have been settled one way or another by Spaniards alone. We never wanted our country to become a battleground for foreign powers. What do you think would happen to you if you were taken prisoner by the Reds? You would be lucky if they only shot you!'

Torres's quiet voice interrupted: 'If it comes to that, what chance would any legionnaire stand if he were to fall into their hands, especially into the hands of the International Brigades? They shot their prisoners at Brunete and Teruel.'

'We realise you can't feel the same as we do,' concluded Cancela, 'but please, Peter, do not speak to me of this again.'

Nevertheless, I knew this was not the policy of the Nationalist high command, who already held several thousand International Brigade prisoners and who released all of them a few months later. After the war I discussed the shooting of prisoners with a veteran officer of the 7th Bandera, which was operating over to our right during the advance on Caspe.

'It's lucky for Peñaredonda that our General Yagüe didn't pass that way during these shootings,' he commented. 'He'd have had him shot then and there and probably all of us too!'

Spanish prisoners, of course, were decently treated by the Nationalists at this stage of the war, with the exception of regular officers of the armed forces, like the man shot by Torres, who were regarded, by a curious process of thought, as traitors. Apart from the difficult question whether International Law can be applied to a civil war, I believe that its rules afford no protection to volunteers from non-belligerent countries. For myself, if I were taken prisoner, I expected no mercy.*

While we were enjoying our rest on the 13th, other forces were mopping up the numerous large pockets of the enemy isolated by the last few days' advance. Although doubtless necessary – and certainly welcome to us – this delay gave the enemy time to reorganise their defence and give us a nasty shock a few days later.

The following day remains in my memory as one of the most horrible of my life. The ghastliness of it is still with me as I write; nor, I fear, will it ever leave me. I can scarcely bear to write it now.

At noon next day we were still resting on our clifftop when I was ordered to report to Cancela. I found him talking with some legionnaires who had brought in a deserter from the International Brigades – an Irishman from Belfast; he had given himself up to one of our patrols down by the river. Cancela wanted me to interrogate him. The man explained that he was a seaman and had got very drunk one night, missed his ship and been picked up by the police. The next thing he knew he was in Albacete and pressed into joining the International Brigades. He knew that if he tried to escape in Republican Spain he would certainly be retaken and shot; so he had bided his time until he reached the front, when he had taken the first opportunity to desert. He had been wandering around for two days before he found our patrol.

I was not absolutely sure that he was telling the truth; but I knew

---

* Captain Don Davidson, an English officer of the International Brigades whom I met subsequently, confirmed that I would certainly have been shot if captured.

that if I seemed to doubt his story he would be shot and I was resolved to do everything in my power to save his life. Translating his account to Cancela, I urged that this was indeed a special case; the man was a deserter, not a prisoner, and we should be unwise as well as unjust to shoot him. Moved either by my arguments, or by consideration for my feelings, Cancela agreed to spare him, subject to de Mora's consent; I had better go and see de Mora at once while Cancela would see that the deserter had something to eat. De Mora was sympathetic.

'You seem to have a good case,' he said. 'Unfortunately my orders from Colonel Peñaredonda are to shoot all foreigners. If you can get his consent I'll be delighted to let the man off. You'll find the Colonel over there, on the highest of those hills. Take the prisoner with you, in case there are any questions, and your two runners as escort.'

It was an exhausting walk of nearly a mile with the midday sun blazing on our backs.

'Does it get any hotter in this country?' the deserter asked as we panted up the steep sides of a ravine, the sweat pouring down our faces and backs.

'You haven't seen half of it yet. Wait another three months,' I answered, wondering grimly whether I should be able to win him even another three hours of life.

I found Colonel Peñaredonda sitting cross-legged with a plate of fried eggs on his knee. He greeted me amiably enough as I stepped forward and saluted; I had taken care to leave the prisoner well out of earshot. I repeated his story, adding my own plea at the end, as I had with Cancela and de Mora.

'I have the fellow here, sir,' I concluded, 'in case you wish to ask him any questions.' The Colonel did not look up from his plate:

'No, Peter,' he said casually, his mouth full of egg. 'I don't want to ask him anything. Just take him away and shoot him.'

I was so astonished that my mouth dropped open; my heart seemed to stop beating. Peñaredonda looked up, his eyes full of hatred:

'Get out!' he snarled. 'You heard what I said.' As I withdrew he shouted after me, 'I warn you, I intend to see that this order is carried out.'

Motioning the prisoner and escort to follow, I started down the hill; I would not walk with them, for I knew that he would question me and I could not bring myself to speak. I decided not to tell him until the last possible moment, so that at least he might be spared the agony of waiting. I even thought of telling him to try to make a break for it while I distracted the escorts' attention; then I remembered Peñaredonda's parting words and, looking back, saw a pair of legionnaires following us at a distance. I was so numb with anger that I didn't notice where I was going until I found myself in front of de Mora once more. When I told him the news he bit his lip:

'Then I'm afraid there's nothing we can do,' he said gently. He was clearly distressed. 'It's best, though, if you yourself witness the shooting. In the first place the Colonel will require it; but more important, it will be easier for the prisoner to have a fellow country-man with him when he dies, especially as he knows you tried to save him.'

I could hardly bring myself to face this prisoner. He was standing between my two runners, but as I approached they dropped back, leaving us alone; they were good men and understood what I was feeling. I forced myself to look at him and was sure he knew what I was going to say.

'We've got to shoot you.'

'Oh, my God!' he whispered.

Briefly I told him how I had tried to save him, and that de Mora and Cancela had also done their best.

'But we simply can not evade the Colonel's orders. I'm truly sorry. Do you want to see a priest,' I asked, 'or have a few minutes to yourself? Can I send any message home for you?'

'No. Just make it quick.'

'That I can promise you. Now turn round and start walking away.'

He held out his hand and, looking me in the eyes said, 'Thank you.'

As he walked away I called up my runners.

'I beg you, aim true. He mustn't feel anything.' They nodded and I looked away as they raised their rifles. The two shots exploded simultaneously.

'On our honour, *mi alférez*,' said the senior, 'he could not have felt a thing.'

I had to make sure he was dead and saw that death must indeed have been instantaneous. When we had buried him I reported to Cancela.

'The *comandante* has asked me to give you a message,' he began. 'He wishes you to know that he deeply regrets the shooting of that Englishman; that he considers it a crime and the responsibility for it must rest for ever upon the conscience of *that*' – he spat out the word – 'gentleman! You know, Peñaredonda went so far as to send a pair of legionnaires to follow you and to shoot you as well as the prisoner if you didn't immediately carry out his order? That is something we'll none of us forget.' He looked at me with real sympathy. 'We are all sorry, Peter.'*

I excused myself hurriedly.

This tragic story has provided a field day for commentators as an example of the Nationalists' inhumanity. Not one of them, so far as I know, thought it appropriate or fair, when quoting me, to mention the great efforts we all made to *save* the Irishman's life. As for reporting Peñaredonda, nothing I submitted would have gone beyond the *bandera*.

I was not left long to my thoughts. In a few minutes a messenger came running from Cancela to tell me that the *bandera* was on the move. Two hours later we were assembled beside the main road that led from Escatron to the important town of Caspe, the last town in Aragon remaining in Republican hands. Here we waited until dusk, when a company of tanks rolled up the road from Escatron. Behind them came a column of lorries, into which we climbed. It was dark when we started towards Caspe, the tanks moving about half a mile ahead of us. A few minutes later we put out our lights. The driver beside me seemed to think that we were bound for Caspe itself, in a sudden dash to take the enemy by surprise; I doubted we should get so far in our lorries, even at night. It was impossible to see anything of the country, for the night was very black.

After half an hour the column came to a halt. I heard the sound of small-arms fire ahead of us. A minute later bursts of tracer flew over us from high ground on our right. This was the first time I had been under fire from tracer; I was fascinated to watch the little red bulbs, each one seeming to approach ever so slowly, then suddenly accelerating to fly past with a very frightening hiss. I began to wish that someone would order us down off the lorries. I heard our tanks moving across towards the enemy positions and saw the flash of tracer from their guns. In half an hour the engagement was over and we were on the move again. There was another brief action a mile or two further on, which held us up for a quarter of an hour while we stayed in our tracks. We finally halted near the hamlet of Chiprana, about eighteen kilometres from where we had started. Leaving our lorries, we climbed to the top of the hills overlooking the road, where we spent a cold and uncomfortable night, alert for possible counter-attacks.

* In my previous account, *Mine Were of Trouble* (1957), I inadvertently misquoted de Mora's words to me, giving an impression that he ordered me to carry out the shooting. I checked it with him in Madrid in 1986. I now reproduce the accurate account.

We made steady progress next morning, moving well ahead of the 5th Division. We met no serious opposition but came under a good deal of artillery fire in the afternoon, most of it from 75s. Towards evening we halted on the fringes of the thick olive groves that cover the approaches to Caspe. The sun was setting when a runner from *bandera* headquarters hurried up to me with orders to report at once to the Major. I found de Mora with his company commanders on the top of a knoll overlooking a wide vale, from which a silvery-green sea of olive trees swept upwards to a distant hill. Briskly he gave me my orders:

'Yours is the leading platoon of the leading company tonight. I want you to make a reconnaissance through those olives ahead of us and try to find out where the enemy are located. Put out scouts in front, but don't let your men get scattered in that close country. Get moving as quick as you can.'

Calling the platoon to attention, I briefly outlined our mission, issued my orders and detailed a pair of scouts to move fifty yards ahead; I took the rest at a trot down into the valley. We had hardly started to move through the olive trees when we were fired on by a machine gun from the hill in front. As the bullets slapped against the trees I felt a sharp stinging pain across my ribs; realising that it was only a flesh wound and that nobody else was hit, I looked round quickly for cover. In front of us was a ditch with an earth bank, one of the many that intersected the plantation. I ordered the platoon into the ditch while I tried to fix the position of the machine gun through my glasses; but I could not find it in the failing light. Unwilling to waste time I gave the order to advance, hoping that the gloom would cover us as we went deeper into the trees. Suddenly we came upon a railway, a single track running at right angles to our advance; about twenty yards to the right was a level-crossing where the main road from Escatron ran over the line. As I halted before crossing the exposed piece of track my senior sergeant caught my arm:

'Listen, sir!' He jerked his thumb in the direction of the road. From behind us I heard the deep rumble of heavy engines coming up the road towards the crossing. 'We're ahead of our own tanks, sir,' said the sergeant, looking worried.

For a moment I failed to grasp the significance of what he had said. Then I realised that the tanks, seeing us ahead of them, would certainly take us for the enemy; in the half light they could not see our uniforms and they must suppose themselves to be the most forward of our troops. This was one of those moments with which textbooks deal so light-heartedly, when the young officer must use his initiative. The decision was taken out of my hands by the sergeant himself; pulling out a white handkerchief he ran to the level-crossing, planted himself in the middle of the road and started to wave it, shouting through a cupped hand at the leading tank. This must have had a nervous gunner; I was running to join him when there was a bright flash and a sharp explosion; the sergeant staggered to the side of the road with his hands to his face. A few seconds later the tank lumbered into view, with its turret open and an officer peering out of its top. When he saw us he halted, horrified at his mistake. At that moment Cancela came up to tell me to discontinue the reconnaissance and rejoin the company with my platoon. The sergeant was carried back to the medical officers, who patched him up and sent him off to hospital; miraculously he had escaped serious injury, although he had a nasty gash in the side of the face. His *pelotón* was taken over by a tall, red-haired Portuguese corporal called Mateu, a good enough soldier but lacking the sergeant's experience.

The company crossed the railway in extended order and began to move at a rapid pace through the olive groves that covered the gently rising slope beyond. We were no longer under fire, but I found it an exacting task to keep in touch with Cancela on my right in the thick country and gathering darkness; our feet sank heavily into the earth, we fell into ditches and stumbled up banks, sweating and cursing in a frenzied effort to keep pace. The graze on my ribs smarted and irked me where my clothes pulled on the caked blood. I tried to console myself with the thought that it was better to be one of the heroic wounded than one of the glorious dead; even so, I found my temper running very short. I had no idea where the rest of the *bandera* was, nor even in which direction we were advancing. As far as I was concerned, the military situation was, in official language, 'obscure'.

Quite suddenly we halted in the last of the fading light. Ahead of us the hill rose sharply and steeply to a conical mound, falling away gradually to our right in regular, unbroken lines of olive trees. A hundred yards or so on our left ran a road, roughly parallel with the line of our advance; we could hear tanks moving along it. One of the rifle companies was sent to occupy the mound, supported by Colomer's machine-gun platoon. We stayed where we were, near de Mora, ready for instant action. It seemed that we had run into heavy opposition and would not take Caspe without a fight.

When we were settled I went to *bandera* headquarters to get one of the doctors to dress the graze on my side. I found them in a small hut with the *padre* and de Mora; the latter was lying down looking very tired. Back with the company I forced myself to eat something and then lay down to sleep. But I found sleeping as difficult as eating. The air was charged with tension and uncertainty; the night was full of the sounds of impending battle: explosions and bursts of machine-gun fire from over the hill and the rumble of tanks along the road on our left. At first I was confident that the tanks were ours; but soon afterwards I was disturbed to hear the sound of engines coming down the road from the direction of Caspe. A few minutes later the last of my complacency was shattered by a series of sharp reports, followed immediately by the hiss and explosion of shells among the surrounding olive trees. The tanks were hostile; moreover they were shooting at us.

At first we lay where we were, hoping the bombardment would subside; on the contrary, it increased rapidly in volume, shells raining on the ground around us or bursting in the branches overhead. I heard the clamour of Colomer's machine guns from the mound and the thud of grenades. Cancela shouted to the company to stand to; I felt better on my feet. The shelling continued for half an hour; then it died away as suddenly as it had started, to be succeeded by a silence almost as unnerving in contrast. I doubt if any of us slept for the rest of that night.

We were on our feet again before dawn. De Mora ordered the company to take up position over on the right and prepare for a strong enemy counter-attack. Our delay on the 13th and 14th had given the Republicans time to pull the bulk of their retreating forces into Caspe; these they had strengthened with four International Brigades and part of a fifth. Pushed far ahead of the 5th Division, our two *banderas* and supporting tanks were now thrown back on the defensive in face of vastly superior numbers; furthermore, the enemy controlled the higher ground. Until substantial reinforcements could arrive we would be batting on a very sticky wicket.

In the first grey light we moved to our new positions, crossing without incident one very exposed piece of open ground, bare of olive trees or other cover. Cancela posted my platoon on the left, Martín's on the right and Marchán's in the centre; at first he had planned to keep mine in reserve, but with the length of front we had to hold and the danger of enemy infiltration on the left, he felt he could no longer afford the luxury of any reserve but that of his own headquarters. Our orders, Cancela explained, were to hold our positions at all costs; rather than retreat we must die where we stood. Remembering the open ground across which our ammunition supplies would have to reach us, I wondered if we should be able to achieve even that usefully.

As the sun rose we heard the first sounds of battle over on our left, where the rest of the *bandera* was engaged. I was relieved to note that the enemy seemed to be very short of artillery; apart from the 37 mm of their tanks I could hear none.

In trying to describe the action that followed I am at a disadvantage which anybody who has been an infantry subaltern in battle will appreciate: I had little idea of what was happening anywhere but in my own immediate vicinity and not always a very clear idea of that; moreover, my mind was so fully occupied at the time that I found it difficult later to recollect the sequence of events.

De Mora could not spare us any machine guns, and so we had to depend on our own Fiats and rifles. I was thankful that the olive groves at least made it difficult for the enemy to use mortars.

Taking advantage of the cover afforded by the banks and ditches, I disposed my platoon with a view to giving the maximum depth to my defence. 'Fire at anything you see moving to your front,' Cancela had said. There was, of course, no time to cut away the olive branches that blocked our field of fire, giving excellent cover to an attacker. I awaited the enemy's assault, trying to dissemble my anxiety in front of the men. I did not have long to think about it. One moment we were waiting, the men crouched behind their weapons, myself scanning the olive groves through my glasses: the next, bullets were hissing through the trees, slashing the trunks, spattering earth from the bank in front of us. I heard Marchán's guns go into action a second before my own. All we could see of the enemy was an occasional glimpse of a crouched figure darting from one tree to another. For a while we held them off; but at the end of twenty minutes, when the firing died down, I had lost half a dozen men and we knew the enemy were appreciably closer.

I sent a runner to Cancela with an account of the action; he returned with orders for me to report in person. I found the Captain looking grave.

'There's a hill just above you on your right,' he said, pointing it out to me. 'Take one of your *pelotones*, get up there as quick as you can and hold it at all costs – at all costs!' he repeated.

I was getting to know that phrase pretty well. I ran back to my platoon, made a quick readjustment of my plan of defence and ordered Corporal Mateu to follow me with his *pelotón* to the top of the hill. There was a small piece of open ground in front of the foot of the hill. As we ran across it a sharp burst of fire came from the left; I felt a searing pain across the front of my throat; a bullet had torn a shallow furrow through the flesh, but I had no time to think about it as we scrambled panting up the hillside. On the top was a small space of open ground before the olive trees began again on the further edge; hurrying across it we dug in on the other side. When I returned to Cancela to report my disposition he said:

'Go and get that wound dressed.'

I hesitated. It had bled profusely, making a picturesque mess on the front of my jacket, but it was causing me no trouble; I felt that this was scarcely the time to bother with trivialities.

'Don't argue,' he said. 'The sooner you go the sooner you'll be back.' And so I went, running all the way.

Bandera headquarters was under heavy fire from the enemy tanks. It seemed that the fuses of the shells were adjusted to explode immediately on impact, so that many of them burst in the trees on striking a branch or even a twig, producing an alarming effect and causing a number of casualties. The sound of fighting seemed to come from all sides. De Mora was looking a little worried. I noticed the *subteniente* sitting by himself, huddled despondently beneath an olive tree, peering through the collar of his greatcoat; he looked like an old, mournful, red-faced sheep. Paulino greeted me with a look of friendly concern.

'You again!' laughed Doctor Larrea when I came up to him. I apologised for bothering him because I could see that he and Ruiz had their hands full, with wounded pouring in from all the companies. De Mora, standing near, looked up.

'I think you ought to go to hospital,' he said. 'Those throat wounds can be very dangerous.'

I hadn't the face to follow up this suggestion and ran back to Cancela. I found that the battle had broken out again; I could hear the sound of continuous small-arms fire from ahead and from the right where Marchán and Martín were closely engaged. As I arrived a runner hurried across from Martín with the news that he was under severe pressure, heavily outnumbered and in danger of being outflanked.

'He's got to stay there,' said Cancela. Sounds of firing came from the hill which I had recently occupied. Cancela told me to take the rest of my platoon up there to join Mateu.

'The position on the left can look after itself; but that hill is vital. We ought to have occupied it before. For God's sake hold on to it, Peter!'

'I'll do my best, sir,' I said, falling over my feet in my hurry to start.

For some reason the enemy had ceased to press their attack on the left, so that my *pelotón* was not engaged when I reached it. We climbed to the top of the hill without difficulty and took up firing positions. Mateu was glad to see us; with his limited fire-power he had been unable to stop the enemy closing in. I cursed the thickly planted olive trees which prevented my seeing where the enemy were, or at what point they were likely to launch their main attack;

their fire seemed to come from straight ahead and from the right, saturating us in a deluge of bullets that was carrying off my men at a frightening rate.

During one of the intervals I found Cancela beside me, come himself to see the situation. I told him quietly that if the enemy were in the strength I believed them to be, I did not see how we could avoid being overrun. He nodded gravely:

'This is a classic Legion situation, Peter, but don't be dismayed.' He raised his voice to a laugh for everyone to hear: 'We'll enjoy our drinks more in Saragossa when we look back on this day.'

'Well,' I said, 'I certainly hope the girls will look better than they did the last time I was there.' Our poor sallies were acknowledged by a few grins from the men. Suddenly one of them attracted our attention, pointing over to the left, where we saw a figure crawling painfully on his stomach across a piece of open ground trying to reach the shelter of some trees.

'Shall we shoot, sir?' he asked.

We studied him for a moment through our glasses, then Cancela said firmly:

'He's wounded. Leave him alone.'

He walked back down the hill, leaving me to make my final arrangements to meet the assault which I knew could not be long delayed. Both my Fiats were still in action, and I reckoned I had enough ammunition and grenades; on the other hand I had already lost half my men, including one of my runners. However, the rest were in good heart and I knew they would stand by me. I resolved that, before we were finally overrun, I would pull my force back to the edge of the hill and make my last stand there, where we could at least deny the position to the enemy. There was a small ditch which would give us some protection. I warned my sergeant and Corporal Mateu of my intention.

'They're on the move again!' cried the sergeant as a fresh hail of bullets started to fly among us. This would be the final assault. While we poured our full volume of fire into the attackers – or what we could see of them – the legionnaires tearing at the bolts of their rifles, slamming them back and shooting as fast as they could, the Fiat gunners firing in long, steady bursts, I ran, crouching, from one *pelotón* to the other, checking the fire to see that we were not shooting too high and trying desperately to forecast the point of the enemy's principal thrust. But from what I could make out they were converging on both sides in equal and overwhelming strength. They were terribly close to us. The explosions of grenades were added to the crackle of small-arms fire. Realising that if we were going to disengage we must do so at once, I gave the order to retire; in a few seconds we had covered the twenty yards to the edge of the hill. We were now ready for what I reflected grimly was, literally, a 'last-ditch' stand. I sent my runner to warn Cancela.

Across the clearing we saw the gaps in the olive groves fill with figures. I noticed one of them steady himself against a tree and take aim, I thought at me; I fired twice with my pistol and he disappeared. I gave the order to fix bayonets. We were a pitiful remnant, a bare dozen; around us the ground was strewn with the bodies of our comrades. In a few moments – minutes at most – the enemy would close and that would be the end. As I unwound the tape from a grenade and slung it across the clearing I understood that at last I was face to face with death; that there was nothing I could do about it. With this realisation there came over me an extraordinary sense of freedom and release from care. A few yards in front of me I caught sight of the red and yellow colours of a Nationalist flag which had been carried by one of our *pelotones*; it was on the ground beneath the dead body of its bearer. Running forward – I realise now, of course, that this was the most puerile dramatics – I seized the flag and ran back with it; calling encouragement to my men, I waved it in a wide arc. Whether this nonsense had any moral effect I am unable to say: a second or two later there was a soft thud beside me, an anguished shout of warning from my runner – '*¡Cuidado, mi alférez!*' – and a violent explosion.

I was knocked backwards clean off my feet to roll over and over down the hill, ending up in a heap in front of Cancela, who, with Torres, was on his way to visit us. I pulled myself up, dazed and shaking, to feel blood pouring down my left arm. I began to climb back, but Cancela reached the top before me; taking one look at the situation he shouted:

'Down off the hill, all of you!'

I feared we should be shot down as we ran, but the enemy were slow to press their advantage. We halted about a hundred yards beyond the foot of the hill, behind an earth bank among the olive groves, where we found Cancela's headquarters.

Nearly a year later I learned that our adversaries this day were a British battalion of the International Brigades; Captain Don Davidson, my informant and one of its company commanders, told me that their own casualties were very heavy.

Although embarrassed by the enemy's capture of the hill, with the dominating position it gave them, Cancela was determined to hold his ground, covering de Mora's right flank. After pulling in the remnants of Marchán's and Martín's platoons, which were in danger of being cut off, he awaited the enemy's next move. But the latter made no attempt to advance further, and confined themselves to raking us with small-arms fire. In the end it was our own artillery that forced us from our new positions, coming into action now for the first time; I suppose it had just arrived. A battery of six 77 mm dual-purpose anti-aircraft guns began to fire at the enemy on the hill. Unfortunately, three shells in every salvo landed in our midst. After what we had been through we were enraged as well as unnerved each time we heard the guns fire to know that within a few seconds we were likely to be disembowelled or maimed by one of our own shells; pressing my face into the earth and shrinking as the blast of the explosions swept over me, I cursed a fate that had delivered me from an honourable if uncomfortable death at the hands of the enemy, only to consign me to ignominious and messy annihilation by our own guns. After a grim ten minutes, during which time we had as many casualties, Cancela took us back another hundred yards, where life seemed peaceful in comparison, with only the enemy's bullets to worry us. Soon even these abated and we reckoned that the guns, with their high rate of fire, must be giving the enemy as bad a time as they had given us.

About twenty minutes later we had our first really happy moment of the day: a section of our tanks appeared through the olive trees behind us, negotiating the difficult country with remarkable agility.

'It looks as if the worst is over,' said Cancela. He turned to me: 'Go and get that arm looked at.'

I was glad enough to obey; the blood had clotted, and the arm was stiff and painful. I moved warily through the olive trees, having no wish to be knocked out at this stage of the battle by a sniper's bullet. I came to the edge of the open ground we had crossed early that morning; among the trees on the other side I saw Lieutenant Terceño, of the 54th, who shouted to me not to linger while crossing it; I saw what he meant when a couple of bullets sang past my head as I hurried over. The tanks were still shelling *bandera* headquarters, where Larrea and Ruiz were working calmly and efficiently, while the *padre* was busy among the rows of wounded on the ground. De Mora looked strained and grim, but he cheered up a bit when I told him about our tanks. The *subteniente* was wailing that he had been hit in the chest by a shell fragment which was hurting him horribly. When the girl *practicante* had cut away the sleeve of my jacket and shirt, prattling happily to me the whole time, Larrea examined the wound; there were no bones broken, but splinters of metal had lodged in the forearm and above the elbow. He looked at me with his hands on his hips:

'This time, damn it, you really are going to hospital! I haven't enough lint and bandages to keep on wrapping up a bloody great beanpole like you.'

When he had dressed the arm and put it in a rough sling he wrote out a hospitalisation order, which he handed to me:

'You'll find a casualty clearing centre somewhere back down the road; just go on walking till you find it.'

De Mora added: 'Be careful for the first part of the way; it's dangerously exposed to fire.'

Accompanied by Paulino who, I was delighted to see, had hung on to my wine *bota*, I walked away from the battle. We went very carefully at first, for Paulino told me that several casualties had been hit again as they were being carried back and a stretcher-bearer had been killed. For the first half mile bullets flew over us, but afterwards we were pretty safe. About three-quarters of a mile back we passed a culvert where the railway ran over a sunken track. Here Colonel Peñaredonda had established his command post, though he alone knew what control he could exercise at such a distance. He greeted me with effusive cordiality:

'Hi, Mr Peter! What's it like up there?'

'Arduous, sir,' I replied sourly. 'You can see it better from up the road.' And I passed on.

Soon afterwards we came to the main road, where we met a column of cavalry, who hailed us cheerfully; they were part of General Monasterio's division, just arrived from Alcañiz. With a light heart I realised that the agony of the *bandera* was over. A mile further on we came to a tent, marked with a red cross, in a small grove of oaks; in a field beside it a battery of 10.5 cm field guns was in action. I gave my hospitalisation order to the medical officer in charge, who told me that I should have to wait some time before an ambulance could evacuate me – he indicated the rows of wounded lying around; I had better make myself as comfortable as I could in the meantime. Paulino spread a blanket for me at the edge of the trees. I fell asleep immediately, undisturbed by the firing of the guns fifty yards away.

In the hospital train to Saragossa, where an ambulance dropped me late in the evening, I found myself sharing a compartment with Antonio Marchán. In the turmoil of the battle I had neither seen him nor given much thought to the fortunes of his platoon; but I had gathered from Cancela that he had done very well. He became a casualty soon after me, with a grenade wound in the hand; it was more painful than mine but did not seem to damp his gypsy spirits. Two days later we were revelling in hot baths and clean, comfortable beds in the General Hospital at Bilbao.

The day after we were wounded Caspe fell to an assault from three directions by overwhelming Nationalist forces. The International Brigades, particularly the 14th (British), had fought a gallant and determined action, inflicting terrible casualties on the 16th Bandera and ourselves; our own company had barely twenty men left, out of 110 with which we had started the battle.

I never saw Colonel Peñaredonda again. He was posted to another command after the battle of Caspe. But I heard of him from my brother officers of the 14th Bandera and also, after the war, from one of his personal *enlaces*. He wasn't a Legion officer, but a regular Army infantryman, and no one could imagine how or why he obtained this command of good Legion troops. His first and only concern, it emerged, was his own comfort and safety; during operations when the rest of us had little or nothing to eat, and were sleeping pretty rough, he had mules carry him every luxury the canning industry could supply, no matter how they impeded our speed and manœuvrability. He never put his own life at risk, depending on reports from runners to give him an idea of how a battle was going. I doubt if any officer can ever have attracted such contempt from his subordinates.

Nemesis overtook him in the Battle of the Ebro, where he was commanding a sector of the front when the Republicans launched their final offensive at the end of July 1938. Surprised by the enemy, his troops were quickly overrun. Instead of attempting to rally them, he jumped into his staff car at once and didn't halt his flight till he reached Saragossa. For his cowardice a court martial cashiered him. Why, I wonder, didn't they shoot him? They could have found plenty of volunteers for the firing squad from the 14th Bandera.

Chapter 11

AFTER THREE DAYS in hospital my wounds ceased to throb and I began to feel almost well again. But it was the middle of May before the medical authorities would let me rejoin the *bandera*;they had been worried at first that the wound on my arm showed signs of festering. I spent most of the interval in the Spanish Red Cross Hospital in Seville, having first got permission to see my brother, still at Gibraltar, for an evening in Algeciras. Towards the end of April the hospital discharged me with a week's sick leave, which I contrived, perhaps unwisely, to spend with friends in Biarritz. It was easy enough to get there because I was going through Nationalist territory all the way to the frontier.

Afterwards I was faced with the problem of getting back into Spain. The Spanish authorities had raised no objections to my crossing into France, nor the French to letting me in, but crossing back into Spain would be more difficult. It was soon made clear to me that I hadn't the remotest chance of getting a French exit visa to return to Spain and officers of the Non-Intervention Commission were patrolling the frontier. However, at a dinner party in Saint Jean-de-Luz a friend pointed out that a simpler way would be for me to walk up the disused funicular that ran to the top of La Rhune, a prominent peak nearby, along which ran the frontier.

'Lots of picnickers walk up there now to spend the day,' he explained. 'Try to look like one of them. At the top you should be able to find an unguarded spot where you can slip across. After all, you won't have to worry about the Spaniards when you're over.'

He promised to take me next morning in his car to the foot of the funicular.

On a fine early summer morning I said farewell to my friend at the foot of La Rhune and began my three-thousand-foot climb. I was wearing civilian clothes, but in an old machine-gun ammunition case, which looked less suspicious than one might think, I had packed my Legion uniform, intending to put it on when I was over the frontier. I hadn't gone more than a couple of hundred yards when I heard a shout and, turning, saw a gendarme coming after me. I put on what I hoped was an amiable smile and waited. When he reached me, out of breath but apparently friendly, I explained I was an English tourist out for a picnic on the mountain. I pointed to my ammunition case.

'I have my lunch in here and,' I added, 'a bottle of good French wine.'

He beamed and waved me on with a cheerful *'bon appetit'*.

It was a dull as well as tiring climb along the railway sleepers, but I dared not deviate in case I lost the way; however, fearing there might be a guard post at the top, I left the funicular a quarter of a mile short of it and cut across the mountainside. I supposed the frontier would run along the crest and when I reached it I saw there were thick woods, already coming into leaf, a little way down the other side; they should afford me excellent cover. I tried not to hurry and began to walk over the crest of the ridge as nonchalantly as I could. My heart was already pounding uncomfortably and it speeded up when I heard a shout from the funicular building over to my right. Pretending not to hear, I walked steadily on without turning round or quickening my pace. I heard a couple of shots, but by now I was well over on to the further side and walking downhill among large boulders, which should give me some cover. I dived into a gully, ran down it for a hundred yards and jumped off a small spur into the shelter of the woods.

When I had cooled off and calmed down a bit I found and followed a narrow track that led south. After half a mile I walked round a corner into a Spanish soldier plodding uphill, his rifle slung from the shoulder. We both stopped.

'Good afternoon,' I greeted him. 'I am *Alférez* Peter Kemp of the 14th Bandera of the Tercio, returning from leave. My uniform is in this case. Please escort me to your guard post, where I can change into it.' His mouth opened in astonishment, to reveal a large wad of half-chewed bread. After a moment he nodded and turned back, beckoning me to follow; but he didn't recover his voice until we reached the frontier post at Vera. Over a beaker of *chacolí*, a strong cider, I explained the position to the officer in charge, who gave me a hearty welcome and sent me on my way to San Sebastian. That was my first but not my last clandestine crossing of an international frontier. I was lucky I didn't have to make it, like many a few years later, with German patrols on my heels.

My travels in search of the 14th Bandera took me to Saragossa, where I met another compatriot, Pip Scott-Ellis, an English girl who had been serving as a nurse with the Nationalist forces at

Teruel and in the offensive south of the Ebro; during the latter she was, like me, attached to the Marroqui Army corps. She had come to Spain with no knowledge of the language and qualified in the Spanish Red Cross examinations for nurses within three months of her arrival. She was now enjoying a well-earned rest after arduous and dangerous work in a field hospital at Escatron under sustained and heavy fire from enemy artillery across the Ebro; for her gallantry and devotion to duty during these bombardments the Nationalist commander recommended her for the award of the *medalla militar*. A cheerful girl with a great sense of humour, I found her a stimulating and sympathetic drinking and dining companion during those few days, and, after the war, in Madrid and London.

I rejoined the *bandera* at last in the village of Villanova de Alpicat, just inside the borders of Catalonia and a few miles west of Lerida; they were resting while replacing the losses they had suffered at Caspe. If I felt any regret for the vanished comforts of Seville and Biarritz, it soon dissolved in the enthusiasm and kindness of my welcome from de Mora and my brother officers; even the legionnaires and NCOs seemed to take me more seriously. Antonio Marchán was already back, with his hand in good shape, and so now the 53rd Company had all its old officers. Another bonus, of course, was that we no longer had to endure Colonel Peñaredonda.

Cancela told me that after I had left, our tanks had swept up the hill I had tried to hold, with all guns firing, and driven off the enemy. When Cancela reached the top he found a scene of total carnage, with no sign of life among the bodies; the shellfire had caused most of the slaughter, which the tanks had completed, and so the company took over the hill without another casualty. He had found the flag on the ground where I had dropped it, the staff broken clean off by the grenade that had wounded me; he gave the flag to me as a souvenir. The *bandera* had not been in action since Caspe.

We were now in occupied Republican territory and the difference was noticeable in the attitude of the villagers towards us. Notwithstanding that '*Requeté*' is derived from the Catalan, the Anarchists had always been the most numerous political party in the province, although the Communist Party and the Trotskyist POUM had a good many supporters. Separatism was almost universal; and so, although they were polite enough to us, I was sure the villagers would not be sorry if the place were to change hands again. Meanwhile I noticed young *falangistas*, of military age and sound physique, busy among the inhabitants recruiting members for their party from communists of a few weeks ago.

Otherwise Villanova was a pleasant enough village, in rich, flat country intersected by canals and irrigation ditches. We enjoyed this idle life, basking in the warm May sunshine, with plenty of good food and wine. But we weren't allowed to enjoy it long. At the end of the month we were back in the line – and in a most uncomfortable part of it.

The line in this sector followed the course of the River Segre, which flows south-westwards past Lerida to join the Ebro beyond Caspe. Twelve miles below Lerida the Nationalists had thrown a bridgehead across the Segre at the village of Seros, where the river flows through a deep ravine, about three hundred yards wide, with steep cliffs rising from either bank. Throughout June and July the *bandera* was holding this bridgehead on the Republican side of the river. It was an uncomfortable and, in more than one sense, unhealthy spot: a semi-circle of trenches on high ground above the river, covering a half-mile perimeter and about the same in depth. Our only line of communication with the ruined village of Seros on the other bank was a narrow iron bridge over the river, under constant enemy artillery fire. There was a level piece of ground by the bridge, on which stood a shell-damaged house which was *bandera* headquarters. Two of our rifle companies held the trenches, with the third deployed round this headquarters in reserve.

It was a hazardous position because the Republicans were entrenched on three sides of us at a hundred or two hundred yards' distance, and although they were second-line troops of poor quality, their situation enabled them to shell and mortar us from all sides, inflicting a steady toll of casualties. It wasn't much better for the company in reserve because *bandera* HQ was a priority target for the enemy artillery; they never managed to hit it because it was situated too close under the cliffs but it was no fun to be orderly officer and have to sit beside the field telephone alone and unprotected while the shells showered down close by. Perhaps the worst discomforts were the intense heat, the bad water and the flies; I had never seen so many flies before, nor have I since – except in the southern Philippines. They hung over us in great black clouds, swarmed all over our food and our faces, and polluted our drink. It says something for my brother officers that during this time there were no quarrels among us, and plenty of talk and laughter.

On 23 July my company was occupying the trenches on the left flank of the bridgehead, a hundred yards from the enemy. It was a day of intense heat. During the morning I had mortared the opposing trenches at Cancela's request, trying to silence a troublesome machine gun. I lunched as usual with the other officers of the company in Cancela's dugout. Afterwards I remained behind to discuss an operation which he wanted me to undertake after dark – to lead a patrol against an enemy working party in front of us. While we were talking the enemy started to mortar our position – I suppose in retaliation for my effort in the morning. Their trenches were so close that we could hear the thuds of the discharges long before the grenades burst; they were using 50 mm mortars, not the more lethal 81 mm. I excused myself to go and see that all my men were taking shelter; then I returned to Cancela's dugout. He was lying on his bed and I sat down on a packing case by the table in the middle of the floor just inside the entrance. I had started to explain my plan, using my hands for gestures, as one does when speaking Spanish, when a mortar bomb burst in the opening beside me. I barely heard the explosion: I was conscious of it only as a roaring in my ears, a hammer blow on the left side of my face and a sickening dizziness as I fell to the floor. My mouth seemed to fill with a sea of pebbles; as it fell open the sea resolved itself into a deluge of blood and the pebbles into fragments of my back teeth; twice more the flood welled up into my mouth to pour in a widening pool across the floor. I watched with a detached bewilderment, changing to near panic. 'Oh God!' I prayed. 'Don't let me die now, like this, in terror!' I took a grip on myself, remembering how someone had once said to me, 'You're never dead till you think you are.' Cancela, on the bed, was unhurt; he provided a comic interlude by standing over me, exclaiming in tones of sincere and horrified concern:

'Are you hit, Peter? Tell me, are you hit?' He pulled himself together; faintly through the singing in my ears I heard his strong voice calling for stretcher-bearers. Slowly I rolled over on my back, then painfully raised my head to examine my wounds; my mouth and throat felt numb and soggy, I could not speak and my jaw hung loose – I realised that it was shattered; there was a bloody gash across each hand, another at the top of my right arm and something at the back of my head. Cancela examined my body and assured me that the haemorrhage was not internal. Heartened by this news and filled with the exhilaration that follows shock and precedes collapse, I motioned away the stretcher-bearers and walked the three or four hundred yards down to *bandera* headquarters. On the way I stopped to rest: leaning against the parapet I looked out north-eastwards along the shimmering band of the river to the old red stone citadel of Lerida dancing in the heat haze. Somehow the sight of that harsh and alien landscape drove into my fuddled mind the firm resolve that I would not die there, far away from home.

At *bandera* headquarters Larrea and Ruiz were busy with other casualties from the bombardment; but as soon as they saw me they shouted to an orderly to lay me on a mattress and make me comfortable. They had their hands full and it was nearly half an hour before they could attend to me. I lay on the mattress, my head propped on a haversack and greatcoat, watching the black clusters of flies settle on the wounds in my hands and feeling the movement of their buzzing through my jaw; I watched them with interest, even fascination, as though from a long way off. By the time Ruiz came to look at me the flies were congealed into the wounds; he worked on me quickly but with surprising gentleness, cleaning and bandaging while he talked to me about the wonderful time I was going to have in San Sebastian when I was well again. Larrea came to help him, and they tried to cheer me by a discussion of the joys of leave and love in a cool climate. After giving me injections of anti-tetanus and anti-gangrene serum, and a shot of morphia, they went away to arrange the evacuation of the wounded. After a while I heard them whispering; they probably thought I was asleep, but in fact I seemed to hear everything with increased clarity:

'It's no good sending Peter back,' one of them said, 'he won't live more than a few hours.'

Into my mind flooded that view of the Segre and the ruined citadel of Lerida, filling me with the determination to overcome this death that threatened me. Slowly I raised myself on one elbow; painfully I turned my head, caught their gaze and held it. Larrea smiled:

'Send him in the first ambulance.'

The following weeks of pain and shock and occasional blessed oblivion have almost faded from my memory, although I still remember some instances of the selflessness and heroism typical of the Spanish character at its most inspiring.

Larrea and Ruiz watched anxiously as their orderlies loaded me on to an ambulance bound for the field hospital at Fraga, a ten-mile journey over rough roads heavily pitted with craters. Every lurch and bump would have thrown me off my stretcher had not a gunner lieutenant with his left arm shattered by shell splinters stood over me all the way, bracing his body with a foot against my stretcher supports while he held me down with his other arm; there was only one medical orderly with us to look after six serious casualties.

At the field hospital I had a stroke of luck in the form of the medical officer, Captain Tomás Zerolo, a brilliant surgeon who, I was to hear later, was famous throughout Europe. Born in the Canaries, he had taken his medical degrees in London; just to hear him talk to me in fluent English raised my morale considerably. But he took a grave view of my condition.

'Look, old boy, I have to operate on you at once to clean up these wounds and remove the fragments of metal that are still there. I daren't give you an anaesthetic' – I've never understood why not – 'but you can have some brandy.'

I couldn't speak, but I shook my head slowly. My throat was so sore – from the white-hot metal of the mortar bomb, I discovered later – that it was agony to swallow even a sip of water and neat alcohol was out of the question. While he probed in the wounds and cut away the infected tissue he talked to me quietly all the time about England and the scenes he loved to visit in London, such as the rose garden in Regent's Park and the superb skyline (now ruined) from Constitution Hill; he talked also of his favourite restaurants, bars and nightclubs – most of which were also favourites of mine. In effect, *he* was the anaesthetic. When he had finished he bound up my jaw so skilfully that the broken pieces eventually knitted together by themselves.

The next two nights and a day were grim because I couldn't sleep. On the morning of the third day Zerolo came to my bedside with a sad and worried look.

'Listen, old boy, I must send you to Saragossa right away. I hate to do it, but I've just had orders to clear this hospital immediately for a heavy intake of casualties.' He slipped an envelope into my shirt pocket. 'This is for the doctor in Saragossa. Good luck to you.'

I was past caring. I couldn't know that the Battle of the Ebro had begun that morning – the Republicans' last desperate throw to stave off total defeat. Although it was a costly failure for them in the end, the offensive's initial success flooded every hospital in Aragon with Nationalist wounded and there was no room for me so close to the front line. Months later Zerolo told me he hadn't expected me to survive that move; I'm certain it was his expertise that saved me.

The journey to Saragossa was an experience I would not care to repeat: two hours on a canvas stretcher in a hot and stuffy ambulance careering at high speed over a road pitted with shellholes, every one of which sent spasms of agony through my jaw. I remember little of my first days in the General Hospital at Saragossa because I began at last to lose consciousness for long periods. But I have a clear picture of the chief oral surgeon, an angry little man with a grey goatee beard and steel-rimmed spectacles, who complained bitterly about the condition of my mouth and asked how he could be expected to operate on anyone whose throat was so badly burnt; he seemed to be blaming me for it. Added to the pain of my wounds and the discomfort of the heat – they told me the noon temperature outside was 108°F – I developed severe urticaria from Larrea's serum. It was acutely painful to swallow even my saliva and I dreaded the liquid meals they made me force down. Most of all I dreaded the morning visits of the dressing trolley; I had an open hole in each thumb, into which they poured neat surgical spirit. Usually I fainted. But the nurse detailed to look after me, the daughter of a regular cavalry officer, was an angel of kindness, who never seemed to sleep; whenever I rang my bell, even in the middle of the night, she appeared immediately at my bedside.

Sometimes I had visitors. The most assiduous was a retired American general, Henry Reilly, who lived near Paris but was visiting Saragossa. With his bright red face, snow-white hair and genial, open manner he might have passed for a particularly amiable senator. Notwithstanding his advanced years and considerable bulk, and the exhausting heat, he would stagger up the stairs to my floor several times a week, weighed down with a crate of beer on his back, the sweat pouring from his friendly and now almost purple face as he cursed the Nationalist government for a recent, particularly silly decree forbidding civilians to shed their jackets in public. It was agony for me to swallow the beer, but his noble gesture compelled me to try. I had several visits, too, from a small, purposeful and very serious Irish girl, Eileen O'Brien, of the 'Irish Christian Front', a volunteer Red Cross organisation that was new to me. Although I wasn't able to talk I loved to listen while they told me what was happening in the world outside my little whitewashed room.

Very soon the hospital was overflowing with wounded from the Ebro battle. They carried into my room a young *Requeté* lieutenant from Navarre with a badly mangled leg; he was in terrible pain, his face green and waxy with sweat. But he never complained of his wound and only told me how delighted he was to share a room with an Englishman who had come so far to fight for the cause of Spain. Waking one day from a prolonged coma, I found he had gone. Eileen told me the reason: with fresh casualties arriving every day, the hospital was overcrowded and one of us two had to be moved to a more distant hospital. I was still unconscious when the order came, but apparently the *Requeté* had insisted that as an English volunteer I must have priority over him and they must transfer him, not me; he was clearly, however, in no better state to travel than I. When I could speak a little later on, I begged Eileen to find him and thank him. She shook her head.

'I can't. He died on the journey.'

At the end of the first week in August I was loaded on to a hospital train, which landed me after a protracted and uncomfortable journey in the General Mola Hospital in San Sebastian. The change was most welcome, however, both because the cool climate of that pleasant seaside resort was a great improvement on the stifling heat of Saragossa and because the General Mola was a base hospital, where the medical facilities were much better. At first I could take little interest in my surroundings because, though no longer in acute danger, I was still in considerable pain and could only sleep after morphia injections, which at least weren't denied me.

I was privileged, also, in the doctors who treated me, notably the dental surgeon, Scherman, a quiet but very competent Austrian, and the famous Irish-American plastic surgeon, Eastman Sheean. The latter had run his own field hospital for the British Army in France in the 1914-18 War; afterwards he went to live in the United States, where he established a fashionable and lucrative practice lifting the faces of the ageing rich; but his real enthusiasm was for travelling round Europe and treating wounded ex-servicemen, which he did without payment and without regard for their nationality.

The nursing in this hospital was under the supervision of elderly nuns, worthy, devoted and kindly souls whose ignorance of and indifference to the principles of antisepsis and general hygiene horrified Sheean; moreover, they had a habit – well intentioned, no doubt – of waking me in the middle of the night when I had only just managed to fall asleep to ask if I would like coffee. Most of the nurses were, in turn, delightful girls who before the war would never have been allowed out unchaperoned; they knew little about nursing, but their attentions and gorgeous looks were an inspiration to our recovery.

About the end of August Scherman, the dental surgeon, told me he must operate on my jaw to cut away the fragments of teeth, bone and metal that remained there and were threatening infection.

'I'm afraid it will be painful for you,' he added, 'because I can't give you anaesthetic for it.'

Again I never knew the reason. However, the day before the operation I had a visit from two British friends who had been staying with a family in Cognac and they brought me a bottle of brandy. I carried the bottle down to the operating theatre next day and asked Scherman if I might use it as a substitute for anaesthetic.

'Certainly!' he grinned. 'In fact, I'll have a nip with you.'

I took an enormous swig to start with, he a small one, and then he started to work on me with probe, forceps and chisel. Whenever the pain became unbearable I signalled him to stop and took a long pull at the bottle. In this manner we nearly finished the brandy. I had suffered less than I had feared during the operation, but I still remember the pain that followed when the alcohol wore off that evening. I suppose a soldier or sailor of the eighteenth century would have wondered what all the fuss was about.

A few days later I was moved from my large ward to a small room with only two beds. As I went in I heard a shout from the other bed:

'Why, Goddamnit, you old bastard!'

Goggi von Hartmann had collected another wound, a bad one; he had taken a bullet in the arm, which had damaged the main nerve, and he was in very severe pain. After a lengthy and excruciating operation with local anaesthetic he found it difficult to sleep, even with morphia, and would swear horribly when awakened in the middle of the night by a blaze of light, to find a smiling nun offering him coffee. We begged the nuns to abandon this practice, but with the obstinacy of the truly pious they took absolutely no notice – for the next three nights. On the fourth night I had scarcely been awakened by their usual visit when I was startled by a couple of deafening reports from Hartmann's bed; a pungent stench of cordite invaded the room, now plunged in darkness, a shower of glass from the shattered bulb fell to the floor, and there came the clatter of broken cups and a sharp scream of terror.

'Next time,' shouted von Hartmann as the door slammed behind the fleeing nun, 'I shoot you, not the light!'

We began to recover our strength soon afterwards and by the second week of September were able to go out in the town. We visited Chicote's most evenings, where Perico gave us a rapturous welcome, and we often dined out, returning only to sleep in the hospital. Such latitude would never have been permitted in a British military hospital, but the Spanish theory seemed to be that it would vastly improve our morale, which it did, without endangering our recovery. My own experience was that a few glasses of diluted gin or whisky deadened the pain in my throat and made it much easier to swallow the soft foods that were all I could attempt. But it was a deceptively short step from there to drinking too much.

'You be careful,' Scherman said to me one day in Chicote's, 'or you'll be getting a red nose and become a dull fellow.'

The Munich Crisis that autumn threatened me with the loss of both liberty and honour. It was the general view among my Spanish friends that if war were to break out the French would immediately attack Nationalist Spain. Still unfit to leave hospital and enlisted in the Legion for the duration of the Civil War, I was in no way prepared to bear arms against my own country or her ally; I could easily find myself in a Nationalist concentration camp, if not before a firing squad. Whatever the faults of the settlement I could only welcome it personally. But I realised more clearly than ever before that I must prepare myself for a far more desperate war.

Early in October, when at last I could leave hospital, I applied for leave to convalesce in England. It was obvious, and the doctors confirmed it, that I wouldn't be fit for active service for another four months at least; there was no point in hanging about Spain and I was as anxious to see my family as they were to have me back. My application would need the personal approval of the Generalisimo, but thanks to the help of one of his ADCs and the support of the Colonel in charge of Medical Services at GHQ I soon obtained it. I remained, of course, on the strength of the Legion but I had two months' leave, to date from my departure from Spain. At the end of November I arrived home.

Delighted as I was to see my family and friends, the progress of my convalescence was painfully slow. When my leave was due to expire, at the end of January, I was still far from fit. I wouldn't admit it to myself, especially after reading accounts of the fierce fighting in Catalonia, in which my *bandera* was sure to be involved. Fortunately for me my friends were well aware of it and brought it to the attention of the Duke of Alba, Franco's representative and later his Ambassador in London. The Duke called me in to see him.

'You are not yet fit enough for active duty, whatever you may think,' he told me. 'I am the Generalisimo's accredited representative and so here you come under my orders. I am ordering you to remain here until I'm satisfied you are fit, and so I have informed the Generalisimo.' These words were typical of the character of that great Spanish diplomat who, with all his preoccupations, took such an interest in the welfare of a very junior officer of the Legion.

And so it wasn't till the end of March 1939 that I arrived back in Spain. The war was over. After Catalonia, Republican resistance collapsed and on 28 March the Nationalists occupied Madrid virtually unopposed. I had still to get my official discharge papers from the Legion and I naturally wanted to say goodbye to my old friends in the *bandera*. Too many, I found, were no longer alive, having perished in assaults on the Republican positions in the Pyrenees; among them was my cheerful, gallant *andaluz* comrade, Antonio Marchán, who fell at the head of his platoon, half his face blown off by a grenade. But Larrea was still there.

'When I sent you off in that ambulance from Seros,' he told me with a great belly laugh, 'I never thought you would live.'

Cancela was still with the *bandera*; but he died some ten years later, I heard, in agony from cancer. De Mora, on the other hand, served with the Blue Division in Russia and survived to retire as a general and Captain General of the Canaries.

The pursuit of my discharge papers took me more than three months, travelling around Spain and Spanish Morocco in search of an officer competent to issue them. It was July before I was formally discharged and could start my journey home. On my way through Burgos I was summoned to an interview with General Franco. To my surprise he received me alone and sat himself down beside me on a sofa – a short, tubby figure with a soft, high, almost feminine voice. I naturally left him to do the talking, which he did almost incessantly throughout the half-hour interview; his two themes were the danger to Europe and western civilisation presented by the spread of communism and the power of the Soviet Union, and his admiration for Britain – the latter astonished me in view of the attitude of my brother officers in the Legion.

I won't discuss in further detail the rights and wrongs of the Civil War; I have already explained my own motives for taking part. Moreover, the subject has already inspired a spate of exhaustive studies and even fifty years afterwards it continues to reveal, more than any other war I can think of, except perhaps Vietnam, the dominance of the closed mind.

I have concentrated on recording what I saw and felt at the time. For me those years in Spain were a rewarding experience, despite the horror and the heartbreak, and the wounds that trouble me still. I count it a privilege to have fought beside some of the best and bravest friends anyone could hope to meet – and against some of the bravest enemies.

It is, however, safe to say the immediate results of that war satisfied almost nobody, not even the victors. Many of us deplored Franco's ruthless suppression of all Republican tendencies and the shocking number of executions in the early years of the peace; and it is poor consolation to reflect that if the other side had won there would have been even more of them, especially during the years of Stalin's purges. But it remains to Franco's credit that he presided over a recovery in his country's prosperity barely dreamt of until his dictatorship; and he left behind a situation in which the skill and wisdom of King Juan Carlos could at last dispel most of the accumulated bitterness of more than fifty years, and achieve a significant reconciliation among Spaniards. On my last visit to Spain in 1986, it was a joy to see, engraved on the new War Memorial at Caspe, scene of fierce fighting in March 1938, the simple inscription: '*A Todos*' – To you all.

PART TWO

WORLD WAR

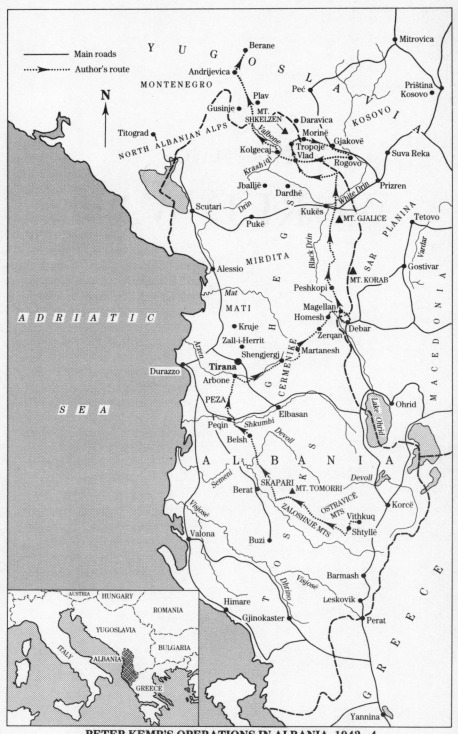

PETER KEMP'S OPERATIONS IN ALBANIA, 1943–4

Chapter 1

'WHAT YOU'RE GOING to do,' Kim Philby told me in his usual patronising tone, 'is train conscripts for the coming war.'

We were in Saint Jean-de-Luz, where I had paused on my way home from Spain at the end of July 1939 and I was having a drink with a group of journalists in the Bar Basque. I had no intention of training conscripts. Whatever Spain might have fitted me for, it wasn't to teach other men how to get killed in a much more modern war. In any case, when war broke out on 3 September I found the Army had no immediate use for me in any capacity; a medical board looked at my hands and my jaw, thanked me very politely and suggested I come back again in six months' time.

In that grey and gloomy September I was very low as I saw my friends, many of whom were Territorials, called to the colours, while my brother was at sea in the carrier *Courageous*, flying Swordfish torpedo-bombers; but apparently I was unfit for anything active. A brief but acute outbreak of girlfriend trouble at the time added considerably to my depression. I was feeling thoroughly unwanted. My friend Archie Lyall tried to help.

'I think you should meet The Dame. She was head of the Red Cross in the last German War, so she might have some useful contacts.'

The Dame was Dame Beatrice Hudson Lyall, his mother and the only person on earth he was truly afraid of. Having spoken to her briefly on the telephone, I could well understand why. 'I'm taking you to tea with her next Sunday,' he went on. 'I shall collect you in a taxi from your house in Brompton Square [lent to me by an uncle and aunt] at 4 pm. Be ready. The Dame is a stickler for punctuality.'

I was feeling distinctly nervous that Sunday afternoon as the taxi bore us off towards The Dame's Kensington house; but not so nervous, I noticed, as Lyall himself. I soon discovered the reason. As the taxi drew up fifteen minutes later he leaned over to me and said with compelling gravity, 'I would ask you, Peter, to keep in mind that from the moment we cross The Dame's threshold I, Archie, am a teetotal eunuch of rather Low Anglican views.'

The Dame was sympathetic but proved unable to help and so I took a temporary job in the press section of the Postal Censorship, sifting material from Spain and Latin America at a salary of £5 a week. It was uninspiring work and when my brother's ship *Courageous* was sunk by a U-Boat at the end of September with the loss of nearly half her crew, I began to wonder if I hadn't been a fool to engage in an alien war in Spain and so find myself unfit now to fight for my own country; in fact Neil survived the *Courageous* disaster, after swimming for two hours in the cold waters of the North Atlantic in the full mess dress which naval officers still wore for dinner in those days.

A few days later I ran into another acquaintance from Spain, Douglas Dodds-Parker. Some years older than myself, he was a Wykehamist who had entered the Sudan political service after Oxford, but had left it in the late 1930s to travel extensively in Europe. We had met in Burgos at the end of the Civil War while I was awaiting demobilisation, and I had taken him round some of the battlefields in Aragon and Castile. Tall, handsome and quiet-spoken, he had a first-class brain and was always stimulating company; he was to become a good friend. I wasn't sure what he was doing now, but he soon gave me a clue.

'Would you like me to give your name to my people?' he asked as we parted. I had no idea who or what his 'people' were and he didn't enlighten me; but they sounded a lot more interesting than Postal Censorship and so I accepted.

A few days later I received a letter from a room number in the War Office, asking me to present myself there for interview. In a room full of desks a staff captain took down every detail of my education and service in Spain. At the end he said, 'I think we can use you – not immediately but later if, as we expect, the war spreads to other parts of Europe; then we shall need officers with your kind of experience. Meanwhile, continue with what you're doing in Postal Censorship until you hear from us.'

I was about to leave when I heard my name called. It was Peter Wilkinson, a Cambridge friend and now a captain in the Army. He was talking to a short, dark, wiry officer with a clipped moustache and alert, intelligent eyes, whom he introduced as Lieutenant-Colonel Gubbins. A gunner who had served in India among other theatres, Colonel Gubbins had just returned from Poland, where he had commanded a British military mission to the Polish Army, now engaged in a desperate struggle on two fronts – against the

Wehrmacht in the West and the Red Army in the East. As one of the founders and later the director of SOE Colin Gubbins was to have a profound, even decisive influence on many thousands of lives, including my own. Now, in clipped, precise tones, he questioned me about the Spanish Civil War, in which we had a friend in common, Pip Scott-Ellis; he at least didn't seem to disapprove of the side I had chosen.

Early in November the Postal Censorship moved to Liverpool, where the lavish hospitality of my Spanish friend, Miguel de Larrinaga and his ship-owning family did a great deal to compensate for the tedium of my office work. In those early wartime days you could have a very good time in Liverpool.

A week before Christmas I received an official letter from the War Office department that had interviewed me – it styled itself MI(R) but to this day I don't know what the '(R)' stood for. It informed me that I would be commissioned into the Army (general list) with the rank of second lieutenant, dating from 19 January 1940, and on that date I should report to the 110 (Horsed) Cavalry OCTU* at Weedon, Northamptonshire. First I had to face another medical board, but sailed through it with an A1 rating.

Before reporting at Weedon I spent a week at home in Sussex and a couple of days in London with Archie Lyall. On the strength of *Lyall's Languages* he had been asked by the War Office to prepare a similar handbook for the use of the British Expeditionary Force in Europe. Entitled *Soldier's Speakeasy*, it included such useful phrases as 'How much is that girl with red hair', but the conventional morality of the War Office led them to reject it. Now Lyall had just been appointed press attaché to the British Embassy in Belgrade. For this assignment he asked to borrow my Spanish civilian cloak.

'You can have it, Archie,' I told him, 'on the one condition that if the Germans invade Yugoslavia you swear to save it, even if you don't save yourself.'

In the event, Lyall smuggled out my cloak the following year, on the day before the Germans invaded. I agreed in return to leave it to him in my will. Meanwhile, over the next fourteen months I would hear reports from Belgrade of a huge, amorphous figure enveloped in a dark blue cloak with green and crimson lining who was a popular spectacle at official receptions and private parties, rallying Serbian support for the Allied cause.

Nineteen-forty ushered in the coldest winter of the war; Weedon on its hill was one of the coldest spots in England and the cavalry barracks, built in about 1745 and condemned in the First World

* Officer Cadet Training Unit

War, was about the coldest building in Weedon. Nevertheless I enjoyed the three months I spent there, notwithstanding the cold, and the strict discipline and training. The equitation instructors knew their job and taught us all to sit on a horse under the most exacting conditions, which many of us were to find very useful later on. Although an officer, I was treated, like the rest, as an officer cadet while in the precincts of Weedon. There were four troops of cadets on this course, including our own; the other three were destined for one or other of the horsed cavalry regiments, but ours, generally called the 'M1 Troop', had been recruited by M1(R) or some similar organisation.

Among the staff at Weedon the figure we stood most in awe of was the RSM, 'Gentleman Joe' Taylor, Royal Scots Greys, a former equitation instructor at Sandhurst and a superb horseman. An austere, clean-shaven Yorkshireman, he had absolute disciplinary powers over us and used them ruthlessly to impose his own fierce standards of efficiency and turnout. No lapse, however small, went unremarked and unpunished. It was with misgivings, therefore, that I heard him call my name at the end of parade one morning in the middle of April. What had I done, or failed to do? When I formed up I was relieved to hear him say, 'War Office for you, Mr Kemp, sir. You're to report there immediately.'

Chapter 2

S OME TWENTY-FIVE miles west of Fort William, at the head of Lochailort and on its southern shore, stood Inverailort House, a large square building of plain, grey stone, whose chill austerity of design reflected the gloom of its natural surroundings. The front of the house faced north on to the sea loch, whose sombre waters, alternately wrapped in mist and whipped by rainstorms, blended with the leaden tones of walls and roof. The back was overshadowed by a grim, black cliff, surmounted by a thick and forbidding growth of trees, which rose from the back door to well above the height of the roof, blotting out the sun from the house at all times except high noon in summer. The rainfall at Glenfinnan, ten miles to the east (where Bonnie Prince Charlie raised his standard in 1745), is the highest in the British Isles; but on the few fine days the shores of Lochailort and the Sound of Arisaig revealed a bleak, wild beauty of scoured grey rock and cold blue water, of light green bracken and shadowed pine, that was strangely inspiring in its stark simplicity and grandeur.

At this remote outpost six of us arrived in May 1940, sent by the War Office, with several more officers and NCOs expert in some unusual or specialised branch of soldiering.

Scots Guard Bill Stirling had the idea that this group should form the nucleus of a new training school; we would start with cadre courses for junior officers from different units of the Army. Colonel Brian Mayfield was to be the commandant, Stirling the chief instructor. But there was no fear, Stirling assured us, of our having to remain instructors for the rest of the war; when we had trained the first few cadres there would be plenty of candidates to take our places, freeing us for operational duties overseas.

With War Office help Stirling and Mayfield had managed to recruit some outstanding officers and NCOs to join us. Stirling's cousin, Lord Lovat, the senior instructor in fieldcraft, took me on as his assistant. His fighting record with the Commandos and during the Normandy landings was later to become legendary. I had already met him at Weedon, where he was in one of the three regular cavalry troops; recently married, he and his wife had lived there in a borrowed caravan through that dreadful winter – an experience that might have broken up most marriages but seemed to cement theirs. Now at Inverailort he proved to be a brilliant instructor and in less than a month taught me more about concealed movement across country than I could have learned elsewhere in a year. He was also wonderful company and his superb wit and sense of humour made him a very popular as well as an effective instructor. Jim Gavin, a sapper, was in charge of demolitions with another sapper, Mike Calvert, as his assistant; the latter had just had the satisfaction of seeing himself reported in the official casualty lists of the Norwegian campaign (the Germans had invaded Norway early in 1940) as killed in action. Three years later 'Mad Mike', at the age of thirty, was one of Wingate's brigadiers in the Chindit operations in Burma.

Our first students arrived in the first week of June – some twenty-five keen but puzzled subalterns, among them Bill Stirling's youngest brother, David, soon to become another legend as the 'Phantom Major' and founder of the SAS in North Africa. From this small beginning developed the succession of special training schools established by SOE – Special Operations Executive – throughout Britain, and in the Middle and Far East, Australia and North America.

The year 1941 began with a great personal tragedy. On 10 January the carrier *Illustrious*, in which my brother was serving, suffered a heavy attack from German divebombers in the Sicilian Channel; Neil was among the dead. The previous November he had piloted his Swordfish in the Fleet Air Arm night attack on the Italian fleet in the harbour of Taranto, penetrating the innermost defences and torpedoing one of the new *Littorio*-class battleships, and disabling her; he was subsequently awarded the DSC. Even before the war he had established a reputation within the service as a considerable naval historian, winning, as a sub-lieutenant of twenty-one, the coveted RUSI gold-medal essay competition on naval strategy – something never achieved before by an officer below flag rank. A column and a half of tributes to him in *The Times* showed that his death was a severe loss to the service as well as to his family. I learned of his death in a telegram from my mother. Numb and sick with shock, and blinded by my tears, I couldn't believe that a crumpled piece of buff-coloured paper could contain so much human misery. My mother, four years a widow, never recovered from the blow. It was a long time before I could bring myself to face the fact that Neil was dead. All my life he had exercised a profound influence on me – in truth I believe he still does. He was the best friend I ever had and, most usefully, my severest critic. As I wondered sadly how I would manage in future without his wise advice and sound judgment, I tried to take some comfort from Clarendon's words on the death of Lord Falkland:

'And whosoever leads such a life need not care upon how short warning it be taken from him.'

I hastened to see my sister-in-law in Dorset and my mother, who was staying with her. My sister-in-law Diana was carrying Neil's son, who was to be born the following August and who, in another war twenty-five years later, was to show fighting qualities of which Neil would have been proud. A telegram from the War Office suddenly called me to London and a new briefing from one of the Staff Officers I had already met in M1(R).

M1(R) was now dissolved and absorbed into the new and much larger organisation SOE. The new organisation had a representative in the War Cabinet, the Minister for Economic Warfare, but its director was a distinguished banker. In these early days comparatively few of its staff officers were regular soldiers; most of the others seemed to have been financiers or solicitors.

The Spanish section, I now learned, was preparing a party to go on an operation 'in which you might be interested'. I was. The prospect of action at last might help to stop me brooding over Neil's death. There would be eighteen officers, and a number of NCO wireless operators and demolition experts; we were to start with a para-military course at Lochailort, where we would learn the details of this operation from the officer in charge.

I was surprised to find that few of my new colleagues had much knowledge of Spain; only a few, who had learned it in Latin America, could speak Spanish. Most had been happy as regimental officers and were not at all pleased to be posted away suddenly, with barely a word of explanation, to Lochailort. After three weeks of intensive training – forced marches over that rough country carrying fifty-pound rucksacks, pretending to blow up bridges with dummy explosive (and once nearly blowing up an important road bridge and ourselves with real explosive that had been substituted in error), map reading, pistol shooting and unarmed combat – we assembled one evening to meet at last our new commander, who had just arrived from London, and learn the details of the proposed operation. He proved to be a large, plump lawyer with an oily smile and an ingratiating manner, who wore the badges of a lieutenant-colonel but tried to impress on us that he was just an ordinary jovial fellow like ourselves. Beginning with one of the oldest dirty jokes in the legal profession he went on to explain that it seemed likely the Germans would soon invade Spain to try and take Gibraltar. If so, there would be a surprise waiting for them: ourselves. He himself would control our operations – from a distance; but he would be with us all the way, in spirit.

We would leave for Gibraltar shortly, to await the German invasion. We would divide into parties of two officers and a wireless operator NCO, each with its wireless set and store of arms, ammunition and explosives, to be carried in a one-ton Army truck. Each party was allotted its operational area, to which it would drive with all speed when the balloon went up – ignoring, apparently, the overwhelming German air superiority which would make the use of any road lethal. Lest we be downhearted, he told us we would be meeting him when we reached Gibraltar.

'As for what the future holds for you,' he concluded in ringing tones, 'I can only tell you' – in a deeper, sterner tone – 'hardship shall be your mistress, danger your constant companion.'

For my partner in this operation, codenamed 'Relator', I paired up with John Burton, a ginger-haired captain in the Lincolnshire Regiment. The partnership was to last a long time, through far more serious operations than 'Relator', and develop into a close friendship that endured until Burton's death in 1985. His quiet manner concealed an obstinate determination, great courage and superb endurance; and beneath his austere appearance he combined a wry sense of humour and genuine personal humility.

Our journey to Gibraltar by sea proved a nightmare. We embarked at Liverpool on a raw, rainy evening in the middle of March, aboard HMS *Fidelity*, previously a freighter of the French mercantile marine and now converted to Special Operations. Her captain, officers and crew were French, but had all assumed incongruous Scottish or Irish names to pass themselves off as Canadians if they fell into enemy hands. Unfortunately nobody on the planning staff had thought to advise any of them that they would be carrying eighteen extra passengers on this voyage, with the result that nobody had provided for us.

A Royal Navy commander who introduced himself as the liaison officer greeted us as we stepped on board.

'It's a damned disgrace!' he spluttered. 'Until I arrived here an hour ago nobody in this ship had the least idea they were going to carry passengers – certainly not *eighteen* of you. There's nowhere for you to sleep, but the crew are clearing space in two of the holds and you'll have to park your campbeds there – lucky you've brought them with you. I'm afraid you'll be hellish uncomfortable. I don't even know if there's enough food for you, because there's been no time to order extra stores and we sail tomorrow.'

'Oh well,' said a cheerful voice, 'I suppose we can exist as far as Gib on gin.'

'I'm afraid not, unless you've brought your own. There's been no time to get customs' clearance for extra liquor and the ship's crew have barely enough for themselves. It's a damned disgrace,' he repeated, and left us.

The prospect of a hungry, thirsty and extremely uncomfortable voyage in March weather at the height of the Battle of the Atlantic was not appealing; nor was the reality. We formed part of a slow convoy that sailed round the north coast of Ireland and well out into the Atlantic. The crew had worked hard to make our quarters habitable; but despite their efforts, the holds with their bare iron decks and bulkheads gave us a grim feeling of being entombed in some doom-laden prison deep below the waterline; if we were torpedoed we would have only the slimmest chance of escape from it. In good weather we would have suffered only minor discomfort, but when we rounded Ireland and entered the Western Ocean we ran into a series of gales that lasted until we passed Cape St Vincent. Through the ill-caulked deckheads rain and seawater poured over us incessantly, drenching our beds and clothes and swirling about the floor with every roll of the ship; moreover, as *Fidelity* carried a formidable armament aloft, she rolled and pitched with a savage, plunging violence, sending our campbeds and ourselves skidding across the deck, and sometimes decanting us into the pools of water that collected at the sides of the holds. I was lucky in that I don't get seasick, but others like poor Burton suffered continuously from it. We found buckets for him and the others, but there was no way of stopping the wretched things skidding all over the hold, overturning, and adding their contents and special aroma to the mess on the deck.

Fidelity was not a happy ship. Officers and crew alike were terrified of their captain, a stocky, black-bearded pirate with a reputation for ferocity which he seemed resolved to impress upon us all. Slung from a belt round his uniform jacket he carried an automatic pistol, with which he claimed to be a deadly shot; he would blaze away at anything that caught his eye – a seagull on the mast, a piece of flotsam on the sea or even an offending member of the crew. He would stride about the bridge, his hands in the pockets of his jacket, his beard thrust out aggressively and a malignant expression on his brick-red face, screaming invective at the officer of the watch, the guns' crew at practice, the quartermaster at the wheel or anybody unlucky enough to cross his line of vision. During these black moods, and they were more frequent than his bright ones, he would aim savage blows and kicks at the nearest officer or man within reach. He never actually assaulted any of us, contenting himself with abuse.

For defaulting officers he had a special treatment: when all were assembled for a meal in the saloon the captain would bellow the offender's name. A trembling 'O'Flaherty' or 'Mackenzie' would present himself at attention in front of the angry little man, who would launch into voluble details of his offence, his character and the less creditable habits of his parents, concluding with three or four heavy slaps across the face in dismissal; often, as the victim turned to go, a well-directed kick in the seat of the pants would send him sprawling among his colleagues.

At least the convoy escaped serious attack and we were alarmed by nothing more menacing than the distant explosions of depth-charges.

All our discomfort, we learned on landing at Gibraltar, had been for nothing. The British Ambassador in Madrid, Sir Samuel Hoare, categorically refused to allow SOE to take any measures in Spain to prepare for our operations, even a reconnaissance of our proposed areas. And so, while our masters deliberated what to do with us we were lodged under canvas on the old racecourse, now called the North Front, beside the RAF airfield, where we occupied ourselves in such training and exercises as the limited space and facilities on the Rock allowed; otherwise there was very little for us to do and far too much time to do it, with the result that most of us spent our leisure in the bars and cafés of Gibraltar, where gin and whisky were cheap at duty-free prices.

This was no life for men geared up to the kind of operation for which we had been recruited. Moreover, although a German invasion of Spain seemed possible – in order to take Gibraltar and close the Mediterranean – we thought it unlikely that if they did we should ever get near our allotted operational areas, obliged as we were to travel there by road in our Army lorries. The area assigned to Burton and me was in Estremadura in south-western Spain, and

I doubted whether I at least could expect a friendly reception from the group we had been told to contact, who were almost certainly Republican fugitives.

The most likely form of attack on the Rock, the authorities believed, was a massive assault by parachute troops supported by heavy air bombardment; it had just proved successful in Crete, although at enormous cost. Its consequence in Gibraltar was an atmosphere of alarm, bordering on panic; everyone was sure the next target would be the Rock. The garrison went on instant alert, there was a curfew from 11 pm till dawn with severe penalties for infringement; extra roadblocks appeared, guarded by trigger-happy sentries, which made it a hazardous business to go out at night, even before curfew; and our orderly officer told me he had received an order, signed by the garrison commander and marked 'Top Secret', instructing us that 'in the event of an enemy airborne invasion of the Rock all tentage will be returned forthwith to Ordnance'.

After the German attack on Russia on 22 June the panic subsided, since it was inconceivable that Hitler would try to invade Spain as well. Along with most of our companions, Burton and I began to look for alternative employment. Meanwhile, we submitted a plan, for transmission to SOE in London, suggesting we should parachute into one of the Basque provinces, where I knew the country and could hope to find friends among former *Requetés*; I had already heard on the grapevine that they were thinking of dropping missions from Britain into northern Spain, in case the Russian resistance collapsed and left the Germans free to turn that way again. While we awaited their reaction, I managed to arrange, through some submariner friends, to go on a patrol in the submarine *Clyde* to the Canaries, where they had information that a U-Boat was lurking; I had no difficulty in getting permission to go.

'If we can creep up on her at dusk or in darkness,' said Commander Ingram, the submarine's captain when explaining the patrol to me, 'it would be fun to try and board her and bring her back here. Then you would come in useful with your cloak-and-dagger stuff.'

I reported on board one morning at the end of June. I was shown to my quarters, a bunk in the comfortable little wardroom, and over lunch I met the rest of *Clyde*'s officers, a friendly group who seemed genuinely glad to be taking a 'pongo' with them; they probably thought it was a good opportunity to study the breed at close quarters. We sailed the same evening, gliding into the Bay of Algeciras under a bright and brassy sun, and turned westwards into the Straits towards Tangier. Once we were clear of the harbour and out into the bay I was allowed on deck, and from the bridge I watched the houses of Ceuta gleaming white on the port beam under the great bulk of the rock Gebel Musa above the town; to starboard on the Spanish coast rose tiers of dark hills clothed in groves of olive trees, and high up on a hillside stood a ruined Moorish watchtower concealing, it was said, a German observation post. It would be an uneventful trip, I decided, at least until we approached the Canaries.

We were abeam of Tarifa when we sighted the destroyer coming from the West; she proved to be HMS *Avon Vale*. I turned from her to watch the various colours on the African coast glow and fade in the evening light. I was aware we were exchanging identification signals with her at a distance of about a mile on our starboard beam and then with a flash of alarm I sensed that something was wrong – a mistake, it seemed, in the colour of the recognition flares. Suddenly I heard the officer of the waterwatch shout, 'God, she's opening fire!' and simultaneously with Ingram's snapped order, 'Crash dive!' there came the whine of a shell close overhead. I felt myself seized from behind and pushed roughly to the opening of the conning-tower hatch. Fearfully alive to the danger I threw myself down the vertical iron ladder, with the next man's boots stamping on my fingers. As my feet touched the floor of the control room and the last man off the bridge slammed shut the conning-tower hatch, there was a violent explosion overhead, followed a second later by the faint sound of a gun. Someone called out, 'Bloody good for her second shot!'

The confined space of the control room, the boat's nerve centre, was crowded with men, each grimly concentrating on his own job: the first lieutenant by the hydroplane controls, anxiously watching the angle of our dive; the helmsman tense at the wheel listening for Ingram's curt directions; petty officers and ratings with their hands on control levers, their eyes on the dials and gauges. Clearly I wasn't wanted there; I made my way to the wardroom and sank down on a settee at the small dining table. *Avon Vale* was still firing, and in the silence I could plainly hear the bark of her guns and the rising hum of the shells as they came at us to burst with a curious metallic ring in the water around us. Over the intercom I heard the warning, toneless and terrifying:

'Stand by for depth-charge attack, stand by for depth-charge attack.'

Bewildered and sweating I wondered what action I should take. Looking up I caught sight of the wardroom steward in the narrow passageway, bracing himself against a bulkhead, and so I braced myself as best I could between the back of the settee and one of the table supports. I was glad to see that he also was sweating. I managed a feeble smile and received a cheerful grin in answer.

The shelling ceased. There was absolute silence throughout. I would never have believed a crowded boat could be so quiet. I couldn't tell if we were still diving, or even moving. No sound came from *Avon Vale* and I tried to comfort myself with the thought that if she were closing to attack we would hear her propellors. After what seemed an eternity we heard the captain's voice: 'Flap seems to be over. Up periscope!'

A minute or two later came the welcome orders, 'Stand by to surface! Blow number one! Blow all tanks!'

I heard the rush of water along our sides as we broke surface, then a draught of air when the conning-tower hatch opened. Soon afterwards I was on the bridge watching *Avon Vale* rolling in the swell while signals of explanation and apology flew back and forth. *Avon Vale* could be proud of her gunnery; her second shot had landed a four-inch shell on our bridge as we were diving, but luckily there were no casualties and only slight damage to the superstructure.

'I suspect, Peter,' Ingram said to me, with a grin, 'that we may have had the luck of Jonah.'

The rest of our voyage was uneventful. We found no U-Boat and spent three days submerged off the Canaries, watching through the periscope the bathers relaxing in the sun and the fishermen in their brightly coloured boats pulling in their nets. We stayed under water during daylight, surfacing at night to recharge the batteries and take some air aloft. Ingram's orders didn't allow him to stay longer and we reached Gibraltar ten days after we had set out.

July passed slowly, in heat, humidity and, for most of the SOE officers on the Rock, frustration. But on 3 August Burton and I received the welcome order to embark for England aboard the converted French liner *Pasteur*, one of the fastest passenger ships on the old New York run. Although we had to sail well out into the Atlantic we were in Glasgow a week later.

The officers of the Spanish section of SOE, where we reported on arrival in London, were in a large block of flats off Baker Street. We had an interview with two staff officers, both former solicitors and partners in the same firm as our previous boss on the Gibraltar mission. One was a solemn naval lieutenant – he eventually became president of the Law Society; the other was an Army captain with a cheerful outlook, whom I would often find around midnight in the popular nightclub, the 'Nut House', with his bottle of whisky in front of him and a blonde on either side.

With Spain preserving her neutrality and no prospect as yet of a German invasion, it seemed unlikely we should be needed there. While SOE decided what to do with us, they wisely sent us on several useful courses – industrial sabotage, parachute training and an undercover agents' course in the New Forest. Then they gave us some leave and at the beginning of October I took the opportunity to get married – to an attractive girl I'd been pursuing since just before the war. Apart from our alas transient love for each other, we didn't have a great deal in common and it was a stormy partnership. It lasted the statutory (in those days) three years.

Chapter 3

THE NEW YEAR of 1942 found Burton and me still in London, telephoning daily to the Spanish section of SOE, to be told there was nothing for us. After Pearl Harbour and the widening of the theatre of war we tried other SOE country sections – French, Norwegian, Polish, Czech, Russian and Far Eastern. Some had work but no vacancies, others no work. Towards the end of February 1942 I ran into a gunner colonel who had been a fellow instructor with me at Lochailort and was now an SOE staff officer.

'I'll give your names to my old friend Gus March-Phillips,' he said after hearing our story. 'He's looking for officers for a scheme of his that should be up your street.'

An interview followed soon afterwards with Major March-Phillips and his second in command, Captain Geoffrey Appleyard. After exhaustive questioning about our past experience we both found ourselves accepted into the 'Small-Scale Raiding Force' in our rank of captains.

March-Phillips was a regular officer in the Royal Artillery who had served in India before the war and seen action on the Northwest Frontier – but not enough of it to compensate for the boredom of peacetime soldiering and social life in the intervals, and so he had sent in his papers and retired to the English countryside to write novels. Recalled to active service, he had won the MBE in France in 1940, after which he joined the newly formed Commandos that autumn. In the spring of 1941, with the help of Brigadier Gubbins, a fellow gunner, he had persuaded SOE to let him fit out and arm a Brixham trawler, *Maid Honour*, and sail her with his own picked crew of seven to Freetown in West Africa – in the middle of the battle of the Atlantic. They completed this hazardous voyage without incident and proceeded to carry out some brilliant *coup-de-main* operations against enemy shipping along the African coast, culminating in the seizure of a large Italian liner with her entire crew, whom they obliged, without much argument, to sail the ship across the ocean to an American port. The operation earned March-Phillips the DSO.

A devout Catholic by religion, by breeding and tradition an English country gentleman, he combined the fire of a crusader with the professionalism of a regular soldier; and the inspiration to conceive great enterprises with the unquestioned ability to carry them out. Slightly built and of medium height, with piercing eyes puckered from straining against tropical sunlight, he had an expression both enquiring and formidable, only a little mitigated by a slight stammer. Despite a hasty temper he had a great sense of fairness towards his subordinates and no malice; in battle he was invariably calm.

He was fortunate in his second-in-command. Of more equable temperament but similar romantic nature, less impetuous but just as obstinate, Geoffrey Appleyard had a flair for planning and organisation together with superb skill in battle and an astonishing – unique, I thought it – ability to instil confidence in the face of danger. Beneath a broad forehead his deep-set blue eyes looked out from a fresh-complexioned face with a calm steadiness matched by the low timbre of his voice. He had the stamina of a championship skier, which his extraordinary willpower put under inhuman strains.

The son of a Yorkshire industrialist, he had entered his father's engineering business on leaving Cambridge. Commissioned in the RASC in 1939, he had met March-Phillips in France and become one of his troop commanders in the same Commando unit. Early in 1941 he had landed from a submarine in the Loire estuary to collect two British agents, and brought them back to safety in difficult and dangerous conditions, for which he received his first MC; he received his second for the *Maid Honour* operation, in which he was second-in-command to March-Phillips.

After the success of *Maid Honour* March-Phillips had no difficulty in getting approval from SOE and Gubbins's enthusiastic support for the Small-Scale Raiding Force. The idea was to recruit and train a force to carry out small raids of about a dozen men across the Channel, under cover of darkness, against selected German strongpoints and signal stations on the coast of northern France. The short-term objects were to take prisoners for information, and to shake the enemy's morale and raise that of our European allies; the longer-term object was, by launching a series of these raids almost every night along the whole coastline from Holland to Brest, to force the enemy to redeploy their troops and so relieve some of the pressure on the Russian front. March-Phillips's immediate intention was to train a nucleus of officers and NCOs in the principles of this kind of warfare and then to give them practical experience by leading them himself in raids across the Channel. As we acquired experience, he explained, we ourselves would train and lead others in these raids, and so the force would expand.

'We're taking over an old manor house in Dorset,' Appleyard told us, 'which will be admirable for our base. Our first raids will be from Portland, Poole and Gosport, and so Anderson Manor, between Poole and Blandford, is perfectly situated. We shan't be able to start our training for about six weeks, so find yourselves something to do in the meantime.'

The first thing to do, we decided, was to get ourselves fit again after so much inactivity in London, and to refresh our memories on demolitions and small arms – pistols and tommy-guns especially. After a series of courses in the Western Highlands we reported for duty, fit and fairly proficient, at Anderson Manor towards the end of April. In the meantime we both attended March-Phillips's wedding in London, where we met some of the others who were to form the nucleus of this small force. The senior among them was Major John Gwynne, Sussex Yeomanry, in charge of planning. A teetotaller and vegetarian who regularly shaved in cold water even when hot was available, obstinate, unwearying and quite fearless, he had a lean, dark face and thinning, almost tonsured hair which gave him the look of some medieval inquisitor – I could almost see his eyes glittering beneath a Dominican's cowl. He fretted constantly under the restraints of his sedentary task and longed to lead an operation in the field. He had some original ideas for it. On one occasion he visited an SOE camouflage station and returned with a *papier-mâché* cow's head, which he proposed to take with him to France, put on his head and push through some hedgerow beside a major road; thus disguised, he assured us, he would count German vehicles and troops passing by. Mercifully his plans for our own operations were more realistic.

A schoolfriend of Appleyard was Graham Hayes of the Border Regiment, who had also won the MC in *Maid Honour*; he was a serious-minded young man of great charm, courage and strength, and a fine seaman who had sailed before the mast in a Finnish grain ship. Anders Lassen, also an old *Maid Honour* hand, was a cheerful, lithe young Dane whose quiet, self-effacing manner concealed a sharp sense of humour and a terrifying ferocity against the Germans, from whom his family had already suffered cruelly during their occupation of his country. His wild bravery was to win him an MC and two bars with us and, later on in Italy, a posthumous Victoria Cross; to this day his memory is revered in Denmark.

Anderson Manor was a fine Elizabethan house with spacious grounds and handsome gardens, about eight miles south of Blandford. In the grounds we constructed our own assault course and pistol range, and started our training very soon after arrival there. For cover purposes we were known as No 62 Commando and wore the Commando green beret, but March-Phillips arranged our training schedule according to his own ideas. The most important aspects had to do with small boats, practising embarkation and landing, mostly in Poole Harbour, and night exercises across country; we would have to operate in non-moon periods and so we trained ourselves to see in the dark, almost like cats. Although discipline was extremely strict during training, off-parade relations between officers and other ranks were informal. There were no punishments, nor were they needed because we knew that the lives of all of us were going to depend on the steadiness of each.

Because we were intended to form the nucleus of a much larger force we had more officers than other ranks; among the former were a Dutchman, a Frenchman and a Pole. Probably the most popular with all of us was Brian Reynolds, a subaltern in the Welsh Guards but an Irishman by birth; although not yet thirty he already had an adventurous history behind him. Well known before the war as a sportsman, *bon viveur* and playboy, he had gone to fight for the Finns when Stalin invaded their country with no provocation or excuse in the winter of 1939. Forsaking the comfort and cuisine of Buck's Club he endured bitter hardship and extreme danger in the icy forests of Lapland and Karelia before making his way to Sweden after the collapse of Finnish resistance. In Sweden he turned his remarkable talents to the service of the Allies, smuggling cargoes of ball-bearings from Gothenburg to Britain in freighters through the narrow waters of the Skagerrak under constant attack from the German Navy and Air Force; on his last run he lost four of his five ships, but his arrival with the fifth prevented a serious gap in British tank production – and won him the OBE. Sadly he was killed the day after the European war ended.

By the end of July we had completed our training and were anxious for action; the plans were ready for our first raids. The Admiralty had assigned to us an MTB, smaller and faster than most of her class, stripped of her torpedo tubes and armed only with two Vickers machine guns; she was known as 'The Little Pisser' and commanded by a keen and very competent young RNVR lieutenant. She would carry, after modification, a light landing-craft lashed to the afterdeck. The idea was that she would take us across the Channel to within about a mile of our target, when we would paddle or row ourselves ashore in the landing-craft.

She presented one serious problem, in that with the landing-craft attached she couldn't put to sea in more than a force 3 wind; and because we could only launch our raids in non-moon periods these limitations of weather and season delayed the start of our operations. However, in the second week of August we mounted our first raid, with half our force, against a small strongpoint on the coast of Normandy. The approach involved some difficult rock climbing, which made March-Phillips, who had observed my deplorable lack of agility as an alpinist, exclude me from the party; Burton too stayed behind because he had injured a calf muscle during training. With anxiety and envy we watched the raiders leave in the dusk for Gosport, festooned with tommy-guns, pistols and grenades. They were back in time for breakfast, exhausted but content with their work. They had crawled under the perimeter wire but had roused the evening guard when trying to force an entry to the buildings; they had slaughtered the guards with tommy-guns and grenades, and after inflicting further casualties on the bewildered and frightened garrison had withdrawn safely. Although they had brought back no prisoners we all felt they had given us a promising start.

Burton and I took part in the next raid. The target was the lighthouse and signal-station manned by the Germans on the Casquets, a rocky islet some seven miles west of Alderney in the Channel Islands. A week after the first raid our new party, about ten of us, assembled for a briefing in the conference room at Anderson, where we studied charts, maps, air photographs and, most valuable of all, a perfect scale-model of the target in plasticine, showing the lighthouse and adjoining buildings in clear detail. March-Phillips, who would command, gave us his operation orders.

We would embark in the MTB at Portland at around 9 pm and arrive off the Casquets before midnight. On approaching the enemy coast the MTB would travel on her silent auxiliary engine and at half a mile from the target she would anchor, and we would man the landing-craft and paddle ourselves ashore. We could expect a difficult landing, with a heavy swell and a fierce tiderace round the rocks. Our coxswain, Graham Hayes, would let go the kedge anchor to keep the boat off the rocks, and Appleyard as bowman would take the painter ashore and make her fast while the rest of us landed. Hayes and another officer, Lieutenant Warren, would remain with the boat. Once ashore we would climb in single file up to the wall that enclosed the signal-station buildings. Inside, we were to split into four parties, each with its separate objective. The largest party, led by March-Phillips, was to tackle the main building, containing the living and sleeping quarters; Burton and I were to make straight for the wireless tower, kill or capture any Germans we found there before they could use the wireless and put the transmitter out of action; and the other two parties were to occupy the lighthouse tower and the engine room. When we had completed our tasks we would all report, with any prisoners, to March-Phillips. A small escort would shepherd all the prisoners to the landing-craft while the rest of us searched the buildings for codebooks and other documents. Nobody knew the precise strength of the garrison, but they were thought to number about eight; there would be ten of us in the attack and so if we could achieve surprise we should in theory be able to overpower them.

Bad weather and engine trouble in the MTB held us up for nearly a fortnight. However, Wednesday 2 September was a fine day with a fresh breeze – all we could ask for. In the last ten days we had rehearsed over and over again our parts in the planned attack, practising silent movement in the dark, scaling walls in full equipment, and disembarking and re-embarking on a rocky shore; and we all had a clear picture in our minds of the details of our target.

After a hurried supper we climbed into our lorry and set off for Portland, singing lustily as we drove through the green and gold countryside – chiefly to distract our minds from brooding on the possibility of disaster. On arrival at the dockyard the lorry halted close alongside the MTB and we hastened on board, disposing ourselves below wherever we could find space, in the forecastle or right aft; Appleyard, who was navigating, joined March-Phillips and Freddie Bourne, the skipper, on the bridge. At 9 pm we sailed.

With the hatches battened down to show no light it was oppressively hot in our cramped quarters. The little boat bounced jarringly over the waves, for the wind had now risen from force 3, when we sailed, to force 4. Most of the others tried to sleep, but I sat up and tried in the dim light to read a thriller.

One of the motors was giving trouble again, obliging us to reduce speed, and so it was after 10.30 when Appleyard knocked on the forecastle hatch and warned us to get ready. When we had inspected our weapons and adjusted our equipment we switched out the lights, to accustom our eyes to the darkness outside. Half an hour later the hatch opened and we were ordered on deck.

It was a clear night, bright with stars. The wind had dropped again and the sea was moderating. Gathering aft of the bridge around the Goatley assault-craft – a flat-bottomed boat with canvas sides which had already proved itself surprisingly seaworthy – we could make out the dim shapes of some rocks on the starboard beam; Appleyard and March-Phillips were on the bridge trying to identify them. The MTB had switched from her main engines to the silent auxiliary. Looking round the horizon and shivering in the chill night breeze, I noticed a flickering light at some distance on our port bow and another – a bright red one – almost directly ahead of us; the latter, I afterwards heard, was Sark. The moon appeared, low in the sky, on our port quarter. Suddenly I caught sight of our target, straight ahead of us; the tall, thin column of the lighthouse, the whitewashed wall and the buildings of the signal-station gleamed palely above the blackness of the rock.

Slowly the MTB moved in, manœuvring to approach from the north-west; at half a mile's distance she anchored. Silently we pushed our Goatley over the stern and dropped quickly into our places, kneeling with our paddles ready. It was five minutes after midnight when March-Phillips jumped down beside me and called softly:

'Right! Push off! Paddle up!'

Now the moon was higher, casting a sharp, clear light over the choppy water between us and the island; we could see it distinctly and must ourselves be visible, I mused uncomfortably, to any watchers there. I dismissed such thoughts and concentrated on keeping time with the others, holding my paddle well away from the side of the boat; I took comfort from the silence of our movement through the water and from the knowledge that we were a small object and therefore difficult to pick out among the waves. It was hard work paddling, for the north-east flood was running fast.

Some twenty minutes after leaving the MTB I saw that we were entering a small bay. There were splashes of white close ahead, where the surf was breaking on the rocks.

'All right, Apple?' whispered March-Phillips. Appleyard's voice called back from the bows, low yet to our tensed minds alarmingly clear:

'Okay. Graham, bring her in just to the right of that white splash of surf.'

I could see the landing place, a smooth and gently sloping slab of rock, lighter in colour than the rest, in the right-hand corner of the bay. As Hayes let go the kedge anchor Appleyard stood up in the bow, the line in his hand. The swell caught us, sweeping us towards the rock; Appleyard leaned forward to jump for the shore. At this moment the kedge began to drag, holding us back. We paddled up with all our strength to shorten the distance, but we could make no headway against the weight of the kedge. I saw March-Phillips glance apprehensively at the buildings above us. We were close under the rock; its black mass towered overhead, the signal-station standing out clearly against the sky. It would be awkward, to say the least, to be caught in such a place, as it seemed we must be if the enemy up there were alert. As the swell lifted us again and carried us shorewards Appleyard jumped with the bow-line. He landed on the rock, slipped on the wet surface and almost fell into the sea; recovering just in time, he scrambled up the cliff to make fast the painter. One by one we followed him ashore, timing our jumps to the rise of the swell, while Hayes held the boat off the rock with the sternline and kedge. Encumbered by our weapons we slithered about, trying to get a purchase on the rock, until March-Phillips hissed angrily:

'Use the rope, you b-bloody f-fools, to haul yourselves up!'

Leaving Hayes and Warren to look after the Goatley and keep a watch on the MTB through an infra-red receiving set, we started to climb the cliff in single file. I followed Burton who, prostrated with seasickness during the crossing, had made a remarkable recovery as soon as his feet touched land. We had avoided the recognised landing points, fearing that they might be set with mines or booby-traps; we were lucky, therefore, to find an easy way up from the shore. Our only obstacle was some coiled Dannert wire, through which we cut our way without trouble. Any noise we made was probably drowned by the rumble of surf and the booming of the sea in the chasms and gullies round the cave. Nevertheless, my heart was pounding with more than exertion as we came into full view of the buildings. Under different circumstances the whitewashed walls and dark roofs would have seemed lovely under the pale moonlight: in those critical moments they loomed cold and menacing, silent and lifeless, yet seemingly ready to spring into life to destroy us.

The entrance to the courtyard was blocked by a heavy 'knife-rest' barbed wire entanglement. Motioning us to follow him, March-Phillips leaped for the wall, heaved himself over it and dropped on the other side. Within a few seconds we were all in the courtyard. This was the moment for independent action. Burton and I tore across the fifty yards of open ground to the door of the wireless tower, where a light was burning. Inside, on the left, a stone staircase led up to the transmitting room. Without a pause we raced up the stairs to a landing on the first floor, where an open doorway led to a lighted room. Burton was through the door in a second, his pistol in his hand; I was hard on his heels, my finger on the trigger of my tommy-gun.

We found ourselves in a deserted room, crammed with wireless sets, generators and equipment; by the operator's stool, which was thrust back from the table, were some signal pads and an open notebook; codebooks were on a shelf on the wall above. I stood on guard at the doorway overlooking the staircase, listening for sounds of firing from the other parties; but everything was quiet. Meanwhile Burton went through the room collecting codebooks, signal-books and other documents likely to be of interest. I heard a sound from the entrance below; raising my tommy-gun I peered over the low balustrade and was relieved to see Appleyard looking up at me.

'All clear here,' I said, 'we haven't seen a soul. How's it gone with you?'

'Splendid! We caught the whole damn bunch with their pants down – or rather, with their pyjamas on. Two of them had just come off watch and were turning in, two others were filling up log books and the rest were in bed. Just as well, after all, that we didn't get here earlier. I've never seen men look so astonished and terrified – not a show of fight among the lot of them. We're taking them down to the boat now.' He came upstairs to join us.

'What about smashing up all this equipment?' I asked. 'Can I use my tommy-gun to blast it?'

'No. There's been no shooting, so Gus wants us to keep as quiet as possible. John had better use his axe while you and I go back to help with the prisoners. When you've made a nice mess, John, pick up the papers you've collected and join us in the main building.'

We had indeed achieved complete surprise. Like the wireless tower, the lighthouse and engine room were both deserted; all seven members of the garrison were in the main building. It seemed extraordinary that they had not posted a sentry, but they explained to us that they had not expected visitors. Nothing could better describe their state of unpreparedness than a sentence from March-Phillips's official report to the chief of Combined Operations: 'A characteristic of those in bed was the wearing of hairnets, which caused the commander of the party to mistake one of them for a woman.'

All the following day and night, we were informed later, Cherbourg was calling up the Casquets and asking all other stations if they had had any signals from the island. It was a month before the Germans discovered what had happened to the garrison. All the prisoners were naval ratings, under the command of a chief petty officer. Among them were two leading telegraphists, one of whom had previously been employed on guided missiles and whose information later under repeated questioning proved particularly valuable.

While some of us made a thorough search of the buildings, collecting documents and destroying arms and equipment – which included an Oerlikon cannon – others rounded up the prisoners and marched them down to the boat. As time was running short the Germans were not allowed to dress; dejected, they were hurried away with overcoats over their pyjamas, one of them keeping on his hairnet until we arrived at Portland, where he proved a willing subject for interrogation.

It was one o'clock when I reached the Goatley, to find the prisoners already embarked. The moon was well up, bathing the Casquets and the sea around in brilliant light; our position now would be desperate if enemy patrol craft were to approach. Although the Goatley was going to be seriously overloaded, with the seven prisoners and ourselves, March-Phillips decided to take the risk rather than waste time sending for the emergency dory. He ordered me to jump in and stand at the bow to help the rest of the party aboard. With the heavy swell, the jump from the rock to the landing-craft varied from five to twenty feet, so that re-embarkation was not easy. The smallest mistake might cause the swamping of the boat and bring disaster on us all. The last man to jump before March-Phillips and Appleyard was the Pole, Orr; he had his fighting knife in his hand and, as he dropped, the boat lurched and threw him against me. I felt a sharp, biting pain in my right thigh as the blade went in. However I had no time to think about it; March-Phillips dropped into the boat and ordered us to cast off. I crawled to my place and began paddling with the others, under the ceaseless rain of invective from our commander.

With nineteen men aboard, the Goatley was dangerously low in the water; but she rode the swell admirably and we reached the MTB safely after thirty-five minutes. The prisoners were hauled aboard first and sent down to the forecastle; I joined them there, helped along by Orr, who was very contrite about the injury he had accidentally caused. The return journey to Portland was uneventful. The prisoners were docile, huddled together in their misery at one end of the forecastle; indeed, there was no comfort for any of us in the cramped and stifling compartment. Orr's knife had penetrated deep and my wound was stiff and painful; when we reached Portland, just before dawn, I could barely stand. After a while an ambulance took me to the naval hospital, where I was immediately put to sleep with a shot of morphia. An operation next morning removed the blood clots and greatly relieved the pain. I thought I was the only casualty of the raid, but I was wrong: Appleyard, following March-Phillips into the boat, had seriously damaged his ankle. These accidents, which temporarily put us out of action, in the event prolonged our lives.

I had just left hospital but was still unfit for operations when disaster struck the Small-Scale Raiding Force. On the night of 12 September March-Phillips led another raid, this time against a target on the Cherbourg peninsula; Burton was in his party and Appleyard navigated although his damaged ankle wouldn't permit him to land. They had attempted the raid the previous night, but had run into fog a mile or so from the target; this part of the coast was heavily defended and it might have been wiser to allow a longer interval before repeating the raid.

The Germans were alert and ready for them. The moment they landed they ran into heavy fire from the cliffs above the beach, from machine guns, mortars, grenades and cannon. Appleyard and the skipper Bourne continued to cruise around as close inshore as the shallow water allowed, until the approach of daylight compelled them to make for home; the MTB was under heavy fire all the time and one of her engines was knocked out. None of the landing party returned; months later we learned what had happened to them. The Goatley foundered while carrying them back to the MTB and all but March-Phillips had swum ashore; he struck out for the MTB, but drowned while trying to reach it. The Germans recovered his body next morning, as they announced in an official communiqué. Letters from the survivors told of the calmness, skill and courage with which he had handled that desperate situation on the beach and organised the withdrawal to the Goatley. All but one of the others were captured immediately, two of them with severe wounds. Hayes managed to escape by swimming to land further down the coast, but after a short time at liberty he fell into German hands and, although he was in uniform, he was placed in Fresnes prison for nine months in solitary confinement and shot in July of 1943.

We had been prepared for casualties but not for catastrophe like this. The death of that gallant crusading idealist and rare quixotic genius who had been our inspiration, together with the loss of so many good friends, was a crippling calamity that almost put an end to our activities. I believe it would have, but for the energetic reaction of Appleyard, who refused to let our grief interfere with his resolve to avenge the disaster and carry on March-Phillips's work. Our masters in Baker Street and at Combined Operations responded with a heartening display of confidence, appointing Appleyard as temporary commander of the Force in the rank of major.

He soon justified their support. Early in October he took a party to the island of Sark, leading the raid in person despite his injured ankle. They spent more than four hours reconnoitring the island; they also captured two Germans. Realising that the route back to the landing-craft passed close by some German defences, Appleyard ordered the prisoners' hands to be tied behind their backs, to lessen their chances of escape. At the most critical point of the journey one of the two ran away; Lassen gave chase in the dark, caught him and before he could raise the alarm dispatched him quickly and silently with a fighting knife. The remaining prisoner gave no trouble.

There was one unfortunate sequel: when the dead prisoner was found, his hands still tied behind his back, the German high command raised an outcry, maintaining that it was contrary to

International Law to tie the hands of prisoners. In retaliation they put chains on some of the prisoners they had taken in the Dieppe raid.

Later in October the Chiefs of Staff gave orders for the expansion of the SSRF, as we had now been abbreviated. We established four more bases along the south coast between the Gosport area and Falmouth. My old friend Bill Stirling arrived from Cairo to take overall command, with the rank of lieutenant-colonel; Appleyard became second-in-command and field force commander; and two navigating officers joined our establishment, one an RAF squadron leader, the other a tubby Breton fisherman with a bright red face, with not a word of English and a dialect very few of us could understand. But he was a friendly little man who took a touching pride in his new RNR lieutenant's uniform, especially the cap, which he never seemed to remove; even when seated on the lavatory (he never locked the door) or sitting up in bed in his thick flannel pyjamas reading a book, he would be wearing that cap perched at a jaunty angle on the back of his bald head.

With our expansion came an important change of policy. In future we would be receiving selected officers and NCOs from other Commandos, to train in the techniques of small-scale raiding and then to lead in our raids. The first to arrive, at the end of October, were from No 12 Commando – Captains Pinckney and Rooney and Lieutenant Gilchrist, each with six NCOs from his own troop. Pinckney, whose brother-in-law was an old pre-war friend of mine, was a particularly competent and courageous officer; Gilchrist – 'Gilly' to all of us – proved excellent company, with a lively sense of humour and a sharp but never unkind wit. I was told to train Rooney's squad, with the help of Brian Reynolds and Sergeant Nicholson, a regular soldier and a most efficient as well as a very popular NCO. We were to prepare for a raid in the very near future.

On 5 November, appropriately enough, we received our briefing. Our target was a German semaphore station on the Point de Plouezec, about fifteen miles north-west of Saint Brieuc on the coast of Brittany. We had plenty of maps and aerial photographs as well as some local intelligence about the station's defences and approaches, which was to prove inaccurate in some important details. The station stood on the top of steep cliffs at the end of the point, which jutted out north-eastwards from the Baie de Saint Brieuc. The northern and eastern sides were defended by concrete emplacements, at least one of which mounted a gun; the only possible landing place appeared to be a small shingle beach below the southern face, where a narrow track climbed the cliff to join a path running inland from the semaphore station. On this side of the station, we were informed, the only defences were a single belt of barbed wire and a small concrete guardhouse just inside the entrance, where there would be a sentry; the entrance itself had no barbed wire to protect it. Local information told us there were neither mines nor booby traps on the approaches. The garrison numbered about a dozen soldiers; there would be ten of us and so surprise was vital.

Appleyard, strictly forbidden to land because his ankle was now in plaster, would come with us in the MTB. I was to command the assault party, with Rooney as second-in-command; Reynolds would be coxswain of the landing-craft in which we would paddle ashore and would remain with us during our attack. Stirling particularly impressed on us that he wanted no casualties in our party; afterwards he took Reynolds and me aside to emphasise this point.

'Obviously we want to inflict casualties and take prisoners if we can. But not, I repeat not, at the cost of casualties to ourselves. It just isn't worth it at this stage, so soon after our losses at Cherbourg. If you decide when you get there that you can't get into a fight without losing men, I assure you I'll be quite satisfied with a recce. No Foreign Legion stuff, Peter, on this party!'

This was no easy assignment. To attack a target well protected by natural features as well as its own defences, inflict casualties and take prisoners, without loss to ourselves, would need a lot of luck. I set about drafting my operation orders. In addition to the usual weapons we were taking a Bren gun, a silenced Sten gun and two large grenades of a new pattern; they had a thin metal casing containing a heavy charge of plastic explosive; they burst on impact with a very powerful blast and would be useful if we had to blow our way through any barbed wire across the entrance.

I worked out a simple plan: immediately after landing, the party was to form a defensive beach-head at the foot of the cliffs, protecting the landing-craft, while I located the track leading to the top. When we reached the top of the cliff Sergeant Nicholson would take up position with the Bren gun, to cover the path inland and to indicate the point where the track led down. This should be about a hundred and fifty yards from the entrance to the semaphore station. The rest of us would approach the target in three groups, one on either side of the path and one in the rear; Rooney would lead the left-hand party, I the right. The last part of the approach would have to be made crawling on our stomachs. If we could get near enough, Rooney and I would kill the sentry with our knives; if not, Sergeant Broderson would shoot him with the silenced Sten. We would then invade the station, the party on the right pausing to clear the guardhouse, while the remainder attacked the main building.

MTB 344 was lying at Dartmouth, ready to take us across on the first night of favourable weather. At midday on Wednesday 11 November, heartened by the news of far more important landings in North Africa, we set off from Anderson to carry out our raid.

After a brief halt at Lupton House, our new base near Paignton, where we had a hurried meal and put on our operational clothing and equipment, we drove into Kingswear in the late afternoon. Stirling and Sam Darby, our new intelligence officer, were on the quay talking to Freddie Bourne, whose boat lay alongside, her engines already running. As soon as the last of us was on board we cast off and started down the estuary. Waving a silent goodbye to Stirling and Darby I settled myself with Rooney and Reynolds in the lee of the dory on the afterdeck. Appleyard took up his usual station on the bridge with Bourne; Rooney's men were below. Savouring my first moments of relaxation since early morning I gazed at the wooded hills above the Dart, watching their colours soften as we drew away in the last clear light of evening; the old castle above Dartmouth stood black against the fading western sky. Soon distance and darkness hid them; only the bright torrent of our wake showed in the blackness of night and water.

I strove to keep myself from worrying about the work that lay ahead of us, reflecting that we had rehearsed every detail of my plan; but now doubts began to crowd upon me. Rooney's men were fine, but we had worked together only for a fortnight; on this difficult approach the slightest misunderstanding or mischance, impatience or carelessness, would destroy us before we could launch our attack. Moreover, despite all that Stirling had said, I knew that we would look extremely foolish if we were to return without taking the prisoners or inflicting casualties; yet I could not overlook his instructions which I knew came from headquarters, to bring my party home intact.

Fortunately I was not allowed to immerse myself for long in these unhappy thoughts. As we cleared start point and increased speed to twenty-eight knots against a force 3 wind and swell from the south-east, the sea began to break green over the whole length of the boat, drenching us through our protective clothing and freezing us as we lay under the inadequate cover of the dory. Before long I was too numbed to think about my troubles and looked forward to our arrival off the Point de Plouezec, which would at least put an end to this discomfort.

The journey took us nearly six hours. For some of the time I stood on the bridge with Appleyard, staring in silence through the spray and darkness, unable to make out the horizon in any direction, so dark was the sky. Two or three times I went below with Rooney to see how his men were faring; finding nearly all of them asleep, I envied their composure.

It was not surprising we had some difficulty in finding our first landfall, the light tower on the Roches Douvres, and wasted an hour making a 'square search' for it; just before ten o'clock we picked it up at a distance of about a mile. From here Appleyard laid a course to bring us directly to the Baie de Saint Brieuc. At half-past eleven we switched on to silent engines, altering course again to approach the Point de Plouezec from the east-south-east. The night was now bright with stars, and as we drew near we could clearly distinguish the headland with its off-lying rocks and islands; on top of the point the squat outline of the semaphore station made a dark silhouette against the sky.

At ten minutes past midnight we dropped anchor about half a mile from the shore; Rooney's men filed noiselessly on deck. Now I realised the hours we had spent rehearsing the launching of the dory had not been wasted; within twelve minutes, without a word having been spoken, we were all in our places and paddling silently towards the shore.

Fifteen minutes later we ran into the cove we had selected for our landing; we were dismayed to find that the beach was not shingle, as our intelligence had led us to believe, but boulders. The tide was ebbing fast and if we left the dory on this beach we would be unable to refloat her on our return from the raid. While Reynolds stayed in the boat, to keep her off the rocks, I took the party ashore and established my beach-head at the foot of the cliffs; Rooney went off on a reconnaissance of the cove, in the hope of finding a more suitable beach. He returned ten minutes later to tell me that there was nowhere else possible. The only solution was to leave Reynolds to keep the dory afloat while we made our attack.

We formed up in staggered file and began to climb the cliff, myself in the lead, Rooney close behind me; but it was soon clear that we could not hope to keep any formation. The track, which had looked so plain in the aerial photographs, did not exist, or, if it did, was invisible in the darkness. We set ourselves to scramble up the face, which I judged was nearly a hundred feet high at this point. It was an arduous climb, for the ascent was almost perpendicular and the cliffs were overgrown with thick gorse bushes whose spikes pierced our clothes, and tore our hands and faces; it was alarming too, for the surface was slippery grass and loose shale, which we could not help dislodging with the sound, to our strained ears, of an avalanche.

After twenty minutes we reached the top, where we lay down to look around us and regain our breath. About a hundred yards ahead

I could make out a line of telegraph poles running parallel with the cliff face, indicating the track which led inland from the semaphore station. We made for the track, moving swiftly across the open ground that separated it from the clifftop; we joined it about a hundred and fifty yards away from the barbed wire and the guard-house. I was reflecting with relief that at least we had encountered no mines or booby traps when I saw Rooney staring fixedly at two small noticeboards, one on each side of the track, facing inland. I went to examine them and read with horror the warning, '*Achtung! Minen*'. Included in the minefields was the route by which we had approached and by which we must return.

I sent Rooney with one of his men to make a close reconnaissance of the defences of the semaphore station. They returned with the gloomy news that the entrance and guardhouse were protected by a double line of barbed wire, which also blocked the path, and by two sentries, who seemed very much on the alert. Our best plan seemed to be to work our way across country on the left of the path and try to get through the wire at some distance from the sentries. This, of course, involved the risk of mines; but we had already crossed one advertised minefield without mishap and so could reasonably hope that the notices were either a bluff or merely a warning of intention to lay mines. Accordingly, after leaving Nicholson with the Bren gun by the path to guard our rear and to serve as a marker for our return, I started to lead the others across the open ground on our left.

We did not get very far. I had covered only a few yards, crouching low and straining my eyes to watch the ground at every step when I all but trod on a mine. It was laid, with very little attempt at concealment, under a small mound of turf. Abandoning our hopes that the notices might be a bluff, we returned to the path. A frontal attack was the only solution; whatever the risks, they were at least calculable; we must trust our luck and skill to bring us close enough to the wire to blast our way through it and kill the sentries before the garrison could turn out. Although I knew that Stirling would not blame me if I abandoned the raid at this point, I agreed with Rooney that it would be pusillanimous of us now to return without putting up a fight.

I split the party into three groups, according to my original plan. I took the right side of the path myself, followed by Sergeant Broderson with his silent Sten; Rooney, Sergeant Barry and another NCO were to move along the left side, abreast of me, while the rest followed a dozen yards behind. I was to set the pace; as soon as I dropped to the ground the rest of the party would do the same, after which we would complete the approach on our stomachs. We had rehearsed all this beforehand and so detailed instructions were unnecessary at this point; Rooney was carrying the No 6 grenade which was to blow our way through the wire and he would have to decide when to throw it.

As we padded slowly up the path I was appalled at the stillness of the night. At a hundred yards' distance the voices of the sentries sounded unnaturally clear; Sergeant Broderson's breathing pounded like a steam engine at the back of my neck and I feared my own must be as loud; but our felt-soled boots and long hours of practice enabled us to tread silently, and as long as the sentries went on talking we could move forward in reasonable safety, although slowly. Whenever they stopped speaking we halted and stood motionless, holding our breath. Thirty paces from them I dropped on to my stomach and, waiting until all the others were down, began to edge forward inch by inch on my elbows and the points of my toes. I halted frequently to listen and peer through the gloom at the line of wire and the silhouette of the guardhouse ahead. Those last yards seemed like miles and it needed all my self-control to move without haste; in that still air the least sound would carry to the sentries' ears and give us away. I was glad to note that Rooney and the others were watching me carefully, coordinating their movements with mine; I could see Rooney's dark bulk on the other side of the track exactly level with me.

When we were ten paces from the sentries we came upon a pair of low posts, one on each side of the track, with a trip-wire hanging loosely between them. I judged that we were unlikely to get any nearer without being heard, but I decided to wait a while in the hope that the guards might move away on a round of the defences. For a full fifteen minutes we lay there, listening to the lazy drawl of their conversation, punctuated all too frequently by periods of silence when they would peer towards us and listen. The nervous strain inside me grew almost intolerable, sometimes bordering on panic when I thought of the peril of our situation; we must carry on now, for I could never turn my party back under the noses of this watchful pair. Clearly we had no hope of killing them quietly. I remember thinking how good the earth and grass smelt as I pressed my face close to the ground; overhead a lone aircraft beat a leisurely way up the coast; from the direction of Paimpol came the distant sound of a dog barking.

Out of the corner of my eye I saw Rooney make a slight movement; then I heard a distinct metallic click as he unscrewed the top of his No 6 grenade. The sentries heard it too; they stopped their conversation and one gave a sharp exclamation. I sensed rather than saw Rooney's arm go up and braced myself for what I knew was coming. There was a clatter as one of the sentries drew back the bolt of his rifle; then everything was obliterated in a vivid flash as a tremendous explosion shattered the silence of the night. The blast hit me like a blow on the head. From the sentries came the most terrible sounds I can remember: from one of them a low, pitiful moaning, from the other bewildered screams of agony and terror, an incoherent jumble of sobs and prayers, in which I could distinguish only the words '*Nicht gut! Nicht gut!*' endlessly repeated. Even in those seconds as I leaped to action I felt a shock of horror that those soft, lazy, drawling voices which had floated to us across the quiet night air could have been turned, literally in a flash, to such inhuman screams.

Though they were to haunt me for a long time, I had no leisure for such thoughts now. In a moment I was floundering through the wire by the guardhouse on the heels of Rooney and Sergeant Barry. The wire, mangled by the explosion, was no longer a serious obstacle. A little dog sped out of the open door of the guardhouse and ran off into the darkness, giving tongue in shrill, terrified yelps. The guardhouse was empty. The two sentries were sprawled on the ground, one silent with his hands over his face, the other calling on his mother and his Maker until a burst of tommy-gun fire from one of my NCOs quietened him; the grenade must have landed close beside them, for their clothes were terribly burnt.

I wasted no time here, but followed Rooney's party past the guardhouse and on to the open courtyard in front of the main building. As I arrived beside Rooney a German loomed up out of the darkness, firing rapidly at us with a small automatic. Rooney and I replied with our .45s, bringing him to his knees; but he courageously continued firing until a burst from Sergeant Barry's tommy-gun finished him off. A door was thrown open in the station building ahead, revealing a light inside and, silhouetted clearly against it, the figure of a man with a submachine gun, poised at the top of a flight of steps. He paid for his folly in presenting such a target, because Sergeant Broderson gave him two bursts from the silenced Sten, toppling him forward on his face; as he tried to rise Corporal Howells riddled him with his tommy-gun.

When my rear party arrived I prepared to send half of them round to the back of the station building, while the rest of us stormed the front. But although only a few seconds had passed since we had started the attack, we no longer had the advantage of surprise; the Germans were organising their defence and, having turned out the lights, began to pour a heavy fire on us from the windows and the open doorway. The garrison was clearly stronger than we had expected. If we stormed the building we would have to cross the open courtyard under heavy fire, with grave risk of casualties; in any case it was doubtful if we were strong enough to overwhelm the garrison now that they were alert. We had killed four Germans for certain, without loss to ourselves; I decided to disengage now, before I had the added difficulty of carrying wounded through the minefield and down the cliffs.

I shouted the order to withdraw. We raced back across the wire and along the path to the spot where Sergeant Nicholson was waiting impassively with his Bren gun. As we hurried through the minefield I was in a sweat of terror lest we should have a casualty here at the last moment; I do not know how we could have carried a wounded man down those cliffs to the boat. In fact we were lucky, but the descent was dangerous enough as we slid and fell blindly in the gorse-covered gullies leading down to the beach. I was greatly relieved that there were no signs of pursuit from above, although the semaphore station was in an uproar and we could still hear the sound of small-arms fire when we arrived on the beach. The Germans had sent up alarm rockets and I wondered whether they would have searchlights to intercept us on our way back to the MTB.

When we reached the dory I saw how much we owed to Brian Reynolds. While we were away the tide had been going out fast, but for Reynolds the dory would have been left high and dry on the boulders, where she would have been almost impossible to refloat. For two hours he had stood waist-deep in the icy water, holding the boat off the rocks; I wondered that he had any movement left in his legs, but he seemed active enough.

We stumbled to our places in the boat; but when Rooney called the roll there were two men missing. Both had been with us when we started down the cliff and so presumably they would join us at any moment – unless they had had an accident on the way down, which was not unlikely. As we sat waiting anxiously, a Verey light shot upwards from the clifftop and fell slowly towards the sea, illuminating the bay, the cliffs and ourselves in a vivid magnesium glare. I began to feel desperate. In such a light the Germans could not fail to see us; my stomach contracted as I awaited the spatter of machine-gun bullets that would announce our discovery. There could be no escape for us once we were seen; was I to lose the whole party for the sake of two men, or must we incur the shame of abandoning two of our companions to certain capture and possible death? Fortunately I was not called upon to make the decision: as the last glow from the Verey light faded we heard a clatter on the pebbles; the two missing men heaved themselves painfully over the gunwhale.

There was no need to urge everyone to paddle his hardest.

We were three hundred yards offshore when another Verey light exploded from the signal-station, lighting up the tense, sweating faces of my companions as though in the glare of footlights. This time, I thought, they're bound to see us and I waited, almost resigned now, for the hiss and splash of bullets. But once again darkness enveloped us, allowing us to go our way. Reynolds had a pair of very powerful night glasses, with which he had been able to pick out the MTB from the shore; when the second Verey light expired he sent our homing signal – three green flashes from his torch. We were on board at half-past three in the morning, ten minutes after leaving the shore, and received a warm welcome from Appleyard who had passed an anxious three hours while we were away. As we turned for home two more alarm rockets went up from the semaphore station, followed by another illuminating flare, but we could see no response anywhere along the coast.

During the homeward journey Rooney and I sat huddled miserably in a pool of water on the bottom of the dory, under the flimsy protection of a tarpaulin. I was feeling the reaction from the excitement of the last few hours; although relieved that I had brought our party back intact I could feel no elation at our small success: instead, I could not rid my ears of the terrible screams that had come from the mangled sentries, or my mind of the grim memory of our return through the minefield and our wait in the dory under the blazing Verey lights. At the same time I could not shake off a nagging, persistent worry that perhaps I had not acted with sufficient resolution; that if I had pressed home my attack instead of giving the order to withdraw we might have made prisoners of the entire garrison.

At seven-twenty, through the half-light of dawn, we made our first landfall on Downend Point; an hour later, on a raw, grey morning, we came alongside the quay at Dartmouth, where Stirling was awaiting us with Darby and a formidable escort of field security police. My heart sank as I saw the latter and wondered how Darby would take the news that we had no prisoners for him. What he said was:

'Go straight back and get some!'

Stirling listened without interruption to my account of the raid. At the end he said:

'You were fully justified in breaking off the action when you did, in view of the score at the time; I will say so in my covering report. It's bad luck that you couldn't take any prisoners, but you must have given the enemy quite a shock, which is one of our objects.'

Revived by an excellent breakfast in the YMCA at Paignton of scrambled eggs and mugs of tea laced with our rum ration, we drove back to Anderson, arriving in time for lunch. I worked all the afternoon and until late in the evening, composing two reports on the raid – a summary which Stirling wanted to show to the Prime Minister and a detailed account for Combined Operations head-quarters. Appleyard told me later that the Prime Minister made the simple comment, 'Good!'; and so I suppose that honour, at least, was satisfied.

That was the last raid the SSRF mounted from England. Stirling planned several others, but by this time the grand design of 'Over-lord', the Allied invasion of Europe, was well under way and Allied agents were landing along the French coast in preparation for it – although we didn't know it at this time. It made no sense to launch more of our raids, which kept the Germans on the alert and showed them their weak points.

Rooney's men had showed up admirably and went off on well-earned leave. I was sleeping badly after the raid, with terrible nightmares of the screaming sentries; and so I was glad when Brigadier Gubbins ordered me to take a small party of our officers, including Lassen, on a parachute course at Ringway. The comman-dant of the holding station where we stayed was a veteran of the First World War and a delightful fellow; but he was a stickler for punctuality and detail, which caused Lassen on the first day to murmur in a worried tone, 'Tell me, Peter, is this a much-bullshit place?'

Not the most punctual of people, I made a special effort to impress the commandant with a show of keenness and efficiency; I was expecting an enthusiastic report from him afterwards and so was not too well pleased to read, 'He is not entirely the irresponsible officer he appears at first sight.'

Early in 1943 Stirling transferred the bulk of the SSRF to North Africa, to become part of the Second Special Air Service Regiment – Bill's brother David had founded the first SAS in the desert in 1941. With Stirling went Appleyard and Lassen among others; both of them lost their lives in action in Italy. I remained in England for a few more months, my eyes on a more distant theatre of operations.

Chapter 4

'THINGS HAVE CHANGED a bit in the last year, especially in the Balkans. We're now looking for people who would be prepared to drop into Greece and Yugoslavia to work with the guerrillas there.'

I was sitting in the Baker Street office of a lieutenant-colonel who had trained with me at Weedon and had just returned from Cairo to concern himself with SOE operations in the Balkans. I had visited Greece during my first long vacation from Cambridge, in 1934, but knew nothing about Yugoslavia, an exciting and mysterious country to me. The need for British liaison officers, as these volunteers were called, was greater in Yugoslavia and so I asked to go there.

It was now the middle of May 1943. I spent the next three weeks in Baker Street, receiving a briefing on the Yugoslav military and political situation from Major Peter Boughley who had worked in that country before the war with the British Council. He had strong political views and a kind heart; his views were right wing, like my own. When the Germans invaded Yugoslavia in 1941 and crushed the Yugoslav Army, a resistance movement sprang up immediately, centred on General Draža Mihailovic and his Cetniks, in the name of the young King Peter; the British government gave official recognition to the Royal Yugoslav government-in-exile in London. Until the invasion of Russia the communists took no part in the resistance. After June 1941, a communist resistance movement grew up rapidly in the mountains, led by the shadowy and then little-known Tito, whose guerrillas called themselves 'partisans'. Suspicion between the two organisations rapidly grew into hostility and, at about this time, open warfare – a tragic waste of the war effort in that country. British liaison officers were being sent by SOE to both groups to try and concentrate their efforts against the Germans. Both had their strong supporters among SOE staff officers: Boughley believed we should send most help to the Cetniks; the partisans enjoyed the backing of the historian Bill Deakin and the head of the SOE Yugoslav Section in Cairo, Basil Davidson, both of whom had recently operated in areas occupied by Tito.

In Boughley's office I met my friend John Bennett from Weedon days. He had worked for SOE in Belgrade until the German invasion, when he had moved to Cairo to take charge of the Yugoslav section there. Recently he had returned to England after handing over to Davidson. He was pessimistic about my prospects in Yugoslavia.

'I don't think you'll enjoy it there, or be able to do anything useful. Nobody now can stop this ghastly civil war. Why not try to go to Albania? A wonderful people they are, with a wonderful country, ideal for guerrilla warfare; and there's no civil war there. I don't think we have anybody there now, but we ought to have. You'll find Archie Lyall in Cairo; he's well placed to give you some idea of what's going on in the Balkans.'

'How did he do in Belgrade?'

'He certainly livened it up. Once he had to entertain a delegation of Anglican bishops. He took them to just about the louchest night-club in town, where the high spot of the evening is a girl doing a bellydance. You can take my word for it that nothing, but nothing, is left to the imagination. The audience encouraged her by shouting *"měsaj!"* – "mix it!" There were no episcopal protests.'

Reporting at SOE headquarters in Cairo I learned there was no chance of my being dropped into Yugoslavia in the next two months because all the vacancies were already filled. Another surprise was to find my Cambridge contemporary James Klugman, once the secretary and inspiration of Cambridge communists, now established in this headquarters as intelligence officer of the Yugoslav section. Having been required, like other recruits to SOE, to sign a document affirming that I had never been a member of any fascist or communist organisation, I was astounded to find Captain Klugman in such a responsible and confidential post. He was certainly good at his job and he used it to render valuable service to the communist cause in the Balkans. After the war, as a member of the Politburo of the British Party, he had special responsibility for the education of young members.

Major Basil Davidson made no attempt to hide his antipathy to the Cetniks and to those who supported them in London. He even suggested I sign a paper to the effect that I had been subjected in London to indoctrination on behalf of Mihailovic; I firmly refused, but it showed the sort of feeling that was to embitter relations between British officers both at headquarters and in the field.

I lost no time in tracking down Archie Lyall. He had escaped from Yugoslavia, carrying a diplomatic bag – and my Spanish cloak – to Athens just before the German invasion and was now a major in the Balkan section of the Political Warfare Executive in Cairo. He seemed to share John Bennett's pessimism about SOE operations in Yugoslavia, and in Greece as well and for similar reasons.

'Try Albania, Peter,' he advised. 'We have two first-class men in there now, both of them friends of mine. I can't think of a better party for you to join.'

He spoke indignantly of the failure and futility of SOE preparations in the Balkans before the German and Italian occupation of those countries, especially in Romania, where they had failed to block the Iron Gates or sabotage the oil wells.

'I've designed a coat of arms for SOE in the Balkans,' he told me. 'Surmounted by an unexploded bomb a cloak and dagger casually left in a bar sinister. Supported by a double agent over the motto: *Nihil quod teligit non made a balls of it.*'

A few days later I heard there were indeed vacancies for Albania in the next moon period – unlike those of the Small-Scale Raiding Force, these parachute operations almost always took place when there was a moon to help visibility. I reported at once to Major Philip Leake, head of the Albanian section. Leake, a former schoolmaster, had held an important post with SOE in West Africa at the time *Maid Honour* was there, and he had worked on several occasions with March-Phillips and Appleyard. A kindly person with a dry and cynical wit, and an infinite capacity for taking pains, he was well fitted to direct this new and still despised country section.

His assistant, Mrs Hasluk, was a grey, birdlike woman in middle age whose frail appearance concealed extraordinary energy and determination. Julian Amery has described her as 'one of those remarkable Englishwomen who make their homes in strange lands, and gain the affection and respect of their inhabitants'.* She had entered Albania as an anthropologist in 1919 and settled near Elbasan in the centre of the country, where she had lived very happily and gained many friends among the people and their leaders until the Italians expelled her in 1939 on the unfounded suspicion of being a spy. When war broke out she had organised an SOE office in Istambul and then in Athens before coming to Cairo to work with Leake. Her love for Albania gave her a special affection for us BLOs (British Liaison Officers); we were

* *Sons of the Eagle*, p 27 (Macmillan, 1948)

'her boys' and in the field we would sometimes receive signals from her, giving us the map coordinates of some beauty spot nearby, where we could enjoy a picnic.

Among her other works she had published an Anglo-Albanian grammar, complete with Albanian fairy stories, which we had to study. Sadly, it was scarcely more intelligible to most of us than the language it was meant to clarify. Albanian, believed to be derived from ancient Illyrian, is one of the two oldest European languages and resembles no other; Albanians affirm it was the language of Alexander the Great. It is certainly one of the most difficult to learn. Very few of us managed to master it, which seriously hindered our work in the field; we were mostly dependent on interpreters, whom we could trust neither to render our own words faithfully nor to give us a true picture of local reactions.

Most of our knowledge of the current situation in Albania came from signals sent by the only British mission in the country. Code-named 'Consensus' and led by two unusually adventurous regular cavalry officers, Billy McLean and David Smiley (the friends Lyall had referred to), the mission had dropped into northern Greece in April 1943 and, with assistance from the British BLOs in that area, had walked across the Albanian frontier with no knowledge either of the language or of what they might find on the other side. After encountering many obstacles and much suspicion they at last established contact with Albanian guerrillas, and set up their own base and their wireless near Korcë in the South, not far from the Greek border.

Albania is about the area of Wales and the greater part of it is mountainous. It is a poor country, where malnutrition is general among the people, who suffer from widespread tuberculosis in the mountains and malaria in the coastal plains. The Albanians – Shqypetars, as they call themselves – are an ancient race, dating from pre-Classical times, and in spite of some five hundred years of Turkish occupation they have always retained a strong sense of nationality; this sense gained strength from frequent encroachments on their territory by their Greek and Slav neighbours. The Albanians are divided into two branches, the Ghegs of the North and the Tosks in the South, both of whom speak varying forms of the same language; the Shkumbi river, impassable in winter, separates the two. At this time the social structure among the Ghegs was tribal, like that of the Scottish Highlands before 1745; in the South a landowning aristocracy, the Beys, dominated a landless Tosk peasantry.

There were three religions in the country: in the South most of the peasants were Greek Orthodox, though the Beys were Moslem;

the centre of the country was predominantly Moslem, while the North was divided between the Catholic mountaineers of Mirdita and Djukagjin, and the Moslems of Kosovo and the wild north-eastern frontier. But religious differences seemed far less important than the rivalries among the clans in the North, between Ghegs and Tosks, and, especially, the deep suspicion of all Albanians for Greeks, Yugoslavs and Bulgars.

The frontiers of Albania, drawn up by the Ambassadors' Conference of 1913 after the Balkan Wars, were roughly the same as today's; they satisfied neither the Albanians nor their neighbours. The principal bone of contention between Albania and Yugoslavia was the province of Kosovo, inhabited by a preponderantly Albanian population, but incorporated into Serbia because of its significance in Serbian history and its strong emotional appeal to Serbian nationalism.* Today the Albanian Kosovars are causing serious problems for the Yugoslav government.

A period of internal unrest followed the end of the First World War and concluded in 1924 with the seizure of power by Ahmed Zogu, a chieftain from the Mati country north of Tirana, who had himself crowned as King Zog of the Albanians. Still in his early thirties Zog had learned the art of government in Istambul in his youth under the tutelage of the Sultan Abdul Hamid; by playing off his Albanian rivals against each other, resorting to methods that Western democracies would hardly approve, and relying on a very competent gendarmerie trained by British officers, he ruled for nearly fifteen years.

Under King Zog Italian influence was strong in Albanian foreign policy, commerce and education – so strong in fact that during my own travels through the country from South to North there were few villages, even in the mountains, where I couldn't exchange a few words of Italian. But Mussolini concluded that Zog was too independent a character to suit his ambitions. On Good Friday 1939 he invaded Albania. Zog and his Hungarian queen Geraldine escaped to Greece with their infant son, and thence to England, where they spent the war. Only in the port of Durazzo was there organised resistance; a battalion of gendarmerie and a few tribal levies under the command of Major Abas Kupi, an illiterate Mati chieftain, held up for thirty-six hours the assault of two Italian divisions supported by a heavy naval bombardment. After the battle Kupi's followers smuggled him out of the country, but two years later he was back in the Mati mountains to carry on a successful

* The Battle of Kosovo in 1389 condemned the Serbs to nearly five hundred years of Ottoman rule.

guerrilla war against the Italians and their German successors until the end of 1944, when he was overrun and driven into exile by the communist forces of the dictator Enver Hoxha.

When Italy entered the war against us in the summer of 1940, SOE started to organise from its office in Belgrade an Albanian resistance movement. But after the German invasion of Yugoslavia in early 1941 it abandoned its efforts for another two years. Meanwhile the little information that filtered out of Albania was collated by Mrs Hasluk in Istambul and passed to Cairo. There wasn't much of it, but what came through indicated that there were armed bands, *çetas*, of Albanians in the mountains; very little was known, however, about the nature of these bands, their politics, locations or activities.

In consequence of the Allied victory in North Africa and the approaching invasion of Italy, SOE began to take a greater interest in Albania, chiefly because of the importance to the Axis of her lines of communication. Cairo therefore sent in McLean's 'Consensus' mission with instructions to report on the situation and strength of the guerrillas, and their potential value to the Allies. From McLean's signals a much clearer picture emerged.

When Germany invaded Russia the communists in Albania, as in other Balkan countries, took to the hills for safety. When their leaders had established a comparatively secure base in the southern mountains near Korcë they began to form partisan *çetas*, recruited from the landless peasants of the countryside and the young intelligentsia of the towns. Their original instructions probably came from Tito, who maintained two representatives with the Albanian communist committee. Following the usual communist practice the partisan leaders wouldn't call themselves communists, at least to foreigners like us. Instead they pretended to be leading a 'democratic' movement which all who called themselves democrats might join. Its nature we soon discovered. As Julian Amery points out, 'In practice, exclusive control of the movement was retained in the hands of a small committee, all of whom were communists.'* This committee appointed the military commanders and the much more powerful political commissars; most of the former and all of the latter were communists.

As Amery also points out, the partisan movement drew its strength entirely from the Tosks; north of the Shkumbi there was little support for communism. But there were various guerrilla groups with which, for tactical and prestige reasons, the communists wished to ally themselves. The most powerful of them were the

* *Sons of the Eagle*, p 54

Zogist Abas Kupi with his Mati tribesmen; the veteran outlaw Myslim Peza, who controlled the hills south-west of Tirana and who had been defying the central government for ten years; and in the mountains north-east of the capital a brave and boozy old Bektashi abbot, Baba Faja, a bitter foe of the Italians, commanded a strong *çeta*.

The communist leadership managed to persuade these three to join the partisan movement. After a joint conference in September 1942 all of them united with the communists in a single 'National Liberation Movement' or LNC (its Albanian initials). Control of the new movement rested with a central council of ten, predominantly communist but including the three Gheg guerrilla chiefs. It was in fact a triumph for the communists, disarming the suspicions of those who didn't share their ideology; it also enabled them to penetrate the forces of Myslim Peza and Baba Faja, both of whom soon became mere communist puppets. This was due to the diplomatic skill, charm and evident sincerity of the brilliant propagandist, Mustafa Gjinishi, one of the few communists I ever found it impossible to dislike.

There was one resistance group in the South which held aloof from the new LNC. Known as the Balli Kombetar, or the National Front, it drew supporters from local landowners and their retainers, from merchants, professional men and teachers, and from the middle-class intelligentsia of the towns; it viewed the LNC with fear and distrust. Its founder was the venerable statesman Midhat Bey Frasheri, a leading figure in the Albanian struggle for independence in the early years of the century, and its leaders included some of the ablest politicians in the country. As Republicans the Ballists had always opposed King Zog, but as staunch nationalists they hated the Italians. Their feelings towards the British were ambiguous: they welcomed our help against the Italians, but they feared, rightly as it turned out, that an Allied victory would result in the loss of Kosovo, temporarily incorporated into Albania, and in communist domination of their country. In order to qualify for British drops of arms and money, they would sometimes go into action against the Axis enemy, but they were always inhibited by the fact that many of their supporters lived in villages near the main roads, where they and their families were most vulnerable to Axis reprisals.

And so when McLean's party entered Albania there were two mutually suspicious and even hostile resistance movements in the South, and it was soon evident that the lavish supplies of arms, equipment and money that SOE dropped to each of them for use against the enemy were being conserved by each for use against the other. In other words, from a war of liberation this was already turning into a war of succession: who would take over the country when the Axis troops left, as it was now obvious they would? Our briefing in Cairo stressed that we were being sent to an area, not to any particular faction; we must ignore politics and regard ourselves purely as soldiers, giving support impartially to any groups there who were prepared to fight the enemy. These instructions, clear and logical enough in the Cairo office, were to prove quite impracticable in the field.

It wasn't until the August moon period that I was able to drop into Albania. SOE parachute operations into the Balkans were now mounted from Derna on the coast of Cyrenaica, where I arrived in the first week of August. At the transit camp near the airfield I met the officers and NCOs who would be my companions on the drop. There were four parties, including my own, going in that month in two aircraft. A squadron of Halifax bombers, commanded by an old Wellington schoolfriend of mine, was standing by on the airfield to take us.

Each of our parties consisted of an officer, a wireless operator and a demolitions NCO. Much the oldest and certainly the toughest was the famous Himalayan climber, Major Bill Tilman, a regular soldier. Short and stocky, with a prominent nose and jutting chin, and a short, fierce moustache, he had volunteered for Albania, he told us, to keep himself in training for his next Himalayan attempt – his previous one had been the last pre-war Everest expedition. He took not the slightest interest in politics and so, while he was always happy to blow up a bridge or ambush a convoy, his passion for climbing and frequent opportunities to indulge it left him happily impervious to the Albanians' bitter quarrels.

Less fortunate in this respect was Major Gerry Field, also a regular; serious-minded and enthusiastic he loathed political controversy and those who indulged in it. He was most unlucky therefore to be allocated the Valona area, where LNC and Balli Kombetar were directing all their energies to civil war, in which they persisted aggressively and with personal threats in trying to involve him.

The remaining mission was led by Major George Seymour, Royal Scots Fusiliers, another regular. He had suffered severe wounds from a land mine at Alamein, where he had commanded a company of Argylls. He took no interest in politics either but believed that all political problems could be solved by any officer with a gentleman's education and a sound knowledge of King's Regulations. Tall and thin, he affected the appearance of a Victorian military dandy and sported a huge handlebar moustache.

In my own party, which bore the codename of 'Stepmother', there was only myself and a demolitions sergeant, our wireless operator having already dropped into Albania; my demolitons expert was Sergeant Gregson-Allcott, RAF, a quiet young man from Eastbourne. Although destined for different parts of the country, all four missions were to drop together to McLean's headquarters at the village of Shtyllë in the hills some ten miles south-west of Korcë; Tilman and Field would go in one aircraft, Seymour and I in the other. Both aircraft would also carry supplies and money for McLean's mission; the money was in gold sovereigns and Napoleons, the only readily negotiable currency in the Balkans.

The outlines of the Halifaxes on the runway looked like monstrous black locusts against the angry yellow light of the dying sun. Beside our own aircraft stood a young RAF corporal, our dispatcher who would check our harness and static lines before we dropped. We followed him up a short ladder under the belly into the reeking metal interior of the aircraft. When we were airborne we settled ourselves comfortably among the bales of blankets and clothing.

It was the night of 10 August. We had spent the last few days at the camp checking our stores, maps and personal equipment. I was armed with a Colt .45 automatic and a new type of submachine gun developed by SOE and named the Welgun.

Some two hours after the takeoff the dispatcher shook me awake.

'You'll be putting on parachutes in about half an hour, sir. The skipper wondered if you'd like to come on to the flight deck first, for a look round.'

Ten thousand feet below the coast of Epirus gleamed white in the moonlight against an indigo sea. It was a beautiful night as we crossed the coast to turn inland towards Korcë and our dropping zone.

'We can be thankful for this moon,' the pilot told me. 'Your dropping zone is in a narrow valley with some nasty hills around it and I wouldn't fancy going through cloud to look for the signal fires. You'd better get ready now. Good luck.'

We had already arranged between us the order in which we should drop. On the first run-in, the aircraft would release the metal containers with the heavy stores from the bomb bays, followed by the free-dropping bundles of clothing; on the next run we ourselves would drop. As senior officer Seymour would drop first, followed by the rest of us, with me bringing up the rear. We had half an hour to wait before arriving over the target. This period, I was to find, was always the most gruelling part of a drop; there was too much

time to think. For all the information we had picked up from
McLean's signals and from Mrs Hasluk, I felt it was into an unknown
country that we were about to launch ourselves; what awaited us
there and how, if at all, we should return was beyond imagining. I
found it hard to resist an encroaching feeling of gloom.

A shout from the dispatcher jerked me out of my thoughts.

'We've sighted the signal fires! We're going to circle now for the
first run-in. We'll be dropping you from a thousand feet, so you'll
have time to look around on your way down.'

The aircraft tilted sharply as she banked and rapidly lost height,
pitching in the sudden turbulence. The dispatcher had opened the
exit hatch in the floor and as he threw out the 'free drop' packages
I just glimpsed a line of fires flashing past on the ground. 'Now it's
your turn,' he told us.

Seymour's party followed each other swiftly through the hole and
we banked again for our last run-in. Gregson-Allcott swung his legs
over the opening and I sat opposite him, both of us watching for
the red 'Action Stations' light in the roof to switch to green. The
dispatcher's hand was already raised. My gloom had vanished; it
was only necessary to concentrate and remember our parachute
training, especially not to look down until clear of the aircraft.

The light went green, the dispatcher's hand dropped and
Gregson-Allcott was gone. The moment he disappeared I swung
my legs over and pushed myself away from the side, stiffening to
take the impact of the slipstream. There were a couple of seconds
while my stomach seemed to hit the roof of my mouth, then the
slipstream hit me in the small of the back like the fist of a heavyweight
boxer. I felt a violent pull in the groin and under my arms as the
parachute opened, and then I was floating gently downwards with
the great white canopy billowing above my head. Instead of the
rush of air the only sound was the hum of the Halifax's engines
growing fainter in the distance.

The moonlight shone on rocky, scrub-covered hills rising from a
long, narrow valley where a line of small fires flickered immediately
below me. As I drifted lower I could hear men shouting in the
valley and the faint tinkle of goat bells from the surrounding
hillsides; there was the scent of thyme in the air. Contented now,
even elated, I beamed upon the soothing, pastoral scene. My complacency
was soon shattered when I saw I was drifting away from
the fires, across a dry watercourse, towards the steep side of a
mountain.

The next thing I remember, I was standing unsteadily on a piece
of sloping, rocky ground, supported on my feet with difficulty by
a grinning, dark, shaggy little man; he seemed to my confused mind

like a satyr, and I would not have been surprised to see goat-feet, horns and a tail. I tried to collect my wits and remember where I was; my head swam, my eyes seemed unable to focus. The word 'Albania' flickered through my consciousness and I found myself repeating it aloud, to the delight of the satyr, who broke into excited pidgin French:

'*Albanie, oui! Vous êtes en Albanie! Vous venez parachutiste*' – he pointed upwards – '*Vous frappez tête – poum!*' He indicated the rock where I was standing, and my parachute and harness strewn upon it. '*Moi,*' he added, tapping his chest, '*moi Albanais. Moi Stefan.*'

At this moment I heard Seymour's cheerful tones behind me:

'How do you feel, Peter, old boy?'

'What happened?'

'You missed the DZ and landed halfway up the hillside. You came an awful smack and hit your head on a rock. It looks as though you've got a bit of concussion. Come along and we'll see if we can get you on to a mule.'

'Would you mind telling me the date?' Somehow it seemed terribly important.

'Certainly! It's nearly midnight, Tuesday 10 August 1943.'

With one of them on either side of me I limped down the hill, over the bed of the watercourse and on to the smooth grass of the valley, where the fires were being doused and all their traces obliterated by Albanians. On the further side a bunch of mules was standing, waiting for the containers to be loaded as they were collected from the dropping ground. Hoisting me on to one of the rough wooden pack saddles, Seymour and Stefan led my mule along a narrow track winding towards the eastern end of the valley. After ten minutes we reached the crest of a low col, where we looked down on another broader valley in which nestled the low white houses of the village of Shtyllë. Approaching up the hill with long, easy strides came a tall figure in jodhpurs and a wide crimson cummerbund, a young man with long, fair hair brushed back from a broad forehead and wearing a major's crown on the shoulder-straps of his open-necked Army shirt. With a charming smile he introduced himself as Bill McLean and bade us welcome to Albania.

'Stefan will take you to our headquarters,' he went on, 'where you'll find the others, as well as some food and drink, which I expect you need. I'll join you as soon as we've finished clearing up the DZ. Your kit will be collected and brought to you there. Afterwards I'll send somebody to show you where you're sleeping.'

'Consensus' headquarters was in the disused village mosque and school, a single-storey mud and brick building consisting of three large rooms and standing on a low outcrop of rock which overlooked the valley to the south-east. In the largest room, lit by oil lamps and candles, was a long trestle table laden with plates of hot food, bottles of Italian champagne and brandy, and flasks of red Chianti – brought from Korcë, it was explained to me, by McLean's Albanian couriers on their bi-weekly visits to the town. Seated at the table on old ammunition boxes and empty parachute containers were members of McLean's headquarters staff, busily entertaining Field, Tilman and their parties. I was glad to hear that I was the only casualty of the evening drop, although Gerry Field had achieved the remarkable distinction of being sick in the air on his way down; it must have been a distressing experience, for it seemed that he descended quicker than his vomit.

By this time I was feeling very sick myself; and so after swallowing two or three mugs of hot sweet tea I asked to be shown my bed. Led by Stefan and accompanied by Seymour, who was sharing my lodgings, I climbed the hill to a small wooden house, where an old woman led us into a narrow, low-ceilinged room; there were two mattresses covered with blankets on the floor. Within five minutes I was asleep.

Chapter 5

I SLEPT WITHOUT INTERRUPTION for thirty-six hours, to awake feeling refreshed and fit once more. After a breakfast of hot sweet milk and maize bread I walked down to the mosque to report to McLean.

Captain David Smiley, his second-in-command, had left the morning we arrived to lay an ambush on the main road from Korcë to Yannina with a Balli Kombetar *çeta*; but in the mosque I found the sapper, Lieutenant Garry Duffy. The other British members of headquarters staff were Sergeant Williamson, McLean's wireless operator, Sergeant Jenkins, a big, bloodthirsty paramilitary expert who had dropped in a month previously, and Sergeant Jones, his inseparable companion who lived in the same street in Liverpool. With them I also met my own wireless operator, Corporal Roberts.

McLean had collected a number of camp followers, some of them Albanians, others Italian deserters; there was a carpenter, an armourer and several Italian cooks, batmen and house servants. More importantly, he had hired a band of Vlach muleteers to look after our pack transport. These Romanian nomads were exceptionally skilled in the management of mules; they were not particularly honest but were expert in the performance of their contractual duties, which they insisted did not include fighting or the exposure of themselves to danger. There were also three Albanian interpreters: Stefan, who had rescued me when I landed – in the daylight he looked splendidly *farouche* with a pair of fierce black moustaches; Stiljan Biçi, a gentle, timid youth who spoke excellent French; and, dominating them both – indeed dominating all the Albanians in our camp – the sinister figure of Frederick Nosi. This young man, still in his early twenties, enjoyed a position of great confidence with the LNC; a thoroughly indoctrinated Marxist of unusual intelligence and with a fluent knowledge of English, he was selected by Enver Hoxha as liaison officer to McLean's mission – that is, as official interpreter and unofficial spy. Few were the messages we sent to

Cairo or to each other that Frederick Nosi did not do his best to read.

Uninhibited by any scruples or family tradition, Nosi was an enthusiastic supporter of the 'historical process' which must lead, according to Marxist theory, to the triumph of communism. Very brave in battle and infinitely ambitious, he trampled on all who might impede his success, allowing no feelings of friendship to stand in his way. He bullied his subordinates, fawned on his superiors and spied on his comrades; towards most of his fellow countrymen he assumed an attitude of intolerant contempt, emphasising his own superiority with his frequent use of the phrase 'we intellectuals'.

On their arrival at Shtyllë McLean and Smiley had commissioned the erection of a long, low wooden structure on the southern side of the valley, under the lee of a steep mountain; skilfully camouflaged with parachutes, it contained a kitchen and sleeping quarters for the NCOs, a wireless room, and separate store rooms for arms and explosives, containers of money and clothing. They christened it 'The Barracks'. There they stored under lock and key the supplies received in drops, which Smiley as quartermaster would distribute to the partisans, keeping an exact tally of each item down to the last pair of socks.

We lived very well in Shtyllë. We could buy all the fresh food we needed from the friendly villagers, as well as luxuries like wine and brandy, and the excellent local cigarettes from Korcë. The mission had established a well-found and comfortable base. How long would the Italians allow us to enjoy it?

On the morning of 19 August, my twenty-eighth birthday, I had my answer: an Italian biplane circled over our valley and soon afterwards we heard gunfire from the east. Through our glasses we could see shells bursting around the monastery on the hill above the village of Vithkug, three miles from Shtyllë, some of them landing on the walls, while the aircraft circled overhead, presumably spotting for the guns. The partisans had placed a garrison there but by lunchtime the monastery was in Italian hands. Partisan losses had been light.

Two days later David Smiley, who by this time had arrived back from his successful ambush, and I walked to Vithkug to see Mehmet Shehu, the partisans' taciturn commander, and finalise arrangements for the attack on the road which McLean had planned with the general staff of LNC central council, the *Shtabit*. The brigade was to leave that evening and Mehmet confirmed to us that his troops were ready. He also told us the *Shtabit* had already moved to an area in central Albania – showing, as events were to prove, a useful capacity for scenting danger.

The target for this ambush was to be the same stretch of road that Smiley had attacked. Although it might seem a rash choice, partisan patrols had reported it was still clear of enemy pickets and there could be no better spot for an ambush; a convoy caught there would be at our mercy because there was no room to turn on the road, which ran between steep, rocky cliffs and a sheer precipice. The plan of attack was simple. During the night of the 22nd-23rd Mehmet would emplace his brigade on both sides of the road, on the heights commanding it and giving a clear field of fire. Everyone was to be in position by sunrise on the 23rd. When a suitable convoy reached the chosen killing ground, the partisans would open fire while mines and demolitions, prepared by Garry Duffy and his NCOs, would close the road ahead of and behind the convoy.

Duffy, whose party had a long way to go, left as soon as our conference was ended. I was to leave at daylight for a meeting on the way with the local Balli Kombetar commander, who had been complaining of increased hostility from the LNC. After the meeting I was to meet the others for lunch at a nearby village.

The first sunlight striking on my back as my mule cleared the ridge above Shtyllë dispelled the bad temper caused by early rising and a hurried breakfast. My companions were Stiljan, the young interpreter, and a guide. After a couple of hours' ride across the desolate, scrub-covered hills, our way led down through a forest carpeted with pine needles into a green valley, where we halted to rest our animals and drink from a clear, cool stream. We climbed again through pine forests on to rolling green uplands reminiscent of high pastures in the Alps in summer. At about eleven o'clock we came into another valley, where a party of armed men awaited us at the entrance to a small village. As I dismounted, their leader, a tubby old man with a stubbly chin, weak, watery eyes and a worried, nervous manner, came forward and greeted me in French, introducing himself as the Balli commander.

He insisted on talking with me alone, reciting a detailed series of complaints against the LNC – almost identical to the complaints the LNC had laid to us against him. With experience I came to expect this kind of story from either faction when discussing the other, except that the Ballists were usually more polite to us. I rode on my way with young Stiljan, my interpreter, to the village where I was to meet McLean and Smiley. I never saw this Ballist leader again; a month later he shot himself in a lavatory.

We joined the brigade in the late afternoon. The winding columns of guerrillas filed slowly along the broad, sandy bed of a watercourse;

oleander bushes grew thick on the banks and a thin stream trickled sluggishly between. We were in flat, open country with little cover from the air; but we travelled undisturbed. Riding a little ahead of McLean and Smiley, I was beginning to feel acutely uncomfortable on my wooden pack-saddle, my feet thrust into improvised stirrups of thick cord. Snippets of Smiley's talk drifted to my ears; he and McLean were back in London rehearsing the drill for mounting guard.

As the sun was setting we began to climb again into the hills. With darkness came a chill wind that whistled mournfully over the bare ridges. It was hard not to lose touch with one another or stray from the track in the impenetrable blackness. Poised on the edge of some escarpment, unable to discern any way down, I was often in despair; but each time my mule carried me with sure feet to the bottom, while I lurched in the saddle, sweating with fright. About midnight we came to a broad plateau surrounded by hills, where we halted.

We were now within half a mile of the road. After a brief conference Mehmet Shehu dispatched one of his battalions to cross the road and take up position on the spur beyond. A few minutes later the rest of us moved forward towards the hills overlooking the valley and the road. Leaving our mules in the care of our Vlachs we followed Smiley to the position he had already selected for us on the forward slope of one of the hills. We had just settled ourselves to get what rest we could before dawn when we were disagreeably startled by the sound of machine-gun fire from across the valley.

'Oh God!' sighed Smiley. 'They've run into trouble. Unless of course they're shooting at each other.'

Half an hour later Mehmet Shehu and his staff approached over the hill, shining torches with a lavish disregard for concealment which infuriated Smiley.

'Our plan has failed,' began Mehmet angrily. 'Our battalion has been surprised by a German post on that hill. We must withdraw. There is nothing we can do here.'

'Oh yes there is!' said Smiley and McLean together. 'You can start by wiping out the German post. There can't be many of them.'

Mehmet shook his head:

'No. It is impossible. My first operation must be one hundred per cent successful.'

'Just what we mean,' said Smiley. 'Look how easy it's going to be to kill those few Germans with all the men you've got – especially in the dark. Then we can have a crack at a convoy tomorrow.'

Mehmet looked at the ground between his feet.

'I have already given the order to withdraw,' he muttered.

We returned to the plateau, where we lay on the ground wrapped in our blankets and sleeping bags. None of us slept. Mehmet found himself confronted next morning by three furious and disgusted officers. He brought his entire staff with him, feeling, I suppose, the need of moral support. Our reconnaissance had already shown us that the German post consisted of a platoon party of from eighteen to twenty men with a light machine gun. With such odds in his favour we could hardly believe that Mehmet would refuse to fight. We urged him to overrun the post that night and carry on with the operation as planned on the following morning.

Mehmet remained unmoved by all our arguments. It was useless, he sullenly maintained, to blind ourselves to the fact that the operation had failed. He argued that although a withdrawal would be a blow to the morale of his men, the heavy losses which would result from carrying out our plan would be a bigger blow. At the end of a morning's argument McLean gave up.

'So eight hundred of your "patriotic Albanians", with all the armament and training we have given them, are to be frightened away by twenty Germans!' he exclaimed.

Without a word Mehmet turned and walked away, followed by his staff and some plainly audible comments by Smiley.

In the early afternoon I spent two hours watching the road through my binoculars. No convoy passed; a few solitary staff cars and one or two Army lorries were the only traffic during my vigil. When I rejoined McLean the brigade had moved off, leaving us alone with Stiljan, Stefan, our mules and their driver.

'You'll be pleased to hear that the brigade has been in action,' was Smiley's greeting to me.

I looked at him in astonishment, for I had heard no shooting.

'Yes, they killed a solitary German who had wandered into a village near here in search of food. He was unarmed, of course.'

We spent another chilly and despondent night in the same place.

'I'm damned if I'm leaving here without having a crack at something,' McLean said to me over breakfast. 'David's got to get back to Shtyllë to receive the drops we're expecting, but if you agree I thought we might try to shoot up a lone staff car. Of course it's a purely boy scout operation, but at least it should work off some of our bad temper.'

Stiljan volunteered to come with us and one of the Vlachs agreed to guard our mules out of sight of the road. We decided to lay our ambush just before dusk, in order to have the protection of darkness for our escape should the action go against us.

In the early evening we made our way slowly towards the road, while the dying sunlight dappled the hills in a splendid contrast of ochre and indigo. We chose a spot a mile north and out of sight of the German position; here the hills reached almost to the road, and fern and bushes gave plenty of cover without obstructing our view in either direction. Leaving the Vlach with our mules behind a ridge some five hundred yards back, we hid ourselves behind a bank above the road; Stiljan crouched beside me, McLean stood ten yards to our right watching and listening.

The sun was set. In the still, clear light before dusk the land seemed deserted; the only sound I could hear was Stiljan's heavy breathing, showing that he was feeling the same nervous tension as I. We had agreed to attack only a vehicle travelling by itself; but now I remembered that it was the practice for a staff car to precede a convoy at a few hundred yards' distance and I prayed that we should not find ourselves in a trap. Besides our pistols and submachine guns, each of us carried two phosphorus smoke grenades to cover our retreat in an emergency, but I had little faith in their protection if we should run into serious trouble.

Faintly from the south came the sound of a car. We heard it a long way off, the noise of its engine rising and falling on the twisting mountain road. I saw McLean staring through his field glasses; then he stiffened.

'It's a German staff car, all alone; don't fire till I give the word.'

The car turned the last bend and came into full view, a grey saloon approaching at about twenty-five miles an hour – a perfect target. As I heard Stiljan cock his Schmeisser I pressed forward the safety-catch on my Welgun. Then McLean stood up, the Schmeisser at his shoulder.

'All right, let 'em have it,' he ordered quietly.

We opened fire simultaneously. Within a few seconds the windscreen and side windows were shattered, the body scoured with the marks of our bullets. The car continued on its way for about twenty yards, then slewed in a cloud of dust and came to a halt at the side of the road. The driver sat slumped over the wheel, two men lay huddled motionless in the back, but from the front seat a figure leaped out and, crouching behind the car, returned our fire with his pistol. Changing their magazines McLean and Stiljan continued firing but at this moment my Welgun jammed; throwing it aside I drew my .45 and began to fire carefully aimed shots at the place where I imagined the German to be. Suddenly I heard McLean shout,

'Give me covering fire, boys! I'm going down.'

'For Christ's sake, stay where you are!' I shouted back; but I was too late. Throwing one of the smoke grenades, which landed well short of the car, McLean scrambled down the slope; Stiljan, urged by me, redoubled his rate of fire. Unfortunately the thick cloud of phosphorus smoke effectively hid the car from our view, although it did not seem to hide McLean from the German; we could hear the crack of his pistol and see the spurts of earth fly from the bullets round McLean's feet. I knew McLean was going down not only to finish off the German, but to collect any documents in the car, and I shuddered to think how we should get him away if he were hit. I threw a smoke grenade, hoping to give him extra cover; but by now McLean himself had thought better of it and was climbing back towards us. In a moment he was safe.

'I think we'd better beat it,' he gasped, 'while the score is still in our favour.'

We raced down into a gully and started to climb the ridge beyond which our mules awaited us. It was a tough journey until we found a gap with a rough track running through it. The mules were grazing peacefully in the shelter of an outcrop of rock, but the Vlach looked thoroughly frightened; he and Stiljan urged us to be on our way at once. I too was anxious to be gone, remembering that one of the first rules of an ambush is not to linger on the scene of the crime. I wasted no time in climbing on to my mule and begged McLean to hurry. We had a wide patch of open ground to cross and although darkness was falling there was still enough light for us to present a very good target. McLean, however, was in no mood for haste. The danger, he maintained, was over and now was the time to relax and rest before the long journey home. Pulling a tortoise-shell comb from his breast pocket he began to pass it in long, leisurely strokes through the thick blond hair that swept back from his forehead.

'Don't be so damned windy, Peter,' he protested with a careless laugh.

At that moment, with the crackle of exploding fireworks, a burst of machine-gun fire struck the rocks beside us. For a moment McLean stood rigid, the comb still in his hair, the smile frozen on his face; then he gave me a sheepish grin and seized the headrope of his mule.

'On our way!' He pointed to a low bank beyond the open ground. 'Meet you on the other side of that.'

The Vlach was already making off at the double, followed by Stiljan and our spare mule, which had broken loose. My own mule took fright and started to follow at a trot across the hideously exposed piece of ground. Feeling uncomfortably naked and conspicuous I tried to dismount; but my right foot caught in the cord stirrup and I could not free it. The air was full of the hiss of bullets and the angry red gleam of tracer flying all round me as I bent helplessly over the beast's neck, my useless Welgun, which was slung across my back, beating painfully against my hips and elbows with every movement. The machine gun was firing from the direction of the road; I could not be sure exactly where it was, nor at that moment was I much interested in finding out. The distance was only two or three hundred yards, but it seemed as many miles with a stream of tracer whistling about my head. The Germans must have found it hard to see us in the gathering gloom; they were shooting high, although one or two bursts struck the ground behind me, ricocheting past with an angry whine. At last I was behind the cover of the bank; I fell rather than climbed from my mule, luckily remembering to keep hold of the headrope. A few seconds later McLean joined me, panting heavily. The rest of our party had disappeared.

Cautiously we peered over the edge. The shooting had ceased and there was no sign of pursuit. We decided to put a safe distance between ourselves and the road, and then to look for a village where we could sleep. Leading our mules we struck northwards away from the road and into the hills. After half a mile we found a track, which we followed for another mile until we felt it safe to halt for a rest. We were about to move on when McLean seized my arm and pointed back down the path:

'There's someone coming!' he whispered, unslinging his Schmeisser.

Listening with my pistol ready, I heard the sound of hooves striking against rock; a moment later Stiljan's slight figure loomed out of the darkness, leading our spare mule. He had not seen the Vlach since the firing started.

'Never mind,' said McLean. 'He'll have the sense to find his own way back to Shtyllë. Let's get a move on.'

With Stiljan as guide we rode on for an hour without meeting anyone. There was no moon, but the stars gave enough light to follow the track. At last we came to a village. The houses were shuttered and silent, the street deserted; glimmers of light showed behind a few of the doors.

'We should be safe enough here for the night,' said McLean. 'Let's see if we can get anyone to put us up.'

Leaving Stiljan to try one of the houses on our right, McLean and I rode up the street and dismounted in front of a large wooden door. McLean knocked and called several times in a clear voice. At first there was no reply, but when he persisted a surly voice from within shouted back, brusquely ordering us away; other voices joined in, angry and frightened.

'I'd better try another house,' sighed McLean. 'You go back and see how Stiljan's getting on.'

I found Stiljan engaged in what was obviously a losing argument with an indignant figure in a half-open doorway. As I came up, the door was slammed in the interpreter's face.

'He will not have us, Captain,' explained Stiljan – superfluously in the circumstances. 'They have heard of the shooting on the road and they are very much afraid, and very enraged with us for causing the trouble.'

We found McLean arguing with a group of gesticulating and hostile villagers. As he caught sight of us he shouted:

'For God's sake, hurry up and get out of here! These people are going to shoot us if we stay any longer.'

Hastily we mounted and rode on our way, the abuse of the peasants following us as far as the outskirts. We tried two more villages in the next hour, but the inhabitants refused to open their doors to us or even to answer our requests for shelter. Finally about two in the morning, we came to a hamlet with a Greek Orthodox church, where at last we found a friendly reception in the house of a priest. After a few hours' sleep on the floor and a breakfast of warm sweetened milk, maize bread and yoghurt we went on our journey in the dawn.

The sun was sinking below the hills as we rode into Shtyllë, to find Smiley in a rage because all the boots Cairo had dropped him the previous day were size six – just big enough, perhaps, for the village schoolchildren. We all worked late into the night, drafting signals to Cairo and checking stores; then, utterly exhausted, we crawled to bed, looking forward to a long lie-in.

Chapter 6

WE NEVER GOT it. We were woken that morning by an Italian bombardment that continued for a full three days, forcing us finally to retreat to Panarit, a village five miles south-west of Shtyllë.

We could at least be thankful that we had escaped with our lives and most of our stores. Much of our personal property had been looted, but if the looters were the inhabitants of Shtyllë we were in no position to blame them; they had suffered worse than we. Those of them who had taken to the hills returned to find their houses in ashes; those who stayed behind were shot by the Italians.

This dilemma was our constant companion in our efforts to promote resistance: if we were to do our job properly we were bound to put innocent people in jeopardy; they had to stay and face reprisals while we found safety in flight. In the service of our country we simply had to harden our hearts. Whether the leaders of the LNC were as squeamish I do not know; in any case our qualms were no protection to the victims.

Our usefulness in this area was over. Both the LNC central council and the first partisan brigade had moved north; the Balli Kombetar were becoming increasingly hostile. It was time for us to split up.

The other members of the mission dispersed to establish a new headquarters for McLean and on 6 September I set out north-westwards with Corporal Roberts, Stiljan, three Vlachs and ten mules for the Berat area in south-central Albania; Cairo hadn't yet answered my request to go to Kosovo and so McLean had suggested I should in the meantime take on the duties of political liaison officer with the LNC, while also keeping in touch with the Balli leaders around Berat.

Some days later, we reached George Seymour's camp, which consisted of two or three tents in a pine wood among the hills and had been established by his advance party. I heard from his NCOs that he was at a village five or six miles south of Tirana and about six hours' journey from here; he was negotiating with General Dalmazzo, the Italian commander-in-chief in Albania, about an Italian surrender. I decided to stay the night in the camp and join Seymour next day. But now I was faced by a crisis. My Vlachs refused to stay with us any longer; with winter approaching, they explained, they must return to their families, who would starve without them. They wouldn't sell me their mules either, because they constituted their livelihood. Their leader was courteous but quite firm, and so I had no choice but to let them go, leaving me with one horse and one mule – insufficient even to carry my wireless set; nor were there any pack animals to be bought in the district. I could only hope we didn't have to move in a hurry.

Leaving Roberts at the camp to help Seymour's NCOs with their load of signals and to recharge his batteries, I set out with Stiljan early the next morning to join Seymour. We travelled for five hours over drab, low hills formed of a powdery black sandstone and covered with stunted mountain oak. We saw no houses other than an occasional charred ruin. The previous year the Italians had launched a punitive expedition against Myslim Peza and destroyed almost every house in these hills.

I found Seymour about noon in the village of Arbone in a house he was sharing with Myslim Peza and an Italian colonel – one of the very few houses to have survived the Italian reprisals. He was looking tired and very ill, his face white and sunken, and there were deep shadows under his eyes. He suggested I remained with him, where there was plenty of work for me. Enver Hoxha and the central council were living in a farmhouse back in the hills, but they visited us in Arbone daily.

For about a fortnight after the surrender of Italy there was one belief held in common by almost everybody in Albania, whether German or Italian, British or Albanian, LNC or Balli Kombetar: that an Allied invasion of the Balkans was imminent. This was not so naïve a hope as it seems in retrospect. I have no doubt that had there been an invasion at that time it would have been followed by a general rising in Albania, with the cooperation of most of the Italian army of occupation. We were therefore surprised that our headquarters in Cairo, usually so prodigal of advice and admonishment, failed to give us any directive at this critical moment. Seeing nothing of the larger picture we abused our office savagely for their neglect.

As soon as he heard the news of the surrender, on 9 September, Seymour hurried to Arbone, where he sent a message to General

Dalmazzo in Tirana requesting his cooperation and asking for a meeting; unfortunately the message was not delivered until the next day, when the Germans were already in occupation of the capital. However, Dalmazzo sent a staff car to Arbone which took Seymour, wearing an Italian Army greatcoat over his uniform, through the German control posts to Army headquarters, where he had a long discussion with Dalmazzo's chief of intelligence. At the same time, in an adjoining room, Dalmazzo himself was in conference with senior German officers, arranging his own evacuation under German protection to Belgrade; not until Dalmazzo had left did Seymour learn the truth.

This deplorable example was followed by other senior officers of the Ninth Army, including at least two divisional commanders; abandoning their men they thought only of saving themselves and their families. The junior officers and rank-and-file, deprived of the leadership they had a right to expect, became hopelessly demoralised. Overcome with terror, large numbers allowed themselves to be disarmed and led into captivity by a handful of Germans; others dispersed to farms and houses in the hills, where they worked for the owners in return for their keep; the more virile among them joined the partisans, who, it must be said, treated them well; a few attached themselves to British missions as cooks, batmen, or grooms.

Although there were comparatively few German troops in Albania they were efficient and mobile enough to dominate the people, disarm the Italians and contain any resistance forces. In the face of German resolution and Allied inactivity, most Albanians simply adjusted themselves to the change from Italian to German occupation.

Their attitude was reasonable in the circumstances. Without Allied help they could not hope to expel the Germans, who would in any case be obliged to leave the country if the war continued its present course against them. Better, surely, to bear with patience a temporary inconvenience rather than try to end it prematurely at the risk of property, security and life. Moreover to many patriotic Albanians it was by no means clear that an Allied victory was in the best interests of their country; they feared – perhaps I should say foresaw – that it would result not only in the loss of Kosovo but also in their own subjection to communist rule.

The Germans played cleverly upon these feelings. Firstly they made very few demands on the civilian population, to whom they behaved with consideration, and secondly they made much political capital out of the Kosovo question. It is a measure of their success that when they set up a puppet government in Tirana they were able to induce Albanians of high principles and distinction to serve in it. As time went on it became more and more obvious that we could offer the Albanians little inducement to take up arms compared with the advantages they could enjoy by remaining passive. I must confess that we British liaison officers were slow to understand their point of view; as a nation we have always tended to assume that those who do not wholeheartedly support us in our wars have some sinister motive for not wishing to see the world a better place. This attitude made us particularly unsympathetic towards the Balli Kombetar, although the latter was a thoroughly patriotic organisation. The Balli refrained from collaboration with the Germans against us; indeed, they gave us much covert help; but they did sit on the fence, hoping to establish themselves so firmly in the administration of the country that the victorious Allies would naturally call upon them to form a government. Indeed, they were naïvely convinced that the British and Americans would be glad to entrust the government to them, in preference to the communist alternative of the LNC. The leaders of the LNC had good reasons for continuing the struggle; but their interests were not Albania's.

During those days at Arbone large numbers of German aircraft flew directly over us, taking off from or landing at Tirana airfield. The plain in front of our house was alive with partisans – several thousands of them – who must have been clearly visible from the air and whose campfires at night could be seen for several miles around. Although they were within easy range of German artillery and presented a perfect target for air attack they made no attempt to dig so much as a slit trench for their protection, despite repeated warnings to Myslim Peza and their other commanders from Seymour and myself; nor could we persuade the *Shtabit* to disperse them amid the cover of the neighbouring hills. I was astonished that we were never awakened in the morning by anything more unpleasant than the singing of the partisans. After a few days, however, Myslim Peza became alarmed for our personal safety and insisted on moving to a farmhouse which overlooked the plain from the shelter of the Peza hills – one of the few that had survived the Italian holocaust of the previous year.

Myslim himself had a highly developed sense of personal security, acquired during fourteen years as an outlaw. He never slept twice in the same place; nor, if he could avoid it, would he spend a night in a house, but would move into the hills each evening with an escort. He had recently been appointed commander-in-chief of all LNC forces in the field – excluding, of course, those of Abas Kupi.

Of all the leaders of the LNC that I met in Albania, with one possible exception, Myslim was the most helpful and the most honest. A man of no intellectual ability or pretensions, he understood little of politics – a weakness which his more cunning colleagues exploited to their advantage; but he was a brilliant guerrilla fighter.

In his own country his people revered him. He was known among them as 'Baba', or Father, and whenever they mentioned his name they would touch their foreheads in the Moslem sign of respect. His frame was slight and emaciated, his dark marmoset's face drawn and sunken; but his small body held enormous strength, his black eyes flashed with excitement, enthusiasm, or anger and his thin, delicate hands were never still.

On both of us he bestowed a warm and generous affection, giving us his utmost help in our military and political problems – a refreshing change from the attitude of his colleagues. Himself an enthusiastic and convivial drinker he was delighted to find in Seymour and myself companions who would share his pleasures. We learned to start our work at seven in the morning in order to be finished by eleven o'clock, when we were invariably interrupted. There would be a knock on the door of the room where we lived and worked, and a small procession would enter: first would come Myslim's wife, carrying a roast chicken, followed by Myslim himself, his ADC and his escort, all carrying bottles of *raki* and plates of *meze*. The session would often last two or three hours, while we sat crosslegged on the floor at a low, round wooden table, discussing whatever problems had cropped up since our last meeting. Myslim's wife, who in defiance of Albanian custom sat through these parties with us, was a small, slim woman of about forty, dark and wiry like her husband; she always dressed like a man, carrying an automatic at her hip, and had shared her husband's outlawry since its beginning. A less sympathetic participant in these gatherings was Myslim's political commissar, a bitter, cantankerous communist who considered it his duty to the Party to thwart us when ever he had the chance.

The first of my tasks when I had established contact with Enver Hoxha was to answer a series of questions from Cairo about the political situation in Tirana. Cairo seemed to attach particular importance to the subject and so, when I was unable to get a clear picture from the central council, I decided without much enthusiasm that I should have to visit Tirana myself. Since it was impossible for me to go in uniform I signalled Cairo for permission to put on civilian clothes; the only reply I received was a repeat of the original questionnaire. I was now committed.

After a good deal of argument Enver Hoxha reluctantly agreed, on the intervention of Myslim, to provide me with a guide and prepare a safe house where I could stay in the city. He made one stipulation: because he would be responsible for my safety I must only see people approved by himself or by my hosts in Tirana. He didn't exactly help my confidence by pointing out how conspicuous I would appear in the town, for not only did I look like a foreigner but I even walked like one; to the vast entertainment of Seymour, Myslim and Stiljan, he insisted on giving me lessons in the 'Albanian walk'. He was not impressed by my progress. On the eve of my departure he turned up at our farmhouse with a certain Mehmet Hoxha, ex-prefect of Dibra, who was lending me a suit of clothes. This gentleman, of whom I was later to see a great deal, was short, broad and stout – in fact, of quite different build from mine.

Shortly before midday on 22 September I set out with my guide, a young Albanian of nineteen or twenty who spoke a little Italian. Mehmet Hoxha's old grey lounge suit hung loosely round my waist, leaving my wrists and ankles to protrude like the stumps of a scarecrow; on my feet were a pair of patent-leather shoes at least two sizes too small for me; my head and ears were covered by a soft, green felt hat. I had grown a sparse blond moustache which drooped discontentedly at the corners of my lip. Seymour tried to console me as he said goodbye.

'I can promise one thing, old boy: you may not look much like an Albanian, but at least you won't be mistaken for a British officer . . .'

It was a day of blazing sunshine; the plain of Arbone lay shimmering under the noonday heat. We plodded slowly and in silence across the fields, over the narrow bridge spanning the river and up into the hills. I was surprised to meet no one on the way, until I remembered that this was the time of day when sensible people rested; perhaps that was why my guide had chosen it. After the first half hour my patent leather shoes pinched and galled at every step, so that I had to call frequent halts to take them off. At first I was glad when we reached the hills and began to climb in the shade of the woods; but each time I stumbled on the steep and broken track, crying out with the pain that gripped my feet, I longed for the sun-baked but easy paths of the plain.

Every moment I cursed more savagely the foolhardiness that had sent me on this journey; I reflected that I was involving myself and my friends in a great deal of trouble and some hazard in pursuit of information of uncertain value. I preferred not to dwell on the consequences of capture. As a parachutist and saboteur I knew that my chances of survival would be slender enough if I were taken in uniform; in civilian clothes I faced the prospect of a squalid and painful end.

Before leaving the cover of the hills we halted in a small copse on the outskirts of Tirana to cool down, recover our breath and brush the dust of the journey from our clothes. I carried no papers and so we had agreed that if we ran into a German picket or were stopped by a patrol I was to look stupid and say only *'Shqypetar, ska dokument'* – 'Albanian, no papers'. We trusted that this simple phrase would allay suspicion, because I could not hope to run away in those shoes of Mehmet Hoxha's.

I could feel my heart pounding as I accompanied my guide into the first streets. I tried to look indifferent to my surroundings and pay no attention to the groups of townspeople who passed; they, I noticed, were paying a great deal of attention to me, scanning me closely and gazing after me with expressions of hilarious astonishment. The only people who paid no attention whatever were the few parties of German soldiers who passed us, marching in step, their heads held high, looking neither to right nor left. My guide, who kept shooting me sombre glances out of the corner of his eye, was getting more and more nervous, obviously sharing my own feelings. Suddenly he brightened; following his gaze I saw a lone *carozza* standing on a corner, with a tired-looking horse and sleepy driver. Painfully but thankfully I climbed in and sank back on the cushions as my guide gave an address to the driver. We rattled through dusty sidestreets, turned into a broad avenue and after a few hundred yards turned off again into a quiet road flanked by prosperous modern villas with bright, tidy gardens. At one of these we halted, and after paying the *carozza*, rang the bell. In a second the door was opened and my guide hustled me into the cool twilight of a large, comfortably furnished room.

A tubby, middle-aged man dressed in a Palm Beach suit rose from an armchair and greeted me warmly in English, introducing himself as the owner of the house; for security reasons I was not allowed to know his name, but I gathered that he was a prosperous businessman who owned some copper mines and that he was a member of the Greek Orthodox Church. He told me later that he had joined the LNC for patriotic reasons, although he detested communism; he seemed to be a staunch anglophile and treated me during my visit with exuberant hospitality. After so many weeks in the hills I wallowed in the luxuries of a comfortable bed and a hot bath, of good wine and food, of thick carpets and soft chairs.

My fellow guests were two members of the central council, both of whom I had met in Shtyllë; they were close friends, who had worked together in France during the first year of the Italian occupation of their country, editing a newspaper for Albanian exiles. Dyshnica was a young doctor of great ability and charm;* Spiro, by contrast, was a sour-faced, black-biled fanatic who would heap abuse and hysterical invective upon all his countrymen who were not members of the LNC. I had disliked him in Shtyllë but was forced to a reluctant sympathy when I learned that he suffered from a chronic and incurable disease of the liver. During the days I stayed in this house I was occupied with a succession of visitors. Although Enver Hoxha had stipulated that I should meet only people approved by himself my host did his best to show me a representative selection of Tirana opinion. Most of my visitors were professionals or businessmen; none was a communist or fellow traveller; all spoke English, French, or Italian and so I was able to converse without an interpreter.

Hitherto, it seemed, the new occupation had weighed very lightly on the people of Tirana, who were therefore disinclined to take any active steps against it. The imposition of a curfew, the establishment of checkpoints on the roads and the compulsory registration of private cars were the only restrictions; civilians were supposed to carry identity cards, but were seldom required to produce them. In the last few days, however, as a result of a number of attacks on Germans in the countryside, the control had tightened considerably; some houses had been searched and the streets were watched by security police in plain clothes. At the same time the German authorities circulated through their Albanian agents grim stories of the ruthlessness of their reprisals and the grim fate that would overtake any Albanian found 'consorting with the enemy'.

One of my objects was to find out what aircraft were using Tirana airfield. Among my visitors was a young man of an illustrious Albanian family, Liqa Bey Toptani; belonging to no political party he maintained good relations with the LNC. Now he volunteered to take me for a drive in his car along the road past the airfield where I would be able to see all I wanted. On the afternoon following my arrival he turned up with a companion in a small black Fiat saloon; he asked me to get into the back, adding apologetically that I should attract less attention there.

We drove through sidestreets and into a broad avenue, past the Dajti Hotel, Tirana's last word in modern luxury, and the chrome stucco palace of King Zog sprawling in its neglected gardens; after half an hour's drive round the town Toptani brought us out on the road leading towards the airfield.

'You'll easily be able to see the aeroplanes through the fence,' he

* It is reported that he was executed by Enver Hoxha after the war.

explained. 'We can drive very slowly and then perhaps on our way back' – he broke off with a gasp, putting his foot on the brake.

Leaning over his shoulder I saw through the windscreen a car drawn up at the side of the road about fifty yards ahead, with German soldiers standing round it.

'I'm afraid it's a control post,' he muttered and began to put the car into reverse. At this moment the car in front began to move on; one of the soldiers noticed us and signalled us to approach. We had no alternative, for behind was a long stretch of straight open road. As he put the car into gear Toptani whispered to me:

'Sit back and look as stupid as you can. I will do the talking – do not say anything.'

Ramming my green hat well over my ears I huddled in a corner, looking cautiously from under my eyelids for cover in case we had to run. There was not so much as a ditch or a tree; there was nowhere we could flee in safety. I had come to Tirana unarmed, believing that a gun was more likely to get me into trouble than out of it. I watched Toptani's companion slide his right hand inside his coat and, leaning forward for a moment, saw his fingers close over the butt of an automatic. I felt quite helpless, and paralysed with fear.

A corporal with a slung Schmeisser put his head through the driver's window and spoke quite civilly in German to the two in front; then he came to my window, looked at me searchingly and asked for my papers. I stared oafishly at him from under the brim of my hat and hissed my piece.

'*Shqypetar, ska dokument.*' He gave me a long, puzzled stare and turned back to Toptani. He was clearly dissatisfied about something and I felt a surge of panic when he turned away as though to shout to his men. At that moment Toptani had an inspiration; from his wallet he pulled out a crumpled piece of paper and waved it in the corporal's face. The German scanned it for a moment and evidently found what he wanted; he handed it back with a friendly smile and waved us on. When at last we were out of sight and I was mopping my sweaty face Toptani began to laugh.

'Really, that German was very unobservant.'

'Why?' I asked.

'Well, he was asking for the registration paper of this car, which has to have a *Feldkommandatur* stamp on it. Unfortunately there are no papers for this car, but I suddenly remembered that I was carrying a document belonging to another car. He only looked at the official stamp and did not notice the details.'

He stopped the car and while he pretended to be fiddling with the engine I managed to have a good look at the aircraft scattered on the field. They did not seem very interesting – a few Messer-schmitt 109s, half a dozen Stukas, about twenty Junkers 52 troop-carriers and some old three-engine Savoias. When we passed the control post on our way back to the town the corporal recognised us and gave us a spectacular salute.

The following evening my host told me I must leave.

'We've received information that the Germans are going to impose a much stricter control in this city; they have already begun to search the houses, section by section. I do not think it is safe for you to stay here any longer. You cannot leave tonight because of the curfew, but you will forgive me if I order your guide to be here after breakfast tomorrow morning to take you back to Arbone.'

Although I had enjoyed my visit I was not inclined to linger after my host's warning. I had the answers to almost all of Cairo's questions and had been promised some useful introductions in Kosovo should I be allowed to go there. At nine o'clock the next morning, having taken leave of my host, I climbed into the *carozza* which was waiting outside the gate with my guide; after my experi-ence of two days before we had decided that this was a safer method of travel in the city than a car. We returned by the same route as we had entered, making our way out of the city unchallenged. By midday I was back with Seymour in the farmhouse, where I thank-fully discarded the patent-leather shoes, and bathed my blistered and swollen feet. Myslim embraced me warmly and laid on a special celebration in honour of my safe return.

Chapter 7

THE TERM KOSOVO in its strictest application refers to the plain near Priština in Serbia where the great battle was fought in 1389 between the Serbs and the Ottoman Turks. More commonly – and in the sense in which I use it – it includes also Mitrovica and the region of Metohija – that is, the towns of Peć, Gjakovë and Prizren. As the heart of the medieval Serbian kingdom the Serbs claim that it is indissolubly linked with the history of their nation; for which reason, more than any other, it was included in the frontiers of Yugoslavia. Albania's claims are based on two generally admitted facts: that it is her natural granary and that the majority of the inhabitants are Albanians, the proportion being between seventy and eighty-five per cent. Yugoslav rule between the two world wars unfortunately tended to suppress rather than encourage or even tolerate Albanian customs, religion and language.

When I arrived there in early December 1943, my application for a posting having finally been successful, my principal task was to explore the chances of forming a resistance movement among Albanians in Kosovo. I already had one valuable contact there, in the town of Gjakovë, near the old Albanian border. He was Hasan Beg Kryeziu, a rich and influential landowner and farmer. He enjoyed good relations with all the Albanian Kosovar political parties, even the communists – at least, that was what I understood. I had met him on my journey to Kosovo in the house of a kinsman in the mountains. He was short and chunky, with white hair and a square, heavy-jowled face, booming voice and jovial manner, and he clearly enjoyed widespread popularity. He was known to be sympathetic to the Allies and he assured me I could count on his support. When I sounded him on the subject, he warned me that the majority of Kosovars preferred a German occupation to a Serb; the Axis powers had at least united them with their fellow Albanians, whereas an Allied victory would, they feared, return them to Yugoslav rule.

Nevertheless, Hasan Beg seemed delighted that a British officer had come to Kosovo and he promised to do everything in his power to make my visit a success. He emphasised the importance of my keeping in touch with him while I was at Deg and to this end he detailed one of his retainers, Shpen Zeçeri, to act as courier between us. This Shpen Zeçeri was a tall, very silent man with undistinguished features whom I generally recognised by the way he wore his white 'egg cup' cap tilted well forward on his head. His master described him as exceptionally trustworthy; I certainly found him discreet, for I hardly ever heard him speak and only once saw him smile.

Hasan Beg also promised to arrange for me to visit Gjakovë in the near future; he would put me up in his house and invite a number of influential Kosovars to meet me. Afterwards we could plan a journey further afield. He would send Shpen to me at Deg as soon as he was ready.

Finally, he warned me that the partisans were most unpopular in Kosovo and their influence was negligible; I should achieve little if I entered the area under their aegis, for they were regarded as agents of Tito, who, like Mihailovic, was detested as an instrument of 'Pan-Slav Imperialism'. Coming from the 'unofficial president' of the LNC in Kosovo this warning was not to be ignored.

On 5 December we separated: Hasan Beg left for Gjakovë and I for the headquarters of Flight-Lieutenant Hands (who had dropped on the same sortie as me and who was now in charge of our operation on the Kosovo border), at Deg, a cluster of dwellings further north, on the bank of the Black Drin. Before we parted Hasan promised to send me a reliable interpreter within a few days; I was also lent an escort, Zenel Ahmedi, to act as my servant and bodyguard for as long as I needed him. Zenel's father had been a great warrior in his time and this was certainly reflected in his son.

I struck westward down the valley accompanied by Zenel Ahmedi and three tribesmen. At the far end the valley widened into open, rolling grassland sloping towards the River Drin, beyond which the mountains of the Catholic country glittered frostily in the sunlight. At noon we met Corporal Brandrick, Hands's paramilitary specialist, with a messenger I had sent four days earlier. They brought with them two horses, a complete change of clothing for me, two tins of English pipe tobacco and a letter of welcome from Hands.

At five in the evening we reached a small village, where we decided to spend the night because darkness was already falling. Our escort brought us to a small house belonging to three young friends of theirs; in the tiny, stuffy guest room there was barely enough space for the seven of us and our three hosts to lie on the floor. I had not been long asleep when I was awakened by the sound of three rifle shots in quick succession; grabbing their weapons Zenel and the others ran outside, to return in a few minutes with the comforting assurance that it was only a tribesman settling accounts with his blood enemy.

After a stiff three-hour climb next morning we emerged on to a high shoulder of rock overlooking a valley that dropped into the deep ravine of the Drin. Halfway down the valley stood a few miserable dwellings grouped around a small mosque; this was Deg. Brandrick led us to a white farmhouse surrounded by a low brushwood wall; at the entrance stood Hands. When I had first met him the previous July in Egypt he had seemed a cheery and self-confident officer with a trace of brashness; but five months of hardship and hazard in the mountains had drained much of his vigour and all his brashness, etching deep lines of strain on his features. Almost his first words were of trouble.

'Old man, it looks as if you've walked out of one spot of bother into another. A blow-up is expected here any day between the partisans and the local chiefs.'

He led me up a rickety wooden staircase to a small, ill-lit and dusty room in the centre of which was an improvised table of boards laid across parachute canisters, with more canisters to serve as seats. In a corner by the tiny window was a wireless set, at which the operator was finishing a 'sked'; on the dirty floor were four old and greasy mattresses, one of which was for me. There was no other furniture. The remaining room in the house was used as a kitchen and sleeping quarters for the four Italians who waited on the mission. The horses and mules were stabled underneath. The owners of the house had left long ago.

Most of the other houses, including the mosque, were occupied by detachments of partisans, who provided Hands with an inefficient and troublesome guard. But there were a few villagers left; under the leadership of their *hoxha*, or priest, they maintained a precarious but apparently satisfactory livelihood by looting Hands's stores whenever he received a supply drop and stealing from his head-quarters in the intervals; when such methods failed they would come to him and beg.

Their depredations, together with others on a larger, better organised scale by the partisans who were supposed to help him receive his drops, had left Hands with scarcely enough food and clothing for his own needs. No supplies could be bought locally. Bad weather was holding up the sorties he expected and for which he had prepared a wide and level dropping ground a few hundred yards below his house, where the valley opened into gently sloping meadows before tumbling into the Drin.

When we had finished tea Hands thrust a piece of paper at me with a sardonic laugh:

'You're dead, old man, in case you don't know it. We had this signal from Cairo last night.'

The message simply said I had been killed in street fighting in Peshkopije. A year later I heard details of the rumour from Captain Alan Hare.

'A wounded partisan turned up in our camp at Biza,' he explained, 'saying that he had witnessed your death with his own eyes. Major Kemp, he told us, was creeping up a street, close to the wall, with his machine gun at the ready; suddenly, round a corner he came face to face with a German, also with his gun at the ready. Both fired simultaneously and both fell dead. The others,' Hare concluded, 'were suitably impressed and sad. I alone knew the story couldn't be true: you would never have been wide enough awake to fire at the same time as a German.'*

There were some three hundred partisans grouped in *çetas* around Deg; most were from Kosovo but a few had come from the Prefecture of Scutari, which they had made too hot to hold them. All were controlled by a newly formed organisation, the 'Kosmet [Kosovo and Metohija] General Staff', under a military commander who had made a name for himself fighting the Bulgars in Macedonia; the political direction – and the effective power – was in the hands of the chief commissar, Mehmet Hoxha – the same man whose suit I had worn in Tirana and whom I had last seen in Dibra. He in turn received directives from Tito.

The ostensible purpose of their presence was to establish a secure base for the winter; their real objectives, according to Hands, were to coordinate operations with Tito's Montenegrin partisans, and to clear the frontiers of Montenegro and Kosovo of all 'reactionary elements'. Hands's view of their intentions was shared by most of the local chieftains and inhabitants who regarded the Kosmet with undisguised suspicion and hostility – in which, unfortunately, they included Hands. He had been obliged to move his base twice in the last month under pressure from the chiefs.

The day before my arrival they had issued an ultimatum to Hands

---

* Brigadier Davies records that while he was a prisoner in Tirana the Germans showed him photographs of dead bodies in British battledress which they alleged to be Riddell's, Simcox's and my own. See p 171, *Illyrian Venture* (The Bodley Head).

and the partisans, either to leave their territory or be driven out –
if necessary with German help.

If we had to leave Deg where else could we go? Beyond the Drin
was Catholic country where the people, if not actively hostile, would
certainly not receive us as friends; for they followed the lead of the
Captain of Mirdita, the most powerful chieftain in northern Albania,
who was an ally of the Germans. Hands asked me, therefore, to
visit the most influential of these chiefs, who lived in a village a
day's journey to the north, and try to arrange a truce that would at
least allow us to remain where we were.

I set out two days later on horseback and reached my destination
at nightfall. On my way I had to cross a wide and swollen river by
means of a frighteningly flimsy wooden bridge; as we stumbled
across it, fifty feet above the flood, I marvelled at the brilliant
turquoise colour of the water pouring over the boulder-strewn
river-bed and the harsh grandeur of the bare limestone cliffs that
frowned over the far bank.

The eighty-six-year-old Bajraktar* was the finest looking Albanian
I had seen; six foot tall, lean and erect with a fierce white moustache
and silvery hair, he towered like some Homeric hero over his
countrymen.

After a night's rest in a comfortable though damp four-poster
bed, I had a protracted meeting with the local chiefs. It was not the
success I had hoped. Although formally polite they treated me, as
a suspected ally of the communists, with deep suspicion. It took me
the whole morning to extract from these dour men an agreement to
leave us in peace at Deg.

Back at our headquarters I was having an uncomfortable bath
next morning in one of the canisters that did alternative duty as
chairs when Hands came into the room.

'Your interpreter's arrived from Hasan Kryeziu. Scruffy bastard,
if you ask me.'

The description, I had to agree, was apt. Eles Yusufi was a dark,
emaciated, sallow and untidy youth with shifty eyes and the furtive,
apologetic expression of an ill-treated dog. He spoke little and
seemed frightened of everyone. He had very little English, but
unfortunately tried to hide his ignorance by mistranslating what he
couldn't understand.

In the second week of December Hasan Beg's silent courier,
Shpen Zeçeri, arrived with two equally silent companions to escort
me to Hasan's house in Gjakovë. I put on an Italian overcoat over
my battledress and changed my green Commando beret for a flat

---

* Hereditary title meaning 'standard bearer'.

Bulgar fez of black lambswool. With us on the journey came Zenel
Ahmedi, Eles and another young Albanian, Sadri, who spoke good
French, and a pack mule that Hasan had sent with his couriers. But
first we had trouble with the partisans, who had learned of my plans
and tried to stop me unless I promised to go to Gjakovë with their
men and to see there only those people of whom they approved. I
refused as politely as my anger allowed and went on my way thinking
the Kosmet could do what they liked about it. What they did, I
soon discovered, was to send word to the Germans that I was in
Gjakovë.

It was much too cold to ride, but Hasan Beg's mule had slowed our
pace and so it was dark when we climbed to the head of a steep
pass, where a stone pinnacle marked the old frontier between
Albania and Yugoslavia. While we rested there to recover our breath
Shpen and his two companions told me how they used to make a
good living before the war smuggling tobacco across this frontier;
now that Kosovo was part of Albania they had lost their livelihood.

The descent was precipitous and dangerous in the dark; we lost
the track several times but our smuggler guides seemed to feel their
way back to it by instinct before we strayed far. Gradually the slope
levelled and the track became a wide and muddy path through
woodland, easy to follow in the light of a rising moon. Soon we
were walking along a dirt road running between hedges with fields
on either side. The countryside was quiet and peaceful in the
moonlight; the only sound was the soft thud of the mules' hoofs
and the distant barking of farm dogs. We had walked for a couple
of hours when Shpen stopped suddenly and began to whisper with
his friends; I made out some scattered buildings ahead. Eles sidled
up to me.

'We must go very quietly now,' he murmured. 'We are entering
the city and there are Germans in that white house on the right.'

Keeping well into the side of the road we advanced stealthily in
single file; Shpen was in the lead, with Zenel and the mule bringing
up the rear. We crossed a bridge over a river, lit by a lamp at each
end; straight ahead ran a wide, well-lit street, which we avoided by
turning right along a path by the river. After two or three hundred
yards we turned sharp left again up a hill until we came to some
large white barracks guarded by a pair of sentry boxes. At this point
our behaviour degenerated into burlesque. Shpen and his friends
crept forward crouched over their rifles, which they carried at the
hip with their fingers on the triggers. I wondered fearfully whether

we were in greater danger of arrest as bandits or as lunatics. Fortunately the sentry boxes were empty; the barracks housed only workers from the chrome mines.

Soon we were prowling through the twisting, cobbled streets of the town like small boys playing Red Indians. Shpen would stop at each corner, peer round it carefully and hurriedly beckon us on; at every street lamp Eles, whose laboured breathing was heavy on my neck and whose Sten gun, I noticed unhappily, was pointed at the small of my back, would trot forward and steer me forcefully across the street in the full glare of the beam, until I told him irritably to leave me alone; and whenever one of the mule's iron-shod hoofs clattered against a cobblestone everyone stopped in his tracks and hissed 'sh-sh-sh!' so loudly and with such agonised urgency that the poor beast stood still and hung its head in shame.

But for the noise we made ourselves, no sound disturbed the quiet of the sleeping town; nor did we see any movement other than our own shadows on the pale, moon-bathed walls of the houses. At midnight we came to a halt in front of a large wooden door in a high, whitewashed wall. Shpen knocked and called up to a lighted window in the house behind; a minute later the bolts were drawn back and a very old man with a long, drooping white moustache let us into a wide courtyard. At a doorway on the far side Hasan Beg was waiting.

He took me upstairs to a living room furnished with armchairs, a large divan and a table; a double bedroom and a bathroom completed my luxurious quarters. I was too tired to eat but was persuaded to drink some unusually powerful home-distilled *raki*.

Hasan Beg was unmistakably nervous. His face darkened and his manner became more agitated as Sphen told him of our trouble with the Kosmet. The partisans had been trying for a long time to make him leave his house and join them in the mountains, seeking thus to deprive him of his contacts among the various Nationalist and Irredentist groups in Gjakovë; now they would spread the news of my presence, hoping that I should be discovered and he would be obliged to flee.

I was horrified at Hasan's words for he was already taking a grave risk in sheltering me. The old servant, on the other hand, who had been listening to our conversation made light of our fears:

'If you want to play at politics, Hasan Beg,' he teased, 'you must be brave!'

Next morning Hasan had recovered his good humour, but he warned me I should have to curtail my stay in Gjakovë and put off a journey around Kosovo which he had planned for me. He had another reason for alarm: a force of Kosovar mercenaries in German pay had descended on the region to purge it of 'hostile elements' and were indulging in an orgy of executions.

Despite his fears he kept me in his house for three days, treating me with a rare hospitality that I had not experienced in years; more important, he brought to see me some of the most influential of the Kosovar leaders. It was typical of Hasan's integrity that he included among them men who differed from him politically and one or two who were his rivals; he had promised to help me in the formation of a common front of Kosovars against the Germans and this object alone guided him in his choice.

Our talks convinced me that we should achieve no more than isolated military action in Kosovo without some Allied declaration on the future status of the province; it was obvious that the Kosovars did not trust us. Nor might I use the argument that would have appealed to them – that by fighting now they could obtain arms from us, which they could use later to defend themselves against communists or Serbs. The most I obtained was a promise from the commander of the Albanian Army garrison to put his men at my disposal in the event of an Allied invasion or a German withdrawal, and an undertaking from the others to furnish me with military and political information in the meantime. One of my visitors was the chief of police and so I would at least receive warning of any German operations against us. Two leaders of the Albanian Irredentists, Ejub Binaku and Professor Suleiman Riza (the party's real *eminence grise*), promised me a second visit to Kosovo with a wide itinerary; as soon as the situation improved they would send for me at Deg.

I left Gjakovë in the early hours of 17 December with the same escort and in much the same manner as I had entered, though without the embarrassing company of the mule. When I reached Deg I was told of the Kosmet's treachery. I smothered my resentment, not wishing to provoke an open breach; but I derived some consolation from the hypocritical enthusiasm with which Mehmet congratulated me on my safe return.

Twenty-four hours after my return to Deg we received a drop from three aircraft. As soon as we heard the approaching engines and the partisan guards had lit the fires on the dropping ground the villagers poured from their houses in search of loot, while the tracks from the surrounding countryside filled with shadowy, hastening figures; some came on horseback, others on foot, the richer ones leading mules to carry their plunder. In places men laid out their own fires, hoping the aircraft would be deceived into dropping their loads on them.

It was a successful drop. The parachutists landed safely on the dropping ground, the containers not far away, but the 'free drops', of which there was a large number, gave us some bad moments; it was an uncomfortable experience to stand in the open in the chilly, moonless night and hear the bundles whistling through the air towards us. The greatest excitement came when a partisan guard fired on a looting tribesman; the man fired back, frightening the partisan out of his life, and vanished with his spoil into the darkness.

The partisans ignored our instructions and took the stores to the mosque, where they stole all the personal kit of the new arrivals and most of the food; they said they were acting on the orders of their political commissar. And so the newcomers' introduction to Albania was the loss of all their belongings. Only one of the three new officers was to remain with me, Captain John Hibberdine of the Cameronians, and I was thankful to have him. His arrival saved my sanity, which had been showing signs of disintegration. Several years younger than me, of slight but sturdy build and great physical endurance, he combined a quiet, thoughtful manner, shrewd judgment and an even temper. He was also a strong stimulus to my morale. That such a stimulus was necessary became apparent to me from the frequency with which I was losing my temper these days over trifles.

Chapter 8

O N 27 DECEMBER Eles, who had been visiting his family in
Gjakovë, returned to say that Ejub Binaku, the Irredentist
leader, was awaiting me in Tropojë, a small town nine miles north
of Deg and the capital of this district; Hibberdine and I set off there
that afternoon with Eles and Zenel. The journey took us nine hours
because Eles, who was supposed to know the way, kept on losing it
and even Hibberdine's patience showed signs of strain before we
arrived at last at the house of the sub-prefect, where we were to
stay. The sub-prefect, a cheerful little man who had lived in the
United States and spoke English, soon revived us with food and
raki; Ejub himself, though friendly enough, spoke very little.

We stayed indoors next day until darkness had fallen on the town;
then, taking leave of our host, we followed Ejub at a hurried pace
through the streets and began the steep ascent of the Pass of Morina
towards the old frontier. The snow, which had been falling lightly
when we left, increased as we climbed the pass to a full blizzard
blown in our teeth by a howling east wind that froze our hands and
faces, and seared our lungs at every gasping breath; icicles formed
on our noses, encrusted our moustaches and hung from our eyebrows. As we neared the summit the snow lay deeper, until we were
plunging above our knees in the drifts; every step was an effort.
The shimmering flakes threw back the light of our torches in our
eyes so that we frequently wandered off the path. We staggered on
blindly up the slope, our heads bowed against the storm, our limbs
numb with fatigue and our lungs bursting.

It was nearly midnight when we knocked on the door of a
farmhouse at the mountain hamlet of Morina, on the Kosovo side
of the frontier. We waited in the snow while Ejub and the owner
whispered anxiously together for nearly ten minutes. There were
visitors in the guest room who must not see us and so we were taken
to sleep in a disused granary under the roof; but not even the
attentions of the vermin which infested the room could keep us
awake for long.

By the time we were dressed next morning the other guests had gone and so we moved into the comfortable guest room. Ejub left for Gjakovë to discuss with Hasan Beg the final arrangements for our journey and reception there; he bade us await his return in patience and not on any account stir from the house without an escort – even then, we must not wander far.

The fear of informers was so great that throughout our stay in Kosovo, even in the country districts, we were isolated from all contact with – and as much as possible from the sight of – people other than the family with which we happened to be staying and visitors specially summoned to meet us. When we wanted a walk to clear our heads – the guest rooms were seldom ventilated, for the Albanians could not endure fresh air in their houses – someone would first make a reconnaissance to see that there was nobody about; we had always to take an escort, not so much for protection as for camouflage and in order to answer any awkward questions if we should happen to meet strangers. Lastly, Ejub insisted that we should always wear some kind of peasant head-dress and put on civilian overcoats to hide our uniforms; I wore my black Bulgar fez, but Hibberdine preferred the white 'half-egg'. To complete my disguise I usually wound puttees over my field boots. Irksome though these restrictions were we could not reasonably refuse to obey them; for the consequences to our hosts and companions if we were taken would be far more serious than to ourselves. We were astonished at the unselfish courage of these people – whether powerful landowners like Hasan Kryeziu, intellectuals like Professor Suleiman Riza, government officials, small shopkeepers, or poor artisans – who risked their lives to accompany and shelter us in an area where even Albanian partisans could not move in safety. Certainly people faced far graver dangers in other occupied countries, but in Kosovo there was no reason why men should expose themselves to any danger to help us. It may seem strange that we troubled to wear uniform at all when we would expect to be treated as spies if caught. The reasons were, first that we had a directive from Cairo not to remove our uniform; secondly that Hasan and Ejub both thought the sight of them would have a useful effect on our visitors' morale.

As chief bodyguard, guide and constant companion on our journey, Ejub appointed his closest friend, Ramadan, a dark, red-faced, thick-set highlander who spoke little and drank a great deal; he was friendly enough, although in his cups he was subject to fits of moroseness, when he would sit by himself with his head in his hands ignoring the rest of the company. But his story, which Ejub told us, proved him a loyal ally and a stout fighter. He had been an outlaw in these hills for twenty years, ever since the gendarmerie had killed his friend, Rustem Bairami; bound by his *besa*, the Albanian code of honour, to protect Rustem he had fought a stiff battle with the gendarmes, killing six of them and only escaping himself after his friend had fallen. Since then he had been a hunted man without a home to shelter or a wife to comfort him. When there was nothing to do he would let his misfortunes prey on his mind; he would start drinking at seven in the morning and continue until lunchtime, when he would pass out quietly until it was time to start the evening carousal.

In the afternoon of New Year's Day 1944, Ejub reappeared at Morina to take us again to Gjakovë; but he insisted we leave Zenel and Eles behind because they would make us too many to travel in safety. We left before dark in an open fiacre, Hibberdine and I well muffled against the cold sitting in the seat while Ejub and Ramadan sat half on the seat and half on top of us. The driver, a cheery, flamboyant figure with a deep voice and a huge pair of moustaches, flipped his whip and the horse started down the slushy road at a spirited trot. Away behind us the great bulk of Shkelzen, the 'Shining Mountain', the eastern bastion of the north Albanian Alps, rose eight thousand feet, its southern face shimmering in the fading sunset with a pearly light. The people who lived in its shadow held the mountain in deep veneration, investing it with a mythology of ghostly legends: a saint was buried on the upper slopes. All the harsh nobility and fierce endurance of this land seemed to shine in the opalescent beauty of those ice-bound cliffs.

In half an hour we had left the hills and were moving across level, open country. We swept through the villages at a fast canter in a musical jingle of bells, the driver cracking his whip and shouting to clear the way. The fiacre must have excited some comment, over-loaded with the five of us and festooned with automatic weapons; Ejub had brought a sub-machine gun for each of us in case we should have to fight, while the driver carried a rifle slung over his back.

We entered Gjakovë at about seven o'clock, driving up the main street with a flourish that caused me acute alarm, which nearly turned to panic when we were halted at a control post manned by Albanian gendarmes; however, Ejub gave a signal to the NCO in charge, who waved us on without a question, though with several curious glances. We turned down a quiet sidestreet, dismounted and began to creep through the streets like conspirators without, however, attracting attention from the few people we met. After a quarter of an hour we knocked on a wooden door in a wall and were admitted to a courtyard leading to a discreet but comfortably furnished house. This proved to be the back premises of a small café and hotel of which our host was the owner.

Our first visitor, an hour later, was Gjakovë's chief of police, which accounted for our easy passage through the gendarmerie post. He told us over a glass of our host's smooth slivovitz that the Germans had reinforced their garrison by a thousand *Sicherheits-dienst* during the last few days and had considerably tightened their controls, both on the roads and in the towns. They knew of the parachute drop which had brought Hibberdine and the others, but their reports greatly exaggerated the numbers and they believed that a party of fifty British parachutists had arrived. Our friends thought they were planning an expedition against Deg, but feared there would also be a house-to-house search through the town in the near future. The chief of police hoped to give us at least one hour's warning of any search and Ejub had a small force of his men in readiness to fight our way out if the worst came to the worst; but we had always to be ready to move at a moment's notice and be prepared to change our lodgings every night.

We moved house every evening for the next three days, covering the whole of the city in the course of our journeys. Ejub and Ramadan would point out the places of interest we passed – the town hall, the prefecture and the German officers' mess among others. They had gained confidence since our first furtive entry into Gjakovë, but I was never entirely happy in the streets; Hasan Beg had impressed upon me that the German garrison had a most efficient counterespionage service among the civilians. The German soldiers we met seldom looked at us, but we attracted – I particularly – many curious stares and backward glances from Albanians. Only once did our guides show alarm, when Hibberdine unthinkingly pulled out a handkerchief to blow his nose. Ramadan whipped it from his hand, crushing it out of sight in his fist; while Hibberdine, realising at once that no Albanian peasant would use a handkerchief, blew vigorously through his fingers, wiped them on the seat of his trousers and, to complete the picture, spat noisily on the cobbles.

During this time our hosts and most of our visitors were minor civil servants and small tradesmen, from which classes the Irreden-tist party seemed to draw its greatest strength. The tradesmen made up to us in professional services what they lacked in political influence; for a barber arrived each morning to shave us and at one house a tailor called to measure Hibberdine for a pair of breeches. Some of our visitors had come to see us from the furthest limits of Kosovo, so that we began to wonder how long it would be before the Germans came to hear of our presence. However, there was no doubt of the enthusiasm which our arrival had excited, for promises of help flowed in from every quarter.

On the evening of 6 January we tramped for half an hour through snowy streets to the house of a leading member of the Irredentist party, where we were to hold an important conference on the following day. I had a momentary pang of anxiety when I saw our reception committee, which consisted of our host and four uniformed gendarmes; however Ejub explained that one policeman would remain in the house with us for the whole of our visit while the other three kept watch outside. The one appointed as our personal bodyguard was a bibulous, red-faced fellow with an enormous 'Kaiser Bill' moustache; he spoke little but sat all day cross-legged on the floor, his rifle across his knees, regarding us with a benevolent and boozy leer which he interrupted at intervals to swallow *raki* from a flask by his side. Whatever use he might have been in an emergency there was no doubt that he took his duties seriously; for whenever one of us went to the lavatory he would follow across the courtyard and stand swaying and hiccupping in the cold until his charge was ready to return. It seemed that he was an equally conscientious husband, for he confided to us that he had begotten twenty children on his wife, although only seven of them had survived.

The following evening we had a conference with the commandant of the Albanian Army in Kosovo, the Mayor of Gjakovë, and Professor Suleiman Riza. Its purpose was to discuss the final arrangements for our travels through the rest of Kosovo, a matter we had long been pressing. With bitter disappointment we learned we had to postpone our journey. The Germans had tightened their controls of the roads so severely that our friends wouldn't take the responsibility of escorting us. Suleiman Riza told us the enemy knew of our presence – thanks to the Kosmet, it appeared – and were looking out for us. His friends were adamant, said Riza, and we, knowing they were no cowards, were obliged in the end to give way and satisfy ourselves for the moment with their promises to build up a resistance organisation; the Army commander undertook to supply them with arms and instructors. I looked at Hibberdine.

'Time to go home,' I sighed.

It was becoming clear to us that we couldn't remain in Gjakovë much longer without bringing unacceptable danger upon our hosts and helpers as well as ourselves. When we returned to Hasan's house the day after our conference he received us with his usual warmth and hospitality, and kept us there for six days; but we noticed a rising tension in his manner and from time to time he would mutter to himself 'Gestapo! Gestapo!' But he wouldn't let us leave the town until he was sure we could circumvent the German controls on the roads. At last on 13 January Ejub Binaku arrived with the news that he had arranged for us to travel south next day; he confessed he wasn't happy about the journey, but told us frankly he dared not let us stay any longer in Gjakovë.

I slept badly that night, waking often to fret about our escape from the town and the journey that lay ahead. These days I seemed to jump at shadows, but I was worried not only for our own safety but because we were risking the lives of so many good friends who had much more to lose than ourselves. A bright morning, however, scattered my fears and I relaxed happily watching the grey-and-white fantail pigeons flash their wings among the bare trees in the garden under the pale blue sky. A pretty, dark-haired little girl carrying a basket on her arm trotted happily along the path below our window, her tiny wooden shoes clattering like a pony's hooves on the stones.

Hibberdine and I were left to ourselves all the morning; Hasan arrived to join us for lunch. When the meal was over we prepared to depart: I wound puttees round my field boots, donned an Italian Army greatcoat and put on my fez – an incongruous and ridiculous figure that could hardly escape attention; Hibberdine, in an old civilian overcoat and white skullcap, would pass fairly well for an Albanian. Hasan, who was not accompanying me, found my appearance much more diverting than Hibberdine, who was.

At four o'clock Shpen Zeçeri came to fetch us, accompanied by Ismail, the old white-haired servant who had teased Hasan on my first night in the house; now the old man surprised me by taking my hand between his two withered claws and kissing it. Hasan said a hurried goodbye in the courtyard, promising to keep in touch with us. Shpen opened the gate, shooed away a crowd of small children who were playing in the porch and beckoned Hibberdine to follow; taking my arm Ismail hustled me after them, the two of us keeping about thirty yards behind.

After the semi-darkness in which we had lived for so long the glare of the afternoon sunlight on the white walls of the closely huddled houses struck painfully on our eyeballs, so that for a few minutes I was glad to let Ismail guide me by the arm. Schoolchildren with satchels over their shoulders were playing on an open space below Hasan's house; they let us pass without a glance. When we entered the narrow, twisting streets I bent my gaze on the cobbles, but even so I could not help noticing the curious stares that I attracted. Ismail, however, was quite unperturbed, even prodding me into calling a *tungjatjeta!* ('greetings') to a pair of gendarmes whom we passed on the outskirts of the town.

Half an hour's walking brought us to a broad dirt road where a fiacre was waiting, similar to that in which we had left Morina; standing beside it were Ejub and Ramadan. Taking an affectionate farewell of our two guides we squeezed into the back. While we rattled over the flat, snow-bound countryside, from which the colour was slowly draining as the sun sank in a fiery glow behind the western mountains, Ejub explained the reason for our hurried daylight departure: the previous evening the German garrison commander had ordered our friend, the chief of police, to put a cordon round the town and search every house. The chief of police gave Ejub twenty-four hours to get us out of the town, warning him that the search had to begin at six o'clock tonight and that the *Sicherheitsdienst* would take part.

Ejub had scarcely finished his story when we came to a control post; turning a corner we saw, about two hundred yards ahead of us, a rough barrier across the road, guarded by a party of Albanian gendarmerie and two grim-looking figures in field grey. Ejub had evidently planned our journey carefully, for our driver, without checking his pace, turned down a rough track to the right which, after a few hundred yards, crossed a river and ran parallel to the road. Although they must have seen us, the Germans made no attempt to interfere. A mile further on we were met by a fine-looking man mounted on a spirited grey stallion with a high-pommelled saddle and scarlet and silver trappings. When he came up to us he wheeled his horse and shouted a greeting; Ejub told us that he was the owner of the house where we were to stay that night.

We stayed there four days until Ejub brought us news from the city that the Germans, who knew of our presence in Kosovo, were combing the whole area for us and had taken full control of all checkpoints on the road. If we remained in Kosovo it would only be a matter of days before we were caught. We decided to return to Deg until the heat was off.

But on our way there a courier from Hasan caught us up with a long letter from Hands and a sheaf of signals from Cairo, which we burned after reading. They told us the melancholy news of the death of Corporal Roberts – my efficient and gallant wireless operator at Seymour's Camp – and of the dispersal of Brigadier Davies's mission by the Germans. (Brigadier Davies had dropped in October 1943 to command all British missions in Albania and set up his HQ at Biza in the mountains of Central Albania.)

During the winter of 1943 the Germans launched a series of determined drives against areas known or believed to harbour British missions. These operations, combined with the fierce cold of one of the severest winters of the war, virtually paralysed the guerrilla movement for four months, and forced British and partisans high into the mountains, where they had a painful struggle even to survive. Davies was obliged to leave his camp at Biza and jettison his equipment, including essential supplies of food and clothing. Pursued by the Germans, abandoned by the swifter moving partisan general staff – deserted even by the partisan guards who were supposed to protect them – exhausted, starved and frost-bitten, Davies and his companions were ambushed on the morning of 8 January by hostile Albanians while they were taking refuge in a high and lonely sheepfold. Davies and two of his officers were wounded, captured and handed over to the Germans; luckily they survived, but remained prisoners until 1945. Colonel Arthur Nicholls, Davies's chief of staff, and Alan Hare, both suffering severely from frostbite, escaped from the trap; but the former survived only three weeks before exhaustion and gangrene extinguished his incomparable spirit. He was awarded a posthumous George Cross. Hare, whose courage and steadiness throughout that terrible journey earned him the immediate award of the Military Cross, escaped to the South, but he lost several toes through frostbite.

A courier from Hasan Beg brought us another piece of grim news: our former host, the sub-prefect of Tropojë, had been shot dead by partisans outside his own house a few days after our departure. His murder was the measure of the Kosmet's gratitude for the protection he had often given them, nor did they ever try to justify it; it was a clear warning to other Albanians of the consequences of befriending us: to us it was a scarcely concealed threat.

We continued our way westward in the direction of the old frontier, reconnoitring to find a suitable base for our operations in Kosovo which, to judge from enthusiastic signals to us, enjoyed Cairo's full support. The shock was all the greater, therefore, when we reached the village near Deg, where Hands had moved his base, to receive another signal ordering us to 'break tactfully' all our contacts in Kosovo including our relations with the Irredentists; our activities, it continued, were causing an 'unfavourable impression' among Tito and his partisans; it ended with the explanation, 'Our [Cairo's] relations with Yugoslav partisans are of overriding importance.' This was something, we felt, Cairo might have told us a lot earlier; only a very special type of staff officer would suppose we could 'tactfully' abandon men who had risked their lives and families to help and shelter us. I sent a frantic signal urging our masters at least to modify their decision and allow us to keep up some contact with our friends in Kosovo. The answer was an immediate and categorical 'No'.

Clearly I could be no more use in the country and my position was no longer tenable. Sadly I sent my last signal, asking permission to return to Cairo and report; it was granted immediately. In Cairo, I still hoped, I might be useful to my Kosovo friends with my first-hand knowledge of the situation in the field. I was not to know then that the British government had finally made up their minds to give Tito unqualified support, with all that meant for Albania – especially Kosovo.

Hibberdine, who was much less compromised than I, decided to remain. Hands arranged a meeting for me with the Kosmet, who were so delighted to be seeing my back that they readily agreed to help me with my journey over the Montenegrin frontier. It was the only way I could get back to Cairo, for travel to the South and sea evacuation was blocked by the swollen Shkumbi river; but Tito's partisans held an airfield at Berane, a town in Montenegro a few miles north of the frontier. To get there I had to cross the North Albanian Alps. It would be rough going, on foot in mid-winter; moreover, Mehmet Hoxha told me, there were concentrations of German and puppet Albanian troops in these mountains all along the border, carrying out an offensive against the Montenegrin partisans. 'In consequence,' he added, 'the repression up there is most severe.'

More affable than I had ever seen him, he introduced me to his courier and two Montenegrin partisans who would act as my escort. The courier, Idris, was an unassuming young man, slim and wiry, who spoke good French; the two partisans seldom spoke at all. Idris told us that avalanches as well as frostbite had taken a heavy toll in the recent fighting and so we should indeed have a lot to look out for. I must take with me, they said, only what I could carry on my back and no other companions. But Zenel Ahmedi, when I told him he must stay behind, refused with such determination and eloquence – his *besa*, he pointed out, wouldn't permit him to leave while I was in the country – that Mehmet agreed he could accompany me as far as the frontier. We were warned to follow the courier's instructions without question; we must travel by night, avoiding contact with anyone on the way. The frontier was closely patrolled by volunteer bands of Albanian 'reactionaries' but we might be able to bribe one or two of their leaders to let us through.

1 February 1944 was a day of cloudless sky and brilliant sunshine in which the great peaks to the north beneath which I should have to travel that night shone in frosty but friendly grandeur. During the morning I reduced my kit to a small haversack, an overcoat and a couple of blankets; for defence I should have to rely on my .45 automatic and the rifles of my escort.

In the late afternoon the five of us began our northward journey.

It was safe to travel in daylight the few miles to the small town of Kolgecaj; but at a house on the outskirts we halted to eat and to await the fall of darkness. We left at eight and walked for an hour across open country until the track entered the deep gorge of the Valbonë, which runs north-westwards along a narrow cleft through the mountains to within a few miles of the old frontier. Idris called a halt.

'Let's rest a few minutes,' he said. 'Ahead lies a march of six hours . . .'

Under a bright moon we resumed our journey, following a narrow path which wound along the cliff-face above the right bank of the river. Below us the torrent foamed and bubbled among the boulders and over the rapids, the roar and hissing of its passage echoed and amplified by the steep, confining walls; above, the moonlight glistened white on the mountaintops outlined starkly against the indigo sky and glinted evilly on the bare rock faces which plunged hundreds of feet into the shadows of the gorge.

On our side the overhanging wall of rock blotted out the light, so that we stumbled helplessly among the loose stones and boulders which littered the path. Soon the going became harder as the track dropped down to the river, then rose and fell again steeply in a series of vicious switchbacks. Hour after hour we struggled on, with only an occasional halt for a drink of water, until my eyes ached with the strain of following the track and I could no longer control the movements of my aching legs; as though drunk I began to swagger and lurch from side to side. I was painfully reminded of the local name for these mountains – *Prokletije*, 'Accursed'.

The moon was already down when we came to a widening of the valley where a ravine ran in from the north. We forded the river and, after climbing several hundred feet up the opposite hillside in order to avoid a village, crossed the ravine and continued up the valley. If there was a track we failed to find it in the darkness; but after an agonising scramble over broken, rocky ground, which drained my endurance, we suddenly found ourselves beneath the white walls of a farmhouse. The owners were evidently expecting us, for the dogs were quickly silenced and we were hustled inside; Zenel and I were pushed into a small room by ourselves because there were strangers in the guest room. The time, I noted, was quarter-past four.

Zenel awakened me to another bright morning with the news that the strangers had left. Soon afterwards Idris entered, followed by a giant of a man with huge black moustaches; this was our host's brother, a *capo band* or leader of one of the bands that had taken part in the attack against the Montenegrin partisans. He greeted me warmly and told me that he would come with us to see me over the frontier.

'We have nothing against you English,' he added. 'Only we don't want the communists here; and so we collaborate with the Germans, who help us to drive them out.'

Idris, I reflected, was an honest interpreter as well as a skilful diplomat.

After a brief lunch of sour milk and maize bread we left the house at half-past three in the afternoon, retracing our steps as far as the ravine we had crossed the night before. Here we turned north and climbed steeply towards the head of the ravine, following a track which ran along the mountainside through a forest of beeches above a narrow, stony stream. Throughout the afternoon we penetrated deeper into the heart of the North Albanian Alps. On every side rose great walls of shining rock pitted with crevices in which grew clusters of stunted pines. Darkness fell and a bright moon swung into the clear sky, glinting with a steely radiance on the naked rock and bathing the peaks in the still, white beauty that moonlight brings to deserts and mountains, and all lonely places.

After four hours' march we crossed a wide, level valley carpeted in snow and began to climb a steep, beech-covered mountain – an exhausting business, for our feet slithered continually on the frozen track. Half an hour's climb brought us out of the trees on to an open, windswept crest where a small stone pyramid marked the old Montenegrin frontier. Here, while we rested, I looked back over the moonlit mountains and deep valleys of Albania, so beautiful in that clear February night that all the fears and disappointments I had suffered there vanished from my mind; in that moment of rapture I felt a futile longing to return.

Led by our guide, the *capo band*, we set off downhill at what seemed to me a mad pace, for the narrow, twisting track of beaten snow was slippery as an ice rink; quite unable to control my speed or direction I continually slithered off to bury myself in the deep drifts at the side or land up hard against a tree. We progressed in a series of these terrifying descents, interrupted by sharp climbs up narrow paths on the side of mountains above sheer precipices, until at half-past one in the morning we reached our destination, a wooden cabin at the bottom of a steep hill. Unable to keep my feet on the slippery gradient, I made the descent from the crest to the cabin on my bottom.

Our host, a Montenegrin, showed us furtively into a small room at the front of the house, apologising in whispers for not being able to offer us the guest room, which was occupied by strangers whom he dared not let us meet – circumstances fulfilling a by now familiar pattern. Throwing myself on the floor without undressing or removing my boots I slept soundly until late in the morning.

We were now on the most dangerous part of our journey, Idris told me, in the heart of enemy territory. Through the little window of our room he pointed out to me a broad lake a mile or two below us and beside it a cluster of houses among the trees; this was the lake and town of Plav. There was a German military headquarters in the town, he explained, and the country all around was thick with fascists. Our friend the *capo band* had already left for the new frontier to find out whether I could cross that night; meanwhile I must stay in the room, being careful not to show my face at the window.

At six in the evening the *capo band* returned to say that his friends would not be on duty until the following night, but that I could certainly cross then. I had resigned myself to another twenty-four hours of waiting and was preparing to go to bed after an excellent dinner when there was a loud knocking on the front door, and I heard a voice shouting for Idris. He hurried out, to return a minute later with a serious face, accompanied by the *capo band*, who looked a little frightened.

'Listen! We must hurry away from here! The German authorities in Plav know of our presence and are searching for us at this moment. We'll move to a village an hour's journey from here – back on the way we've come. Please hurry!'

Wondering if one of our own party had betrayed us or if Mehmet's affability at our last meeting had been a mask for treachery, I hurried out of the house with Zenel at my heels. We scrambled breathlessly up the steep slope I had descended so fast the night before, until we came to a track running along the crest. From here we made good progress, only pausing at each bend in the path to send two scouts ahead. Keeping my eyes fixed on the track I lost all sense of direction and time; but at last we halted near a small cabin while one of our party went in to talk with the owner. Ten minutes later we were inside a dim, stuffy little room with grimy plaster walls and a dirty wooden floor on which a young man and three small girls were lying in a jumble of dirty bedding. We threw ourselves beside them on the ground and slept.

Daylight revealed that our new hiding place had been well chosen, tucked away in a fold of the mountains at the head of a narrow valley with no other house in sight. Thick fir forests clothed the mountainsides, their foliage a soft green in the morning sunlight. In the afternoon the *capo band* appeared, accompanied by a tall, swarthy Albanian whose head and jaw were wrapped in cloths as though he had toothache; he was, it seemed, the *capo band* in charge of the sector of the frontier where I would have to cross.

Through Idris they told me that I could not leave until the following night, when the hue and cry would have died down. Then for the sum of fifty gold napoleons, they would arrange my journey. This was more money than I had; but after some bargaining they agreed to accept thirty napoleons and my promise that I would commend them favourably to the Allied high command! I handed over the money on the spot and took a note of their names, which I subsequently passed to a staff officer in Bari.

Next day it was snowing. Fearful that the weather would provide another excuse for delay I paced morosely all morning up and down the little room, my every movement followed by the grave, saucer eyes of the three little girls. Zenel and Idris joined me for lunch, and Idris relieved my anxiety.

'Major,' he said, 'you leave for the frontier this afternoon. Zenel and I can accompany you no further, but the two Montenegrin boys we have brought with us will escort you to Andrijevica, where Tito's partisans will take care of you. The *capo band* and his friends will go with you as far as the new frontier. Between this frontier and Tito's territory is a wide no-man's-land infested by patrols of Albanians, partisans and Milhailovic's Cetniks – all hostile to each other. That's your biggest problem.'

In the early afternoon my escorts arrived, shaking the snow from their clothes. There were six of them in all, including the two Montenegrin partisans. Idris was leaving immediately for the South; Zenel, in tears, begged me to take him with me, even to Andrijevica, swearing that he could make his own way back through the mountains.

I knew as well as he did that he could not hope to survive such a journey alone. I sat down and wrote a letter to his chief, thanking him for giving me so faithful a servant; sternly I ordered Zenel to take the letter to his master, telling him that it was a message of great importance. Only thus could I persuade him to leave me. Then, unable and unwilling to conceal my own tears, I took leave of that great-hearted young man.

We climbed steeply through the forest until we reached the top of the mountain behind the house. The thickly falling snow blotted out our view but the *capo band* set a fast and sure pace over the hills, along a very narrow track between high walls of frozen snow. At dusk we halted for an hour at a small house overlooking the lake of Plav, and swallowed in silence a meal of eggs and milk provided by the Albanian owners.

It was still snowing when we resumed our journey in the darkness; but the moonlight, filtering through the clouds, was reflected from the snow to diffuse a weird, pale light over the landscape. Soon we descended from the hills into a broad valley and followed the course of a river northwards over open meadows bounded by hedges. Crossing the flat, snow-covered ground in single file we must, I felt, be easily visible to any hostile patrols or sentries. The two Montenegrin partisans acted as scouts, moving about fifty yards ahead of us. Luckily they had sharp eyes. As we were crossing a field they halted suddenly, then signalled us frantically towards the cover of a hedge. Crouching in the ditch beside it I watched a file of men approaching on our left; I had counted a dozen of them when I felt a tug on my sleeve and found the *capo band* at my elbow.

'*Tedeschi!*' he hissed. 'Over there too!' He pointed to a field, where I could make out another and larger party moving parallel with the first. 'But they haven't seen us – not yet.'

Slowly, agonisingly slowly, the two German patrols stalked across the fields on either side of us. Silent and motionless we lay in the shallow ditch, holding our breath and sweating with anxiety. Once we were spotted we could not hope to escape across the open snow; nor could we fight our way out against such odds and without one automatic weapon between us. Fervently I prayed that they would not notice our footmarks.

They plodded steadily past us, seeming to look neither to right nor left. We lay hidden for a full five minutes after the last files had disappeared into the night; then we moved forward in a series of bounds from hedge to hedge, floundering across the open fields as fast as we could pull our feet through the deep snow. Nearly two hours later we came upon the main road from Plav to Andrijevica, a broad band of beaten snow between low banks.

After a brief rest we set off along the road at a good pace; our guides seemed confident that we should not run into trouble on this stretch of the journey – a feeling which, after our last experience, I could not share. But as it turned out they were right, for in two hours of walking we met no one.

Half a mile short of the frontier we turned up a steep track into the hills. We climbed slowly through thick pine woods, picking our way with difficulty in the darkness and striving to make no sound that might attract the attention of the frontier guards. Emerging suddenly from the woods we found ourselves on the top of a precipitous slope among some deserted earthworks. We stood now upon the frontier. At our feet lay a deep valley; a steep, bare hillside rose beyond – a no-man's-land of uncertain breadth and unknown danger.

For a moment we halted, crouched among the earthworks, while our Albanian guides held a whispered consultation with the two Montenegrins. Then, with a word of farewell to the Albanians, I sprang to my feet and launched myself downhill in the wake of the two partisans. So steep was the slope and so slippery the snow that I was soon careering downhill quite out of control; unwilling to finish up with my head in a snowdrift I tobogganed, as before, on my bottom for most of the way, pulling up only when I came to a belt of trees beside a stream at the foot of the mountain.

I found the climb on the other side a nightmare, stumbling painfully upwards through the snow and tormented by the knowledge that our figures were clear targets against the bare hillside. However, although the ground was honeycombed with footprints we reached the top of the mountain without being seen. While I sat down to regain my breath the two Montenegrins added considerably to my alarm by lighting a fire in order to signal the *capo band* that we had crossed the valley safely. I made them put it out.

We walked for half an hour through the hills, seeing many more footprints but meeting nobody, until my guides, who knew the country well, brought me back on to the main road. We were now in partisan territory, where our only danger lay in being shot by a trigger-happy sentry. We therefore kept to the middle of the road, walking in line abreast, singing and talking loudly with a confidence which I, at least, did not feel. Beside us ran the river, swift and dark and noisy in the night. Suddenly, as we rounded a corner, a voice called peremptorily out of the darkness ahead.

'*Stoj!*'

We stopped in our tracks. My companions answered the challenge, exchanging a stream of words with the unseen sentry. At last we advanced slowly towards an improvised pillbox beneath an overhanging rock; two very young partisans seized my hands, and shook them over and over again amid a torrent of friendly greetings.

After a few minutes' rest and talk we continued down the road for two or three miles, challenged repeatedly by sentries, until we came to a collection of small wooden huts which formed battalion headquarters. In a narrow, smoky room, almost entirely filled with an incongruous four-poster bed, I found a crowd of soldiers, among them the battalion commander and his political commissar. The former, a lean, weather-beaten Serb, immediately subjected me to a sharp interrogation in Italian, strangely relaxing from suspicion when he learned from my escort that I held the rank of major; the commissar was a small, squat man with very bright eyes and a *Struwwelpeter* shock of black hair who sat on the bed swinging his legs and smiling into the light. I was handed a large piece of stale bread and an Army water-bottle full of *raki*, from which I was repeatedly urged to drink, by the crowd of partisans who pressed close around me. Overcome with relief at our safe arrival, exhausted by the journey, and stupefied by the heat, smoke and fumes of alcohol, I soon began to nod. Friendly hands removed my boots and carried me to the four-poster bed, where I lay beside the political commissar, scarcely aware of his presence.

At dawn I was shaken into consciousness by a very pretty girl wearing battledress and a partisan forage cap; she gave me some soap and poured water over my hands, fluttering her eyelashes and giggling 'Aristocrat!' as I washed. At eight o'clock I took the road to Andrijevica, following the valley of the Lim, past burnt-out villages where the blackened shells of once prosperous farmhouses bore gloomy witness to the hatred bred by political cleavage and religious intolerance.

At Andrijevica I heard there was a party of British officers at Berane, eight miles up the road by the airfield, awaiting a plane to take them to Italy; it seemed I had arrived in time.

After lunch the following afternoon, 7 February, I started on the last lap of my journey to Berane. A walk of four hours through a thick snowstorm brought me in darkness to a sad and silent town straggling on either side of a broad main street in the middle of a valley dominated by high-forested mountains. My guides left me at a dismal two-storeyed building with a courtyard opening off the street. Climbing a wooden staircase to the first floor I entered a dingy, ill-lit room furnished with a table, a few chairs and three narrow beds; through a thick haze of tobacco smoke I saw four or five men sitting round the table. A tall, lean figure in British Army battledress wearing the badges of a lieutenant-colonel and the ribbon of the DSO rose and introduced himself with a charming smile.

'Good evening! You must be Kemp. I'm Hudson. We've been expecting you for some time now. Have some *raki*.' And then: 'Do you play bridge?'

I never returned to Albania. Within the year communist forces of the LNC and Kosmet had overrun the country. Implacable in their hatred of the British who had nursed them they were determined to destroy all those they considered to be our friends. In the eyes of the new rulers of Albania collaboration with the British was a far greater crime than collaboration with the Germans. The fury of the new regime was directed especially against those Albanians who, as our allies, had submerged their political differences with the communists in a united effort to win their country's freedom. Such men were marked for destruction because their fighting record gave the lie to the communist claim that the Communist Party alone represented the Albanian people in their fight for independence.

From the madness that followed only a few of my friends escaped.

The partisans murdered Hasan Kryeziu and all my Kosovar friends who fell into their hands; but Ejub Binaku escaped to Greece, as, I most sincerely hope, did the brave and loyal Zenel. Over the succeeding years Enver Hoxha turned on his own colleagues and disposed of almost all of them, either by execution or murder, along with countless innocent Albanians. He was following the example of his fellow paranoiac Joseph Stalin, whom he had always admired; in the summer of 1985 he went to join him in, if there is any justice, the furnaces of hell.

I've never been back to Albania, or much wanted to. But in February of 1990 I visited Kosovo, now a part of the Yugoslav Federation as a province of the Serbian Republic. Although I was able to move around openly and in comfort, I found the province only nominally at peace, under a repressive Serbian government. The Albanian Kosovars, who by now number ninety per cent of the population of Kosovo, would probably have preferred it as it was during the war, when they found German rule much more tolerable than Serbian. The Serbs have never accepted the Albanians, regarding them as invaders and as occupiers of their land. My old friends from the war had disappeared, either into exile or into their graves, murdered by Tito's partisans.

The Kosovar Albanians now want to secede from Serbia. Tito, a Croat, had favoured them against the Serbs, and for many years the Albanians had virtually controlled the Kosovo Communist Party, and therefore the province. But after his death in May 1980, control had fluctuated between the two nationalities. It is sadly true to say that each of them, when in power, had treated the other abominably, and so each had bitter and justified grievances.

Reporting for the British press, I had thought naïvely that I could tell the truth about the Kosovo problem. But I found that there were two truths, contradictory and each equally valid – a Serb truth and an Albanian.

The power in Kosovo now rested with the militant Serb, Milovan Miloševic, elected President of the Serbian Republic and Party General Secretary in 1987 on his programme to 'settle the Kosovo question'. He was pursuing a policy of deliberate provocation towards the Albanian population, with a massive police presence, including imported Serbian riot police, and savage persecution of the Albanian Kosovars. Any manifestation of protest by the Albanians was immediately suppressed with baton charges and tear gas. It is as though he wants to provoke them to armed rebellion and secession. They will not put up indefinitely with this kind of treatment. But even moderate Serbs have assured me that Serbia will fight before letting go of Kosovo. Short of a miracle, the most likely end to the dispute seems to be a bloodbath.

Chapter 9

Where war is holier than peace,
Where hate is holier than love,
Shone terrible as the Holy Ghost
An eagle whiter than a dove.

G.K. Chesterson

I ARRIVED BACK IN England in the middle of May 1944, too late to take part in any SOE operations connected with the D-Day landings or the subsequent campaign in north-west Europe, but in time for the V-Is or flying bombs.

Early in August I was enjoying a month's leave with my wife in north Cornwall when a telephone call brought me hurrying back to London. It was from my old friend of Weedon days, Colonel Harold Perkins, who was in charge of the Polish section of SOE. On 1 August the Poles had risen in Warsaw under General Bor-Komorowski, and Perkins was putting together an SOE mission to drop into the city to help and liaise with them; I was to be a member, with the commander of the mission Colonel Bill Hudson. The others included Major Peter Solly-Flood, a brilliant, quick-witted Irishman who had been in Yugoslavia with Hudson and spoke fluent French and German, and Captain Tony Currie – a *nom-de-guerre* intended to conceal his Polish identity; Currie was to be our interpreter and spoke German as well as Polish, but he was also a trained wireless operator, although our two wireless sets were in the care of a young warrant officer of the Royal Corps of Signals, Sergeant-Major Galbraith. We would have to drop in from Brindisi and must be ready to leave in a fortnight. So we were, but political difficulties intervened because Stalin raised the strongest objections to our mission and the Foreign Secretary, Anthony Eden, was not prepared to offend him.

Poland, it must be remembered, was the only Allied country occupied by the Germans which never produced a quisling to work

233

with them; and Polish resistance started throughout the country almost immediately after the Germans – with help at a critical moment from Stalin's Red Army – occupied most of the country. By far the largest and most representative organisation in this resistance was the *Armja Krajowa*, or Home Army (usually known as the AK), which drew support from Poles of every class, occupation and political persuasion. Since the beginning SOE had been dropping agents – so far always Polish – and arms to the AK, which had also accumulated stores of weapons from old Polish Army sources. It was now a powerful, well-organised and disciplined underground army with its units spread all over the country, under the command of General Bor-Komorowski in Warsaw.

In July 1944, Stalin's summer offensive carried the Red Army across Poland to the banks of the Vistula; on 1 August the Russians halted, or were held, five miles from Warsaw. At this point the Polish Home Army rose against the Germans and the entire civilian population of Warsaw joined the revolt. They naturally expected help from the Russians, but none was forthcoming. With brazen cynicism Stalin ordered the Red Army to stay where it was, while the Germans dealt effectively with the AK and reduced Warsaw to rubble. British aircraft dropping supplies to the Poles were not even allowed to use the Russian airfields a few miles away to land and refuel. Until now few had appreciated the virulence of Stalin's hatred for the Poles, ever since their great victory on the Vistula in 1920 had thwarted the strategy formulated by Stalin himself and driven the Red Army from Poland. Stalin, wrote a biographer usually sympathetic to him, 'was moved by that unscrupulous rancour and insensible spite of which he had given so much proof during the great purges'.*

The Polish defence of Warsaw against vastly superior German forces with tanks and artillery was truly heroic, but hopeless in the circumstances, with the Russians denying any help and British supply drops having to take off all the way from southern Italy. After a few weeks Bor-Komorowski and the pitiful remnant of his Home Army surrendered. For the time being, at least, the AK had ceased to be an effective fighting force. With their usual courage and resilience the Poles began to rebuild it from the survivors scattered in small units over the countryside. Their main object throughout the coming winter had to be simply to maintain their existence.

There was one of these formations in south-western Poland, in the pine forests between Czestochowa and Kielce, and Perkins

* *Stalin*, Isaac Deutscher, p 524 (Oxford, 1967)

decided this was the most suitable area for our operation. But it wasn't until October that Major-General Colin Gubbins, now in command of SOE, was able to persuade the Cabinet to let us go without the Russians' approval.

Obviously much of the value of our mission was lost with the fall of Warsaw; but both the Foreign Office and SOE still required independent information, to supplement reports from purely Polish sources, about the political and military situation in the country, in particular about the strength and morale of the *Armja Krajowa*. Our reports, it was hoped, would indicate how the British government could best help the Poles in the face of increasing Russian pressure to abandon them. Perkins impressed upon us that our new role was simply to observe and report; we must not become involved in battle unless we were trapped and had to fight our way out. He also passed on these instructions to the leaders of the AK. The Russian Foreign Office and high command were kept informed of our movements, because we would probably meet the Red Army on its next drive westward from the Vistula.

From the moment we received permission to go we had little time in which to complete our preparations for departure; most of it we spent learning a new system of coding messages. The greater part of our operational kit awaited us in Italy, but we drew our personal arms from Baker Street; we chose American .30 calibre semi-automatic carbines, because they were light, easy to handle and accurate up to three hundred yards – ideal weapons for forest warfare. We were also handed, in an atmosphere of grim and silent sympathy, a small supply of 'L-tablets', each containing enough cyanide to kill a man in half an hour if swallowed, in a few seconds if chewed. We somehow mixed them up with our aspirin tablets and so decided to destroy our store of both.

We flew out to Italy in the middle of October, and were quartered in a village on the edge of the hills above the coastal plain between Bari and Brindisi. We had a long wait ahead of us, due partly to political problems within the Polish government-in-exile in London, but more to the weather. It was five and a half hours' flying time from Brindisi to our target area in Poland – eleven hours' flying there and back, excluding time spent over the target; and so the weather had to be good enough at Brindisi for take-off, clear over the target and good enough for the aircraft to land back at Brindisi. At this time of year such a combination of good weather was uncommon.

It is a considerable nervous strain to have to sit for long in idleness when you are keyed up for an operation of great importance and some hazard; but it is an experience to which most agents became accustomed. Throughout November we controlled our impatience while our future was fought out in London. For me the tedium was much relieved by the presence in Bari of Archie Lyall; also of Billy McLean, David Smiley and Julian Amery who had just returned from a mission to Abas Kupi and the monarchists in northern Albania. They had done valuable work there, and received valuable and enthusiastic cooperation from Kupi; Smiley had fully indulged his passion for blowing up roads and bridges. But from Enver Hoxha's partisans they had encountered nothing but hostility, including serious death threats. On their return to Bari the officers of the Albanian country section had also received them with undisguised hostility and contempt, referring to them openly as 'the fascists' – an intolerable slander, especially from those who had never put themselves at risk in the field; Philip Leake's death in a German bombing raid on the partisans in the spring was proving an irreplaceable loss.

At last, early in December, we received permission to go. A few days afterwards, in the late afternoon, we boarded a Polish Liberator at Brindisi. Wearing thick clothing under our flying suits – the aircraft was unheated – and with our parachutes already strapped to our backs we climbed with difficulty through the narrow hatch under the fuselage and settled ourselves half lying, half reclining, on the metal floor. I experienced again the claustrophobia I had first known when climbing into the Halifax at Derna; this time there was less room and I felt that we were being packed for immolation in a tin coffin.

The dropping zone, which we had settled in detail on the map, was a stretch of open country surrounded by forest about twenty miles south-east of Czestochowa. We asked to be dropped from six hundred feet, which should give us plenty of time to look around on the way down. The two hazards of the journey, we were given to understand, were a German night-fighter belt over Hungary and the possibility of icing up while crossing the great mountain barrier of the Carpathians. We had to be careful, also, not to stray over territory held by the Red Army; for the Russians had given warning that they would fire on all British aircraft flying to Poland.

When we were over Yugoslavia the two waist-gun ports were thrown open and the gunners took up their positions behind the Brownings. One of the gunners started talking to Currie in Polish; he was a squat young man with long dark hair and a perpetual smile on his face, although when I heard his story from Currie I wondered what he had to smile about. His brother had been killed by the Germans in 1939 and his sister sent to a brothel; his mother and father had been arrested by the NKVD and deported to Siberia. He was the sole survivor of the family.

'Now I have only myself to worry about,' he told us with a little laugh; and he caressed the barrel of the Browning.

We met with no night fighters and cleared the Carpathians without incident; but on the far side we ran into thick mist. The navigator, who was also captain of the aircraft, came aft and told us.

'It's just like flying through milk. I can't even see our wing tips.'

For an hour we cruised low over the target area, hoping to catch a glimpse through some break in the mist of the fires that would show us the dropping zone. Our fuel reserve allowed us to stay no longer; in deep gloom we resigned ourselves to another five and a half hours of cramp and cold. We landed at Brindisi at four in the morning, just twelve hours after take-off.

We made two more similarly unsuccessful flights over Poland, the last of them on Christmas Day. I had scarcely fallen asleep in our house after the second when I was shaken awake to see bright sunlight flooding the room and Hudson standing over my bed. It was half-past ten.

'Get dressed quickly! The operation's on again this afternoon. Weather reports are good everywhere, so we've an excellent chance of making it this time.'

Archie Lyall drove with us to the airfield. We stood beside the Liberator while a gaggle of staff officers formed up, trying to cheer us with forced, stiff-upper-lip jokes about dining together afterwards in London. It was left to Lyall to provide the decisive boost to my morale.

'Goodbye, Peter,' he called out as I went aboard. 'And don't forget, if you croak I get your Spanish cloak.'

It was nine o'clock when the dispatcher came aft to open the exit hatch in the floor; he told us that the fires were clearly visible on the dropping ground.

'It is a beautiful night,' he smiled. 'Just like daylight.'

When it came to my turn to jump and the red light flashed for 'action stations' I sat on the edge of the drop praying that I might make a better landing than I usually managed, calming my fears with the thought that I should have at least twelve seconds in which to get ready for it and repeating to myself the password *Michal* by which I had to make myself known to the reception committee. According to our information the Germans had a garrison of eighty SS at a village six kilometres away and another of fifty gendarmerie ten kilometres away; if they had been alerted by our aircraft the night before we ran the risk of an unfriendly reception.

The red light turned green, the dispatcher tapped my shoulder and two seconds later the slipstream hit me as I cleared the exit. When I felt the pull of the opening parachute I looked down for the ground. To my horror I saw that it was very close and coming closer fast. I had just enough time to pull on my lift webs to break my fall before I crashed on to what felt like concrete. For a few moments I lay still, winded and shaken, on the ice-bound ploughland; my left knee hurt abominably and when I tried to get up I found that it would scarcely bear my weight.

At first I thought my parachute must have been late in opening; but it turned out that the Polish pilot, either through an error of judgment or the excitement of finding himself so close to his native land, had dropped us all from a little over two hundred feet. If any of the parachutes had failed to open immediately there would have been a fatal accident.

While I was pulling off my harness and flying suit two figures came running towards me across the dropping ground. When we had exchanged passwords they asked in French if I were badly hurt; after a moment's doubt I replied that I wasn't. Shaking my hand vigorously and slapping me on the back the two young men each put an arm round me and, laughing and chattering, helped me to hobble towards the trees that fringed the field. I had suffered a severe bruising and a fright.

The night air was dry, bracing and intensely cold. The wide, level expanse of snow-patched fields where we had landed gleamed with a pale radiance under the glittering stars, in sharp contrast to the black outline of the surrounding forest. In a few minutes we came upon the rest of the party with a group of fifteen or twenty Poles. Hudson, who had knocked himself out on landing, was dazed and groggy from concussion; he wandered about, muttering in a bewildered, plaintive voice, 'I've wet my pants.' Solly-Flood had hurt his back, and Currie and Galbraith had minor injuries. Currie, who was the first to drop, had been dispatched too soon; arriving on the ground at the edge of the field he had found nobody there. Making his way through the woods he almost blundered into a village; luckily he met a party of youths on the outskirts who, although not members of the AK, guided him back to the reception committee.

The leader of the committee told us that his men would collect all our kit and bury it in a hideout in the woods in case the Germans, their curiosity aroused by the drop, sent troops to investigate; it would be delivered to us safely next day. Accustomed to the thieving of the Balkans we were pleasantly surprised when it was. We lingered only long enough to recover our personal arms before setting off along a track through the woods for about half a mile, until we came to a long, low-built farmhouse. We were shown into a large and well-lit room crowded with men and women of different ages, all of whom gave us such an enthusiastic welcome that I was unable to decide which were our host and hostess. The majority, we heard, were refugees from Warsaw.

Everyone sat down at a long table in the middle of the room loaded with plates of food and bottles of vodka and wine; I found myself next to a handsome, middle-aged woman who encouraged me to drink more than was good for me and to eat more than I wanted; excitement or exhaustion had taken away my appetite. Fortunately she spoke French, for my Polish was unequal to conversation. She was surprisingly well informed about events outside Poland; although the Home Army maintained a news serviced its bulletins contained very little information and seldom reached the country districts; wireless receivers were almost unknown in the villages, so that most of the war news came from the German-controlled press.

As in the Balkans, it was impossible in Poland to escape from politics, although here at least we knew something of Poland's problems and recent history from our studies before we dropped in. My neighbour at dinner must have had her own source of information, for she launched into a discussion of a matter I was to hear raised frequently and with some bitterness. This was the future of Poland's eastern territories, which Stalin was now proposing to occupy permanently. He had even set up a puppet Polish government known as the Lublin Committee composed of Polish communists; not surprisingly, it had given its unanimous approval to Stalin's proposals. In a recent House of Commons debate Churchill, resolved not to damage relations with Russia, had observed that Stalin's actions were largely a result of Polish intransigence. Most Poles acknowledge that Britain could do little to restrain Stalin now that the Red Army was on the Vistula; but they were rightly indignant at being blamed for his treachery and rapacity.

The meal ended with speeches of welcome, to which Hudson, somewhat recovered from his concussion, replied on our behalf. Soon after midnight we continued our journey northwards, escorted by some twenty armed men and three girl partisans.* Nearly all wore some kind of uniform, usually an old Army tunic, either Polish or converted German, with a leather belt and ammunition pouches, breeches, puttees and boots; a few had British battledress. Most of

* The word 'partisan' in this section of the book refers to any armed guerrillas under military discipline and has no political connotation.

the men wore Cossack hats of grey fur, sometimes with the Polish eagle and crown embroidered on the front.

My knee was too painful and swollen for me to walk, and so I was laid on a pile of hay in a farm cart pulled by an old horse. After three miles we stopped at a peasant's house where an old man and his wife were awaiting us. Within a minute of lying down I was asleep.

Early next morning the leader of our escort woke us with the surprising news that two Russian officers were waiting to see us. We found a captain and a lieutenant, both of them quite young, who told us that they had been dropped three months before and were now living in this village. They spoke Polish and German, which Currie and Solly-Flood interpreted for the rest of us; although shy at first, they were friendly and freely answered all our questions. They were wearing civilian clothes and almost their first words were to recommend us to do the same; advice which, as it turned out, we were wise not to take. It seemed they lived on excellent terms with the villagers and with the AK, on whom they relied for their intelligence and for warning of German movements. They appeared to have no very active duties.

Although it was by far the largest, the AK was not the only paramilitary force opposing the Germans in Poland. There was also the AL or *Armja Ludowa* (People's Army), a Polish communist organisation equipped and directed by the Russians. Much inferior to the AK in numbers, efficiency and influence, it was designed to form a nucleus capable of running the country's administration with Russian help after the arrival of the Red Army. Meanwhile, it attempted road and rail sabotage on a small scale, and produced copious propaganda. Poorly trained and led, with inadequate intelligence, it suffered heavy casualties from the Germans; but the AK, which preserved correct if cool relations with it, gave warning whenever possible of German attacks. During the Warsaw rising some AL detachments fought very well, at least at the beginning.

There was also a very much smaller organisation, the NSZ or National Armed Forces, derisively nicknamed 'The Colonels' Party', which was so far to the right politically that even the AK called it reactionary. But they couldn't be accused of collaboration, for they fought with the greatest gallantry in Warsaw. Relations between them and the communist AL were bitterly hostile, and they fought each other whenever they met, taking no prisoners.

The Germans treated members of all three organisations as rebels, so that any Pole taken in arms was likely to be executed. But our friends in the AK told us that they stood some chance of survival if captured by the Wehrmacht; none at all if taken by the SS.

Most savage of all were the German auxiliary troops belonging to the army of the renegade Russian General Vlasov. Vlasov was a Cossack captured at the beginning of the German offensive against Russia in 1941 when so many Russian soldiers were taken prisoner. From these Vlasov recruited an army of Cossack, Ukrainian, Turkoman, Mongol and other Asiatic troops which the Germans employed chiefly on garrison and security duties in occupied countries. Knowing they would receive no quarter if taken, these men fought to the last; such was their barbarity towards the civilian population that they were feared and detested throughout occupied Europe. In this part of Poland there were Ukrainian and Turkoman divisions on the river Pilica and Cossack patrols everywhere. The AK shot any of Vlasov's men they captured, as they also shot all SS; prisoners from the Wehrmacht were usually deprived of their arms and uniforms, and then released.

The country here was not well suited to guerrilla warfare. It was flat and at this time of year covered in snow. The Germans could bring tanks, armoured cars and lorried infantry to almost any part of the area with very little warning; the partisans, on the other hand, were seldom more than five miles from a German garrison. The great fir forests, carefully cultivated for their timber, were intersected at regular intervals by long, straight, broad rides which could be swept by machine guns; there was scarcely any scrub or undergrowth and the trees were bare of branches from the ground to a height of more than twelve feet. They gave concealment from a distant enemy but little protection from close range. The only dense cover was to be found in plantations of young firs that had not yet been thinned.

German operations against the Poles took two forms; the *pacyfikacja*, a punitive expedition against partisans, and the *lapanka*, a round-up of young men and women in the towns and villages for construction work in Germany; Cossack and Ukrainian troops were usually employed in both. The tactics of the *pacyfikacja* were as simple as they were frightening. The area of forest in which the partisans were hiding was tightly cordoned; tanks, armoured cars and heavy machine guns were stationed where they could command all the rides; then infantry in close formation beat through the woods, driving the partisans, like game, on to the guns. The AK claimed that their warning system usually gave them time to leave the threatened area, or that their knowledge of the terrain enabled them to slip through the cordons by night. The *lapanka* was harder to counter, in winter especially, because the partisan units were then reduced to skeleton strength and could provide neither food nor protection for the fugitives.

After twenty-four hours with the two old peasants we moved out at dusk on 27 December with an escort of twenty partisans under an AK lieutenant, whose *nom-de-guerre* was Twardy.* I still couldn't walk and had to ride on the farm cart, which also carried our heavy kit. It was a clear night but freezing hard, and in spite of my thick clothing and gloves I was soon numb with cold. The creaking of the wagon, the crunch of footsteps in the snow and the gusty whinnies of the old horse sounded as if they must carry for miles in the stillness. Propped up against a pile of rucksacks, my pipe in my mouth and my carbine resting on my knees, I wondered uneasily how reliable were our escort's assurances that the Germans were too scared of the AK to move around the countryside after dark. I was certainly jumpy, for whenever the men at either end of our column called out orders or directions in their harsh voices I found myself gripping my carbine, with my thumb on the safety catch, and peering anxiously from side to side into the dark and silent forest.

It was very late when we halted for the night at a cottage on the edge of the forest, with open fields beyond. The owner, a middle-aged Pole who wore the armband of the German-controlled Forestry Service, was a taciturn fellow but very hospitable, and he and his wife sat us down in their small, comfortable parlour and made us drink two bottles of the excellent cherry vodka that appeared to be abundant in these country districts. After an enormous meal we slept in clean sheets.

We were surprised at the quantity and excellence of our food, for we had understood that the severity of the German agricultural levies had left the peasants on the verge of starvation. However, we learned that the peasants, with the help of the AK, contrived to evade the levies, or at least to mitigate their effect; and an ingenious system of barter and black market in the surplus produce ensured that, in the country districts at least, the people did not go short.

We stayed the next two days in the forester's cottage, but we were not idle. Most of the first day we spent encoding telegrams to Italy, which Galbraith immediately dispatched, announcing our arrival and recording such of our first impressions as we thought might be useful. We had visits from AK officers, including the local battalion commander and an officer who had recently returned from a campaign of sabotage in northern Silesia – a dangerous area owing to the hostility of the partly German population. A young lieutenant was attached to us to act as our liaison officer with the AK.

* Nearly all the names of AK officers mentioned in these pages are *noms-de-guerre*.

In the early afternoon we heard the sound of machine-gun fire about two miles away across the fields. Lieutenant Roman, the liaison officer, immediately sent out a patrol and posted double guards on the approaches to the house. In the evening he told us that a troop of Cossacks had been carrying out a *lapanka* in a village nearby.

'One or two villagers were shot and I hear that a girl was raped.' He smiled and shrugged his shoulders.

However, he was sufficiently worried to suggest we should move away from this area; he told us the Germans had heard our aircraft two nights ago and were already making inquiries, and the partisans here were not strong enough to protect us. He proposed to take us the following evening to the neighbourhood of Radomsko, where they were more numerous.

Next morning, 29 December, Currie and Galbraith, accompanied by Roman and his men, carried all our heavy kit except the two wireless sets and their necessary equipment into the woods and buried it in a concealed dugout. We could send for it later when we were more securely established. In fact we never saw it again; Roman was killed by the Germans a fortnight later while he was trying to recover it for us.

We started off at dusk that evening, escorted by Roman, Twardy and his men. It became our habit to travel by night, not only because we were more secure from attack but because there were very few people about to notice and possibly spread word of our presence. Our time of danger was from dawn until late afternoon. But even at night we moved carefully as a small tactical unit with scouts ahead, an advanced section and a rearguard.

We travelled all through the night, sometimes along forest tracks scarcely wide enough for the carts to pass, sometimes across open country over fields shining in the snow, with the faint lights of distant villages blinking at us through the dark. Three times on the way we stopped at peasant houses – twice for a glass of vodka and something to eat, and once when a cart broke an axle in a deep rut. Dawn was near when we came to a group of farm buildings, part of a large estate. Here we had hoped to sleep, but the manager would not have us; Cossacks came there every morning, he told us, to collect hay and so we should be well advised to move on quickly.

It was bright daylight when, tired and frozen, we stopped at a peasant's house in a village five miles further on. The two small rooms were already filled with people sleeping on the floor, all of them refugees from Warsaw. Indeed, all the country districts in this part of Poland were overcrowded with fugitives from Warsaw and from the eastern provinces occupied by the Red Army; it was a serious problem, which had already caused one epidemic of typhus and a general deterioration in health, aggravated by an acute shortage of medical supplies.

Late in the morning, after we had slept, we made our first wireless contact with London, who passed on to us a few messages from our families and friends. We left again in the evening and marched all night. There was no need now to hide our tracks and so we walked beside the carts, glad enough to be able to keep warm rather than sit and freeze as we had done on the last journey; luckily we had all recovered from our parachuting injuries. Marching along with these cheerful Poles I began to feel a sense of security such as I had never known before in enemy country; their infectious self-confidence and inspiring record convinced me that they would neither lead us into unnecessary danger nor fail us if we ran into trouble. In the latter belief I was soon enough proved right.

In cold grey twilight we skirted the small village of Wlynica and approached a large country house standing on a rise in open parkland surrounded by woods. We were evidently expected, for lights were burning in the windows downstairs. Roman went ahead to announce us. In a few minutes he returned and led us up a flight of stone steps into a large, high-ceilinged hall dimly lit by oil lamps and filled with the scent of pine logs; there our hostess was waiting. In many countries over many years I have never seen a more beautiful woman than the slim, dark-haired girl who stepped from the shadows to meet us. Her great, dark eyes set in the face of a mourning Madonna smiled a welcome that brightened the gloom of the dying lamps and coloured the ugly neutral light of the invading morning.

She greeted us in a soft, clear voice and led us to a small room where a meal was waiting. While we ate she asked us about the progress of the war. Her husband, an officer in the Polish Army, had been a prisoner of the Germans since 1939 in an *Oflag* (officer prisoner-of-war camp) in Posen; she counted the days till she could see him again.

We awoke late, relaxed and content. The war seemed very far away in this large and gracious house. Solly-Flood and I shared a room; we had bathed and were finishing dressing, savouring the luxury of comfort, when Hudson came in.

'There are some men coming up to the house,' he told us cheerfully. 'They're in uniform and they look to me like Germans. But no one seems to be worrying, so I suppose it's all right.'

'Lots of the AK wear German uniforms or bits of them,' I pointed out.

Before he could answer, Roman and Currie hurried into the room, their faces tense.

'The Cossacks are here! We've got to hide. Hurry!'

Behind them I saw our hostess looking anxious but calm; she beckoned to Roman and murmured a few words to him before walking towards the hall.

'Follow me,' Roman ordered, and led us at a run up a flight of stairs, along a corridor and up more stairs to a small, bare room with a single high window.

We sat on the floor not daring even to whisper, our ears strained for the sounds of a search; all I could hear was a murmur of voices and the muffled tread of boots in the hall below, but even those sounds seemed faint in comparison with the hammering of my own heart. I did not dare imagine what would happen to Madame Rubachowa if we were discovered in her house; I could not bear to think of her rotting in the horrors of Ravensbrück or Oswiecim – supposing Vlasov's ruffians let her get so far. As for ourselves, we should be lucky to meet no worse a death than a firing squad; Hitler had ordered the execution of all captured parachutists and we could not hope to pass for long as escaped prisoners of war.

The tension grew in the tiny, dim room as the drawn-out minutes passed, and we listened to the shouts and clatter of boots on the two lower floors. Suddenly, with a wild rush of panic, I heard heavy steps on the stairs leading to our hideout; I unbuttoned my holster and gripped my automatic as with agonising deliberation they approached. The door was flung open and two grinning figures stood in the entrance beckoning us out. With almost sickening relief I recognised two of the servants who had waited on us the previous night.

Madame Rubachowa was an excellent hostess and went to a great deal of trouble to ensure our comfort and entertainment. Knowing that we wished to meet as many of her countrymen as might be useful to us in our mission she arranged a large luncheon party, to which she asked a few senior officers of the AK and some younger friends of hers who lived or were staying in the neighbourhood. I suppose the latter could be described as a mixture of local landowners and refugee intellectuals from Warsaw. We commented on the lack of interest that all of them, old and young, showed in the personalities of the exiled Polish government in London – an indifference which we found everywhere in Poland. It has often been remarked that governments-in-exile tend to lose touch with the people they claim to represent; they tend also to lose their respect.

Among the AK officers present was a certain Major Stefan,

commanding the 25th Infantry Regiment. This unit, which was disbanded after the Warsaw rising, retained one detachment of about forty men under arms, commanded by a very young and enthusiastic subaltern, Lieutenant Warta; he and his men were to be our escort in future, replacing Roman and Twardy.

That evening, the last of the year, we left Madame Rubachowa's house while it was still light; it wasn't the last time we saw her. As we plodded across the fields towards the forest I was filled with a curious despondency, I might say a premonition of disaster; at the time I put it down to the melancholy of parting from Madame Rubachowa, intensified by the chill of the dead and snow-bound countryside, and the grim, cold blackness of the fir trees rising out of the thickening gloom. I tried to shake it off during the three-mile journey through the woods which brought us to the village of Katarzyna; but my apprehension deepened as we approached the outskirts and came upon a wide, straight road whose hard surface was clearly designed to carry motor traffic.

In the village we were led to the house of a Madame Dembowska, a middle-aged widow with a shock of white hair above a mahogany face who fussed unceasingly about our food and comfort. The house, which resembled a small chalet, stood apart from the village, among open fields separating two areas of forest, and was surrounded by stables and outbuildings; the rooms were furnished in the heavy, gloomy style usually associated with aspidistras and antimacassars.

Our escorts, whose quarters were in a group of huts on the edge of the nearest woods, invited us to join them after dinner to see in the New Year. When we arrived the small mess room was packed with cheerful, noisy partisans and heavy with the reek of sweat, tobacco and unwashed clothing; the lamplight flickered on the strong faces and sparkled in their fierce, eager eyes. At midnight we all stood to attention and sang the Polish National Anthem.

Next we sang the 'Warszawianka', the stirring call to battle written for the Warsaw Rising of 1830 – the rising whose defeat a year later inspired Chopin's 'Revolutionary' study. Bottles of vodka and plates of *zakaska* were passed round; we drank toasts to Poland and Britain and Anglo-Polish friendship, and to the damnation of our common enemies; our hosts shook us by the hand, slapped us on the back and warmly if unsteadily embraced us all in turn. The smoky, overcrowded room rang with the shouting. The party culminated in a series of *feux-de-joie* from the rifles of our escort. It was this final gesture, I am sure, that brought us trouble in the morning.

Before we went to bed Hudson made it clear to Lieutenant Warta that we should have to depend on him for all instructions concerning our security. He replied that his men made a habit of rising at five every morning and standing to until at least an hour after daybreak; he didn't think it likely that the Germans would be very active on the morning of New Year's Day, but he would see that we were alerted just the same. And so ended 1944.

I awoke soon after seven with a bursting bladder, a natural consequence of the previous evening. I went outside to relieve it and was on my way back to the house when I heard a dull rumbling from the direction of the road we had crossed the previous evening; distant at first, it became noticeably louder as I listened. It was a sound I had first heard in the days of the Spanish Civil War: the sound of approaching tanks. Hurrying into the room where the rest of the party were sleeping I shook Hudson awake.

'Bill, I don't want to alarm you, but I'm pretty sure I hear tanks. And they're coming closer.'

I had hardly finished speaking when one of our escorts burst into the room to confirm my fears. We threw on our clothes, grabbed our carbines and slung over our shoulders the small haversacks containing our signal codes and essential personal kit. Currie and Galbraith seized the smaller of our two wireless sets and the portable hand generator; it would be calamitous if we were to lose our own wireless links with London and Italy. If the Germans were indeed coming after us there was no hope of saving our heavy, more powerful set or any equipment that we could not carry ourselves.

We were not left long in doubt. While we made our preparations for flight the sound of the tanks grew louder; we could also hear the roar of heavy lorries grinding along in low gear. From close at hand came Warta's voice rapping curt orders to our escort. Solly-Flood and I ran out to see what was happening. Turning right outside the door I ran for the shelter of a barn and peered round the corner in the direction of the noise.

I saw four medium tanks, their guns pointing straight at us, moving at a tangent across a field three or four hundred yards to my front; behind them, in a clump of trees, several large lorries were disgorging green-uniformed soldiers. Fascinated by these preparations for our destruction I was brought sharply to my senses by the crack of an exploding shell in a ditch a few yards away; at the same time a burst of machine-gun fire spattered the walls of my barn. As I jumped back into cover I heard, from my left, the clatter of a Bren; with astonished admiration I saw that a detachment of our escort had emplaced itself behind a low bank and was firing on the tanks and the advancing infantry: some twenty-five Poles with rifles and one light machine gun were taking on four tanks and at least a hundred well-armed Germans.

I heard my name shouted and, turning, saw Warta and the rest of our party beckoning to me from the door of the chalet. Warta was talking to Currie in short, urgent sentences; he ran to join his men and Currie translated his instructions.

'We're to make for those woods,' he told us, 'while Warta holds off the Germans. Once we've got clear he will break off the action and try to join us. We have to cross some open ground first, so we must run.'

The patch of open ground between the house and the woods was some three hundred yards wide; we would be crossing it in full view of the enemy and clearly outlined against the snow. Halfway across was a thin plantation of young firs; we sprinted for this, darting from the cover of the chalet like flushed rabbits and sweating with fear as we forced our heavy feet through the clogging snow. If there is any more disagreeable experience than that of running away under fire I hope I never meet it. There is none of the hot excitement of attack, but much more of the danger; the blood trickled icily in my veins and with each step my muscles contracted, anticipating the impact of a bullet; my throat felt dry and constricted, and I had a violent urge to vomit. Bullets in plenty sang over our heads and smacked into the ground all round as we ran. But fortunately the tanks were concentrating their attention on the heroic Bren gunner and his companions; one machine gun would have finished the lot of us. As it was we were beyond effective range of Schmeissers and the riflemen seemed to be poor shots.

We reached the fir plantation without a casualty and paused a moment for breath, sitting in the snow because the saplings were not tall enough to hide us when we stood. Here we dumped the hand generator in a ditch; it was much too heavy for a running man and Currie had done well to bring it so far. It was cunningly hidden and Currie retrieved it himself later the same day.

From behind us broke loud on our ears the sound of battle: long bursts of machine-gun fire, the vicious crack of tank shells and the faint popping of rifles.

'Jesus!' sighed Solly-Flood. 'Aren't we the brave boys? Running off to the woods while the Poles stand and take the rap. This is a shit's job.'

'You know our orders,' snapped Hudson. 'What's more, so do the Poles. Come on, let's go.'

Together we broke cover, spreading out as we ran across the last hundred and fifty yards that separated us from the shelter of the great forest. But the fighting now was in Katarzyna village, around the house of Madame Dembowska, and no one paid attention to our flight.

Ten minutes later, when we had hidden the wireless at the

rendezvous Warta had indicated, we returned to the edge of the wood to peer through the trees at Katarzyna. The firing had died away, thick smoke was rising from Madame Dembowska's farm buildings, and above the roar and crackle of the flames we heard the Germans calling orders in that half-bellow, half-scream which in their Army was the voice of command.

Dismally we wandered back to the large plantation of saplings where we had left the wireless. We were sure we had seen the last of Warta and his men, and it was bitter to feel that but for our presence they could have faded into the forest without a fight. Madame Dembowska, too, would be in trouble when the Germans found all our equipment in her house. The fact that she had not invited us was unlikely to be accepted as an excuse.

These painful thoughts occupied us in silence for half an hour. We were the more astounded, therefore, when Warta himself appeared with the greater part of his detachment – the rest, he explained, were on guard or patrol duties. In the whole action he had lost only one man – the Bren gunner, who had certainly courted death and been killed instantaneously by a machine-gun burst from one of the tanks; his body had been recovered and would be buried in the morning. Warta had broken off the action after ten minutes, rightly considering that he had given us plenty of time to get away. He claimed to have inflicted casualties on the Germans and he must have given them a mauling, because they had not cared to pursue him. By any standards his performance was an epic of skill and valour – those qualities that had forged the tragic drama of Warsaw.

We stayed in the woods for most of the day, with guards posted to warn us if the Germans should return. Now that they knew there was a party of British parachutists in the neighbourhood they might well conduct an intensive *pacyfikacja* and beat us out of our hiding place; we had therefore to be clear of the district before morning.

In the late afternoon we went back to Katarzyna. Madame Dembowska's house was deserted but undamaged; the Germans had confined their destruction to the out-buildings. As we feared, our unhappy hostess had been taken to Czestochowa; we learned later that she was released the next day frightened but unharmed. After the battle the Germans had brought their casualties into her house and Warta pointed with grim satisfaction at the blood-spattered dining-room table on which they had been laid for operation.

All our equipment, of course, had gone; Solly-Flood, who had been a brigade intelligence officer, treated us to a graphic description of German security officers examining with painstaking thoroughness each article of our kit, and evaluating its military and political significance. From our point of view the most serious losses – we did not then appreciate how serious – were our heavy wireless set and petrol generator; the smaller set had not the necessary power and the hand generator that Currie had saved gave continual trouble. We were soon reduced to handing our encoded signals to the Home Army for transmission; only when we returned to London did we learn that neither London nor base had received any of them.

We did not linger in Katarzyna, but in the last daylight began our journey through the woods. We marched fast and with few halts or rests; although it was unlikely that we should meet Germans abroad at so late an hour we took no chances and moved in our usual formation. Warta's senior sergeant had found himself a fine horse, and rode up and down the column all night, checking the distances between the main body and the advance guard and rearguard, keeping an eye on the scouts and encouraging us all in his strong, cheerful voice. He was a man of fine physique and commanding presence with a long experience of partisan warfare; in his fur hat, with his cavalry bandolier and his rifle slung across his back, he looked to me like some famous Cossack hetman.

In the small hours of the morning we reached our destination, the village of Dudki. We had brought with us the body of the Bren gunner and at daybreak we assembled to give him burial. There was no priest, but the service was read by the battalion commander, whom we found awaiting us at Dudki. As we stood around the open grave on a bare mound outside the village, blinking our eyes against the harsh and hostile light of that cold dawn, I wondered, as I think we all did, how we could hope to justify this man's sacrifice. When the body, wrapped in a Polish flag, was lowered into the ground, and the volley was fired and the earth sprinkled, we felt acutely the full shame of our flight. Afterwards Warta told us sadly, 'We cannot even tell his family, because they live in eastern Poland – Russian territory now.'

We left Dudki immediately after the funeral and tramped for two hours through the forest until we came to a collection of scattered farmhouses. In one of these we prepared to spend the day, but at noon Warta hustled us outside and led us at a run into the woods: detachments of *Feldgendarmerei* had arrived at the next village and were asking if any British officers had been seen. Although they did not come our way we remained in the forest until twilight, nursing our ragged nerves among the fir trees.

We dined that night with a very senior officer of the AK, the colonel commanding the Czestochowa inspectorate. A friendly person, he repeatedly assured us that the Poles well understood that Britain was too far away to help Poland should Stalin decide to annex it; but the Poles, he added fiercely, would fight to the last to preserve their independence. At that time it seemed an academic question, for none of us could foretell the horror of the future and none of us remembered Stalin's 1939 pledge to Hitler that Poland should never rise again; least of all could we imagine that Britain and the United States would underwrite it at Yalta.

In the middle of our conversation the colonel quietly informed us that the following afternoon we were to meet the commander-in-chief of the Polish Home Army – the successor to General Bor-Komorowski. This romantic and mysterious figure, whose very name was concealed from us until our return to London, was travelling swiftly and secretly throughout the country, reviving and reorganising those shattered remnants of the AK that had survived the catastrophe at Warsaw. The next day he would be staying nearby; twenty-four hours later he might be in Krakow, Lodz, Poznan or even Warsaw.

In the early afternoon of 3 January we set off from the farmhouse with a strong escort under the command of Warta's senior sergeant; a horse-drawn sledge came with us to bring us home in the evening. It was still light when we arrived at a large and comfortable mansion surrounded by tall trees. Inside we found a blaze of lights and a crowd of people, nearly all of them in civilian clothes; among them I recognised an old acquaintance, Colonel Rudkowski, a close friend of Perkins, whom I had met several times in London and once, briefly, in Italy.

Rudkowski was already a senior officer of the Polish Air Force when war broke out in 1939. He was a short, square man of about fifty-five who combined the fierce patriotism and mature cunning of his nation with the irresponsible and disarming sense of fun of a prep schoolboy. His courage was attested by his two ribbons of the *Virtuti Militari*, the Polish Victoria Cross, his abilities by the post he had held until recently of air officer commanding the Polish fighter group in Britain, and by his present assignment, which was to build the foundations of a new Polish Air Force. He had parachuted into Poland on the night of our arrival in Italy.

Looking in his civilian clothes more like a character out of *Minder* than the gallant and distinguished officer he was, Rudkowski pounced on us in the hall and led us directly to a small, trim library where we were presented without formality to the commander-in-chief.

Of General Okulicki's history I knew only that he had commanded a Polish division in the field under General Anders. What I do remember well is his soft voice, his courteous, almost deferential manner, his quiet, convincing self-confidence, and his passionate sincerity and belief in his own people, and his mission among them. He had no illusions about the difficulties ahead of him and meagre hope for their solution; but as I listened to him I knew that this man would make any sacrifice to nourish the starving spirit of his shattered Army, caring nothing for his own safety in the cause of his country's freedom.

One sentence of Okulicki's still stays in my mind: despite their treachery at Warsaw, he told us, he would continue to treat the Russians as allies and would do all in his power to cooperate with them; but he could not trust their word. Later, in his anxiety to save his country, he trusted them too much.

After the Russian occupation of Poland and the end of the war Stalin invited the leaders of the *Armja Krajowa*, who had gone into hiding, to come to Moscow for discussions on the future government of Poland; the invitation was issued through the chief of the Russian general staff, who publicly gave his word of honour as a general officer of the Red Army that the delegates would come to no harm in Russia and would be allowed to return to Poland without interference. In spite of their natural misgivings General Okulicki and the other leaders of the Home Army felt it their duty, in the interests of Poland, to accept this invitation. On arrival in Moscow they were all immediately arrested and imprisoned in the Lubianka. They were brought to trial on charges of sabotaging the communications of the Red Army in Poland and operating clandestine wireless stations; on evidence which in Britain would not even have secured their committal for trial they were convicted and sentenced to penal servitude for life. General Okulicki died in prison,

We left again long before dawn and after a five-mile march reached Redziny, a few small houses on the edge of a great forest. Our hosts, an old peasant and his wife, moved with remarkable good humour into their kitchen, leaving the other two rooms for ourselves and our wireless equipment. While we were there we worked late every night, drafting and encoding signals to London reporting the action at Katarzyna, our meeting with General Okulicki and information we acquired from our numerous visitors – unaware, of course, that we were losing our sleep to no purpose.

At five o'clock each morning Warta routed us out of bed and led us into the forest, where he kept us until two in the afternoon. This was the usual pattern of our lives for the rest of our time with the Home Army; there were many German and Cossack foraging parties around, and the Poles were taking no more chances after Katarzyna. Throughout the daytime we remained in a perpetual state of alert, ready to move at a minute's notice; we slept, of course, in our clothes.

Our first visitors were two junior officers of the Home Army, Lieutenants Jerzy and Alm; they were to be attached to us in future as liaison officers with the Home Army command. Alm was an intelligent young man from western Poland and he had a story to tell. In order to secure the release of his father, who had been sent to Dachau, he had volunteered for the German Army and had soon won himself a commission. As an officer he had little difficulty in persuading the authorities to free his father, who went into hiding. Alm then obtained a posting to the Russian front, where he skilfully – or luckily – contrived to get wounded just badly enough to be sent to Poland for convalescence; once he was back in his own country he deserted and joined the *Armja Krajowa*. Jerzy was a very tall, thin young man with a quiet, serious manner; a brother of the beautiful Madame Rubachowa, he had all his sister's gentle charm.

Mr Siemienski, our next caller, was a prominent landowner from the neighbouring town of Zytno; he was a saddened, soft-spoken man in his middle or late fifties whose principal interest was farming but who looked more like a university don than a squire. His only son had been killed four months earlier with the AK in battle against the Germans. With him came two young women who worked in the courier service of the Home Army; one of them was his daughter, a pretty, dark-haired girl of about twenty; the other was married to a Polish officer now in a German prisoner-of-war camp. Siemienski was a member of an organisation of landowners whose principal object was to keep the Home Army supplied with food, money, clothing and shelter.

On the third evening of our stay at Redziny we were in the middle of supper when there was a commotion outside and the sound of urgent whispering; Warta swept into the house, followed by Jerzy. The latter spoke without preliminary greeting.

'Please hurry with your meal. We have just heard there is to be a *pacyfikacja* in this area tomorrow morning. We are leaving at once.'

We marched all night in grim silence, for we were all short of sleep and only too liable to snap at one another when we spoke. At first light we arrived, grey-faced and bleary-eyed, at a small settlement of poor peasant houses. Before the war the place had been a colony of *Volksdeutsche* – German settlers – but after the occupation they had been moved to richer holdings near Radomsko and the dispossessed Poles resettled here. Our house was filthy and almost bare of furniture, and we slept on grubby pallets on the earthen floor; but the owners, a small family reduced to a state of apathy by poverty, did their best to make us comfortable. In return for their hospitality we gave them a few sovereigns, which they accepted courteously but with seeming indifference; obvious suffering had apparently drained them of all feeling.

During the three days of our stay we became infested with the most prolific and ferocious crop of lice. For the Spanish, Albanian and Montenegrin louse I had learned to acquire a certain tolerance; but these creatures bit with an increasing and fanatical fury that excluded all hope of sleep.

On 11 January we returned to Redziny. The Germans, having caught no one in their net, had withdrawn; but we did not relax our security measures during the five days we were there. Any temptation towards slackness that we might have felt was soon dispelled by the regular appearance every morning and afternoon of a pair of Storch reconnaissance aircraft; they flew steadily back and forth over the village, and it was soon clear to us that they were trying to locate our wireless. General Okulicki had warned us of this very danger. We had plenty of traffic for Galbraith's skeds: every day we received fresh reports from different sources on military, political and economic conditions; but we could not risk operating the set while the aircraft were around, and so we were obliged to hand most of our messages to Jerzy or Alm to be sent on Polish links.

The presence of the two aircraft seemed to confirm our suspicions that the Germans already had a good idea of our whereabouts; we braced ourselves for an unpleasant period of *pacyfikacja* and pursuit. It never came. Instead, on the night of 13 January we were startled to hear the sound of heavy gunfire rolling towards us from the east. As the hours passed the barrage intensified to such a climax that we knew it could mean only one thing: the Russians were attacking on the Vistula; a new offensive had begun.

Chapter 10

NEITHER THE POLES nor ourselves – not even, it seemed, the Germans – had expected the Red Army to begin its drive towards the Oder before the spring; nor could we foresee that it would meet with so little resistance. The bombardment continued all night without interruption. During the next two days numbers of enemy fighters and bombers flew overhead, but the Poles told us the Germans were withdrawing. Warta kept us in the woods from early morning until dusk, for we were so close to the battle now that he had every reason to fear an intensive round-up by security forces; but so swift was the German retreat that we were left in peace.

On the 15th we heard that Russian tanks were on the western bank of the Pilica, which meant that they had breached the last line of defence before the Oder and the German frontier; we could expect them to reach us within twenty-four hours. Our standing orders, when this happened, were to present ourselves at the nearest Red Army headquarters.

The same afternoon Jerzy brought us an invitation from his sister to a party at Wlynica. We should not be returning to Redziny, and so we piled all our kit on to one farm cart and ourselves on to another, and set off soon after dark. We travelled slowly and with extra caution, every man on the alert for signs of trouble; we avoided all villages and roads, keeping as much as possible to the forest and pausing for a thorough reconnaissance whenever we had to cross a patch of open country. The district was crawling with enemy patrols and we had no wish for a brush with desperate Cossacks or SS; nor could we be certain of the temper of any *Armja Ludowa* forces we might meet at this moment of their masters' triumph.

We did in fact run into just such patrol soon after we had started, in the depths of a very dark wood; they were belligerent at first and called on us to surrender. We leaped off our wagon and took up battle stations at the sound of peremptory shouting and the menacing clatter of rifle bolts; but after a brief parley they decided that we outnumbered them and let us pass.

Madame Rubachowa's party was going briskly when we arrived. Her guests included almost everyone we had met there before and many more of her friends from the district. The atmosphere was much less restrained than on our previous visit; there was music and dancing, and tables laden with vodka, champagne and food of every kind. But the evening sparkled with a forced, determined hilarity that was terrible and tragic; the underlying tension and anxiety crackled from room to room.

We had hoped for a final interview with General Okulicki and Hudson had accepted tonight's invitation partly in the hope of meeting some representative of the GOC. But he was disappointed, for the only two senior officers present were our old friend Major Stefan, Warta's commanding officer, and the deputy commander of the Czestochowa inspectorate, neither of whom could – or would – give us any idea of the general's whereabouts. They had received no fresh instructions and therefore proposed to carry out those they had been given several months ago – to disband all partisan units on the arrival of the Russians and go into hiding. The hostile tone of recent Russian broadcasts left them in no doubt of the treatment they might expect from the Red Army.

As the evening progressed, the pace of the party quickened to a macabre and frenzied gaiety whose implications could no longer be concealed. However much these people hated the Germans – and there was not a man or woman in the room who had not lost at least one close relative fighting against them – they literally dreaded the Russians. Tonight they were saying goodbye to the world they had always known. The German occupation had brought unbelievable hardship to their country: Russian rule, they foresaw, meant its extinction.

The dancing grew faster and wilder: waltzes and foxtrots were abandoned for the whirling, stamping folk dances of Poland – the *krakowiak*, *oberek* and *kujawiak*; glasses were filled, emptied at once and immediately filled again as people drank with an intense, desperate urgency, as though they would never be drinking again, as though they must not leave a drop for the invading Russians. Beautiful and solitary among these fantastic bacchanals wandered our hostess, her air of gentle melancholy dissolving in a friendly smile as she talked to each of her guests. She told me that she would leave for the North as soon as the party was over and make for Poznan, where she hoped to find her husband.

It was after midnight when we left Wlynica and took the road to Katarzyna, as we had done on New Year's Eve; Warta and his men accompanied us, for they had been ordered to remain with us until the arrival of the Russians. We stayed in a small cottage near the village: at such a time it might be wise to sleep away from large houses.

We awoke to a noisy morning. From the north, where the main road ran west towards Czestochowa, came the rumble of tanks and the continuous roar of motor transport, often punctuated by bursts of machine-gun fire and the thunder of artillery; the sky above us was filled with the whine and drone of aircraft, and to east and west the air vibrated with the thud of heavy bombing.

Our hand generator had finally broken down, but Galbraith's batteries had just enough charge left in them for a last contact with London; this contact brought us a brief signal, confirming our orders to hand ourselves over to the Russians, and reassuring us that our names and location and the nature of our mission had been communicated to the Russian political and military authorities, as well as to the British military mission in Moscow.

At noon we learned that Russian armoured spearheads were already well to the west of us; there seemed no reason to keep our escorts with us any longer – indeed there was every reason to let them disband and hide themselves while they could. They had refused to leave us the day before when we had made the same suggestion, but now it was easy to convince them; they left us the same afternoon, each one shaking us firmly by the hand and giving us a cracking salute before he marched away proudly into a future of danger and doom.

Our problem now was to find the Russians without running into any of the large groups of defeated Germans, Turkomen and Cossacks that were wandering about the country; Vlasov's troops, especially, would be in an ugly mood. Hudson decided to send Currie and Solly-Flood to try and make contact with a Russian divisional or corps headquarters; they left soon after the Poles, telling us to expect them back in the morning.

Much to our surprise we received an invitation to dine that night with Madame Dembowska; we had thought that after New Year's Day she would want no more of our company. Hudson, Galbraith and I set off for her house before it was quite dark, keeping a careful lookout on the way. It was well that we were vigilant, because we saw the Russian patrol before they saw us – in a wood a few hundred yards from Madame Dembowska's house; there were two soldiers moving slowly through the trees, their tommy-guns at the ready. It was unnecessary as well as dangerous to try to avoid them, and so we stood still and called to them, waving in what we hoped would seem a friendly, carefree manner.

They came towards us slowly and suspiciously, their guns pointed straight at our stomachs and their fingers on the triggers. When they were close Hudson, who spoke some Russian, explained who we were and showed them a card with which each of us had been issued in London, displaying a Union Jack and a message in printed Cyrillic letters which began, I remember, '*Ya Anglichanin*'.

They shed some of their hostility and accompanied us the rest of the way, still keeping us covered in a manner suggesting that they would stand no nonsense. I hate to speculate on Madame Dembowska's feelings when she opened the door to us; first we had brought Germans to her house: now we were bringing the Russians. Perhaps she had expected them anyway and hoped that our presence would have a restraining influence, because she welcomed us with warmth. One of our guards now left us to fetch his officers, while his companion made himself comfortable squatting on the floor of the dining room. There were three or four other guests for dinner, all of them farmers or professional men from the district.

We were starting to eat when a Russian captain and two lieutenants walked into the room and saluted smartly; they were all from one of the armoured formations which had been leading the advance and were for the moment resting in reserve. The captain, who acted as spokesman for the others, was a rangy young Ukrainian with a frank and humorous face; Madame Dembowska asked them rather nervously to join us for dinner – an unnecessary invitation, for they told her in a firm though friendly manner to fetch a lot more vodka and be quick about it.

At the end of the meal we toasted each other, and the British and Russian leaders; the captain himself proposed the health of President Roosevelt – as well he might. He then launched into a long set speech, obviously carefully rehearsed because he paused from time to time to ask his colleagues whether he had omitted anything.

It was a very successful party for all except poor Madame Dembowska, whose entire store of vodka was drunk in the course of the evening – without, I must add, producing any noticeable effect on her Russian guests. Before we left, the captain invited us to drink in his mess the following evening.

The mess was in a small wooden house on the outskirts of the village. The captain introduced us to his brother officers, about a dozen of them standing at a long table laden with snacks and bottles of what appeared to be cherry vodka. Handing each of us a half-pint tumbler filled to the brim and indicating that he expected us to drain it in one swallow, the captain called us to drink the first toast: '*Pobeda!*' – Victory! Happily I raised my glass and poured it straight down my throat; a moment later, if I had had any voice left, I would have screamed.

P.G. Wodehouse somewhere describes the effect of a Jeeves pick-me-up – I quote from memory – 'as if someone had touched off a bomb in the old bean and then taken a stroll through the stomach with a lighted torch', a very fair description of what we had just swallowed. It burned like molten lead and tasted of petrol. It was in fact, we discovered, a mixture of the neat spirit used as the basis of vodka and petrol from their vehicles – camouflaged with fruit juice. Our hosts went on to finish all the bottles, without any more help from us. I couldn't speak for the rest of the evening.

Early next morning, 18 January, a Dodge truck arrived outside our house to take us to the Russian Army corps headquarters at Zytno; in it were Currie, a Russian major and two soldiers. The major was far from friendly, and curtly ordered us to pack up our things and get into the truck.

Currie warned us that our reception at headquarters was not going to be an affair of handshakes, vodka and caviar. He and Solly-Flood had been received with arrogance and suspicion; they had been taken before a major-general and subjected to a long interrogation; the general had called them liars, made them hand over their arms and identity cards, and sent them under guard to the house of Mr Siemienski, where Solly-Flood was now detained.

Apart from a brief delaying action on the Pilica the Germans had put up little or no resistance; their object had been to withdraw their forces intact behind the line of the Oder. They seemed largely to have succeeded, because we saw very little destroyed or abandoned equipment and only two columns of German prisoners, of about fifty men each.

Corps HQ at Zytno occupied two small rooms of a peasant's cottage. Forcing his way through a crowd of lounging guards and orderlies, who stiffened to attention as he passed, the major led us to the inner room, where a lieutenant-general and several staff officers were standing before a large, coloured wallmap of the front. The general, a lean, dark man of thirty-five or forty with an intelligent face and a very quiet voice, courteously acknowledged our salutes and pointed to some hard chairs round a small table; his interest was confined to the course of the battle. An officer with a field telephone in one hand passed a series of reports to the corps commander, who commented briefly on each, while another officer marked the map with coloured pencils. The general gave his orders confidently and without hesitation; nothing seemed to be put in writing.

We rose to our feet as the door opened to admit a thick-set officer with a pale, flabby face who wore on his greatcoat the gilded epaulettes of a major-general. He made no attempt to acknowledge our salutes, but sat down across the table from us and stared at us for a while without speaking; a faint sneer twisted the corners of his mouth.

He brought with him a Polish-speaking subaltern, who interpreted for him, as Currie did for us. Hudson explained who we were, adding that Moscow had already received all our particulars; he showed his identity card, but the major-general refused to look at it, saying that it was probably a German forgery. We were then subjected to a barrage of questions: what was the name of our organisation in London and who commanded it? What were the times of our skeds, what frequencies and what codes were we using? Most sinister of all, who were our Polish contacts?

Hudson politely explained that we weren't allowed to give this information, even to our allies, but he could easily check our *bona fides* through Moscow; the general laughed unpleasantly. It was obvious he didn't seriously doubt our story, but was being deliberately offensive; he was not an Army officer, we were sure, but a political general of the NKVD (the predecessor of the KGB). At the end of the interview he ordered us to hand over all our arms, documents and wireless equipment, dismissing our protests with contempt and laughing at Hudson's threat to take up the matter with Moscow.

We were sent under escort to Siemienski's house, which seemed to have been taken over as the administrative headquarters of the Army corps. Troops thronged the building; in the grounds were parked vehicles, guns and Katiusha multiple-rocket batteries, which we were never allowed to approach. We found Solly-Flood, still seething from his treatment of the night before, and Siemienski and his daughter, his mother and his niece, who welcomed us with joy and relief – either because they had feared for our safety or because they hoped for our protection; perhaps both. Siemienski's niece was an attractive blonde of about the same age as her cousin; Madame Siemienska, a small, while-haired old lady with fine, delicate features, walked erect and proud among the noisy Mongol soldiers as though she were not even aware of their presence.

We lived, ate and slept in a large ground-floor room at the front of the house, formerly the drawing room but now denuded of most of its furniture. We were committed to the charge of a Russian major, who in the three days that we stayed there never let us out of his sight. There was, of course, no privacy for any of us – the Siemienskis or ourselves. They bore their humiliation with a fine dignity and good humour.

The Russians had requisitioned all the livestock in the district without compensation and so there would be no means of cultivating the land in the spring; the Red Army's method of living off the country during an advance was as devastating as their 'scorched earth' policy in retreat.

These troops belonged to Marshal Koniev's Second Ukrainian Army; among them was a high proportion of Mongols. I believe their behaviour was no worse than that of other Soviet armies in occupied territory; there seemed to be little difference between their treatment of the peoples they were supposed to be liberating and those they were conquering.

The soldiers quartered on Siemienski behaved towards him and his family with calculated brutality and contempt. They broke up his furniture for firewood, they pilfered every article of value and marked or spoilt what they did not care to take away; they urinated and defecated in every room, sparing our living quarters only because the major in charge of us stopped them; the hall, the stairs and the passages were heaped and spattered with piles of excrement, the walls and floors were splashed with liquor, spittle and vomit – the whole building stank like an untended latrine. It is a pity those communists who declared that they would welcome the Red Army as liberators never saw that particular army at its work of liberation.

Towards the girls, whenever they were out of our sight, they showed a deliberately boorish and arrogant manner, insulting, threatening and sometimes hitting them. The officers behaved better; the girls could always put them to shame by the use of the phrase, *nie kulturny*, for the Red Army officer was very touchy about his 'culture'. But the officers had no authority over their men off duty. On parade and in action orders were obeyed instantly and to the letter; here, however, the officers seemed to mix with their troops without distinction of rank, and their few attempts to check indiscipline and hooliganism were either ignored or, as we ourselves observed, answered with ridicule and defiance. To us they made no pretence at being friendly; one bumptious little captain told us with spirited conviction:

'Don't worry. When we've beaten the Germans we're going on to fight the British.'

He at least did not doubt our nationality.

For Madame Siemienska, however, the troops displayed a reluctant respect; she was, I have said, an old lady of formidable personality and her obvious indifference to whatever fate might overtake her, coupled with her unconcealed scorn for her captors, filled them with surprise and awe. On the evening before we left she came into our room and, sitting down at the piano, began to play some Chopin; soon the Russian officers, and then the little Mongols, gathered round until there was scarcely room to move in the close-packed circle. With great skill and a fierce exultant pride she played the 'Revolutionary' study, the 'Death of Poland', the Polonaise and the first two Ballades. She ended with the 'Warszawianka' and the Polish National Anthem. Then, with a stiff little bow she wished us goodnight and, looking straight ahead of her, walked quietly through the ranks of applauding Russians.

On the afternoon of 21 January we left Zytno in a truck, escorted by the major and an armed guard. We spent that night in Radomsko, where we dined with two Russian colonels who noted with apparent sympathy Hudson's complaints against our treatment as prisoners instead of as allies. Prisoners, however, we remained and were even prevented from speaking to the owners of the house in which we slept.

Our status was made clearer the next day; in a town some sixty miles to the south-east we were handed over to a major of the NKVD and two subalterns, who kept us confined under guard for five days in a small and dirty room; only once were we allowed outside the house, when we were taken for a brief walk under the supervision of one of the subalterns, a supercilious young man with very close-set eyes who wore a Cossack hat and talked German to us in tones of studied insolence. We were firmly segregated from all contact with the Poles; our protests were disregarded and when we asked to speak to a senior officer the major simply laughed and told us to shut up. He was a swaggering, loud-voiced thug, clearly happy in his work.

The final humiliation came on 26 January. We were crammed into the back of a lorry with a dozen Russian soldiers and a glum, tubby little man with a red face who wore the blue uniform of General Vlasov's army; he seemed to be an officer and spoke fluent Russian. He sat on the floor in deep gloom, his head on his chest and his hands plunged in the pockets of his greatcoat. The soldiers addressed him as 'Vlasov' and from time to time prodded good-humouredly at his tummy with their rifles, which did nothing to cheer him up. A few miles from Czestochowa, which was our destination, the lorry stopped beside a long, low, stone building, and all but two of our escort climbed down.

'Come on, Vlasov!' they shouted cheerfully. 'This is you.'

I felt sorry for the little man as he climbed very slowly and deliberately back over the back of the truck, lost and lonely and afraid; his guards marched him through the gloomy prison gates while we drove on our way. I was beginning to feel quite sorry for myself.

The lorry stopped outside a grim stone building surrounded by a high wall with a gateway guarded by two sentries. The major and his Cossack subaltern led us through, across a courtyard and into a gloomy, dimly-lit stone passage with doors along one side. Here they handed us over to a sergeant, who signed a receipt for us and led us to one of the doors, unlocked it with an enormous key and motioned us inside; the guards urged us forward at the points of their tommy-guns. We stepped into the cell, the heavy door crashed to behind us and from the other side we heard the laughter of our captors.

'Well, boys, this is it,' sighed Solly-Flood. 'There's only one question now: which is it to be – Siberia or the firing squad? Personally, I'm not sure I wouldn't choose the firing squad.'

The cell was about twelve feet long, nine feet in breadth and twelve feet high, with a stone floor and bare, whitewashed walls; stout boards nailed across the window shut out the daylight, but a powerful naked bulb hung from the ceiling, throwing a hard, bright glare in our eyes day and night, for we had no means of turning it off. Against the wall on each side of the door was a triple tier of bunks with mattresses of straw covered by pieces of old sacking; they were alive with vermin. Through a slot in the door, cut at eye level and fitted with a shutter on the outside, the guards peered at us and mocked our helplessness.

'*Soyusniki!*' they jeered. 'How are you feeling – *allies?*'

Seated on the bunks we discussed our fate with indignation and anxiety, in which I am not ashamed to admit that anxiety predominated. We had the greatest confidence in Perkins and General Gubbins, but what could they do if the Russians chose to deny all knowledge of our existence, or to report us as dead? While we were debating, we heard, from a few yards down the corridor, a woman crying out in anger and despair; with horror we recognised the voice of the Home Army courier, married to a Polish officer, who had visited us with Siemienski and his daughter. We heard her give her name to the interrogating officer or NCO; then we all broke spontaneously into loud and random chatter, for we wished to hear no more . . .

At six in the evening we dined; that is to say, a pair of guards stood in the doorway and handed us each a piece of stale rye bread a little larger than the average restaurant roll, and a filth-encrusted tin canteen half-filled with luke-warm water in which floated a few grains of barley. This was the staple prison diet and we had it twice a day; when I asked the sergeant of the guard for some vodka he slammed the door with a volley of abuse which unfortunately I could not understand.

Worry, lice and the unrelenting glare from the ceiling kept me from sleep for most of the night; a thunderous banging on the door, accompanied by shouts and more abuse, roused us in the morning. The door was thrown open and a couple of guards with levelled tommy-guns ordered us outside. Led by an NCO and prodded on by the guards we were hurried along the passage to wash in the courtyard. On the way we met a group of Poles, among whom we recognised two who had been our fellow guests at the Wlynica party; we passed them without a sign. In the yard each of us was given a bucket of water, in which, after breaking the ice, we washed superficially and with haste, for the temperature at this early hour was well below freezing. After our wash we were escorted to the latrine, a shallow trench surmounted by a wooden pole and only too evidently never cleaned; we had to use it under the cynical stares of our guards. Then we were locked in our cell for the day.

Such was our prison life. The NKVD had taken over the building from the Gestapo only two days earlier – with all fittings. Luckily we still had two packs of cards and so were able to vary the monotony, as once before in Montenegro, with endless rubbers of bridge; I have never played the game since. Poker was impossible because we did not even have matches for chips; somebody suggested using lice, but that proved impracticable because they would never stay put.

From time to time, usually at night, we would be called out for interrogation; this burden fell principally upon Hudson, and upon Currie who accompanied him as interpreter, because Hudson had given all of us the strictest orders to answer no questions of any kind. He himself firmly and fearlessly refused to speak to any Russian officer below his own rank, which was full colonel; in the face of threats from the bullying major and his colleagues he remained stolidly silent, to their appeals to reason dourly indifferent. Finally, with our help he drafted a personal letter of protest to Marshal Koniev, which he persuaded the major to forward to Army headquarters.

We never knew whether this letter reached the marshal; but Hudson's intransigence impressed the Russians and our treatment began to improve. The food remained the same, but we were lodged in a larger, brighter cell upstairs with bars across the windows but with glass to let in the light. The junior officers who visited us were sometimes polite; we even overheard one of them telling an NCO that he considered our previous treatment scandalous. Finally Hudson was interviewed by a Russian colonel – or by an officer dressed as a colonel – who showered him with sympathy and wholly unconvincing excuses. The guards also became quite friendly; they were Asiatics who felt no embarrassment at being required to switch suddenly from their former hostility.

On 12 February our imprisonment ended. Escorted by the major, now a model of courtesy and consideration, and his two subalterns, we embarked in a Dakota of the Soviet Air Force and flew to Kiev, where we boarded a train to Moscow. Throughout the journey the major fussed over us like an old hen, anxious to make sure we had no chance of speaking to any civilians. At nine in the morning five days later we arrived at the Moscow terminus, to be whisked in an NKVD police van through the snow-bound streets to a grim, heavily guarded building which, to our total despair, we identified as the Lubianka; however, our stay there lasted only a few minutes before we were taken off to the Ministry of Foreign Affairs and handed over, after several hours' wait, to a captain of the British military mission. For the first time in a month we could rest easy.

We recognised, of course, that compared to the fate of most prisoners of the NKVD, like our poor Polish friends, our sufferings had been light – little more than humiliation, discomfort and near starvation – but the nagging uncertainty about our future, the ever-present threat of a firing squad or a labour camp had weighed heavily upon us all. I'm certainly glad I didn't know then what I learned after the war, that SOE parties taken by the Russians in Hungary had been liquidated on the spot.

The officers of the British military mission in Moscow were horrified at our appearance. First they sent us to their medical officer, who made us strip and, after a bath, thoroughly deloused us, burnt our old clothes and fitted us out with new battledress. Then they set out to compensate us for our past discomforts and so successful was their lavish hospitality that over the next two months I do believe we were in more danger of death from alcoholic poisoning than we had been from the Germans or the NKVD.

At no time did the Russians offer us either an explanation or an apology for our treatment. But we had a clue to their motives when we learned from some of the participants that the future of Poland had figured prominently on the agenda of the recent Yalta Conference; the Russians had made sure that no report from us should emerge in time to influence the discussions. Furthermore, I very much doubt if we would ever have been released but for the forceful and persistent efforts of General Gubbins, Perkins and Lord Selborne, who as Minister of Economic Warfare represented SOE in the War Cabinet.

It took two months for the British Embassy to get us the necessary exit visas, but on 17 March we boarded a Soviet Air Force Dakota for Baku and Tehran. In Cairo five days later I lunched with David Smiley, who told me McLean was on his way to Kashgar in Sinkiang and Julian Amery was now in Chungking as political adviser to General Carton de Wiart. Smiley was travelling to the Far East to drop into Thailand, where there was an incipient resistance movement against the Japanese.

'Why don't you come out there yourself,' he suggested, 'and join me?'

PART THREE

THE WORLD
AFTER WAR

PETER KEMP'S POSITIONS IN THAILAND AND LAOS, 1945–46

Chapter 1

T HE TWO COLONELS in our Far Eastern section in Baker Street gave me a cordial reception.

'We'll signal Smiley immediately,' they promised. 'Just give us a couple of weeks to arrange your transfer to this section and book you an air passage to India. Meanwhile, why don't you go on leave? You could probably do with it after that Russian prison. Here's Juliet, by the way, who's just back from our headquarters in Calcutta – she can probably give you a few useful tips.'

Juliet was a trim and self-possessed young woman with soft brown hair, faultless curves and inviting dark blue eyes. Most of her advice on the Far East proved inaccurate; she did, however, give me a few tips of more lasting value and made post-prison life suitably agreeable.

There was nothing more to keep me in England. Perkins had no need of me – he had in fact gone to Prague on a diplomatic assignment. My marriage, after three shaky years, had finally collapsed and now that I was single again – or in the process of becoming single – I had no right, even if I had had the wish, to stay at home while married men with families were fighting a particularly nasty war in South East Asia. I decided to spend my leave in Ireland with cousins of my mother who lived at Bray, south of Dublin.

'Splendid idea!' said the two colonels. 'Just the sort of change that will do you good.'

Neither they nor I had reckoned on Irish hospitality. On my return to London, feeling distinctly shaky, I approached my doctor for a prescription to restore my health. He wrote one out for me, which read simply, 'Say "No thank you", three times daily.'

Young man, I told myself, go East. A week later I was in India.

SOE in South East Asia was known as Force 136. As a part of South East Asia Command, or SEAC, its headquarters was in Kandy, where I went for my briefing on the situation in Siam. Although, under pressure from the Japanese, who had occupied the country in 1941, Siam had declared war on Britain, there was strong anti-Japanese feeling among the population; many high officials in the administration and senior officers of the armed services were working secretly for the Allies. A guerrilla organisation, the 'Free Thais', was already in existence; it was lying low for the moment but when the Allies mounted their attack on Singapore, which would be soon now that the Burma compaign was drawing to a successful close, the Free Thais, under SOE direction, would have a vital operational role to play in Siam against the Japanese lines of communication from their bases in Indochina to Malaya. British officers were needed to train and arm these guerrillas, and prepare airstrips and dropping zones in the jungle. Force 136 missions in Siam were under the command of Brigadier Victor Jaques, a lawyer who had practised in Bangkok before the war and continued to live there during the Japanese occupation, sheltered by the Regent in his palace; under the noses of the enemy he had maintained wireless contact with Calcutta and built up a formidable subversive organisation throughout the country.

The Siamese country section was in Calcutta where I would find Smiley. He had dropped into north-east Siam in the last days of May, but had been terribly burnt three weeks later by the premature explosion of one of SOE's new toys – an incendiary briefcase designed to burst into flames and destroy the documents inside in the event of enemy ambush or surprise; Smiley was packing documents into it when there was a short circuit and five pounds of blazing thermite spread all over him. For a week he lay in agony, unable to sleep, with first-, second- and third-degree burns, and a hole in one arm full of maggots; he was, of course, without medical attention. At last he was picked up by an aircraft of the Siamese Air Force and taken to an airstrip, where a Dakota landed and flew him to Calcutta. By this time he should be nearly well enough to return to the field.

It was the end of July before I reached Calcutta, where a sweaty, overworked and very irritable staff officer told me Smiley had gone to Simla to finish his convalescence as a guest of his old friends, the Wavells at Viceregal Lodge. In the same office I ran into my old friend John Hibberdine, who was expecting to drop into the south of Siam; it looked as if there was to be a pronounced Albanian background among the Siamese BLOs.

Forty-eight hours after my arrival I received an urgent summons from Smiley to go to Simla to discuss plans. It was accompanied by an invitation from Lady Wavell to stay at Viceregal Lodge. I flew to Delhi and reached Simla on the morning of 3 August. Although the marks of his burns were terribly evident, Smiley had made an astonishing recovery; strolling among the dark green, fir-covered hills, with the gigantic Himalayan snows nacreous and opalescent on the distant skyline, we planned in eager detail the course of our future operations in the field.

We very nearly did not get into the field. Hiroshima shattered our pleasant pipedream and sent us scurrying back to Calcutta as soon as Smiley had been passed fit by a medical board.

I was delighted to learn I was to drop in with an old friend, Rowland Winn, at this time a major in the 8th Hussars; I had known him during the Spanish Civil War when he was a correspondent for the *Daily Telegraph* on the Nationalist side. He too had been in Albania, where he dropped during the winter of 1943, unluckily breaking a leg on landing; it was a month before a doctor could reach him, during which time he lay in great pain and without anaesthetic in a shepherd's hut in the mountains.

He held strong and quite unshakeable views on such important subjects as bullfighting, of which he was an enthusiastic *aficionado*, and he had a deep love and knowledge of Spain and the Spaniards. He would argue his opinions with a pugnacity only matched by his personal courage. His manner seemed abrupt at times and his comments candid rather than tactful, but he was a generous and loyal friend; an uncompromising idealist, he also displayed a devastating wit that made him an indispensable companion in the trying circumstances of our work. In appearance he was short and stocky, with a pronounced limp from his parachute accident, and his dress was a curious blend of fastidious elegance and untidy neglect; thus, he seldom brushed his hair but neither in Albania nor Siam would he travel without a bottle of Trumper's aftershave. His independent manner and unorthodox turn-out sometimes shocked professional soldiers, but his fighting qualities won their admiration – as they were later to win him an MC in Korea.

We were flying from an airfield near Calcutta and as it was to be a daylight drop we took off at 11.30 in the morning at the end of the first week in August. I was feeling far from well, suffering from mild bacillary dysentery. Luckily, there was a kindly RAF doctor on the airfield who, seeing I was not prepared to go to hospital, dosed me heavily with sulphonamides and mepacrine; and during the flight Winn generously poured down my throat the entire contents of the flask of Courvoisier which he had brought from

Europe and carefully saved to drink in celebration of his arrival in Siam. Whether or not this combination of drugs and alcohol accorded with strict medical theory, it certainly alleviated the discomforts of emptying my stomach into the Bay of Bengal through a very draughty hole in the Liberator's tail section, and contemplating the hazards of monsoon flying among cumulo-nimbus clouds that could, and sometimes did, tear off an aircraft's wings. Force 136 missions in Siam owed much to these RAF crews, who were for a long time our only means of supply and flew in the most frightening weather conditions and across the most dangerous mountain and jungle country to drop us our stores.

Our dropping zone was an open stretch of ricefields, or *padi*, near the small town of Sakon Nakorn in north-east Siam, about fifty miles west of the Mekong river, which formed the frontier between Siam and French Indochina. A Free Thai reception committee would be waiting there to take us through the forest which covered most of the area. We had been warned to keep well clear of all Japanese troops because it was by no means certain they would surrender, even after Hiroshima and Nagasaki. If and when they did, however, Calcutta would signal us and we could turn to more peaceful and rewarding tasks, such as the liberation and relief of Allied prisoners of war in our area. I wasn't taking a wireless but Winn had a set and a first-class operator, the amiable Sergeant Lawson, known as 'Spider', a cheerful young man who had served with SOE in Greece.

From the Bay of Bengal we turned east in the afternoon to cross the jungle-covered hills between Burma and Siam. At six in the evening we were over the target and in the clear light our pilot soon picked up the smoke signals in the dropping ground. We got ready to jump. Since my last drop someone had invented a new way of leaving the aircraft – a wooden slide like those in swimming pools, which came down from the roof of the fuselage to the exit aperture. The parachutist swung his legs into the trough and lay there with his hands gripping the sides, and when the green light flashed he put his hands on his chest and slid out through the hole. When Winn, who was dropping first, took up his position on the slide I noticed his lips were moving, as though in prayer; he caught my eye and so I bent down to hear if perhaps he had some last message for me. What I heard was:

In the mangrove swamps where the python romps
There is peace from ten till two . . .

The light flashed green and he slid out of sight, still reciting.

A few minutes later I was floating down in the last of the evening light with an acute pain in my crotch, which had taken most of the strain when my parachute opened. Deciding that I wasn't irreparably damaged I looked towards the ground; for a nasty moment I thought I was going to land on the roof of a wooden hut, but I just missed it and landed with a tremendous splash in a paddy-field. Soaked to the skin and blinded with muddy water, I was helped to my feet and out of my harness by three smiling Thais. When I could see again I was rewarded by the spectacle of Rowland Winn, spattered all over with mud and paddy stalk, standing erect and adjusting with meticulous care the green and gold forage cap of the 8th Hussars which he had been carrying inside his bush shirt.

He introduced me to the leader of the reception committee, a young Siamese policeman who, under the pseudonym of Kong, held a captain's commission in the British Army. Kong led us to the hut on whose roof I had so nearly landed, where the packages and containers were now assembled.

'Please sort out your kit as quickly as possible,' he asked us speaking in quick, jerky sentences. 'We ride from here ten kilometres through the forest. There are Japanese around; their patrols are very active still and last night they burnt a village only a mile away.'

Mounted on small, sturdy ponies we rode across the paddy towards the forest; the four of us, accompanied by Kong and another Siamese, went ahead while the rest followed with our kit. These Siamese ponies – all of them were stallions because, so Smiley told us later, it was considered bad form to ride a mare – moved like Andalusian horses, with a curious gait that was a blend of walk, trot and gallop. They went at a surprisingly fast pace and, for a short person, were comfortable to ride; but my long legs reached almost to the ground and, when I forgot to keep them clear of the pony's feet, received some painful kicks.

It was already dark when we entered the forest, but the half moon shining through the trees cast a pale, dappled light on the muddy track that wound through the tangled undergrowth. Our horses splashed, and sometimes swam, through deep pools and across swollen streams; once we crossed a creek on a wooden bridge whose posts and railings alone showed above the water, and once we swam a broad river. Twice only did we halt: when the unhappy Lawson was thrown from his pony into a dark and slimy puddle, and when Winn's forage cap was swept off by an overhanging branch. Otherwise we rode in silence at a steady pace, inhaling the heavy, scented warmth of the sodden forest while glow-worms and fireflies flashed in the misty darkness; at intervals the rain showered upon us, cool and soothing.

At ten o'clock we came to a village in a clearing where we were to spend the night; the headman, surrounded by a curious and whispering crowd of men and women, gave us a graceful *namasti* greeting and led us to a long, narrow wooden building raised on piles to a height of twelve or fifteen feet above the sodden ground and approached by a flight of steps leading to an open veranda. This was the schoolhouse, where we were to sleep.

In construction and design it resembled many other houses in north-east Siam. From the veranda we passed into a large room, bare of furniture except for a table and benches down the centre; the table was laid for a meal and mattresses were spread against one of the walls. The floor was spotlessly clean, the boards scrubbed almost to a polish. Food was set before us – cold boiled rice with pieces of chicken, meat balls, eggs and chillies; also a bottle of what Kong called 'Siamese whisky', a potent rice spirit with a sour, not unpleasant flavour. Already comatose from illness and fatigue I could not bring myself to eat or drink more than the mouthful that politeness demanded; the effects of the doctor's pills and Winn's brandy had long worn off, leaving me weak, sick and feverish. During the last hour of the journey I had been barely conscious and at the end unable to dismount without help. Winn and Lawson undressed me, laid me on a mattress and heaped blankets upon my shivering, sweating body.

We rested all next day; by the evening, although still weak from loss of blood, I was beginning to recover – and we had to keep moving. Over the next two days, we made good progress through the forest and finally arrived at a wide expanse of water, a river in flood, where *pirogues* – hollowed tree-trunks, each one a masterpiece of skilful workmanship – awaited us. We were paddled silently over the surface of the water, the half-submerged forest around us reminding me of pictures I had seen of the Florida Everglades; after two miles we landed at a house beside the water and had lunch.

Kong had received a message from Smiley saying a lorry would be awaiting us that afternoon about a mile from this house; while we rested he sent a scout to look for it. I reflected that, whether or not the Japanese surrendered, we would be pretty safe from them as long as we stayed in the forest. Our Siamese friends made extensive use of scouts and their intelligence systems seemed excellent; we ought to have plenty of warning of Japanese movements and in this vast area of forest we would have no difficulty in hiding.

Kong's scout returned to say that the lorry was waiting. We set off on foot, but mid-afternoon in the tropics is not a good time for a walk, especially during the monsoon; and so when an old man driving a bullock cart offered us a lift we climbed up thankfully beside him. Our escort of guerrillas trudged along on either side, apparently quite content.

We found Smiley's truck, a bright red Chevrolet, parked beside a rough track that ran from the verge of the forest through a wide expanse of waterlogged paddy-field. We climbed into the back, where we were soon joined by the twenty men of our escort, and tried to stave off bruises and abrasions as the vehicle lurched and plunged in the ruts and pot-holes. At length we came on to the straight, brick-coloured *piste* that was the road between Sakon Nakorn and the rail-head at Udaun; Japanese military transport used this road and police patrols were frequent, and so our guards made us lie on the floor and covered us with a tarpaulin. After a quarter of an hour the lorry stopped and we were allowed to emerge from hiding, sweaty and half-suffocated. We were hustled off the road on to a forest track, which led us in a few moments to a village. There we found Smiley with his wireless operator, Sergeant Collins, and a wiry, lightly built Siamese with a gaunt, tormented face, whom Smiley introduced to me as Pluto.

I had already heard of this man. Tiang Sirikand, alias Pluto, was one of the founders of the Free Thai movement and its leader in north-east Siam, where he had been born of an influential family about thirty-five years before; Parliamentary deputy for Sakon Nakorn, close friend and staunch supporter of the Regent, Pridi Panomyong, he had given valuable service to the Allies and in particular to Smiley, who liked and admired him for his kindness and integrity. He was a forceful if humourless personality, with great powers of organisation; his enemies accused him of communist sympathies, I think unfairly.

His grim, swarthy face relaxed in a smile of unusual warmth as he greeted us and, turning to me, remarked:

'Smiley tells me it is your birthday today. We have arranged a celebration for you.'

In the excitement and fatigue of the last few days I had forgotten that this was indeed my thirtieth birthday, 19 August 1945.

'Now,' Smiley told us, 'I want Rowly to go to Naung Khai, north-west of here, and Peter to go to Nakorn Panom, to the east. Both towns are on the Mekong river, which, as you know, forms the frontier between Siam and the province of Laos in Indochina; each town is the capital of a province. You'll meet the two provincial governors here tonight and leave with them tomorrow; I myself am going to Sakon Nakorn with Pluto. Peter, you'll be the worst off, having no wireless contact; but Calcutta have promised to drop in a set and operator for you as soon as they can.

'I'm afraid that, until we get orders from Calcutta, I can only give you the vaguest instructions. Find out all you can about your districts and about the places across the river in Laos – that means Vientiane for Rowly, and for Peter Thakhek and Savannakhet further south; especially get all the dope you can about Japanese prisoners of war. We can keep in touch through the Siamese, who can be trusted not to open our letters – unlike the Albanian partisans.'

At seven o'clock, after toasting our reunion with a few whiskies, we walked over to the schoolhouse for my birthday party. If I describe it in detail it is because it was typical of almost every party I attended in north-east Siam – and they were many, for the Siamese are a friendly and laughter-loving people. A great crowd of men and girls was gathered there to greet us, and a roar of welcome hailed our entry into the large classroom, where there were long tables loaded with food and drink. Seeing the roast sucking pigs, ducks, chickens, plates heaped with meat, vegetables and fruit, and the huge tureens of rice, I found it hard to believe that we were in a small village in a rain-soaked tropical forest.

Before dining we were led out on to the veranda, where stood several great earthenware jars filled with rice beer; a thick layer of rice floated on the top of each jar and from each protruded several thin bamboo drinking straws; the jars were colloquially known as *changs* (elephants) and the bamboos denoted their tusks. All this we were told by Pluto, who, beaming with enthusiasm, made us all drink plentifully from each *chang*; the beer tasted slightly sweet and deceptively mild.

On the veranda we met the governors of Naung Khai and Nakorn Panom. The former was small and slightly built with an impressively quiet and friendly manner; the latter, named Ta Win, was taller, broader, stouter and more effusive than his colleague. He had very thick lips and an excited, bubbly way of speaking. Although he knew a little English, he had with him his interpreter, Sang-a, an emaciated little man with a hoarse, nervous giggle and a twitch, a little too anxious to please everyone.

We dined standing at the tables, as at a buffet, and helping ourselves. There was a remarkable variety of food; in addition to what I have mentioned there was pork, water buffalo, barking deer, fish, eels, snails, frogs, bamboo shoots, coconuts and every kind of tropical fruit; and there were small dishes of a chilli sauce so powerful that anything flavoured with it turned to fire in the mouth. While we were eating, girls brought us glasses of *lao kao*, a fierce rice spirit, which they offered with a charming little bow. As soon as our glasses were empty they were refilled, the girls taking it in turns to serve each of us; Siamese women are uncommonly pretty, and in the face of their enticing smiles and mischievous dark eyes I found myself unable to refuse, with the result that my head was swimming and my eyes were a trifle glazed by the end of the meal. It was foolish of me, so soon after dysentery, to drink so much; but the warmth of my welcome made me forget my illness.

I suffered no more than a hangover from that night's intoxication. Smiley comforted me.

'Don't worry. You're pretty well expected to get plastered on these occasions. I've often enough had to be carried home to bed myself.'

Chapter 2

THE INHABITANTS OF the fifteen provinces of north-east Thailand have close ties of race, language and culture with the Laotians on the other side of the Mekong, and many have relatives on both sides of the river. As a result, commerce and transit across the nominal frontier were at this time almost unrestricted.

The area is a plateau averaging five hundred feet above sea level, most of it covered in forest of a type which geographers call 'dry monsoon forest' and the Siamese call *padeng*; this forest assumes in the dry season a stark and lifeless appearance because the trees shed their foliage, and only the undergrowth retains a certain tarnished green. It is for the most part a forlorn and desolate region, whether sodden under the monsoon rains or dusty and desiccated in the winter months, monotonous to the eye, with scarcely a break in the colourless forest landscape save for the few acres of paddy-fields near the villages. Only under bright moonlight have I seen it beautiful.

All but three per cent of the population lived in villages, most of which lay some distance from the road and were approached by tortuous tracks through the forest. The Vietnamese, many of whom lived and worked on both sides of the river, inspired in Thai and Lao alike a strong and fully justified fear and hatred whose roots stretched far back in history. Smiley told me that Pluto's guerrillas shot any Vietnamese they caught, suspecting them of spying for the Japanese – in this connection it is worth remembering that Ho Chi Minh, like the Indonesian Sukarno, received a high decoration from the Japanese. The Chinese, on the other hand, were tolerated if not greatly loved; they owned the hotels and restaurants and, along with the Indians, the shops.

Nakorn Panom in the dry season was a clean-looking little town; but now under the monsoon the first impression was of damp, mud and gloom, alleviated by the satisfaction I felt at having arrived safely in my operational area. I had travelled there in a rickety old bus with Governor Ta Win, the interpreter Sang-a and a small party of guerrillas. On the way we had passed several lorries full of Japanese troops, who paid no attention to us but looked straight ahead of them with blank expressions on their faces.

The town itself consisted of a muddy main street lined on either side with shops and running north and south beside the Mekong, with a few small sidestreets leading down to the river or dwindling away westward into country tracks. To the west the ground rose gently from the river bank and the town, past open fields and scattered houses to a small landing strip on the verge of the forest; on the other two sides were banana plantations and coconut palms. The Wat lay half a mile to the south; about the same distance to the north lived the Annamese, earning their livelihood chiefly on the river. There was one hotel, owned of course by Chinese.

We turned left in the main street and bumped slowly through the pot-holes, past the stucco fronts of the governor's office and 'Hall of Justice' to the governor's house, a yellow, plaster-fronted, two-storey building in European style, with a cool, green garden shaded by coconut palms. It faced on to the Mekong, at this season nearly a mile wide and flowing swiftly over hidden sandbanks in a series of swirling eddies and whirlpools. On the other side the white houses of Thakhek showed clearly, picked out amid a blaze of green. Behind them rose a range of dark, jungle-covered mountains, grim and threatening, their summits swathed in black, grey-streaked clouds, lit at intervals by jagged, purple flashes of lightning; the thunder rolled to our ears across the mud-brown river.

The day after my arrival the governor took me to the officials' club and introduced me to his assistants: the deputy governor, the captain of police and his lieutenant, the sheriff, the harbourmaster, chief customs officer – there was a duty on goods arriving from Indochina – and the schoolmaster, a quiet, shy little man who introduced himself modestly as the 'Director of Humanity'. The governor decided it was safe for me to set up my own headquarters. Japanese troops seldom came to Nakorn Panom – only when crossing the Mekong from Thakhek; we would have plenty of warning of their arrival and there was a company of guerrillas in the town. And so he had prepared for my occupation the officials' rest house, a large bungalow standing on the open ground that rose to the west of the town. Like most government buildings it had walls of cream-washed laterite, with a cool, wide veranda that led to a long dining room and several bedrooms. Behind the house was a small airstrip. Commanding a wide view across Nakorn Panom and the river to Thakhek and the mountains of Laos, it was an ideal headquarters and I moved in there the same evening. The governor gave me a small staff of servants, assisted by convicts from the local prison to ensure my comfort, and a guard of two policemen and four guerrillas for my security.

During my first week I was able to gain some idea of the situation on the other side of the river. I sent agents to Thakhek, men who had relatives over there; and I drove with Governor Ta Win to Mukdahan, some fifty miles south of Nakorn Panom, on the Siamese bank of the Mekong, to brief others to bring me news from Savannakhet. My inquiries established that there was in Thakhek a number of French civilian internees but no prisoners of war; that there was a force of French and Laotian guerrillas living in the jungle south of Thakhek, commanded by a certain Captain Tavernier; that there was a similar force near Savannakhet under a Lieutenant Quinquenel – and that all were in urgent need of food, money and medical supplies. I also received a great deal of information that turned out to be false. The problem of sifting true from inaccurate reports was one I was never able to resolve the whole time I was on the frontier; I was at the mercy of my agents, who turned out as often as not to be double agents.

This question of double agents became more difficult when the struggle began between the French and the Viet-minh, because the Siamese, on whose advice I was largely dependent for my recruiting, were hostile to the French cause as well as to the Viet-minh.

I was soon obliged to disobey my orders to stay underground. On 25 August the police lieutenant brought me a message that two Frenchmen in Thakhek had been condemned to death by the Japanese and were about to be executed. To save their lives I felt I must act at once. Calling on the governor I asked him for transport across to Thakhek, intending to present myself to the Japanese commander, a Captain Nakajima, and dissuade him from carrying out the sentence. The governor and the police captain, who was with him, implored me not to go; almost in tears they protested that if anything happened to me the consequences to themselves, and perhaps to their country, would be disastrous. I could, they pointed out, achieve as much and probably more through a letter, which they promised to deliver in Thakhek immediately.

Their arguments seemed reasonable and so I abandoned my original idea – not unwillingly, I may add. Instead, I wrote to Captain Nakajima, warning him that he would be held personally responsible for the safety of his prisoners and asking to be allowed to visit them. The governor added a letter of his own. He agreed that if we did not receive a satisfactory reply by the following morning I might go in person. I also relayed the news to Smiley, who had moved from Sakon Nakorn to Ubon, about a hundred and fifty miles down the Mekong.

I spent an anxious day. At about seven o'clock in the evening I was sitting on my veranda watching the green and lilac colours on the hills of Laos deepen to purple and indigo in the twilight; at intervals the cackle of a gecko lizard on the ceiling broke in upon the stillness to jar the rhythm of my thoughts. I sprang eagerly to my feet as a police lieutenant approached with the two messengers who had delivered my letter to Thakhek. They brought me an answer from Captain Nakajima, written in good English and courteously phrased, regretting that until he received instructions from his superiors he must decline my request for an interview and for the release of the prisoners; but he assured me that in the meantime they would come to no harm. After a further exchange of letters, in which I was joined by Smiley, who paid me a visit the next day, the two condemned men were released from close arrest.

Dining with the governor one evening I met an American, Dr Holliday, a Presbyterian missionary who had lived in Siam for fifteen years before the war and previously for thirteen years in China. Having left the country before the Japanese occupation he had dropped back there in April to form an intelligence network for the American OSS (Office of Strategic Services – later the CIA) and he now held the rank of major in the US Army. He was one of the very few OSS officers in Siam, this theatre of operations being the agreed responsibility of the British South East Asia Command. A stocky, well-built man in his early fifties, with a bronzed, square face, a strong jaw and a quiet, friendly manner, he was held in great affection and respect by the Siamese people, whose language he spoke fluently.

He explained to me the reason behind the governor's anxiety that I should not cross the river.

'These people are terribly afraid for their independence. They feel they're in bad odour with the Allies – even though it wasn't their fault they were sold out to the Nips. They are responsible for your safety and they think that if at this critical time something should happen to you, or to any British officer in Thailand, they would lose their independence.'

'But surely if I put it in writing that I take full responsibility myself, that I've gone *against* their advice . . . ?'

'That makes no difference. They still feel they would be blamed.'

It was becoming difficult to avoid the Japanese on my tour of the area; it also seemed unnecessary. While visiting the sheriff of Mukdahan I was embarrassed to find myself in a street crowded with their troops. I received some dirty looks from the officers; by the men I was ignored.

On 29 August Smiley passed me the codeword 'Goldfish'; on 2 September came the news of the Japanese surrender. By that time Japanese forces in my area had moved south to Ubon, where Smiley immediately found his hands full. Outside the town there was a large prisoner-of-war camp, full of British, Australians and Dutch. Although the efficient and tactful administration of Colonel Toosey, famous for his efforts to make life in the camps endurable (he was later decorated), relieved him from responsibility inside the camp, Smiley had the task of receiving and sorting the daily parachute drops which supplied it, and of ensuring the smooth cooperation of the Siamese civil and military authorities which was so necessary for its welfare.

Another of his duties was to supervise the disarming of some eleven thousand Japanese and the shooting of their horses, which were in terrible condition, having been shamefully neglected by their owners. He was astonished, therefore, to see the Japanese soldiers in tears as they shot their horses, and then to watch them remove their caps and bow for two minutes before filling in the graves, which they covered with flowers.

Two days after my arrival at Nakorn Panom I saw a Dakota flying low over the opposite bank of the Mekong and soon afterwards I heard it had dropped two French parachutists, a man and a girl. On 29 August I received a letter from a Lieutenant François Klotz, saying he was in difficulties and would like to meet me. Through the governor I arranged a rendezvous in a small village up river, where the governor would take me in his launch to meet Klotz. Two days later we set out after lunch in the launch, an ancient craft with a canvas canopy on metal stanchions to protect us from the sun; it puffed and spluttered noisily up the swollen, tawny river, making slow progress against the strong currents. We reached our rendezvous in the sweltering heat of mid-afternoon and waited on the veranda of a hut while the launch went to fetch Klotz from the far bank.

Half an hour later he appeared, a dark, thick-set young man of about twenty-five with strong, heavy features and a sombre expression; his speech was slow, his voice hoarse but soft, his command of English nearly perfect. By birth he was Alsatian; he was very tired.

He belonged to a French organisation similar to our Force 136.

Together with his wireless operator – 'who is a she', he explained – he had been dropped by the Dakota we had seen on the 22nd, into the hills about ten miles north of Thakhek.

'For the first few days we lived in a cave,' he told me. 'But now we have moved to a village. Since our arrival my operator has been unable to make contact with our base at Rangoon, although she has been trying six skeds a day. She is very disheartened. Now my hand generator is broken and I cannot recharge my batteries.

'On the 27th I went to Thakhek – in uniform of course – to ask the Japanese to let me see the French prisoners. The Japanese commander was very correct – gave me lunch but would not let me see the prisoners. He mentioned your name, but without comment. Afterwards he drove me in a car outside the town and I went back to my village.'

He added that there were very few Japanese left in Thakhek and none, except deserters, in the country around.

It seemed to me that Klotz would be much more comfortable and able to operate more effectively if he set up his headquarters in my house. The governor readily agreed and promised to charge his batteries at Nakorn Panom; in any case I was expecting a wireless very shortly. We arranged, therefore, that Klotz and his operator should join me in the course of the next few days.

On 3 September I had a message from Smiley asking me to meet him at Ubon, where he had a wireless set and operator for me. In the evening I had a visit from a Lieutenant de Fay, one of Tavernier's officers who commanded a group of Laotian guerrillas in a village on the Mekong above Thakhek. He gave me a clear picture of the situation on that side of the river.

Thakhek, although the capital of the Laotian province of Cammon, contained a very large Vietnamese – or Annamite, as the French called them – population, which in fact outnumbered the Laos; in the countryside, on the other hand, there were comparatively few Annamites, for they tended to congregate where there was some form of industry to give them employment. There was no love lost between the two races. The majority of Laos stood by the French, whereas the Annamites detested them and, having collaborated actively with the Japanese, were now organising themselves into a communist movement, with a declared intention of expelling the French from the whole of Indochina; this movement was the Viet-minh. Now the Annamites, having obtained large supplies of arms from the Japanese, would, after the departure of the latter, control Thakhek. Tavernier's troops were too weak and poorly armed to drive them out; indeed, they would be lucky to hold their own.

Tension was increasing. The Viet-minh were mustering their forces and had already attacked isolated groups of Franco-Laotian guerrillas, protesting that it was the French who were attacking them. Most serious of all at the moment was the position of the French internees in the town, some forty men, women and children who had been confined in the convent under Japanese guard. But now Captain Nakajima had withdrawn his guards, leaving the prisoners in the care of the *Chaokhoueng*, the Laotian provincial governor. This official had no means of protecting them, being himself at the mercy of the Viet-minh, whose leaders – or 'delegates', as they chose to style themselves – had declared their intention of holding the internees as hostages against the French. The attitude of the Viet-minh towards these defenceless people became so menacing that one of the women wrote a letter to de Fay, which he showed me, imploring him to intervene at once.

As a Frenchman de Fay could do nothing; and I could do little enough. However, I immediately wrote to the Annamese delegates warning them not to harm the French civilians; I gave myself the arrogant title of 'Allied Representative at Nakorn Panom', for I knew that the Viet-minh were hoping to enlist Anglo-American support. I wrote to Captain Nakajima, asking him to put some troops at the disposal of the *Chaokhoueng*. Clearly the only solution would be to transport all the internees to the Siamese side of the river, where the governor readily agreed to receive them. This was a situation which I had to discuss with Smiley. I resolved to go to Ubon next day.

A message to Pluto secured me a car and driver for the journey; early the following evening I reached the large wooden bungalow on the outskirts of Ubon where Smiley had established his headquarters. Impressed with the gravity of the situation he agreed to follow me to Nakorn Panom and accompany me across the river to try and evacuate the internees.

In the morning I went with him to visit the prisoner-of-war camp. Talking to those men who had suffered so much, I was filled with admiration for their high morale; for the calm, detached manner in which they talked of their years of misery, overwork and starvation, and described the brutalities of their guards, particularly the Koreans – the savage beatings and the horrors of water torture. They seemed to feel no bitterness, no urge to indulge in reprisals against their former gaolers.

Among the Japanese some discipline still remained; the officers, who took orders from Smiley, continued to exact obedience from their men. But in the evenings there was a good deal of drunkenness among all ranks; a few days before my visit the colonel commanding

Japanese troops in Ubon, who was unpopular, was badly bitten by an intoxicated private in a brothel.

I left Nakorn Panom after lunch, reinforced at last by a wireless set and operator, and a codename with which to preface all my messages to Calcutta – 'Sackcloth'. Jock Rork, the operator, was a tall, rangy, red-haired sergeant in the Royal Corps of Signals with nearly twenty years of service behind him. A man of independent and contentious character, with more than a streak of obstinacy, he was expert at his job, warm-hearted and fearless. We travelled in a three-ton lorry which Smiley had given me and reached Nakorn Panom after dark. There I found Klotz and his operator, Edith Fournier, a cheerful, fresh-faced, buxom young woman clothed like the rest of us in olive-green battledress and jungle boots, and wearing the badges of a second lieutenant of the French Army. They had arrived that morning.

I was awakened next day by a messenger with a letter from Captain Tavernier, written from the village of Ban Tung, about twenty miles south of Thakhek. He told me that he had been appointed civil and military governor of the province of Cammon, with a task of restoring order there as quickly as possible, and asked me to help in persuading the Japanese commander in Thakhek to allow him and his troops to occupy the town immediately; to this end he suggested a meeting with me and named a village on the far bank of the Mekong, where some of his men would await me and take me to his headquarters. He also begged me to send him arms, medical supplies – especially for malaria and dysentery – and money, all of which he needed urgently.

The Japanese had occupied French Indochina in 1940 with the acquiescence of the Vichy authorities who at that time ruled the colony; the French Colonial Army had orders not to resist. Until March 1945 the Japanese were content to use the country as a base, leaving the administration in the hands of the French, whose soldiers retained their arms. But on 9 March they struck. They arrested every French official and officer they could lay hands on; and they murdered the great majority of those they caught. Pockets of the *Armée Coloniale* resisted and were overwhelmed. With a few exceptions the Annamese units surrendered or deserted; but the Laotian troops remained loyal to their officers and went with them into the mountains and the jungle to continue resistance. Short of arms and ammunition, with little food and less medical equipment, plagued by every form of tropical disease, those gallant little men stood by their French officers and NCOs. They could do little actively against the Japanese; they could hardly remain alive. But they survived.

Tavernier's needs were urgent; but more important was the

danger threatening the French civilians in Thakhek. I wrote back to Tavernier, saying I would meet him as soon as our hands were free of this problem.

Smiley arrived on 6 September, and the following afternoon he and I, with Klotz and the governor, crossed the river to Thakhek in the governor's launch; the governor had been so worried by the situation in Thakhek that he had insisted on accompanying us there. At the residency the *Chaokhoueng* was waiting, an unhappy little figure in a white shirt and baggy pantaloons of purple silk. After a short talk, which made us realise the poor man was much too frightened to intervene with the Viet-minh on behalf of his French charges, he agreed to take us to see the internees.

Ignoring the groups of scowling Annamites who sauntered through the streets with slung rifles, we came, after a walk of ten minutes, to the convent, a long, low, wooden building beside a white-washed chapel. A thin, fair woman of about forty came out on to the veranda to greet us; this was Madame Collin, widow of the French resident who had been beheaded in March. She was the acknowledged spokeswoman of the rest by virtue not only of position but of character, for she was a person of indestructible serenity and kindliness.

We were at once surrounded by a pathetic throng of women and children, wretchedly clad in worn and shapeless garments little better than rags; they threw their arms around us, clasped and held our hands or simply stared in apathetic or bewildered disbelief. Some, in an agony of fear, called on us to protect them from the Annamese; others kept silence, only betraying by the tears that poured down their cheeks and the sobs that shook their bodies the desolation of their hearts. All of them begged for news of their husbands; we had to say we knew nothing, for we could not tell them that we believed all their men to be dead.

There were eighteen women and fourteen children – boys and girls between the ages of four and fourteen; there were five nuns, whose steadfast faith and devotion had sustained them all through the past grim months, and there were some forty Eurasian orphans whom they had taken under their care. All these lived, sleeping on the floor, in a long dormitory that had been, I think, the refectory.

Living with the priest, in a room adjoining the chapel, were three men, all civilians and very lucky to be alive. One of them, the electrician in charge of the power station, had been under sentence of death. On 22 August the Dakota which dropped Klotz had flown over Thakhek to drop leaflets. The electrician unwisely waved to it, was seen by an Annamite and reported to the Japanese; that evening he was arrested, together with his wife and child, and taken by car to the fourth kilometre stone on the road south of the town. Realising that he was going to be executed he warned his family to run for safety as soon as the car drew up; they leaped out and ran towards the jungle but the woman and child were quickly recaptured and shot. They were buried beside the kilometre stone. He himself wandered for two days in the forest until, driven by hunger and exhaustion, he approached the hut of an Annamese charcoal-burner and begged for help; the Annamite, after hacking him about the arms with a machete, handed him over to the Japanese, who were going to kill him when our letters reached Captain Nakajima. The slashes on his arms were open to the bone.

'I think, gentlemen, you have only just arrived in time,' said Madame Collin in her quiet voice. 'The Annamite guards who have replaced the Japanese have become extremely menacing. They show us their knives and make gestures of cutting our throats.'

We looked across the courtyard to the gateway, where a group of villainous-looking young men in grey topees squatted in the dust, their rifles between their knees, while others wandered up and down casting furtive glances in our direction.

'We'll go and see the Annamese delegates now,' announced Smiley. 'Then we'll take all these people across to Nakorn Panom tonight.'

While he and Klotz were conducted to the delegates, and the *Chaokhoueng* and Governor Ta Win went to the quay to organise boats and crews for the evacuation, I stayed at the convent in case the guards should take advantage of their absence to make trouble.

It was getting dark when Smiley returned to say that all was ready and the governor, Ta Win, awaited us by the river with boats and crews for the evacuation. Under the direction of Madame Collin and the nuns the packing began in a bustle of excitement and relief. Suddenly there was an interruption: we heard a bark of orders as a Japanese patrol marched through the gate and halted beneath the veranda. An NCO beckoned to Smiley, Klotz and me. As we reached the bottom of the steps, the patrol fell in on either side of us and at an order marched us away amid the despairing wails of the women. We turned and waved to them, shouting that we should soon return, but the Japanese jammed their rifles in our backs and snarled at us to keep moving. Several of them were obviously drunk.

We marched to a house on the waterfront, up a flight of stairs and into a bare room furnished only with a desk, at which sat a young Japanese captain with straight, dark hair and a handsome, almost Latin cast of face. He bowed to us and introduced himself as Captain Nakajima. In jerky, broken English he explained that he had not yet received the precise terms of the surrender treaty and that without orders from his superiors he could not let us evacuate the French civilians.

Angrily we protested against the manner of our arrest and the behaviour of his patrol. Smiling thinly, the captain apologised and promised that the offending soldiers would be punished; but although he would place no further restrictions on our movements, he bluntly refused to let us remove the French. Smiley undertook to get him the necessary orders from the Japanese colonel at Ubon; meanwhile he demanded that the Annamese guards at the convent be replaced at once by Japanese and that the captain hold himself responsible for the safety of its inmates. Nakajima agreed and, while we waited, detailed the guards and ordered them to escort us back. Gravely he bowed us out.

'Obviously,' growled Smiley, 'he's been tipped off by the Anna-mese and is scared of them because they outnumber his men.'

Back at the convent we watched the mounting of the Japanese guard and the expulsion of the Annamese, who left with surprising docility. But our troubles were not yet over. A commotion on the veranda brought us running, to find a drunken Japanese soldier trying to tear a wristwatch off one of the nuns. Smiley, who arrived first, tried to remonstrate with him, whereupon the Japanese, an ugly look on his face, drew his bayonet; I felt for my pistol. At that moment the corporal of the guard walked up to us, took the soldier by the arm and spun him round, hissing at him angrily; the soldier lurched and muttered, but the corporal slapped his face and continued to slap until the man staggered away, grunting.

'Stay here,' ordered Smiley, 'I'm going back to report this to the captain.'

A quarter of an hour later he returned with a grim-faced Nakajima and another patrol; the offending soldier, after a further bout of slapping, was marched away, his place being taken by an evidently sober guard. Smiley and Klotz returned to Nakorn Panom, the former on his way to Ubon to secure the necessary authority for the release of the refugees, the latter to ask Calcutta for an immediate drop of food, clothing and medical supplies on my airfield. I remained in the convent – where I stayed with the priest, who opened two bottles of his Communion wine in my honour.

We had heard that there were French families stranded at some tin mines twenty-five miles north of Thakhek. Klotz had managed to borrow from the *Chaokhoueng* an ancient, dilapidated Citroën, and he and I set out in it for the mines a couple of days later. Its engine popped and spluttered indignantly as we drove through the neat, shady streets of Thakhek and out on the laterite-surfaced *Route Coloniale* 13. After following the course of the Mekong we turned due north and began to climb into the hills, where the road ran through thick, overgrown forest, intersected by numerous tracks and varied occasionally by bright green patches of paddy or banana plantations; ahead of us the distant mountaintops shone blue and clear on the horizon, with patches of jungle on their lower slopes glowing emerald in the sunlight.

We met several convoys of lorries carrying armed Annamese to Thakhek. Each truck displayed a large red flag and the young men riding behind gave us the clenched fist salute as we passed. Approaching the mines we were stopped several times by control posts, also decorated with the red flag and manned by youths in grey pith helmets; when I said I was a British officer they let us through without argument.

It was getting on in the afternoon when we reached the small cluster of bungalows that formed the living quarters of the mine officials. As we stepped out of the car a grey-haired Frenchwoman ran towards us gesticulating and sobbing piteously; her face was ravaged with lines of despair. Taking us each by the arm she led us into one of the houses. Lying on a bed, wearing only a nightdress, was a girl of seventeen or eighteen; she was very pretty, but her face was sunken and waxy, her dark eyes hollow and lustreless.

'My daughter,' said the woman. 'Look!'

She lifted the girl's nightdress and pointed to the bluish puncture of a bullet wound about two inches below the navel. The girl looked at us without speaking, without interest. Her mother led us to another room, where lay a man of about fifty, a sallow death's-head who gazed at us in silence, but with terror in his eyes.

'In God's name,' cried Klotz, 'what has happened?'

Pulling herself together the woman told us the dreadful story. She and her daughter had lived alone in this house since March, when the Japanese had taken her husband; the wounded man lived in the next bungalow with his wife. On 22 August a party of Japanese, probably deserters, had burst in upon them, looted their houses and, in a fit of wanton cruelty, shot their daughter in the stomach with a pistol, put two bullets into their neighbour and murdered his wife.

'Obviously we must move them at once to Nakorn Panom,' said Klotz. 'But how can we take two badly wounded people, as well as this woman and ourselves, in a small Citroën? They won't survive the journey.'

'Let's try to borrow or hire something from the Annamese,' I suggested. 'Even a truck would do and they have plenty of those. I know they aren't friendly, but there must be somebody among them with a spark of humanity.'

I was wrong. We tried for an hour, approaching every lorry we saw and begging at least the kindness of a lift for one of the wounded and one of ourselves. At best we met with indifference, at worst hostility.

'We can't leave them here, François,' I said. 'There's no alternative but to take a chance with the Citroën. Let's ask them how they feel about it.'

'But of course, gentlemen,' whispered the girl. She gave us a charming smile; only her eyes betrayed her fear.

'As for me,' murmured the man, 'I care nothing if only I can get out of here.'

They told us that there were some half-dozen more French civilians at the tin mines of Boneng, a few miles up the road. At the moment we could do nothing for them, but we resolved to come back with sufficient transport as soon as possible.

Gently we carried the girl into the car and placed her on the front seat; she made no complaint, despite her obvious suffering. Klotz took the wheel and the rest of us squeezed in behind. It was nearly dusk when we started; before we had covered five miles we were in darkness. The lights made a faint, ineffective glow.

'This battery is *kaput*,' Klotz called over his shoulder. 'I can hardly see the road, and if we run off it and have to stop we'll never get her started again. We must look for a villa, or even a hut, where we can lie up for the night. In the morning we can find villagers who will push her until she starts.'

We drove at barely more than walking pace for another two miles until, across a paddy-field on the left of the road, we saw a light that seemed to indicate some dwelling.

'Keep the engine running, François, while I go and see if we can stay there.'

Although not usually a provident person I had remembered to bring a lamp. I made my way along a narrow path beside the field until I came to a small hut on the verge of the forest. A wiry, middle-aged Lao came down the steps carrying a torch of flaming brushwood. I pointed to the road and beckoned him to follow me, which he did without the least sign of surprise. When we reached the car he listened quietly while the wounded girl's mother, who spoke his language, explained our trouble. Then he smiled and she translated his reply.

'He says we must stay with him for the night. He is a poor man and has little to offer us, but he will do his best to make us comfortable. There is a village four kilometres down the road to Thakhek. Tomorrow you can walk there and hire men to push the car.'

Very slowly, with the greatest care, we carried the girl along the path, the Lao preceding us with his torch; the wounded man followed, supported by the girl's mother. Even when we carried her up the steps of the hut the girl gave no sign of the pain she must have felt. There was only one room but it was spotlessly clean, as were the straw mats which were all our host could provide for bedding. I have seen many wounded in my life and have been seriously wounded myself; but never have I met such fortitude, such indominable spirit as that young French girl showed throughout her ghastly journey. Whenever either of us tried to sympathise or apologise for her discomfort, she answered gently, 'It is nothing, *monsieur*,' and gave her soft, enchanting smile. The man, also, must have been in terrible pain; but he seemed too sunk in misery to care.

In the morning Klotz and I set off on foot down the road to get help, leaving the others in the care of the Lao. We found the village on a track about half a mile off the road. The headman, who spoke pidgin French, procured us the men we needed; but it took time to assemble them, for hurry is a word unknown in the Laotian vocabulary. Klotz decided to make his way separately to Thakhek, to send help to us in case we could not start the car. He took a *pirogue* down a small river which flows into the Mekong and reached Nakorn Panom in the evening.

It was afternoon before we started the car and bowled down the road to Thakhek. Although light-headed from relief that our troubles were nearly over, as well as from lack of sleep, I took the journey very slowly, to avoid jolting the wounded. When we arrived at the quay I was thankful to find Smiley and Rowland Winn supervising the embarkation of the convent refugees and their very considerable quantity of luggage. Smiley had returned the previous night from Ubon with his order to Nakajima and with a Japanese officer to see it carried out; on his instructions Nakajima's men had cleared the streets of Annamites who, despite their superior numbers, seemed to have a healthy respect for the Japanese. Winn had arrived from Naung Khai for a party which I had arranged but had forgotten in the emergency to cancel.

With the help of the Japanese, who carried the baggage, we finished the embarkation before dark; on the other side the governor, chief of police and doctor were waiting with a large party of labourers, several lorries and a dozen bullock carts. Within two hours all the refugees were installed in the hospital, which the governor had requisitioned for them; they were, naturally, almost hysterical with relief and poured out their thanks to us all in such profusion that I thought we should never be allowed to leave.

The doctor examined the two wounded and made them as comfortable as possible; but he could not operate on them, lacking the instruments, anaesthetics and – by his own admission – confidence. We sent an urgent signal, asking for a Siamese Air Force plane to land on my airstrip and take them to Bangkok. The aircraft arrived ten days later; when I saw them again in Bangkok, in early November, they had both made a complete recovery.

Winn, too, had been busy at Naung Khai. At Vientiane the Franco-Laotian forces, under the veteran Commandant Fabre, were faced with stiff opposition, not only from the Viet-minh, although they were active enough, but from the 'Free Lao' movement. This organisation, in alliance with the Viet-minh, had declared an independent state of Laos, free from all French control, and had nominated a provisional government under the premiership of Prince Phetsarath, a member of the royal house of Luang Prabang. Winn, who was working closely with Fabre, giving him what help he could, had to leave us the next day to arrange the evacuation of French civilians from Vientiane.

It was late on that night of 10 September before we went to bed. We rose early to prepare for our journey to Boneng to rescue the remaining French civilians. Smiley, Klotz and I recrossed the Mekong, and went immediately to see Nakajima. He was now only too anxious to help. At Smiley's request he provided us with a lorry and a Japanese escort with a light machine gun, under the command of a lieutenant.

On the road we met few signs of life except an occasional water buffalo with a small boy perched upon its back and a few peacocks which flitted across the road, gay and glorious in their bright plumage of blue and green. We were stopped by some Annamese guards, who told us that there was a battle going on at Boneng between their troops and the French, and begged us to stop 'this French aggression against our people'.

As we approached Boneng we heard, above the noise of the engine, the sound of rifle and machine-gun fire. We left the lorry on the outskirts of the village and advanced through the town in battle order, the Japanese looking very grim behind their machine guns, and the three of us doing our best to look resolute and undismayed.

The fighting was centred round the village school; a small Franco-Laotian force was holding out against some hundred and fifty well-armed Annamites, who with four machine guns were pouring an intensive if inaccurate fire into the wooden building. We approached the Viet-minh commander and Smiley ordered him to cease fire; after a moment's hesitation and a long look at our escort he obeyed. It now remained for us to parley with the French.

Telling Klotz and me to stay where we were, and ignoring our anxiety for his safety, Smiley broke cover and walked boldly towards the schoolhouse, waving a white handkerchief and calling out at intervals, *'Ne tirez pas, je suis officier anglais.'* With our hearts thumping we watched him walk slowly up the steps to the barricade across the door. He spoke for a few moments to someone inside, then beckoned to Klotz and me to join him.

We found a young French officer of Force 136, Lieutenant Gasset, a Eurasian sergeant and ten Lao soldiers. Gasset told us that he had entered the mines to rescue the French civilians there, but had been fired on by the Annamites, who had taken the civilians as hostages; he had evidently fought a good action, for his casualties were only two men wounded, whereas we saw, lying in the road outside, the dead bodies of four Annamites and there were four more wounded.

Returning with Gasset to the Viet-minh lines we began to discuss with their commander some way of ending the conflict. During our talk the Annamese insisted on producing for our close inspection the very messy bodies of their dead. Eventually we persuaded the Annamese to hand over their hostages and Gasset to return with his men to the mountains, leaving his two wounded Laos in our care.

The hostages were a man, four women and two children, all of them naturally very frightened. We lost no time in packing them and the two Laos into our lorry and driving away with our escort, happy in the fond belief that we had completed our work on that side of the Mekong.

Chapter 3

NEXT DAY SMILEY returned to Ubon, while Klotz occupied himself with the problems of Tavernier around Thakhek. Our refugees adapted quickly and happily to their new conditions at Nakorn Panom. In the single bare room that ran the whole length of the hospital they spread their mattresses and scanty possessions on the floor, grouping themselves by families in defiance of all the good sisters' efforts to segregate the sexes. A few days of rest, decent food and, above all, freedom from fear, worked amazing changes in their appearance, especially among the women. After observing the effects of a little make-up and a lot of ingenuity on one or two of the girls, I began to regret that present circumstances did not allow me to take advantage of my position as their liberator and protector.

The Siamese authorities did all they could to help them and provide their basic needs, and on 15 September we received our first parachute drop for them, with food, medicine and clothing. They stayed with us until the beginning of October, when all but the nuns and their orphan charges left for Ubon, where a French officer met them and took them to Bangkok. The nuns proposed to stay with us until conditions in Thakhek improved. An eighteen-year-old Eurasian girl, Jeanette, attached herself to my headquarters to help Rork and Edith Fournier with their heavy load of cipher work; she proved remarkably good at her task.

A signal from Calcutta informed us that Chinese troops of Chiang Kai-shek's army would soon arrive on the other side of the Mekong to disarm the Japanese and occupy French Indochina as far south as the 16th parallel until French troops were available to take over those duties; the Chinese were advancing from the north and might arrive in Vientiane and Thakhek at any moment. This news worried the Siamese, who feared Chiang Kai-shek might have designs on their own country. Nor did it please my French friends; and Calcutta warned us that there was considerable danger of friction between the French and the Chinese. We must, they added, tread very warily in our dealings with the Chinese; but we should be prepared to 'give the French all possible assistance' without, some bright staff officer had inserted, getting involved ourselves. The French, we learned, needed our support badly 'in view of the American attitude to Indochina'. The American attitude was summarised by the historian Chester Wilmot when he wrote in *The Struggle for Europe*, 'Roosevelt was determined that Indochina should not go back to France.' After Roosevelt's death President Truman continued this policy, as we ourselves were to find out shortly.

In about the middle of September Smiley, now a lieutenant-colonel, procured for me from Bangkok a jeep, a three-ton truck, two motorbikes and several drums of petrol; and so communications were no longer a problem. A week later I paid Winn a visit at Naung Kai; the occasion for my journey was a party for his twenty-ninth birthday, but the real object was to discuss the problems facing both of us across the Mekong.

Winn had evacuated from the other side a large party of French civilians, who were now under the care of the governor of Naung Khai pending their departure to Bangkok; they were going by air, because the aerodrome at Naung Khai was large enough for Dakotas. Commandant Fabre's troops were in occupation of Vientiane, but they were not allowed to remain there long. At the end of the month the Chinese arrived in strength. Almost their first action was to invite all the French officers to a dinner party. At the Chinese headquarters in the residency, where the tricolour was flying in their honour, Fabre and his companions were courteously shown into a room and immediately surrounded by Chinese soldiers with levelled tommy-guns. They were relieved of their arms, equipment, money and watches, and ordered to quit the town instantly on pain of arrest. After some argument Fabre himself was allowed to stay, together with his wireless set and operator; but he had to send the rest of his force ten miles away, for he had been ordered to avoid incidents with the Chinese.

Defenceless and surrounded by enemies Fabre was vitally dependent upon help from Winn, who received parachute drops, including arms, and smuggled them across the river by night to a rendezvous with the Franco-Laotians in the jungle; more than once he had to smuggle not only arms but parachutists, for the French had no suitable dropping ground at their disposal. It was fortunate that the governor of Naung Khai was sympathetic.

Winn's visits to confer with Fabre exposed him to grave personal risk. The distance from the landing stage opposite Naung Khai to Vientiane was nearly fifteen miles – it was impracticable to make the journey direct by boat owing to the distance and the strength of the current; the Chinese had requisitioned all transport and so

Winn had to walk or bicycle. On the way he often found himself a target for Free Lao or Viet-minh snipers. When, later on, he received a jeep his journeys became easier; but at the beginning of November he ran into an ambush and nearly lost his life.

To add to his worries, a few days before my visit an American OSS mission of ten officers and NCOs under a Major Banks had dropped without warning on the aerodrome at Naung Khai. Ignoring Winn they had established themselves in the town and prepared to receive supply drops. They had no authority from SEAC to be in Siam. Although perplexed and a little irritated by their discourtesy Winn was much more worried by their behaviour to Fabre and his officers, who at this time had not yet occupied Vientiane. From his base at Naung Khai Banks crossed the river on several occasions, and in the most insulting manner ordered the French to keep out of the town and to 'cease their aggression' against the Ammanese and Free Laos.

Fortunately for Winn, though not for me, Banks decided to move his mission to Thakhek.

'They have just left for Nakorn Panom,' he told me amiably. 'You should find them there when you get back.'

I soon found my anxieties were justified. Banks set up a temporary headquarters in Nakorn Panom and received a drop for his mission on my airfield, in violation of the terms of an Anglo-American agreement on Indochina. Much worse, in my absence he had scared the French refugees out of their wits by telling them he would have them returned to Thakhek. It took me a while to reassure them; however, a few days later Banks took himself and his mission to Thakhek, which he made his base, and we all relaxed, though not for long.

The Japanese had left the area and Thakhek was now in the hands of the Viet-minh, who welcomed Banks with an enthusiasm which he immediately set out to justify. Having assured their delegates that he was going to put an end to 'French aggression', he went to see Tavernier and brusquely ordered him to withdraw his troops from the neighbourhood of Thakhek.

'He spoke to me as I wouldn't dream of speaking to a servant,' complained Tavernier. 'In front of my own soldiers and the Annamites, all of whom understand French. He called me a pirate and threatened that unless I withdrew my men he would send Chinese troops to disarm us. In order to avoid an incident I withdrew.'

Banks used the same methods to oblige the French to abandon Savannakhet. The delighted Viet-minh immediately launched a series of sharp attacks on the French posts around these towns, forcing the French to pull back further into the jungle. I tried to persuade Banks not to encourage the Viet-minh, who had been truculent enough before his arrival. He was a spare, sallow man in his early thirties with thin lips, a sneering mouth and close-set, flickering eyes; he seldom looked at me when he spoke. I reminded him that both our countries were allies of France, and that Tavernier and his men had held out with great endurance against the Japanese, with whom the Annamites had been collaborating during the occupation.

'So did the French collaborate,' he snarled. 'I was betrayed myself by a traitor in France and damn nearly lost my life.'

He continued to make speeches in Thakhek, encouraging the Viet-minh in their 'struggle for freedom'. But I should emphasise that the rest of his mission were very different from their commander, being courteous and friendly and – on the few occasions when they were allowed to be – helpful. But they seemed overawed by Banks.

On 27 September – a date I'm unlikely to forget – Klotz and I decided to visit Tavernier to hand over some medical stores; Klotz wrote to warn him of our visit. We would pass through Thakhek on the way, to pick up a car for part of the journey and carry out some commissions for the French. Banks had told Klotz to keep away, but he had replied with some heat:

'I can certainly go to Thakhek if I wish! I am a French officer and Thakhek belongs to France.'

We borrowed the governor's launch with his two Annamese boatmen; the American Lieutenant Reese, who had come over that morning, was our only other companion. The monsoon was coming to an end and the afternoon was cloudless, still and warm; the hills behind Thakhek smiled peaceful and welcoming, a bright quilt of green and gold. The houses on the waterfront seemed deserted and asleep. We jumped ashore and walked up the ramp.

As we stepped on to the road we heard a high-pitched command, 'Halt!' From a doorway on the left issued a platoon of Annamese led by a short, lightly built officer with a drawn pistol, whom I recognised as one of the Viet-minh delegates, known as Tu, formerly an employee of the electricity plant. In different circumstances he would have been a ludicrous figure with his dirty khaki shorts, the grey composition topee that seemed to be the uniform of his kind and his self-important, pseudo-military manner. He strutted up to us and made a signal to his men, who spread out facing us with levelled rifles.

'*Bien!*' he yapped, grinning to show a mouthful of uneven blackened teeth rotting in red, betel-stained gums. He turned to me. 'Who are you?'

'I am a British officer, as you know.'

'And you?' to Reese.

'American.'

'You,' he said to Klotz, 'are French?' Klotz nodded.

'Very well. The British and American officers may go free. They are our allies. The Frenchman is under arrest and will come with us. The French declared war on us yesterday in Saigon.'

'Don't be ridiculous,' I protested, trying to sound calm and confident. 'The British, American and French are all allies, and we are certainly not going to let you arrest our friend. Isn't that so, Lieutenant?' I called to Reese, who had made his way through the rank of Annamese and was now leaning against the wall of a house across the road. Reese shuffled his feet and looked unhappily at the ground.

'I don't know,' he muttered. 'I guess we're neutral.'

He looked miserable. I was and still am convinced that he was acting under orders, and that it was not physical cowardice that made him withhold his help from us at this moment.

I do not believe I have ever felt so utterly defeated. With Reese on one side of him and myself on the other, it would have been possible to conduct Klotz back to the launch; I was sure the Annamese would not risk harming a British or American officer, and in this way we could have screened Klotz from their fire without much danger. Now I had to try to do it alone, for it was unthinkable to leave him to certain murder and probable torture. What I would have given at that moment for just one section of troops!

'François,' I said quietly in English, 'you and I are going back to the boat. There doesn't seem any future in staying here.'

He smiled and took his hand off his pistol holster. I turned to the delegate, trying to keep my voice steady to conceal my fear.

'Monsieur Tu, since our presence here is unwelcome to you, my friend and I are returning to Siam. *Au revoir.*'

I made him a stiff bow and, putting my arm around Klotz and trying to keep myself between him and his enemies, turned and started to walk towards the ramp.

'No!' screamed Tu. 'You may go, but he stays here.'

'Keep moving,' I whispered, 'and pretend we haven't heard.'

Klotz nodded, his face expressionless, his eyes calm. I do not like to imagine his real feelings during those moments; I remember too vividly my own. But he gave no sign of fear; his frame beneath my arm was unshaking and relaxed. Behind us we heard the rattle of rifle bolts as the Annamese closed in. Please, dear God, I prayed, look after us now.

There was a shout from Tu, followed by a fusillade of shots about our ears. I felt the blast of a rifle on my right cheek and realised with a sudden surge of elation that they were firing past us or into the air. It was, after all, a bluff. Only a few yards ahead of us lay the launch under her dirty canvas awning; she was deserted, but if we could reach her safely and cast off from the bank, the current would take us downstream with enough steerage way to reach the Siamese side. I was now walking almost directly behind Klotz to give him the maximum of cover; it seemed we had got away with it.

There was a fresh burst of firing; a figure ran up on my left, thrust his rifle under my arm into Klotz's back, fired once and disappeared. Klotz staggered and let out a terrible, despairing gasp.

'Oh Peter!' he whispered. 'Oh Peter!'

A wide crimson stain spread thickly over the front of his shirt; a torrent of blood poured from his mouth. I tried to hold him, but he swayed forward out of my arms and lurched with weakening steps down the ramp on to the landing stage; there he dropped on all fours and began to drag himself towards the launch. I ran after him and lifted him towards the thwarts on to the raised afterdeck; he lay there face downwards, the blood trickling from his mouth. Within half a minute he was dead.

Trembling with rage I ran back up the ramp. Tu and his men had vanished, but Reese was where I had left him, leaning against the wall; he had been joined by a major who was Banks's second-in-command and by two NCOs.

'I hope,' I said, trying to keep my voice under control, 'I hope you're proud of your Annamite friends. That' – I pointed to the corpse on the launch – '*that* is the direct result of your work.'

'Gee!' squealed the younger of the NCOs, 'gee, this is terrible! Let's get the hell out of this place.'

'I guess,' said the major slowly, 'we better have a company of Chinese paratroopers down here right away. I'll go call Hanoi.'

Having failed to save Klotz's life I must at all costs rescue his body before the Viet-minh came to claim it as a token of their triumph. I was thankful to see the dowdy, sorrowful figure of the *Chaokhoueng* approaching with the two Annamese boatmen, who, not unnaturally, had run away when the trouble began. While they started the engine and swung the bows into the stream I sat down beside Klotz, brushing away the flies that were already clustered on his bloodstained mouth and back, and on the congealing pool on the deck; they rose in a cloud with a low, resentful buzz.

All the way across I sat watching the dead face of this man who in such a short time had become a close friend. It seemed a tragic waste that after fighting throughout the war he should die now with a bullet in the back after global hostilities had supposedly ceased. I could not know then how many of his countrymen – and thousands more Americans – were to follow him over the next thirty years. Remorsefully I thought of how he had trusted my judgment when his own instinct had been to draw his pistol and stand his ground. If I had stood with him, threatening to shoot the first Annamese to lift a rifle, might he not, I now wondered, be alive? I am still haunted by the thought that it might have turned out better that way.

At Nakorn Panom I sent one of the boatmen with a note to the governor, asking him to have the body delivered to the nuns and to arrange a military funeral for the following afternoon; leaving the other man on guard at the wharf I walked to my headquarters.

Rork and Edith Fournier were on the veranda waiting for me; they had heard the shooting.

'Where is François?' Edith's voice was very low.

I could hardly bring myself to look at her: 'François is dead.'

She stood quite still and silent while the tears flooded into her eyes and fell in great glistening drops slowly down her cheeks. When I had told her what had happened she whispered, *'C'est la deuxième fois, mon Dieu, c'est la deuxième fois!'* On her last mission, in occupied France, her chief had been taken by the Gestapo. There was nothing I could say to her. Leaving her with Rork I shut myself in my room, fell upon and bed and for a few minutes gave in to my own despair.

Pulling myself together I asked Edith to come with me to the hospital and break the news to the refugees and nuns before Klotz's body arrived. We covered the quarter of a mile distance without speaking. At the hospital we were surrounded by an anxious crowd, who stared in horror at my blood-stained clothes. When they heard that Klotz was dead there was a stunned silence, followed by a chorus of cries and sobs from the women; but their sorrow gave way to a rising clamour of indignation when I told them of Lieutenant Reese's 'neutrality'.

While we were talking, the governor arrived with the chief of police and the doctor. The doctor had already examined the body, which was now on the way to the hospital; he said that Klotz had been shot through the base of the heart and no power on earth could have saved him. The governor was almost in tears himself with distress. It appeared that the messenger to Tavernier had been intercepted by the Viet-minh, who had read Klotz's letter and prepared the ambush to meet us; by the time the governor knew, Klotz had been killed. The order for Klotz's detention had been given by the chief delegate, Long.

I sent word to Smiley, asking him to come as soon as possible; with his rank and authority I felt he might have some influence on Banks.

The nuns would lay out the body and we would keep vigil over it in watches during the coming night. The funeral was arranged for the following afternoon, at the Catholic cemetery north of the town; the police would provide a guard of honour.

At midnight we left for the hospital. I had ordered Rork not to stay long, for he had a lot of signals to send in the morning; but Edith insisted on staying the rest of the night and I could not prevent her. Klotz was lying on a campbed, dressed in a clean uniform; he looked serene and peaceful, his strong features softened in the dim candlelight. We took our places among the shadowy figures thronging the small bare room; all the officials of Nakorn Panom came to stand guard for a part of the night.

As the silent hours passed and I watched the still face on the campbed, I found I was no longer tortured by the terrible memory of that blood-drenched figure staggering down the ramp at Thakhek. Instead, I remembered François gently lifting in his arms the wounded girl at the mines; François reading me passages from Descartes, and patiently and unsuccessfully trying to explain what Frenchmen meant when they discribed themselves as *Cartésiens*; both of us sitting over our rum on the veranda in the cool night, singing French Army marching songs.

We were about to leave for the funeral when Lieutenant Reese arrived at the house, grim-faced but very smart in his uniform. He saluted me gravely.

'I've come, Major, to attend Lieutenant Klotz's funeral.'

Edith turned and walked out of the room.

'That's very good of you, Lieutenant, I'm sure. But do you know what you may be letting yourself in for? The French here are pretty indignant . . .'

'I know. But I'd like to be there.'

He walked with us to the cemetery. There he stood alone, his eyes on the ground, while the silent tide of hatred welled all round him. At last the priest began the service and everyone turned towards the open grave. When the coffin had been lowered, wrapped in the tricolour, the volley fired and the earth shovelled over, Reese turned to face the trench, saluted and marched away.

The grave was marked with a plain wooden cross inscribed with Klotz's name and the date of his murder. It was not allowed to remain there long. The Annamese, whose town adjoined the cemetery, could not let their hatred rest with his death; time and again during the next three months they uprooted the cross and took it away, leaving a few splinters to mock his trampled grave. Each time we replaced it they would do the same.

When we had thanked the governor and all his officers, Edith, Rork and I walked slowly homewards along the road by the Mekong bank. Gazing at those hateful hills above Thakhek which only the previous day I had thought so beautiful, I felt Edith's tight grip on my arm.

'*Nous le vengerons*,' she whispered fiercely, '*nous le vengerons!*'

Before we reached the main street we met Smiley, driving a large Cadillac saloon which he had taken from a Japanese general. My telegram had found him at Mukdahan, where he had gone to take over the Japanese ships on the Mekong; he had driven here at full speed.

When he heard my story he wrote a note to Banks asking for an interview in Thakhek the next morning and for an escort to take him from the boat to OSS headquarters. He ordered me to stay behind and in the circumstances I could not argue. But I tried to stop him going alone, because I had heard that the Viet-minh had announced that any officers, of whatever nationality, who had been helping the French would be arrested if they came to Thakhek.

I was very glad to see him back in the afternoon.

'What did you think of Banks?' I asked.

Smiley grimaced.

'He can't tell the truth. He swore to me that he had never called the French officers bandits or ordered them to give themselves up to the Annamese; but he didn't know I had in my pocket a letter written by him to the French at Savannakhet in those very words. By the way, Peter, you're not to go to Thakhek again. The Viet-minh are after your blood and they've put a price on your head.'

Chapter 4

E ARLY IN OCTOBER Banks and his mission left Thakhek for the south and I never saw him again. Smiley was right about the Viet-minh attitude towards me. Interested in locating their positions facing Tavernier south of the town, I borrowed the governor's launch one afternoon and cruised up and down close to the other bank of the river, studying the shore through my field glasses. This pleasant pastime came to an abrupt end when, without warning, several machine guns opened up on us, fortunately firing short. Sang-a, the only other passenger, threw himself on the floor – wisely – and lay there gibbering. I did not have to tell the helmsman to turn away; before I could give the order he had the launch headed at full speed for home.

One of the suggestions I had made in my signal on the night of Klotz's death was that supplies of arms should be dropped to me to smuggle to Tavernier; two days later Calcutta agreed and told me to stand by for a drop on 3 October; I had also asked to receive French parachutists, as Winn had been doing at Naung Khai, and transport them across; but this was not agreed until some weeks later. I was particularly warned not to divulge the fact that I was smuggling arms; I was to pretend that the containers held medicines, food and clothing – as a few of them would. I decided to visit Tavernier immediately to plan our gun-running operation.

Tavernier's headquarters was at Ban-Tung, a few miles south of Thakhek and east of the Mekong, and so I asked him to have men and horses waiting for me on the far bank of the river. On 1 October I borrowed the governor's launch and crossed over in the morning. Tavernier's men were waiting – six young Lao soldiers under a French NCO.

We rode along narrow winding tracks through thick undergrowth, frequently having to lean over our ponies' necks to avoid branches and creepers that overhung our path. After half an hour we began to climb gradually into the hills. We had covered about ten miles and climbed a thousand feet when we came suddenly upon the familiar banana plantations that marked the outskirts of a village; here we were challenged at an outpost by three Lao soldiers with an old Hotchkiss light machine gun. A few minutes later we came into a wide clearing dotted with huts and a few small houses, which was the village of Ban-Tung. Laotian soldiers – barefooted little men in shorts and dark blue berets – walked between the huts in twos and threes, or squatted in groups in the doorways, chatting and laughing; all had the same alert, expectant look. Dismounting, I followed the NCO to the largest of the houses, which was Tavernier's command post, and waited on the veranda while he announced me with an impressively smart salute.

Captain Ferdinand Tavernier was a tall, dark officer of about my own age; lean and ascetic in appearance, prematurely bald, with tired eyes blinking behind thick horn-rimmed glasses, he seemed a good deal older. He spoke in a quiet, rather high voice and he very seldom smiled; he had no English.

I had brought with me a few medical stores and told him that there were more waiting for him at Nakorn Panom. He was pathetically grateful.

'You know, Major, there is not one of us here who is not sick. All of us have recurring malaria, most have amœbic dysentery and our small stock of medicines was long ago exhausted. We have had no supplies since the Japanese *coup* in March.'

Making a note of his most urgent needs I asked, 'Have you had any cases of bacillary dysentery?'

'Oh yes, plenty. But they all died.'

We arranged that he should come to Nakorn Panom the day after the drop; we would load his stores on to one of my lorries and drive to a point about fifteen miles south of the town, where he would have men and *pirogues* waiting to transport them over the river.

'This is wonderful news!' he exclaimed. 'We really are desperate here. Since our Major Banks gave them such encouragement the Annamites have been pressing us hard; with the few weapons I have I cannot stand up to them and now I am running out of ammunition. I could, of course, retire deep into the mountains, but that would mean leaving the population here, who are our friends, to be massacred.

'Do you think you could also get me some money to buy food? We cannot continue to live indefinitely on the charity of these people. And my soldiers have not been paid since March.'

There was no other officer with Tavernier, but I was introduced to his NCOs. Sickness, undernourishment and fatigue made them look like walking corpses, but they were all cheerful, and full of hope and enthusiasm. The most impressive figure was the *padre*, a short, square Frenchman with a huge black beard, a deep voice and an apparently inexhaustible fund of energy.

On the way back to the launch I was riding at the head of the party; as I leaned forward to pass under an overhanging branch I heard a sharp cry from the man behind: '*Attention, Commandant!*' Looking back I saw, coiled along the branch I had just passed, a large snake. That was the only live snake I saw in the Far East outside the Pasteur Institute in Bangkok.

My carefully disseminated cover-story about the arms was shattered during the drop by one of those pieces of bad luck which always seem to catch me out when I embark upon deception. The two Liberators made their dropping runs from west to east, turning at the end of each run when they were over Thakhek. Owing to a fault in the release mechanism one of the containers got stuck underneath the aircraft, falling a few seconds later on the far bank; it was retrieved by the Viet-minh, who thus received a present of eighteen stens, as well as valuable material for propaganda, of which they made immediate use.

The next morning the governor came to see me in a state of extreme indignation, forbade me to move the arms I had just received and placed a police guard over them. Even Smiley was unable to mollify him; the most he would allow poor Tavernier to take were the containers that actually held only food, clothing and medicine, and the money which I had received on his behalf.

I sent an early signal to Calcutta, asking for instructions to be sent from Bangkok for the release of the arms; but it was a fortnight before they arrived. Even then the governor insisted that the operation should be carried out at night and well away from the town. I therefore wrote to Tavernier asking him to send *pirogues* and men to a small village on the Siamese bank of the river, a little way upstream of our original rendezvous; they were to await me there at midnight on 20 October; I decided to accompany the arms across the river and see them delivered personally – partly to satisfy myself about their condition, and partly because it would give me the opportunity of having a further talk with Tavernier and assessing his future requirements.

I could scarcely hope for complete secrecy in smuggling the arms, after the publicity that had attended their arrival; the governor, however, tactfully removed our police guards at dusk on the 20th and so gave us the chance to load the containers on to our lorry under cover of darkness. It was a slow and exhausting business but, exhilarated by the thought that we were doing something, however small, to avenge poor Klotz, we put our backs into the work.

Leaving Edith Fournier behind to operate the wireless, Rork and

I set out for the rendezvous shortly after eleven, with Rork at the wheel.

'I hope to God the French are there on time,' I commented as we bumped over the pot-holes on the road leading southwards from the town, and left the last huts and plantations behind. 'I shan't feel happy so long as this stuff remains on Siamese soil. Those Annamite bastards must have a pretty good idea of our plan, and I wouldn't put it past them to try and intercept – in which case I don't at all care for the thought of waiting around on our own in the dark in the middle of the countryside.'

'No more do I, sir. D'you really think they'll try something here? I don't think the governor would like that much.'

'No, he certainly wouldn't. But I don't want to take chances, just the same. Of course, they may try to catch us on the river – they ought to be able to see all right with this moon.

'That reminds me,' I went on. 'In my letter, I gave Tavernier to understand that I would be returning tomorrow by the same route and you'd be picking me up in the truck at this same village. Now of course that would be a dotty idea. If the Annamese are really out to get us, it's the obvious place they'd choose to lie in wait.'

'But how will you really get back?'

'Quite simply. Before we left home tonight I wrote a line to the governor – I have it on me now – asking him to send his launch tomorrow morning to collect me from the other side and take me direct to Nakorn Panom. You will please deliver it to him personally first thing in the morning.'

'I will, sir. But will he agree?'

'Certainly he'll agree. I've explained that I'm afraid of trouble from Comrade Tu and his pals, and that's something he's as keen to avoid as we are.'

We drove on in silence until we came to the track leading to the village where I was to meet Tavernier's men; it ran off to the left, just before the road crossed a narrow wooden bridge over a watercourse. Rork slowed down.

'Better turn her round,' I said, 'so that we're facing homewards in case of trouble.'

'We're a bit late for that, sir. Look!'

In the moonlight I saw two figures standing by the posts on either side of the bridge; at the same moment two more appeared from the bushes at the entrance to the track. I fumbled for my pistol and was about to shout to Rork to put his foot on the accelerator when, with an almost sickening flood of relief, I noticed the berets and uniform shirts of Tavernier's Laotians.

There were more than a dozen men awaiting us, not all of them soldiers; in command was one of the NCOs I had met on my first visit. Under his direction they set to work swiftly and quietly, opening the containers and carrying the weapons and boxes of ammunition down the few hundred yards of track to the river. When the last empty container had been replaced in the lorry I gave Rork my note to the governor.

'Mind you hand it to him personally,' I repeated.

'I will, sir, never fear. Good luck to you now.'

He drove off into the night. Slinging my carbine on my shoulder I followed on the heels of the French sergeant, picking out the pale ribbon of the winding path between dark clumps of thorn bushes. Once or twice I stopped and looked around uneasily, to reassure myself that we were not being followed; but the fields lay still and peaceful in the milky moonlight. We slowed our pace when we entered the coconut plantations on the outskirts of the village, making a wide detour to avoid the houses. A gentle breeze rattled the palm fronds overhead and brought to our nostrils the heady, sweet scents of the tropical night mingled with the reek of wood smoke from dying fires; from close by came the snarling bark of a dog, followed by a brief chorus of yelps that gradually died away into silence.

Six or seven large *pirogues* were lying at the water's edge. The work of loading was completed with the same speed and silence as before. There was no sign of life from the village as we climbed aboard and paddled away from the bank; even the dogs had ceased their howling and the only sounds in the still night were the gentle splash of our paddles, the gurgle of water against the hulls and the faint whispers of the Laotian crews.

I reclined in the centre of my canoe on top of some salvaged parachutes and propped my back none too comfortably against a small pile of ammunition boxes in the stern. For the first part of the journey we set a course slightly upstream, to take advantage of the current later on. From my position, roughly in the middle of the flotilla, I kept an anxious watch for our enemies, but the only signs of human life other than ourselves were an occasional *pirogue*, obviously engaged in fishing, and one or two lights on the further bank – probably the fires of charcoal burners; the only movement that caught my eye was the shimmer of the moon on the swiftly gliding water and the dancing points of light where the river raced over the shoals among the blue and silver shadows of the sand-banks.

In the middle of the river, a little more than halfway across, lay a small island, a long, low strip of jungle whose tree-fringed shore showed dark against the distant background of the Cammon Hills.

As we approached it we began to alter course to pass below its southern tip.

'Who lives there?' I asked the French sergeant, who was sitting immediately in front of me.

'Oh, nobody. The fishermen use it sometimes and we too, when we cross the river, halt there to rest ourselves a while. But tonight,' he flashed me a smile over his shoulders, 'with this valuable cargo perhaps we had better hurry on our way.'

As I watched the trees glide past I strained my eyes to peer into the gloom of the undergrowth, wondering if any hidden enemies were lying in wait for us; but I could see no movement in that strip of silent jungle. I lay back with a sigh, and marvelled again at the moonlit beauty of this mighty and mysterious river which ran for nearly three thousand miles from the Tibetan plateau to the South China Sea. What a romantic setting, I gloated, for a smuggler!

We were rounding the tip of the island, less than two hundred yards from the shore, when an abrupt challenge rang out from the darkness, shattering my reverie; I clutched at my carbine as a burst of machine-gun fire ripped up the water a few yards away. A second burst slammed into the leading canoe, toppling the bow paddler straight over the side; the steersman slumped slowly forward and sideways and, as he fell, the canoe heeled over and capsized with a great splash and flurry of foam. The third occupant appeared for a moment in the water, grabbing frantically at the slippery bottom of the dug-out as it spun away on the current; but he stood no chance and in a few seconds was swept from our sight.

The sergeant bellowed an order in Lao, and our *pirogue* swung sharply downstream, almost tipping me overboard as the crew drove their paddles into the water to speed us away from that murderous trap. The little island, which had seemed a moment earlier so quiet and aloof, was now erupting with the ragged crackle of rifle fire and the vicious stammer of the machine gun; the sound of the fusillades rolled across the river to echo back to us from the distant hills.

I imagine that a smuggler can have few more disagreeable experiences than that of coming under heavy fire at close range in a flimsy canoe on a fast and turbulent river. As the bullets smacked into the water around us, or zipped frighteningly past my ears, or whined in angry richochet among our scattering flotilla I let go of my carbine and lay back as far as I could, gripping the gunwales tightly to brace myself against every lurch and twist of our plunging craft. I was acutely conscious, also, of my proximity to the ammunition cases and wondered unhappily whether it would be more comfortable to be blown to glory or drowned in the Mekong.

I picked up my carbine and, wriggling over on to my stomach

facing the stern, began to shoot back at the island. There was not the least likelihood, of course, of my hitting anybody – except perhaps the paddler in the stern, whose nervousness increased noticeably with each shot I fired – but I thought it showed the right spirit and at least it made me feel better. The paddler, with bullets flying past him from both directions, was rapidly approaching hysteria; moreover, my efforts were endangering the balance of the boat. I rolled over again on to my back and tried to lie still, praying feverishly that we should soon be out of effective range.

Fortunately the enemy's fire, after that early unlucky burst, was not very accurate. Untrained troops, as the Annamese were, tend to fire high, especially at night: fortunately, also, they seemed to have only one machine gun and they had no tracer to help them correct their aim. They had probably hoped to take us by surprise on the island. Clearly visible as we had been at first in the moonlight, now that we had scattered we presented more difficult targets; moreover, the strong current, combined with the efforts of the paddlers, was rapidly increasing the range. Their shots went wider with each minute of our flight and soon they ceased to trouble us, although they continued to blaze away sporadically in our direction almost until we landed.

It was indeed a miraculous escape and I poured out my thanks to providence for the sergeant's decision not to stop for a rest on that island. In the capsized canoe we had lost two Lao villagers and one soldier, as well as a number of stens, and some food and clothing; otherwise our only casualties were two men slightly wounded, both of them able to walk.

As I checked the stores next morning with Tavernier, he said to me: 'In future I think it better if we use no couriers but mine to carry letters concerning the delivery of arms. The Annamites will always try to intercept our correspondence, and in Lakhon [the French name for Nakorn Panom] you do not know who you can trust. But I can always send men of proven fidelity. So next time you have some material for me, send me word and I will send you a courier to whom you can entrust the details of a rendezvous. It will take a little longer, but it will be much safer.' I could only agree.

As I had expected, the governor's launch arrived to take me back and a very worried man came to meet me at the landing stage at Nakorn Panom. I tried to make light of the incident, although I knew he would learn the full story soon enough. But when I reached home Edith Fournier was looking very grave.

'I hear you had trouble on the river, Peter.'

'Yes, a little. Someone had been tipped off, I'm afraid.'

'They had indeed. It is as well you did not come back the same way this morning. The *curé* of the church by the *ville annamite* was here. Although he is an Annamite himself he is a good friend of ours and he hears a lot of things. He was very worried because the Annamites had arranged another little reception for you at that village where you and Rork went last night.'

A few days later I received an enthusiastic letter of thanks from Tavernier. The Viet-minh had launched a heavy attack on Ban-Tung the night after I had left. Thanks to the arms, and more particularly the ammunition, I had brought him he had been able to hold his ground; but for their timely arrival lack of ammunition would have forced him to withdraw. In the following weeks I took him several more consignments; some of the arms I received by parachute drop, others came from Smiley, who was able to draw on Japanese dumps. Each time we varied our rendezvous, using Tavernier's couriers as we had arranged; there were no more incidents.

Thereafter, as long as I remained on the frontier, a large part of my time was spent in running arms to the French – both to Tavernier and to Quinquenel, with whom I arranged a secluded rendezvous on the river south of Mukdahan. These officers needed everything we could send them; they were continually engaged in savage battles against superior forces, and their own command in Saigon was in no position to help. But on 19 October they received their first reinforcements: sixty-four French parachutists dropped on my airfield and, after an enormous lunch which Tavernier attended, they were ferried across the river in *pirogues*. By the time our missions left the area, at the end of January 1946, the French were able to take the offensive; two months later they were in possession of Thakhek and Savannakhet.

With Quinquinel I met a thick-set, broad-shouldered Laotian with whom I was to strike up a most rewarding the entertaining friendship. Chao (Prince) Boun Oum of the ancient royal house of Champassak – a kingdom in southern Laos which the French had suppressed before the war – had the outlook of a western intellectual combined with the instincts of a Laotian patriot. Intensely francophile – he had been educated in France – he was convinced that his country's future lay in Franco-Laotian cooperation and he had played a leading part in the resistance against the Japanese; eyewitnesses gave me lurid accounts of the Prince wading with his retinue across the breast-high waters of the Mekong with a machine gun held above his head, in the face of Japanese air attack. In the south of Laos he inspired a devotion not far removed from worship. Strangely, he seemed to hold no resentment against the French for their suppression of his kingdom. He was very proud of his ancestry, however, and wrote, in French, detailed histories of Champassak and its royal line, going back at least twelve hundred years to the time of the Khmer Empire; I still have copies of several which he gave me. Along with a fleshy face and thick lips he had some impediment in his speech which rendered him hard to understand even, I was told, in Laotian and in French nearly impossible.

At about the end of October, at long last, a medical officer arrived on attachment to my headquarters.

Captain Donald Gunn, RAMC, was quiet, most conscientious and extremely efficient; he was about twenty-six and had previously worked behind the Japanese lines in Burma. His confident, unruffled manner, dry sense of humour and abundant common sense vastly increased his value to our party. Sickness and enemy action took a constant toll of the French forces; to Nakorn Panom, Mukdahan and Naung Kai they brought their casualties for treatment and evacuation by air to Bangkok. Gunn's life was an exacting round of journeys between the three stations; after driving all night to attend a batch of wounded he would often have to drive back sleepless through the following night for further work elsewhere. In the intervals he found time to help us with the problems of administration, and the reception and disposal of parachute stores; he didn't seem to need rest.

Smiley had cultivated excellent relations with the Siamese Air Force, especially with the station commander at Korat, Wing-Commander Manop Souriya, who was known even to his brother officers as Nobby; the wing-commander, who had passed through West Point and served an attachment to the RAF before the war, proved himself a firm friend. Aware of our difficulties with communications, he obtained permission from his superiors to send an aircraft and pilot to Ubon for Smiley's personal use. The aircraft was a dual-control Mitsubishi Advanced Trainer, an obsolete monoplane of doubtful reliability, with seating for one passenger in comfort and a precarious perch for a second in the tail; it did not prove as useful as we had hoped, because it spent most of the time on the airfield at Ubon or Korat undergoing repairs or awaiting spare parts. We were none too happy to learn that the pilot's name was Pilot Officer Prang.

My first flight in the machine was on 31 October, when Smiley and I were summoned to Bangkok, he for a conference with General Evans and Brigadier Jaques, I for my first meeting with the Brigadier. We took off from Nakorn Panom after breakfast, with Smiley sitting behind the pilot and myself squatting on a discarded parachute, prey to acute discomfort and claustrophobia. Our first call was at Udaun, thirty-five miles south of Naung Kai where we had an appointment with Winn. We reached it in an hour, flying at a thousand feet and followed the narrow pink strip of laterite road that ran almost straight through the feathery carpet of forest.

Planning to lunch at Korat, nearly two hundred miles to the south, we left Udaun at noon and climbed to five thousand feet, to cross a high range of mountains. After an hour's flying we saw them beneath us – jagged outcrops of rock thrusting malevolently up towards us through the bright green profusion of hostile jungle; deep-shadowed gorges twisted sharply between the peaks. If the engine fails now, I thought, we haven't a hope of making a landing.

Of course it did fail, in a series of sharp, angry backfires while Prang fiddled furiously with various switches on the instrument panel; then it cut and left us gliding through the air in a grim and fearful silence. Smiley turned round in his seat to catch my eye, the corners of his mouth twisted comically downwards as he pointed to the savage mountains below. RAF pilots had told me that if your engine failed while flying over jungle and there was no paddy in sight, the best chance was to land on top of bamboo.

'Do you see any bamboo down there?' I asked. Smiley shook his head, obviously thinking that terror had deprived me of my wits.

At that moment the engine spluttered into life and we breathed again. But not for long. Five times in the next half hour this terrifying performance was repeated, while we steadily lost height, until, at two hundred feet above the ground, clear at last of the mountains, we saw ahead of us the comforting expanse of Korat aerodrome. There was no safety margin for a circuit and so we came straight in, landing with the wind in a frightening succession of vicious bumps, breaking off a wheel and slewing sideways on the starboard wing in a cloud of choking red dust. Leaping from the aircraft Smiley and I stood shaking and sweating on the runway while Prang climbed slowly down and gazed at us in silence with a bashful, apologetic and wholly disarming smile.

Strong drinks and lunch with Nobby restored our nerve sufficiently to fly on with Prang in another aircraft. We reached Bangkok in the last of daylight and in time for a spectacular party given by Force 136 in the palace of one of the royal princes. I had never thought our frontier life uncomfortable, but I was staggered by this sudden projection into luxury, and felt awkward and scruffy in my faded battledress beside the trim little Siamese officers and the British in their well-tailored uniforms. The women dancing under the coloured Chinese lanterns or gliding across the lawns in the clear, warm, scented moonlight seemed each one an Aphrodite of voluptuous sensuality. Sadly I noted that none of them showed the least interest in me.

The following day passed in an endless succession of conferences. Force 136 was going into liquidation but a few of our missions in Siam, including those on the north-east frontier, were being retained in a new organisation, under the direct orders of the GOC, General Evans. Smiley and Winn were returning to England at the end of November, the former to attend his staff college course, the latter for demobilisation. I was asked to take over Smiley's command, an offer which delighted me; I should be the only remaining officer with experience of the north-east frontier and, having no urgent reason to return home, I felt that I must stay to give all possible help to our Franco-Laotian Allies who had inspired me so deeply.

We left Bangkok after lunch on 2 November and landed at Korat without incident; when we took off again Smiley, who had flown his own aircraft before the war, was at the controls. We were gaining height over the aerodrome when there was a violent jar on the port wing; as the aircraft shuddered and banked at a dangerous angle I peered over the cockpit, to see a long, deep gash in the leading edge, about halfway along. Smiley quickly adjusted the trim and returned to land safely. It turned out what we had collided with a very large bird, which fortunately had struck the wing and not the propeller; but the dented metal had jammed the connecting wires to the ailerons and we were lucky to have avoided a crash.

After half an hour's delay we left in the machine which had brought us to Korat two days before. By now we were both thoroughly apprehensive of Siamese aircraft, or at least of Advanced Trainers, and we only began to breathe freely when we saw to starboard the hill above Sakon Nakorn, a round, furry pimple in the forested plain, and flew over a reed-fringed lake where in August I had tried to shoot duck. The mountains of Laos loomed closer through the haze and I sighed contentedly when I caught sight of the houses of Nakorn Panom straggling down towards the mudbanks exposed by the subsiding waters of the Mekong. I was not even alarmed when, as we swung in to land, the engine spluttered once or twice and cut. We glided in and bumped gently over the landing-strip to a halt.

'What was the cause of that?' I asked Smiley a little later.

'Oh, it seems they forgot to fill her up at Korat. She was clean out of gas when the engine cut. Aren't we the lucky ones?'

Chapter 5

For it is better for us to die in battle than
to behold the ruin of our people and our
sanctuaries.

Maccabees

IN THE NEW Year of 1946 a peace treaty was signed between
Thailand and Britain, and so our presence became unnecessary
as well as unwelcome. However, I was given command of a small
mission to occupy the East Indian islands of Bali and Lombok,
whose Japanese garrisons had not yet surrendered. Their intentions
were still unknown to South East Asia Command, who sent us in
there to clarify them.

'In other words,' explained General Mansergh, who commanded
Allied forces in East Java, 'if they cut your throats we'll know we'll
have to launch a full-scale invasion.'

The Japanese surrendered immediately and we remained in those
beautiful islands for another four months, preparing at first for the
arrival of the main occupation force, which was Dutch, and, in my
case, conducting the civil and military government.

In June, I flew home for demobilisation and ceased to be a soldier.
The following November I remarried. If remarriage is, as they say,
the triumph of hope over experience, my hope, at least, was fully
justified, though I'm afraid few could say the same for hers. Cynthia
was a wonderful wife and put up with me for twelve years. She
should have had a medal.

I had found a job after demobilisation with Miles Aircraft at
Reading, who sent me to represent them in Rome in May 1947. But
in the autumn I fell ill with serious pulmonary TB and my Italian
doctor sent me to a sanatorium in Davos in Switzerland. This
sanatorium enjoyed a high reputation, though I could never understand why. There was no discipline and the patients therefore didn't
observe any. The nursing was appalling. In the whole sanatorium

there was only one night nurse, and she was an alcoholic drug addict. There was no restriction on how much patients might drink: in fact, one patient died there not of TB but of alcoholism. Nemesis came just before I left in the form of some young Turkish patients who arrived under an exchange scheme between the two governments. When these young men got drunk, they stripped off their clothes and rampaged through the building naked, in pursuit of any female patient they found. The management thereupon posted notices advising inmates that in future each of them would be rationed to one bottle of spirits per patient per day.

In February 1949 I discharged myself and returned to England – not much fitter and a great deal poorer. At the end of that year, back in Rome, I had a relapse of TB. This time the Army accepted my condition as a war disability and secured me a bed in the excellent sanatorium at Midhurst. Six months later I was discharged and have suffered no relapse since.

One of the conditions of my discharge from Midhurst was that I shouldn't take up work for six months or a year. My friend Rowland Winn offered us his house in the south of Spain for my convalescence: he himself had rejoined his old regiment, the 8th Hussars, to go with them to the war in Korea, where he won his MC at the battle of the Imjin River. After an idyllic year in his house overlooking the Straits of Gibraltar we returned to London in September 1951 and rented a flat in Onslow Square. Looking for a job – for Miles Aircraft had gone into liquidation – I was lucky to run into Tommy Weldon.

'If you're looking for a job,' he said, 'why not join me?'

Thus, in November I joined the Imperial Life Assurance Company of Canada, who put up with me until I reached retirement age in 1980; I worked under Tommy Weldon in the branch he ran in St James's Square, and I enjoyed every minute of it; the company was unusually tolerant of my *Wanderlust* and, provided I brought them business over the year, made no objections to my travelling. And so, when the Hungarian Revolution broke out in October 1956, I determined to get myself to Budapest somehow and do what I could to help there.

For the previous eleven years the countries of Eastern Europe had endured a repression crueller and more thorough than any since the rule of the Mongols; this was a consequence of the disastrous Yalta settlement. During Stalin's lifetime they had endured it with resentful but helpless resignation; but after his death in 1953 there appeared the first signs of revolt, albeit abortive, among the satellites. That same year workers' riots in East Berlin were bloodily suppressed; and in the autumn of 1956 similar events in Poland brought some changes in the government and a slight, though temporary, easing of Russian control.

Hungary had suffered unspeakable horrors under the murderous regime of Stalin's appointed viceroy, the odious Mátyás Rákosi – Enver Hoxha was an enthusiastic fan of his. For sheer wanton and sadistic brutality Rákosi's rule was unsurpassed at the time. But Stalin's death brought no immediate relief to the Hungarians. Rákosi remained in power until July 1956 and his Soviet-trained secret police, the AVH ('Avo'), continued to terrorise the people with a cruelty shocking even by communist standards. Although Rákosi was dismissed and officially disgraced in July 1956 for his 'mistakes', his successor was another Stalinist, Erno Gerö – the 'General Walter' of the International Brigades I have already mentioned – and the power of the Party, and of the AVH, remained unchallenged and unchallengeable.

Until Tuesday 23 October 1956: on that day the Hungarian nation rose against its Russian and Russian-appointed masters in a spontaneous and virtually unanimous outburst of fury and national pride. Almost the entire population was behind the Revolution, whose inspiration and leadership came, ironically enough, from the students and workers – the two sections of society most 'favoured' under communist rule.

Although the causes of the Revolution lay in the horrors of the previous eleven or twelve years, the incident which provoked the rising occurred on the evening of 23 October, when a group of AVH fired on an unarmed crowd demonstrating outside the radio building in Budapest and killed at least twelve of them. The furious crowd attacked the AVH and seized their weapons; they received more arms from the Hungarian soldiers sent to disperse them and from military arsenals which were thrown open to them. Within hours an enormous army of freedom fighters had assembled under leaders they chose for themselves. The Hungarian Revolution had begun, to thrill Western public opinion and fill the columns of the press – and be forgotten within two months.

In the early hours of the following morning, 24 October, Russian tanks entered the streets of Budapest. There followed five days of fierce fighting between the Hungarian freedom fighters, including boys and girls of twelve years and upwards, and Russian troops assisted by units of the AVH. The Hungarians fought with a courage and ferocity typical of those people when they have been pushed too far, and when their country and traditions are in danger. They had no anti-tank guns, but they had automatic weapons and, devastatingly effective in the confined conditions of street warfare, grenades and Molotov cocktails with which they disabled many of the Russian tanks. Stupidly the Russians had sent in their tanks unsupported by infantry, rendering them vulnerable to this kind of attack. The hero of this battle was Colonel Pál Maléter, commanding the Killian Army barracks in Budapest, who at a critical moment led his tanks and infantry into the fight against the Russians and probably decided the outcome. The Russians abandoned the city. At the end of the 'first phase' the freedom fighters controlled all the province of Transdanubia, stretching westwards from Budapest to the Austrian border, and all the western frontier crossings.

Although determined to go to Hungary, fired by the same enthusiasm as many others for this heroic cause, I was realistic enough to understand that I couldn't hope to be much use to it if I went in a private capacity; I must find a newspaper to represent and so be able at least to tell the outside world what was happening. But all the leading British papers by now had staff correspondents in Hungary. However, I approached the proprietor, Douglas Woodroffe, of the Catholic weekly, *The Tablet*, which took a special interest in Iron Curtain affairs, and discovered he had nobody in Hungary – his usual correspondent was in Poland; I had known him before and he readily agreed to send me – 'if you can get in'. The next morning I was on the plane to Vienna; from there I should have to play it by ear.

The 'first phase' was drawing to its successful close and the fighting dying down. On 28 October the new Prime Minister, Imre Nagy, ordered a ceasefire; the AVH would be dissolved and negotiations would begin for a total Russian withdrawal from Hungary. Arriving in Vienna I was lucky enough to meet a British journalist who offered me a lift in his car on the following day.

'But I can only take you as far as Györ,' he warned. 'That is only thirty miles beyond the frontier. You'll have to hitch-hike the remaining hundred to Budapest; you won't need a Hungarian visa now,' he went on. 'The freedom fighters control the frontier post at Hegysalom and they're only too happy to let in Western journalists. So we'll start tomorrow directly after lunch.'

'Welcome to Hungary, sir,' smiled the young man who stamped my passport at Hegysalom. He was wearing plus-fours and looked like an undergraduate. In the mellow sunlight of late afternoon, under a pale blue, cloud-flecked autumn sky, we drove across the great Danubian plain towards Györ. In the villages the houses were draped with the red, white and green of the national colours; in the centres of the flags were gaping holes where the Soviet red stars had been excised. Groups of happy, noisy people standing by the roadside waved and shouted to us when they saw the Union Jack painted on the bonnet of our car. At every village there was a checkpoint manned by young freedom fighters, many of them boys of fifteen or sixteen, armed with rifles or tommy-guns; having been warned that they could be trigger-happy we pulled up carefully each time, but when we showed them our passports they waved us on with cheerful greetings. Their real interest was in preventing the escape of members of the hated AVH and so they were more concerned with traffic travelling the other way. We entered Györ just before dark and my friend dropped me off at the hotel in the main square.

In this town I was immediately aware of a new feeling of tension. An air of anxiety hung over the crowds in the streets and on the square; the little knot of people round the hotel doorway wore strained and worried faces. I soon found out why: news had arrived of Russian reinforcements pouring into Hungary. All the same, when I asked the receptionist what the hotel was called, he answered with a shrug: 'It has no name now. Last week it was the "Red Star" hotel, but' – and he smiled faintly – 'we have no red stars in Hungary any more.'

I went to the bar for a drink before dinner, only to find that they served nothing stronger than coffee; the government of Imre Nagy had banned the sale of alcohol throughout the country. They were trying to negotiate a treaty with the Russians and dared not risk any more explosions of anti-Soviet feeling. For a while I sat at a table in the noisy, stuffy room, where the lights glimmered opaquely through a pall of cigarette smoke, and studied the intent, excited faces of the groups seated near me, huddled over their coffee or lemonade.

An important cathedral town and provincial capital, Györ was at this time the headquarters of the newly formed National Revolutionary Council of Transdanubia – the authority in charge of affairs in western Hungary. After dinner I crossed the crowded square, thronged with anxious men and women listening to the bulletins interspersed with music that blared from loudspeakers, and walked into the town hall, where the council was in continuous session.

All was bustle and confusion inside the building, with a smiling crowd of people in every room and on the stairs; messengers were continually arriving with news of Russian troop movements or hurrying out with orders from the council. I was introduced to the President, who bore the inappropriate name of Attila – for he was a heavily built, puffing, red-faced man with long, drooping blond moustaches and an air of melancholy foreboding that was only too well justified by events; a few weeks later the Russians hanged him.

On a large wallmap in an inner room, where his colleagues were in conference, he showed me the latest positions and lines of advance of the Russian columns. Already it looked as though they were moving to seal the southern and western frontiers; yet there were still a few optimistic councillors who believed that they would withdraw as soon as a treaty had been signed. Others were not so confident and one young man, a doctor of philosophy, told me in perfect English that he was leaving in the morning for Austria.

'It is one thing to be brave,' he explained with a smile of apology. 'It is quite another to be stupid.'

It was nearly two o'clock when, having seen enough, I took myself gloomily to bed.

I awoke from a fitful, nightmare-troubled sleep to a slate-grey sky and the sound of heavy rain hammering on the cobbles beneath my window. But it was another sound that had awakened me, a sound that had haunted my dreams for twenty years: the heavy, measured rumble of approaching tanks.

I dressed hurriedly and ran to the crossroads by the square to watch them go by, squadron after squadron of Russian T-34s and the newer, streamlined T-54s, on their way westwards towards the frontier; although the tanks were not battened down for action, the grim expressions on the hard-faced, helmeted drivers and crews seemed to show that they were expecting battle. The streets of the town were almost deserted and the few people I met hurried by with downcast eyes; their faces wore a look of doom.

There was no traffic on the main road, either, to give me a lift to Budapest and I returned unhappily to the hotel for lunch. There I had a bit of luck. I was finishing a goulash when a party of four joined me at the table – two Englishmen and two Hungarians, one of them a very pretty girl; they were on their way by car to the capital. The owner of the car, Nigel Leigh Pemberton, an affable young man with a round, cherubic face, offered to take me with them.

'It'll be a hell of a squash,' he warned me. 'I've only a Morris Minor and there'll be three of you in the back; but if you haven't much luggage I daresay we'll manage.'

'Why are you going to Budapest?' I asked him. 'Are you a journalist?'

'Indeed I'm not!' He snorted at the suggestion. 'I'm an opera singer – or rather I'm studying in Vienna to become one.'

'But surely there's no opera in Budapest at the moment? Or do you mean to become the Caruso of the barricades?'

'No, thank you! I'm just here as a chauffeur. This chap' – he nudged his companion – 'is going there on some newspaper errand and I said I'd drive him.' His companion, a blond, taciturn youth, gave us such a dirty look that I forbore to ask the name of his paper.

'The trouble is,' Nigel went on, 'I'm supposed to be back in Vienna for a concert the day after tomorrow and now it doesn't look as if I will be.'

'Why do you say that?' I asked quickly.

'We ran into a column of Russian tanks just after leaving Hegy-salom. As we passed the leading tank it slewed suddenly right across the road – damn nearly rammed us – and stayed there, blocking the way. We only just got by in time and the chap in command – a real little Tartar he looked – shouted something rude at us; but he let us go on. It seems pretty clear they're going to turn back anyone approaching the frontier now.'

'Who are your two Hungarian friends?'

'He's a doctor from the South and she's his fiancée. They stopped us on the road and asked for a lift to Budapest. It seems her younger brother was a freedom fighter and was desperately badly wounded in the fighting there; they don't expect him to live. I gather there were just the two of them – orphans, you know – and she's hoping, poor girl, to get to him before he dies.'

It was nearly three o'clock when I squeezed into the back of the Morris with the two Hungarians and we started off. In my halting German – for they spoke no English – I tried to apologise for the extra discomfort I was causing; but they seemed too deeply wrapped in their own troubles even to notice my intrusion. They sat huddled together, taking comfort from the warmth and closeness of each other, the girl's pretty, dark head on his shoulder and his arm tightly encircling her slim waist.

The rain had ceased before lunch, but the sky was still overcast and stormy, and the weather had turned bitterly cold; a keen wind was blowing from the East, carrying the promise of snow. The road ran straight and level, following the Danube across the bare plain, past sad brown stubble fields and patches of sombre, dark, leafless woodland. In the villages the flags still hung from balconies and windows, but the streets were almost deserted. The soldiers and young freedom fighters who stopped us at the checkpoints were smiling and friendly, and seldom bothered to ask for our passports; but there were few people to wave to us as we went by.

There was scarcely any traffic on the road. At the entrance to a wood we passed a black saloon car, battered and abandoned, its windscreen and windows splintered; on the panels of its front doors were painted the letters 'AVH'. We drove on through the afternoon while the sky grew darker and the first flurries of snow beat upon our windscreen; when twilight settled upon the empty landscape it was snowing heavily and soon we had to grope our way forwards blindly against the glare of our own headlights, thrown back at us from the thickly falling flakes. I felt sorry for Nigel, straining his eyes into the murk ahead, but he kept the car moving at a steady pace. Suddenly the engine faltered, spluttered and coughed, then rallied for a moment as Nigel trod hard on the accelerator; the next minute the engine cut and we glided to a halt by a low, snow-covered bank at the side of the road.

Luckily it was not more than a quarter of an hour before we saw the glare of powerful headlamps lighting up the road behind us and a minute later a large limousine pulled up in response to our signals. There emerged from it an enormous figure in clerical collar and black gaiters, and a wiry little man in a leather windjacket; it was a Lutheran bishop from eastern Hungary, on his way back to his diocese, and his chauffeur. The latter proved to be a trained mechanic and while he was dealing with the fault in the Morris I had a few words with the bishop, a heavy-faced, phlegmatic prelate who spoke a slow and measured English.

'The Russians have now entirely closed the frontiers,' announced this ponderous man in complacent tones, as though he had just learned of an unusually full attendance at Harvest Festival. 'More divisions have entered Hungary today from the Ukraine. Perhaps we shall have some interesting times, eh?' He gave a dry and mirthless laugh, shook my hand solemnly and climbed back into his car; his chauffeur joined him and they disappeared swiftly into the night.

The snow had ceased to fall and lay only thinly on the ground, so we made good progress for a while. We were in the hills that guard the western approaches to Buda – the old half of the city – when a flashing torch in the darkness ahead caused us to pull up once again. In the light of the headlamps we saw a stocky figure in a green uniform standing in the middle of the road.

'Another checkpoint,' we groaned and reached for our passports. The girl sighed and moved away from the doctor as the torch shone in our faces and a hoarse, peremptory voice shouted a challenge through the window.

We handed over our papers and I said, 'I am an English newspaper correspondent.' The policeman or soldier, whichever he was, made no reply. He looked at the documents, then threw them back at us and stood glowering through the window. He was swaying slightly and he had an evil look on his face.

'Hungarian or Russian?' I asked the doctor in a whisper. He shook his head, evidently as bewildered as I. I began to feel distinctly uneasy. I had heard that the Russians had occupied these hills in strength and, if the doctor could not identify his uniform, it seemed likely that this man was a Russian – probably some kind of military policeman, for he was not wearing the usual Army uniform. In the darkness it was impossible to tell whether he was alone, but he would certainly have friends within call. At any rate, for the moment he represented authority; and clearly he was far from sober.

He peered through the open window beside me and shouted something in Hungarian at the doctor. I caught the sickly-sweet smell of *barack* on his breath. As the doctor stared at him in astonishment he whipped a heavy automatic from the holster at his belt and thrust it in through the window. The barrel was only a couple of inches from my face, swinging in an unsteady arc from one of us to the other, the hammer was back at full cock and, with that trembling finger on the trigger, the gun was liable to go off at any second.

The guard's spite seemed to be directed mainly against the two Hungarians; he kept repeating the word *'Magyar!'* with vicious emphasis. At another barked order the doctor opened the door and climbed slowly on to the road. Still shouting the guard urged him forward with gestures of his pistol until he stood in the full glare of the headlamps. The poor man stayed there staring into the lights, his hands at his sides, yet he somehow maintained a quiet composure that showed no sign of fear in the face of imminent death. The guard, working himself into even wilder paroxysms of sadistic fury, covered him at point blank range; at any moment I expected to hear the sharp report of the pistol and to see the slight figure in the headlights crumple in the snow.

The girl, who had been whimpering quietly, gave an anguished, despairing cry and, leaping from the car, ran to her fiancé; putting her arms round him she hugged him closely to her and, while the tears rained down her face, tried to place herself between him and that menacing pistol. Gently he moved her aside and, with an arm around her shoulder, turned to face his persecutor.

The three of us who were ignorant of the language had not at first realised what was happening, especially since we could see no cause for the guard's sudden outburst. Now we sat silent and paralysed with the horror of the scene, terrified to make any move that might precipitate a double murder; the guard was obviously not open to reason, even if we could have made ourselves understood; while the least attempt at interference would probably set off that trigger. On the other hand, we could not just sit there and do nothing. Nigel leaned out of the window and called to the guard in German; the latter, in the same language, brusquely told him to shut up, adding with a snarl: 'If any of you makes a move I will shoot them both.' It was clear he meant it.

He turned back to the two lovers huddled together in the bright glare of the headlights, and stood swaying and cursing, alternately sighting along the barrel of his automatic and straightening up to deliver an incoherent diatribe in Hungarian. I felt a cold rage steal over me at the vile cruelty of this drunken animal; I was trembling violently and my hands were cold and damp with sweat. The strain was becoming unbearable; at any moment it would snap.

And then, from the trees by the side of the road, emerged a young man in a smart grey uniform, wheeling a bicycle; he had a handsome, friendly face and an air of lazy self-confidence. He spoke sharply to the guard in Hungarian. There was a long, tense pause and we held our breath while the two men glared at each other in angry silence; I could feel the sweat pouring off my forehead and running down my nose, but I dared not make the least movement to wipe it off. Then, slowly and sulkily, the guard replaced his pistol in its holster and stood muttering surly protests at the ground. The newcomer strolled over to the Hungarians and, after a few words, and a brief examination of their papers, patted the doctor on the shoulder and motioned them back into the car. When they were inside he came up to Nigel's window and, with an apologetic smile and a deprecating shrug of his shoulders, waved us on our way.

To avoid further checkpoints we left the main road and travelled by side roads to the outskirts of Buda, where we dropped the doctor and the girl. They were as puzzled as we were by the guard's behaviour. He was no Hungarian, they were sure, but a Russian in Hungarian uniform; he had spoken with a thick Ruthenian accent. We never heard whether the girl saw her brother, whether he died, or whether he lived, like so many other gallant young freedom fighters, to suffer imprisonment, torture and the hangman's rope.

The consul in the British Legation to whom I told our story later that night was sympathetic but incredulous.

'Of course I've heard there are these drunken types on the roads,' she said airily, pouring me a stiff whisky from a bottle in her desk, obviously kept for visitors. 'But you're the only journalists who seem to have met one.'

The Lutheran bishop proved to be right: the Russians had indeed closed all the frontiers and were pouring troops into Hungary. They were occupying the airfields and would soon, with cynical effrontery, refuse landing permission to the Secretary General of the United Nations.

These facts were not yet generally known, but already when I arrived in Budapest the frantic euphoria of the early days was beginning to give way to an atmosphere of foreboding. Among the journalists in my hotel the optimists, such as my former SOE colleague Basil Davidson, confidently maintained that the Russians were going to pull out and that the recent troop deployments were only to protect their withdrawal; but the realists, including Sefton Delmer's *Daily Express* team – though Tom Delmer himself expressed no opinion in public – gloomily predicted the Russians would never swallow their humiliation so easily but, in the words of one of them, 'come back and clobber this town'.

On Saturday 3 November there was a press conference in Buda on the progress of negotiations for the Russian withdrawal. I was not invited but among those who attended was Basil Davidson. He was at lunch afterwards in the hotel, where I joined him, and he radiated satisfaction and confidence.

'Everything's settled,' he told us. 'The Russian troops are pulling out. The're having another conference tonight to discuss the logistics of the withdrawal.'

It didn't turn out quite like that. The Russians had indeed invited Nagy and Maléter, the new Defence Minister, to their headquarters to discuss troop withdrawals. The intermediary had been the Soviet ambassador, one Yuri Andropov, later head of the KGB, and finally Soviet President and Party leader; he guaranteed safe conduct to the Hungarian leaders and so they went. A reception committee awaited them under the infamous Colonel-General Serov, the organiser in 1940 of the deportations from the Baltic States. Maléter was immediately arrested along with his aides – the same kind of deception by which ten years earlier Stalin had lured the Polish leaders Mikolajcik and General Okulicki into prison; Nagy managed to take refuge in the Yugoslav Embassy, only to be handed over to the Russians. Nagy and Maléter were imprisoned and eventually hanged.

At the time none of us knew about the arrests. But early the following morning I was awakened in my hotel by the sound of machine-gun fire and the explosions of shells. It was soon clear the Russians were launching a full-scale assault on the city. The 'second phase' had begun. In this attack the Russians used artillery, aircraft and tanks – this time closely supported by infantry – and they came in irresistible strength. The Hungarians didn't stand a chance. Their few Army units were quickly overwhelmed. The 'free world' had lavished praise on the freedom fighters: now they lavished sympathy, but nothing else; sympathy is little use against armour. Besides, Britain and France were now involved in the Suez operation and a bitter dispute with the United States. The media soon lost interest in Hungary. I heard from a well-informed source that the

Russian troops who came in to crush the Revolution received their marching orders at least twenty-four hours before the outbreak on 23 October, in which case the AVH provocation could have been deliberate. If they had already got wind of the impending Suez operations, the Russians would know that they might count on a free hand in Hungary.

Nevertheless, the Hungarians fought on. The entire population seemed to be fighting. Students and workers manned houses and barricades, and the Russians had to blast their way through, house to house and street to street. But after a week of desperate and heroic resistance the Hungarians were inevitably run into the ground. But they still preserved their defiance. The workers of Csepel, an industrial suburb, called a general strike and kept it up in the face of Russian threats and reprisals for another month.

On that Sunday morning, 4 November, British journalists were told to report immediately to the Embassy; the Ambassador, who had provided transport, spoke to us all. He feared Russian reprisals might extend to include Western journalists – which happily they didn't – but he emphasised that he would be held responsible for our safety and so he asked us to remain in the Embassy at least for the next two or three days until the situation clarified. At first the fighting was quite near the Embassy, but it drifted away and eventually we dispersed to our hotels. Meanwhile we were allowed to send daily a pooled dispatch on Embassy links.

A week or ten days later most Western correspondents returned home, sickened by the tragedy and their own inability to help its victims. The Russian vengeance was terrible. Thousands of freedom fighters were arrested; many were hanged, many tortured – special torture cells had been built under Rákosi's regime, with the floors constructed so that the blood would drain away quickly. In order to conform with the concept of 'Socialist Legality' boys and girls under eighteen, the minimum age for the death penalty, were held in AVH prisons until their eighteenth birthdays – sometimes for as long as six years – and then sent to the gallows. Thousands were packed into cattle trucks and transported to Soviet labour camps. Hundreds of thousands fled to the West, dodging the frontier controls, leaving a shortage of talent in Hungary that still persists.

I felt reluctant to join the general exodus of journalists quite so soon; there was still plenty to report, especially the continuing arrests and deportations, which I felt I owed it to the Hungarians to try and publish. When I told the Ambassador I was staying on, he said, 'As long as just a few of you chaps can hang on here the Hungarians won't feel themselves completely abandoned.' I wasn't too happy when he added that the Russians would likely have a file on me, since I had been a prisoner in their hands in Poland. However, it seemed little enough to do for this brave people.

Although there were no postal or telegraph services, strangely enough the telephone lines were still open, and it was possible to call London and pass dispatches or messages. This was not very satisfactory for a weekly like *The Tablet* and much too expensive. And so, with Woodroffe's full approval, I persuaded the *Sunday Express* to keep me on. I didn't, however, achieve a lot of success with my stories, for Hungary by now was second-class news at best; the headlines were for Suez – rather naturally. But I persevered and received valuable help from the Reuters correspondent, Ronald Farquhar, a true professional, who was staying in the same hotel.

One morning in mid-November one of my contacts asked me to accompany him to his flat.

'I have something to show you, if you are interested in the Russian repressions.'

On the bed in the single room of his flat were sitting two boys and a girl. They were dressed alike in windcheaters and trousers tucked into their boots. They appeared to be in their late teens, though it was hard to determine their precise ages through the ravages of starvation, exhaustion and fear that lined the features of them all. I hope I never see again such stark terror as was written on those pathetic young faces. Before my friend spoke I knew pretty well what he was going to say.

'I thought you would like to meet these three freedom fighters who have been on a deportation train. Only they escaped on the way to the Russian frontier and managed to get back to Budapest. But they can't go home because the AVH are looking for them. They will tell you their story themselves but first let me introduce you. This is Balázs, the eldest, who is their leader. He is just nineteen.'

He indicated a well-built youth with fair hair, and a frank and friendly expression, who rose unsteadily to his feet and shook hands, relaxing his weary features in a charming smile. The other boy, whose name was Dénés, was short and wiry, with a sallow complexion, thin lips and a gleam of ferocity in his pale eyes; he spoke jerkily, with quick nervous gestures. Magdi, the girl, was small and plump and, despite the ghastly look of strain on her face, remarkably pretty.

'Dénés and Magdi are engaged to be married.'

'Good God! How old are they?'

'Seventeen and sixteen. Our people marry very young these days, you know.'

Their story was similar to that of thousands of young Hungarians in those terrible weeks – except that these three had been luckier, so far, than many others. Before the Revolution Balázs had been a medical student, Dénes a mechanic; the three of them had been friends since childhood. When the fighting started on 4 November they found themselves part of the garrison of a block of buildings to the south of the Gellért hill. The garrison held out for six days and, so they told me, accounted for six tanks and three or four hundred Russians. When at last resistance collapsed the three friends had escaped from the ruins, only to be picked up a few days later by a Russian patrol.

Their captors were on the point of shooting them when, for some unexplained reason, a Russian officer intervened. Instead, they were packed into a train, along with several hundred other young people, and sent off towards the Ukrainian border. On the way, however, the train was derailed; Hungarian partisans had blown up the track. In the confusion they escaped once again and, after many days, reached Budapest, where they all lived. But the AVH had already been to their homes to look for them and would certainly return, and so their terrified families had sent them away to hide with friends. They had spent the last few nights in hiding, but now the net was closing in and they could stay no longer in Budapest.

If the AVH caught them they would be lucky to be shot, with their record. One of their comrades, they told us, had escaped before being put on the train, but had been recaptured immediately and handed over to the AVH. They had stripped him naked and beaten him to death in front of the others.

Their only hope was to flee the country. They had friends in Győr, a hundred miles to the west and about thirty miles from the Austrian frontier, who would look after them and, they felt sure, be able to get them across the border. But how were they to get to Győr? How could they even get out of Budapest, where lay their greatest danger? A friend had brought them to this flat, but they certainly would not be safe here for long.

'Time is running out for them,' said my friend. 'Is there *anything* you can do to help them get out?'

Looking at the agonised, haunted faces of those three children, I knew I could not bring myself to abandon them to a hideous death without at least making some effort to save them. An idea began to take shape in my mind: not a very bright idea, but it might have a chance.

I had persuaded my newspaper to let me hire a car; they were not easy to find in Budapest, but I had managed to procure one belonging to a friend, who was also able to supply me with petrol.

It was a rickety old Skoda in very poor condition, but so far it had not broken down on me. I had attached to the bonnet a Union Jack obtained from the Legation.

'Now,' I said to them, 'I have a suggestion for you: I am willing to drive you in my car to Györ. There is a possibility that when they see my British flag the guards at the checkpoints will let us through; there is the further chance that if they do stop us they will be satisfied with my British passport and press card, and won't bother about anyone else in the car. I have seen that happen before. I admit it's a pretty desperate gamble and you may very well be caught. So if you have any other plan of escape I strongly advise you to stick to that. Otherwise, if you'd like to try your luck with me, you're welcome.'

There was a short pause while they talked among themselves; and then, somewhat to my surprise – and dismay – the three of them crowded round me, shaking my hand and pouring out their thanks in a chorus of relief. Now that they had accepted, there was no going back for me. I began to experience a distinct sinking feeling. I didn't suppose for a moment that my British passport would give me the least protection if I should be caught smuggling this particular sort of contraband and I was frankly appalled at the enormous responsibility for those three young lives that I had taken on my shoulders. However, it was done now.

'Can you be ready to leave in an hour's time?'

'*Igen! Igen!*' they assented ecstatically. 'Yes!'

'What about a rendezvous?' I said to my contact. 'It had better be on the Buda side of the river because the guards on the bridges might stop my car, but they don't seem to bother much about pedestrians, at least in the daytime.'

The others agreed and after a short discussion we chose the Joseph Bem Square, named after the Polish general who played a leading part in the Hungarian revolution of 1848. It stood on the Danube embankment and was small enough to avoid any risk of missing each other, and busy enough for us not to be conspicuous; it was also on our way out of Budapest. They raised one objection – that it was only a few hundred yards from the notorious AVH headquarters and prison on the Fö Utca; but, as I pointed out, for that very reason it might not be as closely watched as other parts of the town. I described my car carefully and told them I would be waiting in it on the north side of the square at half-past one.

There remained the language problem. Dénes and Magdi spoke only Hungarian, but Balázs had a working knowledge of German; my German was poor but, having no Hungarian, I had been forced to practise it in recent weeks and it had improved considerably. We would probably manage all right.

As he let me out of the flat our friend wished me luck on the journey; but he gripped my hand with an intensity of feeling that did nothing to improve my confidence.

'Of course,' he added, 'much will depend on the guards you meet at the different control posts. Some of them are only Hungarian soldiers, whom the Russians are using for this work; they should not give you too much trouble. The Russian guards will be more difficult, but they are often very stupid. The AVH, of course, are the most dangerous, but fortunately there are still not too many of them.' He smiled grimly. 'They have not yet made up their losses from the Revolution.'

I raced back to the hotel. Upstairs in my room I wrapped up a parcel of food and a bottle of brandy, slipped a toothbrush in my pocket and walked outside to my car.

By the time I had filled up with petrol it was almost half-past one. I rattled over the Chain Bridge across the Danube without interference from the guards at either end and turned right, down the narrow, gloomy Fö Utca, past the forbidding stone facade of the AVH building with its heavily barred windows and pair of dark-blue-uniformed police in the doorway, and came out into the Bem Tér, dominated by the equestrian statue of the general in a green space in the centre. I drew up by the pavement on the north side and waited with the engine running.

My *protégés* were not there. At first I was not alarmed: they might easily have been held up, or they might have arrived before me – I had been a few minutes late myself – and, rather than attract attention by staying in the square, they might have gone for a short walk, intending to return in a few minutes. But after a quarter of an hour I was feeling uneasy. It was conceivable, though not likely, that they were waiting on another side; and so I got out of the car and, leaving it unlocked in case they should turn up in my absence, walked slowly twice across the square and then along each of the sides, keeping a good look-out all round me. There was the usual number of people about, hurrying along on business or strolling in twos and threes savouring the crisp, clean air and the pale winter sunshine; but there was no sign of my three.

I returned to my car to find a small group gathered round, staring curiously at the Union Jack. They smiled at me as I got in.

'*Ongol* [English]?' one of them asked.

I nodded, smiling back.

'*Ongol sajtó* [English press].' There was a low chorus of approval and one or two insisted on shaking my hand. But it wasn't the moment to be smiling; I was attracting far too much attention to stay there any longer. Besides, it was after two and it was obvious that my passengers were not going to turn up; either they had taken fright and abandoned the plan, or something had happened to them on the way. After a moment's indecision I waved to the friendly loiterers and drove off as fast as I could to my friend's flat.

They were all there, sitting side by side on the bed, the picture of dejection and fright.

'What the devil happened to these three?'

'They arrived a little early in the Bem Tér – and you, it seems, were late. They say there were many police about and then they saw some Russian soldiers come into the square, and they were too frightened to stay there any longer. So they came back here.'

'I saw one or two policemen, certainly, but not an unusual number. And there were no Russians while I was there.'

'Perhaps they were especially nervous to find themselves so close to the Fö Utca. What are you going to do now?'

'We'd better start at once – it's half-past two and curfew's at nine. That gives us more than six hours to do a hundred and thirty miles; it should be time enough provided the car doesn't break down. Thank God for this milder weather – the roads should be pretty well clear of snow. I've parked the car right outside the door; tell them to pile in as quick as they can – Balázs in front with me.'

'I'll come down too and wave you goodbye from the door – it will look less suspicious.'

A few minutes later I was driving once again towards the Danube, with my three passengers in the car and a very uncomfortable feeling inside me; my hands on the wheel were damp and slippery. The more I thought of it the more preposterous seemed the risk, the more appalling the responsibility I had undertaken. However, I forced myself to put on a confident grin, which was answered by a smile from each of the boys and a rather nervous giggle from Magdi.

I decided not to chance another crossing of the Chain Bridge, but to make for the Kossuth Bridge about half a mile upstream, by the Parliament building. We came into the square in front of the bridge, where a section of Russian tanks was permanently stationed; and then, as we mounted the bridge itself, a Russian soldier stepped into the middle of the road, signalling me to stop. My heart was pounding and I could feel the blood mounting to my face as I pulled up and began to fumble for my passport; at length I found it and handed it to him through the window, calling out '*Angliski jurnalist*' in as confident a tone as I could manage. He was a short, spotty-faced youth, very shabby in his dirty, quilted jacket and felt hat with its loose earflaps; I was glad to observe that he seemed rather bored as he glanced through the pages of my passport, which obviously conveyed nothing to him. Suddenly he shot a question through the window. Balázs translated: 'He wants to know where we're going.'

I dared not hesitate. *'Kulugy Ministerium,'* I rapped out. The Ministry of Foreign Affairs, where I often had occasion to call, lay directly on our route and it was a happy inspiration that made me think of it now. The soldier turned to shout something to a group of his fellows across the road; then he stepped back and waved us on. I could not trust myself to look at my companions as we drove across the bridge to the control post on the other side. Here, however, we were not even stopped and as I turned right to run along the Danube embankment my hands were shaking so much with relief that I could hardly steer the car.

Our road led north, beside the Danube, past the famous Hill of Roses where stood the luxurious villas, built by rich noblemen and merchants, which in recent years had housed high officials of the Party and the AVH. Soon we came to the suburb of Obuda, or Old Buda – the site, I am told, of the original Roman settlement. But I was not at that moment interested in history or archaeology; what held my attention, and brought a fresh spasm to my tortured nerves, was a barrier across and road and, beside it, the mud-coloured uniforms of a Russian picket.

As we slowed to a halt I tried to reassure my passengers with another confident smile, but I noticed that Balázs's face had gone very white.

'*Avo!*' he whispered fiercely.

I followed his gaze and saw a short, stocky, dark-faced man with a black toothbrush moustache, wearing a leather windcheater, ill-cut cloth breeches and brown jackboots; he was leaning against the barrier post by the side of the road picking his teeth.

'Are you quite sure?' I whispered back, for the man looked harmless enough to me. Balázs nodded glumly.

As I reached again for my passport I found myself praying silently that somehow we should be delivered from this dreadful situation; I prayed also that Balázs and his friends would keep their heads and stay where they were, for any attempt to run away now would effectively seal our fate. Already one of the Russians was at the window, one hand outstretched for my papers, the other on the butt of the tommy-gun that swung from his shoulder; a second soldier stood in front by the bonnet, scribbling something in a notebook – presumably the number of my car. The AVH officer –

if he was an officer – continued to pick his teeth, but I saw him looking curiously in our direction.

The Russian opened my passport and looked carefully at the photograph, and then back at me; I took off my hat to assist the identification. Apparently satisfied, he took the document over to the AVH official, who removed his toothpick and flipped through the pages, evidently checking my visa; he seemed to take an age examining it. Partly to take my mind off the agonising suspense, partly to give an impression of nonchalance, I lit a pipe, though my mouth was so parched that smoking it was out of the question.

When I looked up again the Russian was back at the window, handing me my passport and the barrier was slowly rising to let us through; the Russians stood back from the car. But the AVH agent, I saw, had left his post and was walking slowly towards us. It would never do to let him get any closer. From a distance he had seen my Union Jack and that, together with my passport, had temporarily satisfied him; but the moment he was near enough to see my passengers clearly, he would identify them as Hungarians and not the Englishmen that the Russians had presumably taken them for. There was not a second to lose. Putting on my friendliest grin, I waved to them, shouted, 'Thank you very much!' in English and let in the clutch.

We ground forward beneath the barrier and I accelerated steadily but not so fast as to give the impression of panic. I gripped the wheel in an agony of tension, my ears straining for the sound of shouting from behind and expecting at any moment the impact of bullets against the car. Only when we rounded a corner that hid us from view of the check point did I relax; I heard Balázs's breath forced out in a long low sob of relief and a high-pitched, almost hysterical laugh from Magdi. I felt as weak as a jelly myself; I wondered how much more of this sort of thing our nerves would stand. Then I remembered the bottle of brandy I had brought from my hotel room, and told Balázs to unpack it and pass it round.

A mile further on, where the road left the river and turned north-westwards into the hills, we came upon another control post; my spirits sank. I had congratulated myself too soon on our escape at the last checkpoint; if the AVH official had really been suspicious, or had second thoughts, all he needed do was telephone to the guards here to hold us. I stopped the car and was preparing myself for the worst when Balázs suddenly gave a gasp of relief.

'*Magyar!*' he exclaimed, and I saw that the young soldier walking towards us wore a Hungarian uniform. He was a tall, pleasant-faced lad and he gave me a friendly smile as he took my passport, glanced at it and handed it back. He said something to Balázs and I gathered that he was asking if we had passed through the last control post; then he said, '*Büdös Orosz!*' and spat, and we all laughed, for *büdös Orosz*, a phrase I had heard before, means 'stinking Russians'.

We had agreed that, once we were clear of Budapest and the suburbs, if we were stopped on the road we should pretend that I had picked up my three passengers a few miles back and was giving them a lift to their homes in a village a few miles further on – in other words, they would pose as countrymen and make no mention of having come from Budapest; obviously the story would not stand up to serious examination, but it might just get us by. Now I told Balázs to ask this amiable young man if he knew where we were likely to meet the next checkpoint; the guard gave a knowing grin and replied that he thought there were no more Russian posts before Szony, a small town on the Danube across the river from Czechoslovakia; but, he added, there was bound to be a very strict control there because it was a frontier town. I decided to try and make a detour round it.

For a while the road climbed steeply through wooded hills where the watery sunlight filtered through the bare branches and shone yellow on the patches of snow that dappled the ground. I told Balázs to pass round the brandy again.

Ten minutes later we were brought once more to a halt. So far there had been little traffic on the road, but now I saw ahead of us a line of cars halted behind a large lorry; there were people standing about beside them. Dear God, I prayed, not another checkpoint, *please*! I stopped behind the rearmost vehicle, my heart beginning its familiar, uncomfortable pounding. Along the right side of the road ran a ditch and in the ditch was a platoon of steel-helmeted Russian soldiers; they were manning the parapet, their rifles at the ready, and they had a light machine gun trained across the road on a long, low, white building that looked like a barracks, about a hundred yards away on our left. There were no signs of any actual fighting and nobody else seemed to be taking cover; anyway, as far as I knew, all fighting in Hungary had been over for a fortnight. But the soldiers' faces looked grim and threatening behind their levelled rifles and the air was charged with menace; one of the men's helmets had fallen off and rolled on to the road, where it lay unretrieved on its side, its leather lining turned towards me.

For a long time nothing happened. It certainly did not look as though we had blundered into a battle, more likely some military exercise; unless – and I shuddered at the thought – they were making a really detailed check on all the cars ahead of us. I looked at my three companions; they seemed pretty rattled, as was natural, but they showed no signs of running away. In any case, there were now other cars drawn up behind us and so it was impossible to turn back, even if it had been wise. We had no alternative but to sweat it out.

The soldiers crouched silently in their ditch, looking straight ahead of them. At last I heard shouts from the vehicles in front and the sound of engines starting up; the column began to move slowly forwards, only the big lorry remaining stationary. As the car in front of me drew level with it I saw a Russian officer and a soldier standing in the road; they were making no attempt to check the cars, but simply waved them on one by one like traffic policemen. A moment later we were past them; the column was thinning out ahead of us and with a great surge of relief I trod hard on the accelerator.

Soon we were clear of the hills and the country opened out on either side in a wide rolling plain; the late afternoon sun shone straight in our faces as it slid down towards the horizon. We had not much daylight left and I had to hurry if we were to reach Györ before curfew. I prayed we would not be held up again.

It was my haste that was our undoing. We were travelling fast around a corner when we came upon one of those open level crossings that are a common feature on the Continent and that are so difficult to see approaching; before I could slow down we were on to it. As the car crossed the rails there was a shattering jar and with a series of grinding, clanking jolts we came to rest at the side of the road. It hardly needed Dénés's brief inspection to tell us that the front axle had snapped.

Savagely I cursed the car, my reckless driving, and the sadistic fate that had brought us safely through so many dangers only to leave us ignominiously stranded in the middle of an unknown and friendless countryside. The despair on my poor companions' faces wrung my heart.

I pulled myself together; there was no giving in at this stage. I sat down on the bank at the roadside and began to think. It was out of the question to go on in my car; even if we could get it to a garage the job of repairing it would take days. But this was one of the main highways to Austria and even in these times there was a certain amount of westbound traffic; there was no reason why we should not hitch-hike to Györ, even if we had to do it by stages. No one was likely to recognise these three so far from Budapest. As for the car, I could probably arrange with the first garage we passed to collect it; I could retrieve it later, or have it driven back to Budapest.

My friends at first were sceptical, but they agreed that there was no alternative. However, they pointed out that most private cars on the road were owned by officials of one sort or another and we must be careful not to stop one belonging to the AVH. We unpacked the parcel I had brought and sat down to eat while we waited; the food and brandy soon improved our spirits, and we were feeling almost cheerful again when we heard the sound of an engine approaching from the east.

It was a heavy diesel lorry, fully laden, with its cargo concealed beneath lashed tarpaulins. Seeing our predicament the driver pulled on to the side of the road, and three hefty and jovial men clad in overalls got out; they were full of sympathy, especially when they learned that I was English. They told me they were bound for a village only two kilometres further on, where they said there was a good garage; they could tow the car there and I could make my own arrangements with the proprietor. When I agreed, delighted to have one problem off my hands, they produced a stout wire cable and attached my car to the lorry.

Several cars had passed, travelling in the direction of Budapest, but nothing had come the other way. At this moment, however, a large grey saloon car appeared around the corner, crossed the railway line and pulled up beside us; on its door was painted a Red Cross. Its two occupants got out and walked up to us. One, the driver, was a short, oldish man with wispy grey hair, a lean face and tired eyes, the other, who was middle-aged and heavily built, with a comfortingly placid and benign expression, addressed himself to me and, in excellent French, asked if they could help.

When I explained that we were trying to get to Györ he conferred with his companion.

'We are not going so far as Györ,' he said at length, 'but we can take you to Szony. I will arrange for you to sleep there and you can continue your journey in the morning.'

I thought this an excellent idea; it was already twilight and we might not get the chance of another lift after dark. In any case we could hardly hope now to reach Györ before curfew at nine, but Szony was only twenty-five miles from Györ and so we would have accomplished by far the greater part of our journey; moreover, in a Red Cross car we would have little difficulty with checkpoints unless we were very unlucky. I began once again to see a gleam of hope.

But when I put the idea to Balázs he was strangely reluctant; he kept muttering '*Avo, Avo*' under his breath and seemed afraid that this was a trap to hand them over to the police. I pointed out that the AVH were not likely to be using Red Cross cars for their business and, as he grudgingly admitted, these men hardly looked like AVH agents.

At length he agreed and we piled into the saloon – myself in front with the driver and his friend, and the three young people in the back. The lorry had already started off with my car in tow, the driver and his mates indignantly refusing to take a penny for their services. We stopped for a moment at the garage, where the proprietor promised to repair my car as quickly as possible and look after it until I could collect it or send someone for it from Budapest; then we drove on into the gathering darkness.

It turned out that the driver and owner of this car was a Budapest doctor, on his way to a village just this side of Szony to visit a patient; his friend was the director of a factory or group of factories – I could not work out which – and was going there on business.

'We shall spend the night in this village,' announced the director, 'and I shall arrange for all of you to stay there too, with some good friends of mine. They are trustworthy people,' he added significantly.

After about half an hour we stopped in another village, outside a house with a telephone sign. The doctor and his friend got out.

'We are going to make a call to Szony,' the latter explained, 'to tell my friends you are coming.'

As soon as they had disappeared panic seized the three in the back; they were convinced that they were going to be betrayed and that this telephone call was to an AVH headquarters. Poor things, I sympathised with their fright, although on this occasion I didn't think there was any need for it; when Balázs got out of the car and followed the two men into the house I made no effort to restrain him. He seemed reassured when he came back.

But any grounds we might have had to fear treachery disappeared during the rest of the journey. We passed two control posts and at neither did I even have to show my passport. If our new friends had wanted to betray us they would have done so then. I found myself blessing the fate I had so recently reviled.

Any chance I might have had of bringing the three Hungarians to safety on my own had vanished with the breakdown of my car. Even to reach Györ they would need other help than mine, for the director had told me that the road between Szony and Györ was strictly controlled. I could see no sane alternative but to confide in our new friends and beg their help or at least their advice. It was a risk, of course, but one that I was convinced we must take and if it succeeded it might pay off handsomely. I was sure they would not betray us now and suspected they knew the truth anyway.

It was about half-past six when the car drew up outside a small house a little way off the main road.

'Wait here a moment, please,' ordered the director as he followed the driver inside. As soon as they had gone I put my idea to Balázs. To my surprise he raised no objection and after a brief discussion the others agreed too. When the director reappeared I beckoned him into the car and, in a very few sentences, explained our position.

For a few moments he was silent, looking solemnly at the four of us. Then he said, 'We will discuss this inside and see what we can do.' We followed him into a small room, austerely furnished with a table and straight-backed wooden chairs, where an old man and his wife greeted us with warm smiles, and brought us bread, salami and a bottle of *barack*. I offered them some of my Cognac, but the old man shook his head and pointed laughingly to the *barack*.

'He says you must try his apricot brandy,' translated the director. 'He made it himself and he says it is much better against the cold.' It kindled a fire immediately.

While we ate, the others talked in whispers in a corner, glancing frequently in our direction. Eventually the director came over to me.

'I am going now,' he said, 'to make some arrangements for tomorrow. I will come back in one or two hours. Don't worry.' He disappeared with the doctor into the night.

The time seemed to pass with infinite slowness. I tried to read a thriller I had brought with me, but I could not concentrate or take any interest in the plot; the problems and adventures of the hero, an amateur detective, seemed insipid and unreal in the light of our own. At last I heard the car outside and a moment later the director strode into the room. He looked pleased with himself.

'All is settled,' he told me with a broad smile. 'Tomorrow morning at eight o'clock your friends will take the train from the station near here to Györ. I have arranged for them to be met at Györ by reliable people, who will take them across the border.'

'But should I not go with them as far as Györ?'

'Better not. You would only attract attention. The train is not very strictly controlled and they will be quite all right on their own. We will go down to the station to see them off. Please do not worry.' He laughed. 'You know, my friends have a very good organisation!'

I was so overwhelmed with relief that I hardly knew how to thank him; as for the others, it was the first time I had seen them really cheerful. The director told us that Balázs and his party would leave the house on foot soon after daybreak, accompanied by one of his friends; the station was only two kilometres distant and the guards at the checkpoint on the way did not bother about pedestrians. He and I would follow on afterwards, and meet them at the station. I made Balázs memorise the name and address of an English friend of mine who had a business in Vienna, and promise to get in touch with him as soon as they arrived.

Soon afterwards the director took his leave, promising to return for me in the morning, and we lost no time in going to bed. I had a room to myself and hardly had the strength to undress.

When I awoke in the faint grey light the old man was standing by my bed; he had brought me some bread and hot milk, and a glass of *barack*. While I was dressing the director arrived to tell me it was time for us to start; Balázs and the others had already left. I tried to make the old man accept some payment for our lodging, but he would not hear of it; so I followed the director out into the raw, foggy morning.

The countryside was still and peaceful at this early hour; there was no traffic on the main road, which ran straight ahead of us in a long grey sliver through the fog. We trudged along in silence until we came in sight of a cluster of houses and the red and white posts of a checkpoint; on our right I could see the grey waters of the Danube and the latticed iron girders of the bridge that led over into Czechoslovakia.

'We turn right after the control,' said my companion, 'and follow the road towards the bridge; the station is just below it.'

There was a pair of guards at the checkpoint, a Russian and a Hungarian, standing with slung rifles in the middle of the road. They made no attempt to stop us, though the Hungarian asked where we were going; he seemed quite satisfied with the reply.

We were almost on to the bridge before I realised it; the squat bulk of a T-54 tank blocked the entrance, the long barrel of its powerful gun pointing straight at us; a scowling group of Russian soldiers stood alertly round it. We turned sharply left down a steep incline and found ourselves in the station.

To my horror there was no sign of Balázs, Dénes or Magdi. They ought to have been there long before us. I saw the look of stupefaction on the director's face and all my worst fears returned; either they had lost their nerve at the last moment and turned back rather than risk the checkpoint – in which case why had we not met them on the road? – or by some mischance they had been stopped and detained. In the circumstances the latter seemed the more likely.

'What shall we do?' I asked in despair.

'There is nothing to do but wait here until the train leaves. Perhaps they will turn up yet.'

We paced up and down the platform to keep off the early morning chill and calm our nerves. There was quite a large crowd of travellers standing about or sitting on their luggage, and as it drew on to eight o'clock the number grew; but our friends were not among them.

'Luckily the train is always late,' said the director. 'Nevertheless they should be here.'

Eight o'clock came and still there was no sign of them. Anxiously we scanned each fresh group of faces on the platform; then came the whistle of the approaching engine. The train pulled into the station in a cloud of steam; there was a great hissing and clanking, a clatter and banging of doors, and the crowd surged forward into the carriages. Suddenly the director clutched my arm.

'There they are – just in time!'

The three of them were pelting down the slope, followed by a fourth figure, whom I took to be their guide. We ran up to them and bundled them into the nearest carriage, just as the train started to move.

'Well, what happened?' I asked as we turned away. 'Were they stopped at the control?'

'No, they passed the control without difficulty. But when they saw that tank and those Russians on the bridge they lost their nerve completely. Nothing would make them go on. They ran away and hid in a field, and it took my friend all this time to persuade them to come on to the station.'

'One can't really blame them. I suppose. All the same, it's lucky the train's always late.'

Two days later I telephoned my friend in Vienna.

'Your pals have arrived,' he told me. 'They're staying with us here for the moment. They're a grand bunch and the little girl's a smasher – you dirty old man!'

A fortnight later I had to present myself at the Ministry of Foreign Affairs.

'Your visa expires today,' I was told. 'Permission to renew it has been refused. You must leave today.'

'Today?' I protested. I had no car. 'But how? It's a hundred and thirty miles to the Austrian frontier. It's after midday now. I have no transport – and there's a blizzard blowing.'

'That's your problem. But heaven help you, Mr Kemp, if you are still in this country after midnight.'

I explained my plight to the British Embassy. They had no wish to bail me out of the Fö Utca, and so they sent round a Land Rover and driver to take me to Vienna. We just made the deadline and crossed the frontier at Hegysalom with fifteen minutes to spare.

For all its tragedy and suffering I believe the 1956 Revolution did in the long run bring some benefit to the Hungarians. The Kremlin, which had believed that Hungarian resistance would be easy to suppress, received a severe shock and it treated the Hungarians ever after with some respect. This attitude probably enabled Kádár to introduce, though slowly and carefully, his liberalising reforms; the Russians, for their part, never thought again of pushing the Hungarians too far.

Chapter 6

SOON AFTER MY return from Budapest I was overtaken by a crisis of my own making. My wife, who had supported me loyally 'in sickness and in health' for over twelve very trying years, now decided enough was enough; her decision had nothing whatever to do with Hungary, but a lot to do with my excessive fondness for alcohol. Dr Scherman's warnings to me in Spain in 1938 were becoming disturbingly true. And so we parted; but we remained and still are extremely good friends.

'"Piracy and Rebellion in South East Asia"?' mused the agent who handled my efforts in literature. 'Well, it sounds a promising subject, but I'm not sure whether it would make a book – rather a series of articles.'

Nevertheless, within a month he called me. 'I've found a publisher for your subject – a paperback firm. They're prepared to take it on *and* give you an immediate advance of £1,000 to cover air fares and expenses.' In 1960 £1,000 was a lot of money – quite enough for my likely needs. On 9 August I took off from Heathrow on a Qantas flight to Singapore.

I had done no serious travelling since Hungary, devoting myself in the previous four years to my Life Assurance work. It was a pleasant enough occupation and brought me into contact with congenial clients who more often than not became good friends; and my colleagues in our office in St James's were themselves excellent company. But by 1960 I was feeling again the urge to travel and the firm, as usual, raised no objection.

My destination was the Philippines, for it was in the southern islands of Mindanao and the Sulu Archipelago that I hoped to find the bulk of my material. I had an invitation to stay with the British Ambassador in Manila, John Pilcher, whom I had known fifteen years before, in Rome.

John Pilcher was an able diplomat whose wit and friendliness made him a popular ambassador with the Filipinos, who particularly warmed to those qualities. He had the expression and the figure of the Chinese god of good luck. With him and his cheerful wife Delia as my hosts it was inevitable that I should enjoy my stay. It also proved very useful. The Pilchers took me to a succession of parties, where I met a fair cross-section of the diplomatic, military and social hierarchy of Manila – Filipinos with romantic Spanish names who spoke no Spanish but talked to me in English with a pronounced transatlantic accent. Much more importantly, they introduced me to the legendary wartime guerrilla leader, Colonel 'Chuck' Parsons, who had landed by submarine on Mindanao soon after the Japanese occupation to raise a resistance movement there and who kept it going throughout the war, in spite of all Japanese efforts to capture or destroy him. He gave me a warm reception as well as many valuable contacts in the Moro country; their knowledge of the country and influence among the people were to ensure my safety during my travels there.

At this time the Moro rebellion, which later developed into a civil war, had not yet broken out. But I was warned that it was far from safe to travel in that region. The people of the southern Philippines originally received the name of 'Moros' from the Spaniards, who conquered the islands in the sixteenth century and who named the unruly Moslems of Mindanao and Sulu after the Moors of North Africa whom they had already been fighting for about five hundred years. These Philippine Moros, converted to Islam by missionaries from Arabia, were a proud and independent race with a fanatical hatred of all infidels and foreigners. They were ferocious fighters, whom the Spaniards never entirely subdued and who continued to trouble the Americans after the latter expelled the Spaniards at the end of the nineteenth century. They were great pirates and slavers – indeed, slavery still existed illegally in their territory. They, with the Sulu islanders, formed the dreaded Illanun pirates who were the scourge of the waters around Borneo and Malaya until the Brooke rajahs of Sarawak finally broke them in the last century. Now, although there wasn't yet a full-scale revolt in Mindanao and Sulu, both were infested with armed bands of outlaws who, I was told, had no great aversion to robbery or murder.

I left Manila in about the middle of September and flew by stages to Illigan on the north coast of Mindanao. There I hired a car and driver, and so arrived, at the beginning of October, at Dansalan, the capital of the Moro province of South Lanao, on the shore of Lake Lanao, one of the most beautiful lakes I've ever seen. Here I stayed with Father Brenan, a missionary to whom I had an introduction from friends in Manila. He was a priest of the Order of St Patrick, who had spent a long time among the Moros of Lanao and by his courage, charity and obvious dedication to his work among them had earned their sincere respect. During the days I spent in his small house on the outskirts of Dansalan he accompanied me in his Land Rover or on foot on journeys all over the country, some of them to remote parts where no Christian Filipino could travel safely. But in his company I felt, and was, completely safe. I never even saw an armed outlaw.

I did, however, confirm that slavery, though illegal, still existed in Lanao. A captain of police called to see me in Father Brenan's house, bringing with him a very frightened Christian girl aged about twelve. He and his men had found her in a house in the mountains with a Moro family, who had bought her from some men who had abducted her from her home in one of the islands up north. She had been living with this Moro family as a slave for nearly seven years, treated abominably, overworked and fed on scraps, and beaten if she offended her owners. The police had hidden her and cared for her well, and so she no longer looked starved, but she was still very frightened; her former owners were looking for her and would certainly kill her if they found her. The trouble was, the captain told me, that local sentiment approved of slavery and had no respect for the law; the police must therefore keep her hidden until they could arrange for her to be sent safely to the North, out of danger. The captain assured me this girl was only one out of many cases they knew about or strongly suspected.

From Dansalan I made my way slowly to Zamboanga, the main port of Mindanao, situated in the extreme south of the island; formerly a thriving town in the days of Spanish rule, it was now a dilapidated, dying and most depressing place to visit. There I took a ship for Jolo, the capital of the Sulu islands, and stayed for several days with the hospitable Fathers in their well-found mission house nearby. After visiting other islands in the Sulu group, by passenger ferry and by small local craft called *lipas* – a kind of canoe with a sail and stabilising outrigger, with an astonishing turn of speed before a following wind – I fetched up on the island of Sibutu, almost the most southerly of the group and about the nearest of them to British North Borneo, where I was heading. Sibutu was a long, low-lying island with a few coconut palms along the shore and jungle covering the rest; there was a village – only a few wooden houses on stilts – and a wharf. Two Oblate Fathers ran a school on the island, where they allowed me to stay while they tried to arrange a passage for me across to Borneo.

Although I hadn't yet managed to meet any outlaws and not a

single pirate – so far as I knew – I had by now a fairly good idea of my intended subject. Piracy was widespread in these waters, it appeared, and the pirates preyed on the extensive barter trade between the Philippines, Borneo and Celebes; they attacked both smugglers, of whom there were plenty, and legitimate traders, and they were seldom caught by the various government naval forces sent to suppress them.

Now my hosts told me there was a small trading vessel, called a *kumpit*, crossing from Sibutu to Semporna on the east coast of what was then known as British North Borneo and they had persuaded the master to take me with him; we were to leave Sibutu on the night of Monday 10 October. A *kumpit* had a very wide beam and a shallow draught, propelled originally by sail with a small auxiliary engine; some *kumpits*, used by smugglers and the pirates who preyed on them, had several powerful outboards, enabling them to escape from naval and customs ships to the shallow waters inshore, where they were usually safe from pursuit.

I left the Fathers' school on Monday evening to walk down to the wharf where my *kumpit* lay. My hosts sent a few of the students with me as guides. Our way led through a coconut plantation. I was walking a short way ahead of the leader, who carried a lantern, when I saw in the half darkness what looked like a long palm stalk lying across the path. Luckily I had a good torch and thought it might be wise to make sure before I trod over or on it. Just as well I did, for in the torchlight it proved to be a large and very angry snake. Later, in the Sarawak Museum I was able to identity it, or something like it, as '*Lachesis Waglerii*', labelled 'highly venomous'. Now it coiled, reared up at me, and swayed for a few moments before suddenly uncoiling and sliding off into the undergrowth, hotly – and rashly, I thought – pursued by my young escort with their lantern. They didn't catch the snake but enjoyed telling me how lethal it was.

At the wharf I found my *kumpit* with its captain and crew of six or eight, all of them Samals, the best seamen among the Moros. Their *kumpit* had only a six hp inboard diesel engine and another *kumpit* in tow, and so I reckoned the journey might take a bit longer than the eight to twelve hours I had been told to expect – I hoped not too much longer. I had no provisions for the journey – there weren't any to spare on Sibutu; there was, of course, nowhere to sleep but on the open deck and the only loo was over the side into the sea. I had expected nothing better.

We were under way at last at about 8 pm but our top speed with the tow was a mere two to three knots. I was the only passenger, apart from two women and a child who were probably the family of one of the crew. The journey took a lot longer than twelve hours – in fact, from Monday night until midday on Thursday, because we ran into a violent storm on the second day, with heavy seas and a fierce, south-westerly headwind. These were treacherous, shallow waters studded with reefs of sharp coral that could easily tear the bottom out of a boat, and so it was lucky we had such a skilful crew and a captain who knew his way through or around the shoals; lucky too that a *kumpit* is a superb sea boat. Even so, twice the storm threw us against reefs, and twice the boat was holed and the sea flooded the engine well, smothering the diesel. But on each occasion the crew managed to plug the hole and restart the engine, working in the darkness, and drenched with the seas and the rain while I did my best to keep my torch steady enough to guide them. The battering of the heavy seas was frightening and I pictured a horrible end for us all in the water as the razor-sharp coral tore us to pieces. Only the exemplary seamanship of master and crew, who never once showed panic or even serious alarm, saved us from disaster.

We limped into Semporna at four o'clock on Thursday morning. There was a government launch there which, after I had warmly thanked the captain and crew of the *kumpit*, took me south to Tawao, a busy port and commercial centre on the estuary of the Kalabakan River. There I reported to some astonished police, customs and immigration officers.

'You were bloody lucky to survive that storm in a *kumpit*,' they commented. 'You must have had a damn good crew. Anyway,' the immigration said, 'you should be properly cleared by the Philippines immigration to leave the country. We ought to send you back to Manila. However . . .' And so I entered North Borneo.

I spent a fortnight in Borneo and Sarawak before taking a boat on to Singapore. I had intended to fly back to England as soon as I reached Singapore but on second thoughts I decided to pay a visit first to Laos, to see my old friend Prince Boun Oum, who had worked so loyally with the French and ourselves on the Thai-Lao frontier in 1945–6. The Prince was now the political leader of a revolt against the new Laotian government of Prince Souvanna Phouma – a revolt of which the military commander was another acquaintance of mine from 1945, General Phoumi Nosavan. I knew little about this situation, but felt it might provide some more much-needed material for my book.

Any detailed explanation of the Laotian political scene would now be both tedious and irrelevant. In August, when I left London, I read of a political *coup* in Laos, led by a young captain of paratroops, Captain Kong-Lae, which had overthrown without bloodshed the strongly pro-Western government in Vientiane. There were fears, but no clear evidence, that the *coup* was contrived and supported by the Laotian communists of the Pathet Lao, with the backing of the Vietnamese communist regime in Hanoi. The new Prime Minister, Prince Souvanna, was certainly no communist, but many in Laos and in the West feared he had lost control to the communists. Their fears turned out eventually to be unfounded, but at that time it did look as if the communists might become dangerously powerful under the new regime, and the Vietnamese communists might gain control of the country – as of course they did fifteen years later. That, at any rate, was how the situation appeared in 1960 to me and many others. It gave me a strong incentive to go to Laos now.

In Bangkok I learned that the present headquarters of the rebels was Savannakhet, on the Mekong opposite Mukdahan in Thailand. Of course I knew both towns well from 1945, when I had been running supplies to the French. On Sunday 24 November I took the train from Bangkok to Ubon, David Smiley's headquarters in 1945. A new but cramped and crowded bus took me from Ubon to Mukdahan, where I arrived in the early afternoon with my mouth, eyes, nose and hair full of red dust from the laterite road. This was all 1945 country to me and as I contemplated the familiar scene I could hardly believe it was fifteen years since I had been there – it seemed like yesterday. But the crossing of the Mekong, which used to take up to three-quarters of an hour with two men paddling hard, now lasted ten minutes in a *pirogue* with a powerful outboard.

On the Laotian shore I received a smart salute and a civil handshake from the policeman who had been watching my approach. But in the police post I ran into difficulties. Why had I come without a visa to enter Laos? I must go straight back to Bangkok and get it from the Laotian Embassy there. I pointed out that the Embassy represented the Vientiane government, against whom his people were in revolt.

'Perhaps. But you must go back to Bangkok for your visa.'

After a good deal more of this the logic penetrated and I was escorted to the police barracks, where I met a full colonel, the chief of police for the Savannakhet region. With great courtesy he asked me the object of my journey; I told him I was a writer and added that I was an old friend of Prince Boun Oum. He appeared impressed.

'But you really ought to have gone to the Embassy in Bangkok for a visa.' Silence again. At last he relaxed. He regretted it was too late to see the Prince now – it was after 5.30 – and so I should go to the hotel and report back to him early in the morning, when he would arrange for me to see both the Prince and General Phoumi.

I had never been to this hotel before and very soon I was hoping I never would go there again. Covered in dust and sweat, very hungry and very weary, I had a sponge-down and a disgusting meal, and threw myself into my bed about ten o'clock, praying for a good night's sleep. I had begun to drop off when there was a thunderous rapping on the door, and in came a small, ape-like porter with an ingratiating grin on his face and no less than six girls trooping behind him. Before I could utter he had paraded them all for my inspection.

'Go away!' I groaned and gestured towards the door. 'I want to sleep.'

He stood there for a few moments, then went out, followed by his troupe.

About twenty minutes later, just as I was going off to sleep, the hammering on the door was repeated, and in he came with the same grin and five or six more girls. After a few minutes of my shouting at him he led them out – only to return, this time when I was fast asleep, with yet another selection. I wasted no words but leaped out of bed, seized him by the collar and literally threw him out. The girls followed in silence.

At least, I reflected with satisfaction as I drifted off again, I had been admitted to Laos, however illegal my method of entry.

Prince Boun Oum seemed delighted to see me.

'One doesn't forget people,' he told me, 'with whom one has worked closely, no matter how long ago.' We talked until well into the afternoon and arranged to meet next day with Phoumi in the latter's bungalow, which also served as a headquarters.

I remembered Phoumi also from 1945, though with rather less affection than I had for the Prince. Phoumi had then belonged to a 'Free Laos' organisation in opposition to the French but not in collaboration with the Viet-minh. Now he was looking fit, prosperous and smart in his general's uniform, whereas in 1945 he was scruffy and half-starved. He told me he had attended the French staff college at St Cyr. I have to confess that on this occasion I took to him a lot more than I had before – or than I have ever since. A cynic might say, with some justification, that on this occasion he simply pulled the wool over my eyes.

Phoumi's troops now held the royal capital of Luang Prabang on the Mekong well to the north-west of Vientiane, the administrative capital, which Kong-Lae's paratroops still occupied. The only communication to Luang Prabang from here was by air. I had always wanted to see the royal capital with its famous, beautiful and ancient temples, and so I asked Phoumi if he could arrange a seat for me in one of his aircraft. He readily agreed, but warned me that there might be an enemy attack on Luang Prabang at any moment. But if I was really keen to go, I should report the next morning at the airfield where there would be a flight for me.

After much confusion and delay, which I had found inseparable from such journeys, it was noon on 30 November before I took off, in an old C47 Dakota of the Laotian Air Force. It was a beautiful, clear day when we started and we followed the course of the Mekong without difficulty. But as we came nearer to Luang Prabang a blanket of cloud covered the river and the mountains through which it flowed. As the pilot began to descend into the cloud the turbulence increased alarmingly. I knew the C47, although old, was a tough and reliable aircraft, but I couldn't be sure of the quality of Laotian Air Force maintenance. We were now flying low through the mountains and soon I couldn't even see our wing-tips. But from time to time, through gaps in the cloud, I caught glimpses of a brown river snaking in and out among the hills, and of little *Montagnard* (mountain tribesman) villages on the forested slopes. Sometimes, much too close for my comfort, I would catch sight of great black buttresses of rock jutting out towards us from the steep mountainsides which towered above and dropped below in sheer precipices. The young Lao pilot was expert at picking his way surely through the valleys, or rather gorges, banking and losing height in a series of tight left turns that seemed more suitable to a fighter plane than an ungainly C47. At one point he told us on the intercom that visibility was deteriorating and he would have to turn back, but almost immediately he found a gap in the cloud and brought us down to land on the Luang Prabang airfield. The time, I saw, was 3 pm.

I handed Phoumi's note of introduction to a young Army captain wearing gold parachute wings on his red beret who had met me in his jeep and drove with him to the rest house, known as 'the Bungalow', in the town. I spent the next morning looking at some of the temples. Though very impressive, they weren't as ancient as their sites, having frequently been burnt by raiding outlaw bands during the last century.

The threatened attack on Luang Prabang by troops from Vientiane occurred very soon after my arrival. It came from the north, east and south. But it failed entirely because the young commander, also a parachute captain, of the southern and main thrust chose a critical moment in the battle to desert with his men to the defenders. He was immediately promoted lieutenant-colonel. I met him the same night in the bar of the Bungalow, very happy, rather drunk and quite uproarious, bellowing for drinks all round.

From Luang Prabang I arranged a flight four days later to Savannakhet, where I took leave of Boun Oum and Phoumi before returning by bus and train to Bangkok. I had intended to go home after a few days in Bangkok, but while I was there news came through of a full-scale attack on Vientiane by Phoumi. On the night train to Udaun, the railhead for Nongkai, across the Mekong from Vientiane, I found Michael Field, the *Daily Telegraph* correspondent; like me, he was hoping to get into Vientiane with or even before Phoumi's attacking forces. It didn't prove easy.

We crossed over to Laos by *pirogue* from Nong Kai, as Rowly Winn and I used to do in 1945; but at the Laotian landing point, Tadeu, we were promptly arrested by a group of Phoumi's police, who proposed to keep us under detention. However, we persuaded them to take us to see Phoumi himself at his battle headquarters nearby. He was a good deal less friendly than he had been at Savannakhet, but he ordered our release; however, he told us we could not enter Vientiane that day. We recrossed the river to Thailand, where we hired a rickety old car to take us some thirty miles up river towards Vientiane, and crossed over again by *pirogue* to a little village on the Laotian side, Kong Nhang. Once again we failed in our attempt to enter Vientiane and had to return to Kong Nhang for the night. It was a hideous night. We slept on the very dirty floor of a hut with a roof but no outside walls; it was very cold and a chill wind blew over us, piercing our thin tropical clothing. We hadn't an overcoat or blanket between us. When we asked the headman for a blanket he shook his head and answered in French:

'There are no blankets. But [brightening a little] we can get you some girls.' We groaned and prayed vainly for some sleep.

At last daylight came and we staggered to our feet, still cold and miserable, and set out on foot for Vientiane, listening to the sound of explosions from the city. We managed to dodge all Phoumi's control posts and, hurrying through the outskirts, made for the centre of Vientiane under a ferocious artillery and mortar bombardment.

There followed two more days of bombardment and confused fighting in the streets, where any outside activity became extremely disagreeable if not hazardous owing to Phoumi's armoured cars, which had a habit of spraying the streets with machine-gun fire at the least sign of human activity. At times we felt we were the targets of both sides; but in fact Kong-Lae's troops were retreating fast to the north, abandoning the city. Nevertheless Phoumi continued the bombardment quite unnecessarily, in what could only be a savage demonstration of military might designed to overawe the inhabitants.

The evenings brought me some relief and cheer when I would join the journalists, British, American and Australian, in the bar of the old Constellation Hotel, where I had managed to find a room, and carouse with them until the small hours.

When the fighting, or rather the shelling, subsided Phoumi was firmly if temporarily in control of Vientiane and the Laotian government. Casualties had been high among the civilian population – unnecessarily high. I doubt if the military on either side had suffered very many.

Chapter 7

T HE *News of the World* has a reputation for a certain levity in
its treatment of domestic news; foreign news, on the other
hand, at least in the Sixties, it took very seriously indeed. And so I
was delighted when in the early summer of 1965 I received a
telephone call from that paper suggesting a meeting with the proprietor, Sir William Carr, and the editor to discuss the possibility
of my making a tour of South East Asia on their behalf. Their idea,
they explained, was that I should visit as many countries as possible
in the three or four months of my stay out there, and they would
require a total of twelve articles on the theme of communist pen-
etration and subversion in the region; I should try to spend some
time in each country. Vietnam, where the Viet-minh of North
Vietnam and their satellite movement in the South, the Vietcong,
had progressed from guerrilla warfare against the South Vietnamese
government to open confrontation on the battlefield, would be of
particular interest and importance. Finally, they wanted me to cable
every article, not post it, because they didn't think the airmail was
fast or reliable enough and for this reason I should cable from
Singapore or Hong Kong, where the Commonwealth rate was still
only a penny a word.

Apparently they had chosen me for this job through the
recommendation of my friend Charles Letts, with whom Sir William had discussed the project on a recent visit to Singapore. I had
done no travelling since 1961, when I spent six very disagreeable
weeks in the former Belgian Congo, now Zaire, for an English
Sunday paper long since defunct. The Belgians had only recently
withdrawn, in precipitate and undignified haste, from their colony,
leaving their nationals to the vengeance of the Congolese. Although
the country had become a bit quieter, the Congolese National Army,
formerly the *Force Publique*, was still in control of the streets and
roadblocks; but they were certainly not in control of themselves. It
was a perpetual hazard to go out, either on foot or by car; for these
soldiers, half-crazed most of the time with *chanvre*, a raw hashish,

would stop Europeans and often take their money and valuables, and sometimes beat them up. There was no redress. I was lucky to escape such treatment – I was also very careful – but I don't think I've ever been more relieved to get away unscathed from any country. However, I accepted with enthusiasm this assignment from the *News of the World*, with the usual cooperation from my company; I flew to Singapore on 9 June.

This was an interesting time to be in South East Asia. Singapore, which still formed a part of the Federation of Malaya, was about to break away, as it did while I was out there. And President Sukarno of Indonesia, already embarked on an aggressive policy of Javanese imperialism – though not himself a Javanese – had attacked the Federation and sent his troops into Borneo, after declaring a state of *Konfrontasi* with Britain and Malaya. 'He wants to recreate the ancient Javanese Empire of Madjapahit,' a journalist commented to me. The British sent troops and naval forces to oppose him and, soundly defeated but far from chastened, Sukarno withdrew to his old frontiers. In the hope of strengthening his own position he now began to make overtures to the Communist Party and the Chinese, with strong support from Chairman Mao. Sukarno's new policy, already unpopular with the Army, eventually led, at the end of September that year, to an attempted *coup* by the communists, which the Army suppressed, though not before some of its most senior officers had been murdered. There followed several months of savage bloodshed in which hundreds, if not thousands of communists, suspected communists and Chinese were slaughtered throughout the islands – Bali suffered very severely, I was told. The Army obliged Sukarno to retire from active politics and established an Indonesian government under General Suharto, which is now on less hostile terms with the West.

Meanwhile, I had at first hoped to go to Borneo and get permission to accompany British troops on operations there. But the military authorities in Singapore, though very polite, didn't encourage the presence of journalists in the theatre of operations.

'We would be responsible for your safety,' the colonel in charge of press relations told me, 'and if you were unable to keep up with the troops on a patrol, for instance, or were wounded, someone would have to risk his life to help you. You might cause us casualties.'

I took his point, of course, although it was the opposite of the American attitude I later found in Vietnam; in the light of events maybe the British were the wiser. I abandoned the idea anyway, because even if I were to succeed, it would take much too long to arrange.

Surprisingly, though, I had no difficulty in arranging a visit to Indonesia. I had no intention of trying to cover the war from the Indonesian side, but my paper wanted an article on conditions there. They were appalling: poverty, misery, near starvation and a pervading sense of hopeless and purposeless stagnation among the peasantry and workers – all this in a country which had once been among the richest and best fed in all the East. The architects of this misery and chaos – Sukarno, his ministers, senior officials and many of his generals – lived in conditions of luxury and idleness that further encouraged the incompetence of their administration.

I thought it might be a relief from the gloom and frustration of Jakarta to pay a visit to Bali. It was a sad mistake.

Balinese life had suffered some grim changes under the oppressive and puritanical rule of Sukarno and the Javanese. Himself a notorious womaniser, Sukarno would allow no such relaxations to his easy-going subjects in Bali; women were obliged to cover their breasts in public – something they had seldom bothered to do except on formal occasions. A friend of mine from London, visiting Bali, found a notice posted in the airport at Den Pasar stating, 'Visitors are reminded that it is an offence to photograph women with breasts uncovered, *whether on purpose or by mistake*'. Any kind of political discussion, however harmless, was dangerous and might well lead to arrest and worse.

'I should be so happy to invite you to my house,' a Balinese acquaintance would apologise to me. 'But I dare not.'

If I were to meet any of them in public, almost his first words would be, 'Please, no politics.'

Finding the atmosphere of fear in Bali as saddening as the gloom of Jakarta, I soon returned to Singapore to cable my impressions. On the flight there the air hostess handed me a copy of the *Surabaja Daily News*, in which I read an account of a royal visit to Jakarta, in which their correspondent described the royal personage as 'smartly dressed in a grey lounge suit and wearing a carnation in his bottomhole'.

Both Cambodia and Burma were barred to me, the former because the ruler, Prince Sihanouk, had taken offence at some unflattering reference to him in the Western press and was admitting no journalists; Burma's dictator, General Ne Win, was admitting no foreigners, Eastern or Western, to his country. Vietnam was therefore the obvious choice for my next visit – South Vietnam, of course, for I would never get a visa from Hanoi to enter the North.

Early in August I flew to Saigon, where I stayed in the old Hôtel

Continentale, a pleasant, airy building in the French colonial style with a wide veranda-café in the front. Unfortunately, the beer was also in the old French colonial style and so almost undrinkable; for a good glass of San Miguel from Manila you had to go to the bar of the pretentious new Caravelle Hotel or its roof café, from which you could listen every night to the thunder of artillery shelling, probably ineffectively, suspected enemy concentrations outside the city. Saigon was crammed with troops, most of them belonging to the ARVN, or South Vietnamese Army. The ARVN had been having a bad time lately, its convoys ambushed and shot to pieces by the Vietcong and its infantry repeatedly decimated in battles with the NVA, or North Vietnamese Army. Its morale was near breaking point and only the arrival of reinforcements from the US saved it from collapse.

The rights and wrongs of the Vietnam War is a subject already overworked in print and on the screen, where the issues have been distorted to a degree I haven't seen since the Spanish Civil War and the truth is unlikely to emerge for a generation at least. One important point, however, is consistently ignored by critics of the American action; South Vietnam never attacked the North; the North, on the other hand, with help and encouragement from China and war material from the USSR, had begun to attack the South soon after the 1954 Geneva Agreement – at first with Vietcong guerrillas and then with regular troops of the NVA.

The US was bound by treaty to come to the aid of the South if the latter were attacked. They intervened in Vietnam to fulfil their treaty obligations – although they were surely unwise as well as ineffective in the vast scale of their intervention and the manner in which they tried to fight the war. Both those mistakes played into the hands of the Vietnamese communists.*

But the fundamental American mistake, the consequences of which the Americans were now having to bear, was their original support for Ho Chi Minh and the Vietnamese communists in 1945; one early victim of this policy was my friend François Klotz. The Americans had soon recognised their mistake and were now doing their best to rescue the countries of Indochina from a serious, if long-term communist drive by Hanoi to take them over. At this time, in 1965, public opinion in the US was very largely behind the President and the morale of the US armed forces in Vietnam was very high.

* The clearest and best informed discussion of these matters that I have read is in Sir Robert Thompson's book, *No Exit from Vietnam* (Chatto and Windus, 1969).

'We're fighting communism here,' a soldier or airman would tell me, 'so's we don't have to fight it in our own back yard.'

As soon as I had arranged the necessary military authorisation I took the opportunity to accompany a flight of US Air Force ground-attack aircraft on a bombing mission near the Cambodian border. These were slow, piston-engined aircraft, which were considered best for that kind of work. I sat beside the pilot, a colonel who had fought in the Second World War and Korea, and had logged over five hundred 'combat hours' before coming to Vietnam, and so I reckoned I was in safe hands. We flew south-east of Saigon, and bombed and destroyed a group of seven huts in a jungle clearing which the colonel assured me was an ammunition dump; certainly I saw a number of secondary explosions, which could signify ammunition blowing up. We also made some fearsome power dives over the target and whenever we pulled sharply out of one, I blacked out.

'Never mind,' said the colonel when we had landed, 'the last guy I took on one of these was sick over both of us.'

A few days later I flew north to Pleiku in the Central Highlands, where there was a sizeable compound of US military advisers on a plateau by the town; for Pleiku was the headquarters of the Vietnamese 2nd Army corps. There was a special forces' camp in the jungle nearby, which I wanted to visit. Because of the American attitude to journalists I had no difficulty in arranging it. Everyone seemed to be expecting the Vietcong and NVA to launch a great 'monsoon offensive' against Pleiku and the provincial capital, Kontum, further north, and Hanoi had been infiltrating regular troops of the NVA from bases in Cambodia into the whole area. Duc Co, the special forces' camp about thirty-five miles from Pleiku, commanded the important *Route* 19 from Cambodia and so was of vital importance to the defence. It had been under siege by the enemy for the past six weeks and almost overrun several times; the ARVN had recently landed two airborne battalions near the camp to relieve the pressure.

Colonel Williams, deputy adviser to the 2nd Army corps, hitched his carbine on his shoulder and waved me towards the helicopter standing on the pad with its rotars turning.

'I've ordered the pilots to get us in there at all costs,' he told me cheerfully. Not much liking the sound of 'at all costs', I clambered into a seat at the rear between the two machinegunners who sat huddled over their guns at the open hatches on either side; beside me sat the senior US adviser at Duc Co, Captain Richards. The chopper lifted in a crescendo of noise and made for the hills to the south, flying at first over hilly country with the villages of the *Montagnard* tribesmen perched on the hilltops. After fifteen or twenty minutes we came over wild, jungle-covered mountains intersected with narrow, steep valleys. This was Vietcong territory. Our pilots took us down to treetop height, to present as difficult a target as possible to VC machine guns, of which there were said to be plenty, while our own gunners depressed their barrels, ready to spray any area from which we might take fire. We skimmed across the jungle and as each treetop loomed ahead, it seemed we must crash into it; indeed, as it passed beneath us I was sure I could hear the swish of branches we had carried away. But at last we were pretty safe from ground fire, and at last the trees thinned and we saw ahead the red earth airstrip of Duc Co.

We landed in a cloud of dust and ran towards the gate of the camp.

'Better not hang around here,' called Captain Richards as he shepherded us away. 'They've got mortars and a .50 calibre machine gun covering the airstrip.' As we hurried through the gateway several sharp explosions behind us confirmed his words. 'Don't linger here either,' added the captain as we stood watching the chopper take off on its return flight to Pleiku. 'Charlie has a mortar zeroed on this gate and a very accurate sniper. He shot three of our men on this very spot, clean through the head – one, two, three, just like that!'

In the mess, a wooden hut with roof and walls reinforced by sandbags and timber, Richards, an affable young man who seemed to enjoy his heavy responsibilities, introduced me to the rest of the team, a subaltern and ten sergeants; one of them, of Polish extraction, had fought in the Second World War with the British Army. They greeted me warmly, especially because, they said, I was the first journalist to be spending a night with them. The garrison consisted of some four hundred local levies, Vietnamese and *Montagnards*, under a Vietnamese captain. These *Montagnard* hill tribes had an inherited dislike of the Vietnamese, who despised them and called them '*moi*', 'savages', but they came to terms with the South Vietnamese, following a more conciliatory policy by the latter. Formerly loyal allies of the French, they seemed to have transferred that loyalty to the Americans, who considered them both brave and skilful fighters. If they had disliked the South Vietnamese, they loathed and feared the communists of the North – who gave them good reason for it. The notorious massacre of Ban Ma Thuot is a case in point. This *Montagnard* village was a district capital in the highlands, which Hanoi ordered the Vietcong to destroy as an example to others. They swept through the village at dawn, carrying flamethrowers, with which they destroyed every house and incinerated the inhabitants, all of them civilians; there were very few survivors. A British TV company, to its credit, showed a film of the ruins.

I spent twenty-four hours in the camp at Duc Co – a comparatively quiet period, as it turned out, because the besiegers were preoccupied with the two ARVN airborne battalions. But the enemy was all around our camp, as they would from time to time remind us by sending mortar bombs or bursts of machine-gun fire into the camp. Luckily our guards seemed to have uncanny ears and could hear the discharge of a mortar – their shouted warnings would send us diving for the nearest bunker; but there was nothing to be done about the machine guns except keep out of the way. At the height of the siege, Richard told me, the fire had been almost incessant, day and night.

After an uncomfortable and noisy night in the command bunker, listening to the thump of mortar bombs overhead, I returned in the chopper to Pleiku. A few days later the ARVN sent more troops to reopen *Route* 19 and raise the siege of Duc Co.

'How would you like to fly in a mission with an FAC ship?' they asked me in the mess at Pleiku a couple of evenings later.

'Very much,' I answered, with no very clear idea what an FAC ship was. FAC, I discovered, stood for Forward Air Control, and the aircraft's mission was to cruise over a battle area and select and pinpoint suitable targets for bomber and fighter attack; it coordinated between ground forces and aircraft, and its slow speed enabled it to locate targets more easily. The tiny, frail-looking aircraft which was waiting for me on the airfield a few days later seemed about the size of a pram, much too flimsy to trust myself to in a three-hour flight over defended enemy positions while we directed air strikes on to them.

For half an hour we cruised high over our target area while another FAC ship finished directing its strike; then I heard my pilot talking on his radio to our bombers. A moment later he began to throw the little aircraft around in a series of sharp twists and banks that did no good at all to my stomach.

'We're taking ground fire,' he explained shortly. I had learned the Vietcong seldom used tracer against aircraft, fearing it would betray their positions, and so I couldn't guess how near us their fire came. But a little later he levelled out and called to me over our intercom,

'We're going in now!' We went into a steep dive, pulled out a few hundred feet from the ground and loosed a smoke rocket as an aiming point for the bombers. We climbed immediately to get out of their way as they swooped down to release their bombs, which I saw bursting in a group of orange flashes around the smoke flare. Climbing again to above the smoke of the bombs, we flew off to pinpoint our next target.

This could be a tedious experience for the passenger; but it could also be hazardous, because the pilot had to fly in a straight line at a constant level and fairly near the ground, in order to pinpoint the target accurately and send its map coordinates; and so it presented an easy target to the defences. The rest of our flight attracted no more ground fire and we landed back at the airfield about two and a half hours later. The pilot congratulated me warmly.

'That wasn't a dangerous flight, surely?' I protested.

'But you're an *old man*, Mr Kemp,' he explained.

I was very nearly fifty.

My fiftieth birthday I celebrated in Hong Kong with an old friend, Colin Peel Yates, a retired captain of the Royal Navy who now held the post of Director of Protocol in the government of the colony. He told me he had been notified of my visit by the Foreign Office in London, on whom I had paid a courtesy call before leaving London. He read me their description of me:

'Personable, erratic and of romantic right-wing political views.'

When I had finished cabling to my paper I returned to Vietnam and spent another month travelling round the northern part of South Vietnam to Hue, the capital of the former Emperors of Vietnam, near the border with the North, and Danang, where I was allowed to accompany US marines on patrols outside their newly established perimeter. A month or so later I was in Singapore again, on my way to Thailand and then home.

Back in England with my series of articles completed, I became ill and remained so throughout the following year, 1966. Around the end of 1966 I could no longer pretend even to myself that I didn't know the cause: I was drinking too much and had been for too long. I was drinking now without even enjoying it; I was addicted and it was affecting my work. And so I went to my doctor, spent about a week in hospital and remained on the wagon for the next six or seven years. I came off it very slowly on to beer and have been lucky enough to enjoy my life ever since, drinking moderately and happily and, above all, smoking my pipe. The pipe was a wonderful, life-saving comfort to me, especially during those years of total abstinence, which in consequence I never found depressing. Anti-smoking fanatics, please note. I must add that I could never have overcome the drink problem without the sustained support of true friends. The most influential in this respect was a girl I met shortly after my divorce: Elizabeth Moore probably saved my sanity and almost certainly my life. It can't be easy to wean a veteran drinker off the bottle, but she persevered in the face of very considerable discouragement until at last I could see for myself I had no alternative but to lay off. She has remained ever since those days my closest friend and my most candid critic.

In December 1972 I paid my last visit to South East Asia, this time on a Travelling Fellowship from the Churchill Memorial Trust. Laos was the country I chose for my study, which I hoped might develop into a book. I had some experience of the kingdom and a great affection for the people. Because they were now at war I decided to begin with an examination of the royal armed forces in action – 'The Lao as a fighter' – and so I became involved, though only as a spectator, in the fighting between the royal Laotian government, aided by the Americans, and the Pathet Lao or commu-nist Lao whose principal and only effective support was the North Vietnamese Army. It has been the misfortune of Laos throughout its history to be either a buffer or a battleground between its larger and more powerful neighbours – principally Burma, Thailand and Vietnam. The Laotian kings acknowledged the suzerainty of the Emperors of China and in former times paid them tribute; but the Chinese gave them little protection. It was the Vietnamese the Laos most feared and hated, and the communist Vietnamese in particular, who were now the greatest threat to their independence – in the tragic outcome a wholly successful threat.

Before I left England I met through a friend Sir Robert Thompson, who had formerly been British adviser to President Diem of South Vietnam and was now special adviser on Vietnam to President Nixon; he was one of the greatest authorities, also, on counter-insurgency operations of which he had a wealth of practical experience dating from the days of the Malayan emergency, for the defeat of which he was largely responsible. Sir Robert arranged to put me in touch with senior members of the US military and civil missions in Laos, whom he also advised of my date of arrival there. I reached Vientiane, via Bangkok, about two weeks before Christmas and put up at the new hotel on the Mekong, the Lane-Xang or 'Million Elephants' – one of the many titles of the king of Laos was 'Lord of the Million Elephants and the White Parasol'.

I had begun to make arrangements for my journey during the previous summer. Among other preparations I had embarked on a crash course in the Laotian language, prepared for me by my friend Stuart Simmonds, Professor of South East Asian Languages and Literature at the School of Oriental and African Studies in Bloomsbury. Professor Simmonds was a quite exceptionally gifted teacher and by December I had absorbed enough Lao, including the five different and vital tones, to carry on simple conversations with Bangkok taxi drivers, most of whom were Laos, not Thais; the two languages are much alike. I also read some of the history of the region and a few simple books on Hinayana Buddhism, which is the religion of both Thailand and Laos.

I also met in London the counsellor of the British Embassy in Vientiane, Robin Fearn, and his wife Sally, who asked me to dine with them and their three young sons on Christmas Day; they were excellent company and I was happy to be rescued from a lonely and rather cheerless Christmas, especially as I was only just recovering from a virus infection picked up soon after my arrival. The Fearns were to prove themselves true friends later on; when I fell ill again with the same virus, they nursed me back to health in their own house.

Sir Robert Thompson had been as good as his word and at the end of December the US military mission flew me to Pakse, HQ of the Fourth Military Region (southern Laos) of the Laotian Army, a small town south of Ubon and further south than I had ever been before. Members of the mission met me on the airfield, put me up in one of their houses, and gave me a briefing on the military situation and the programme they had prepared for me.

About seventy-five miles north-east of Pakse stood – or once had stood, for it was by now in ruins – the small town of Saravane. It formed at this time the focal point of the front-line defences of southern Laos and so had suffered repeated attack, capture and recapture by both sides, especially during the previous two months. It was now in government hands, but the enemy were attacking it in force, heavily supported by artillery and mortars, and rockets. The defenders were picked troops of the royal Army, principally two '*Groupes Mobiles*', and numbered some two to three thousand men. The Americans now suggested taking me there next day. The enemy had encircled the town and its defences, and so we should have to go in by helicopter. In Vientiane I had already met a journalist who had witnessed some of the fighting in the streets of Saravane, a Scotsman who worked for a New York paper, and after his vivid account of the whistling of bullets past his head and the whine of shells I wasn't entirely looking forward to the experience.

We took off early in the morning and landed in a dry paddy-field after another hair-raising flight at low level clipping the trees to avoid anti-aircraft fire. Knowing how close the enemy was and that our choppers has sustained most of their losses while landing and taking off, we jumped out just before we touched down and ran, scattering as the aircraft lifted off without lingering. A walk of less than a mile through woods and fields brought us to the command post of Major Ting, who now commanded *Groupe Mobile* 41. The major, a tough, stocky Kha tribesman from the mountains near Saravane who had been soldiering all his life, gave me a cheerful but to me incomprehensible reception – he spoke no English or French – and through an interpreter gave us a thorough briefing on the local military situation, which he appeared to have well in hand. His principal worries seemed to be the enemy's great superiority in artillery and the increasing exhaustion of his own men, who had been heavily engaged in action, with very little rest, for two months. The briefing over, we lunched together under a tree while enemy shells and heavy mortars exploded a few hundred yards away as his men fought off another NVA attack. When the attack subsided Ting led us to his forward positions, where I found his troops, for all their weariness, remarkably cheerful and confident.

The NVA were certainly the most dangerous of the enemy forces and the success of enemy attacks depended entirely on the strength of the NVA component in them. Like most other people I spoke to on the subject, Ting had a poor opinion of the fighting quality of the Pathet Lao. The value of the PL to those who controlled it from Hanoi lay in its political, not its military organisation. Its titular leader, Prince Souphannavong, was a member of the Laotian royal family and a relative of the Prime Minister, Prince Souvanna, but he had a Vietnamese communist wife, a lady of overpowering character like many Vietnamese women, and she had almost total influence over her husband. The PL proved useful to Hanoi as a vehicle for political leverage and, after 1975, for handing over to Hanoi complete control of the country.

I spent about ten days in Pakse and toured the military region, travelling up to the Bolovens Plateau in the cab of the leading lorry of the first convoy to go there by road since they had cleared the enemy from it – an experience more interesting than enjoyable. I also went south to visit the ancient Hindu temple of Wat Phou, which stands on a steep mountainside south of Champassak, the principality of my old friend Boun Oum. It is said to date from Champa times – around the end of the eighth century AD.

Towards the end of my stay in Pakse I was asked if I would care to fly on a night operation in a 'Spooky'. This, it appeared, was a converted Dakota carrying in the side of the fuselage three Gatling 'mini-guns', each capable, they told me, of a rate of fire of two thousand rounds a minute. The operation would be in support of our ground troops in Saravane, which was again under heavy attack. The aircrew would all be Laotians, which might advance a little my researches.

'Senator Bill Buckley,' the CO of the US mission told me by way of encouragement, 'flew in one of these not long ago.'

'Did he come back?'

'Sure. I think he enjoyed it.'

We took off at 7.15 pm. I was sitting up forward in the navigational seat, on the port side, the same side as the mini-guns. I soon discovered the reason for the nickname 'Spooky'; it was just that, sitting there in the darkness, with no sound but the muffled purr of the engines, waiting for the moment to attack. Half an hour's flying brought us over the target area, which the flares we dropped lit up like daylight, illuminating the tree-lined banks of the river just west of Saravane, where the enemy were attacking; I could even see clearly the flashes of their mortars and the stabs of flame from automatic weapons. In the light of the flares we began our attacks on selected targets, making in all about a dozen runs and banking steeply to port to fire our guns in five-second bursts, pouring down scarlet streams of tracer on to both banks of the river and creating one of the most spectacular fireworks displays I'd ever seen. I was thankful I wasn't on the receiving end. I wouldn't let myself even speculate on what might be coming back at us from the ground; we were attacking, I knew, at a height of three thousand feet – well within the range of the lightest anti-aircraft weapons, of which I had learned in a lecture that afternoon that they had a good supply. At least I saw no tracer coming our way; but I learned next day that on previous occasions we had lost entire aircraft and crew from anti-aircraft fire on these operations.

Ten days later I flew again over Saravane, but in daylight. By then the town was in NVA hands once more. I flew 'back seat' in a FAC ship piloted by a young Royal Laotian Air Force lieutenant. He frightened the life out of me by flying slowly and straight over the town at nought feet while he called down and observed air strikes by piston-engined Laotian Air Force light bombers. Some of their bombs landed near enough to blow us off course and nearly give me a heart attack. Afterwards he did the same to an NVA troop concentration in some woods west of the town. I didn't enjoy either of these performances while they lasted, especially after a talk I had had before with the US air operations officer. He had told me not to take a parachute because we should be flying too low.

'I expect there will be somewhere we can crash land if we're hit,' I replied with an attempt at a cheerful look.

'Right,' he said. 'But nobody has ever *survived* a crash landing in one of these flimsy little kites. Ready to go?'

Apart from a brief visit in August and September of 1973 to Cambodia, Laos and Vietnam, I've never returned to South East Asia, a part of the world I always loved and where I felt at home. Now, except for Thailand, there are few of the countries I knew where I could expect to be either happy or welcome. Laos is a colony of Hanoi, controlled through puppets by the detested Vietnamese; the horror of Cambodia remains in all our minds; and Vietnam itself is a Stalinist state, a regime more ruthlessly oppressive than – and just as corrupt as – any that have gone before. 'Re-education centres' take the place of Stalin's gulags. We hear now that it is relaxing gradually under the influence of *glasnost*, but for how long will the process continue? The communists did not, of course, win Vietnam on the battlefield: they won it on the American and European home fronts, by massive and skilful propaganda, supported by the misdirected sympathy of the Liberals and the left. The Viet-minh Tet offensive of February 1968 was probably the turning point, with all the television coverage and international publicity it attracted. The US military made a great mistake in ignoring its effect, dismissing it as a disastrous failure because of the appalling casualties it caused the Viet-minh. Uncle Ho himself disposed of that one. Replying to a high-ranking Czech communist who asked him how he could endure such heavy losses among his people, he said they didn't worry him – 'because more babies are born every day in Vietnam than men and women are killed in the war'.

Ho is dead, but the Boat People are very much with us. The shocking stories we read of the risks they ran to escape, and the dangers and suffering they endured at sea, must surely make us wonder about the nature of a regime that drove its subjects to such lengths. Political and economic conditions in Vietnam are at last improving, but I wonder if those politicians and publicists – not always of the far left – who in Britain, America and Europe loudly and constantly demanded American withdrawal from Vietnam slept less soundly when they read of its consequences. My guess is, not a bit.

I travelled no more, apart from occasional holidays, until the autumn of 1976, when I went to Paraguay to write articles for the *Spectator* and other papers on the subject of the Tupamaros, a Uruguayan left-wing urban guerrilla movement which had kidnapped the British Ambassador in Montevideo, Sir Geoffrey Jackson. Sir Geoffrey endured a long and atrocious captivity with extraordinary fortitude before his release. The movement was strongly anti-British and anti-American but by no means pro-Russian. Although the Tupamaros achieved considerable notoriety both within Uruguay and outside, by 1976 their unity was cracking and they were experiencing a good many defections. A number of these defectors, well-educated, middle-class young men, had taken refuge in Paraguay with the connivance of the Stroessner government. I was to interview them – in Spanish because very few of them spoke English – and write some articles based on their stories. I had to see them in secret, for their own protection, because the Tupamaro movement, in the manner of all terrorists with defectors, had sentenced them to death. What emerged from the defectors' accounts was that the Russians had infiltrated their own agents into the Tupamaro leadership in the hope of swinging the movement behind the communists. Failing to do so, they resolved to destroy it and eventually they did so by manipulating it skilfully into direct confrontation with the armed forces of the state – a battle it was bound to lose. To all intents and purposes the Tupamaros ceased to exist. The lesson was that Moscow would not tolerate a left-wing guerrilla movement it couldn't control; another who had to learn this lesson the hard way was Che Guevara.

I was surprised to find that President Stroessner enjoyed at this time considerable support among the Paraguayan people. The reason, it was explained to me, was that before he took power neither property nor life were safe, especially in the countryside.

'Men would descend on your house,' several farmers told me, 'violate your womenfolk, take anything they wanted from you and disappear. They were never caught. Our lives were a misery of fear.'

Things were little better in the towns.

'Stroessner put a stop to all that,' one woman told me. 'That's why we support him now.'

Since then, like most dictators, he had let power go to his head.

His rule became more and more oppressive and corrupt, his methods more ferocious. In the end, few regretted his overthrow.

The Paraguayans seemed a delightful people. I was charmed by their cheerful friendliness and impressed by their fierce pride in being Paraguayan, and in their Indian as well as their Spanish heritage. Guaraní, along with Spanish, is the official language, with notices and signposts written in both; there is even a Guaraní theatre. In the seventeenth and eighteenth centuries Paraguay was the scene of a rare experiment, by the Jesuits, in promoting the welfare of a colonised people. For over a hundred and fifty years they created and developed farming settlements worked and later run by the Indians under the missionaries' supervision. They encouraged the Indians to come in from the forests and settle; and they gave the brightest of them a good classical education. They also built splendid churches, using surprising Indian skills in building, sculpture and painting. Unfortunately the whole experiment collapsed after the expulsion of the Jesuits in 1767 from Spain and consequently from the Spanish colonies. But that was far from the only example in Latin America of the benign influence of Catholic missionaries in mitigating the harsh and selfish rule of the Spanish settlers.

Although not a warlike people, the Paraguayans showed remarkable resolution in the defence of their country after they became independent of Spain in 1811. They were involved in 1865 in a disastrous war with their neighbours, Brazil, Argentina and Uruguay, and they fought bravely against impossible odds. I drove through a town north-east of the capital and looked at a large stone monument in the square. It was erected to commemorate some five thousand children, none of them over ten years old, who had held the town against a Brazilian army – the adult men were either dead or fighting elsewhere – until the last child was killed. As a result of this war Paraguay suffered eight years of foreign occupation and the loss of much of its territory; out of a previous population of 800,000 only about two thousand grown-up men survived the war, alongside some 200,000 women – a situation which impelled the Pope to give his formal approval to the practice of *concubinaje*.

In 1980, when I reached the official retirement age of sixty-five, I gave up full-time work for Imperial Life, although I continued with them part time. This gave me more time for travel and for writing. Central America seemed at this time to be a promising field to combine both; it was becoming a focus of international interest and concern, a prime target of communist subversion, and the scene of two major and several smaller guerrilla wars; moreover, my knowledge of Spanish would be a useful asset. And so, in the spring of 1982 I approached the editors of the *Sunday Telegraph* and the weekly *Spectator* with the suggestion that I should travel on their behalf through the Isthmian republics and produce articles for them on the situation; both of them agreed and in April 1982 I flew to Mexico City on the first stage of my journey.

There was plenty happening in Central America for me to write about, as there had been for several years past. Soviet policy under Brezhnev and his immediate successors, repressive at home and among the satellites, was pursuing an aggressive line overseas, particularly in Africa and in Central America. And in Castro's Cuba the Russians had the perfect means for their designs in Central America – it was close to their target, with a Spanish-speaking population, and a core of skilled operatives in espionage and subversion, trained by the KGB and known as the DGI. The North American department of the DGI was in charge of subversion in Central America, and its immediate objective was Nicaragua. Fidel Castro, increasingly dependent on Soviet aid to preserve his mismanaged and fragile economy, had long abandoned any pretensions to independence. Che Guevara's ill-starred attempt at revolution in Bolivia was probably Cuba's last independent venture; thereafter Castro acted under Soviet direction.

Autocratic or oligarchic rule has persisted in Central America since pre-Colombian times; Aztecs, Toltecs, Mayans and Spaniards have imposed it with varying degrees of brutality. Turbulence is also endemic to the region, and has persisted into recent years through the wide gap between rich and poor, and the indifference of the former to the plight of their less fortunate countrymen. Consequently Central America was an ideal field for revolutionary activity. Perhaps after the 1990 Nicaraguan elections and the rout of the Sandinistas, things may take a more peaceful turn in the Isthmus.

Epilogue

Ὡς ἡδὶ τὸν σωθέντα μεμνῆσθαι πόνων.
(How sweet for a survivor to remember his troubles.)

Euripides

I THINK OF 1986 as a year of anniversaries. July was the fiftieth anniversary of the outbreak of the Spanish Civil War: October brought the thirtieth of the Hungarian Revolution. I was to cover both occasions, once again, for the *Sunday Telegraph* and the *Spectator*.

Although I had been back to Spain on several occasions since 1939, I found the atmosphere there in July 1986 refreshingly changed, as I have already indicated. The Civil War and its aftermath had left most Spaniards deeply mistrustful of extremist parties and political philosophies, either of the right or left, and thanks partly to the enlightened leadership of King Juan Carlos, partly to a new understanding of popular political responsibility, the transition to a democratic system had been completed.

Spaniards, while relieved that Francoism had been left behind, viewed the Communists with suspicion and, remembering the cynicism and brutality of their behaviour in the Civil War, with dislike and distrust; the Falange, especially since the farce of their failed *coup* in February 1981 and the clownish antics of the Civil Guard Colonel Tejero, commanded no influence except among a few *Camisas Viejas*. I found everywhere else a wish to forget the Civil War and put aside the old antagonisms and bitterness.

But in the Basque provinces it was different. True, the former antagonisms had gone, but only to be replaced by new ones. The main issue now was between those who accepted Basque autonomy within the existing Spanish state and those extremists who demanded nothing less than a separate, fully independent Basque Republic. How the separatists expected to survive on their own in the modern world has never been clear to me. Nevertheless, separatist feeling had grown alarmingly even among former Carlists I used to know – to whom it had been anathema during the Civil War – and in Navarre, the old heart of Carlism. It was especially strong among the Basque clergy, who once abominated the idea. During the Civil War one of the Navarrese battlecries was 'For God and Spain!' Today God plays a very small part in Navarrese life and Spain, as represented by the Madrid government, is regarded almost as an enemy – by some as *the* enemy. The intense patriotism of 1936 has given way to a narrow provincialism. The Carlist movement is virtually dead, and the parish priests who in 1936 inspired and recruited the *Requetés* are today too often recruiting agents for ETA terrorists. Father Vicente would be turning in his grave.

Separatism has its IRA in the shape of ETA, whose apologists, the *Herri Batasuna* party, like Sinn Fein, pretend to deplore violence but never fail to defend the terrorist atrocities of ETA. ETA has suffered some serious reverses since the French and Spanish authorities have been cooperating closely in counter-terrorist operations on each side of the frontier, but it is by no means finished; and I was dismayed at the sneaking sympathy for the terrorists shown by old friends of mine with whom I had served in the fighting around Madrid or in the mountains of the North.

What had become, I wondered, of the old Carlist *Fé y Ideal* for which thousands of *Requetés* had fallen fifty years ago?

Budapest, too, had changed radically – and was and still is changing – from thirty years ago. When I arrived there in October 1986 I found, in place of the gloom and terror of 1956, new hope and a relaxation in the attitude of that brave and battered people. There were still restrictions and a degree of censorship, particularly in the publication of views or news unwelcome to the authorities, but nothing to compare with the other Soviet satellites. There was no restriction on contacts or conversation with visitors from the West, and I was deeply impressed and moved by the sincere friendliness of all Hungarians I talked with, and the forthright criticisms they voiced about the regime and its still irksome restrictions; they had no fear of being overheard and several of their leading journalists told me I might quote them by name in anything I wrote for the British press. The shops in the famous Vaci Utca were a fair imitation of Bond Street, with plenty of stock imported from the West, although their prices, for Hungarians, were prohibitive. Only in the back streets did I see traces of 1956 – shattered windows and walls still showing the pockmarks of bullets. Much of the improvement was due to the policies of János Kádár, General Secretary for the last thirty years of the Hungarian Communist Party.

Kádár, originally detested and reviled by almost all Hungarians as the Soviet puppet who presided over the arrests and executions that continued for two years after the Russian invasion, had gradually redeemed himself by his enlightened policies afterwards. He knew the Russians well, and knew how far and how fast he could move in the process of reform – he knew also, only too well, the consequences in that pre-Gorbachev era of overstepping the limit. By slow stages he had now transformed Hungary into the comparatively free society I found there in 1986.

There was no evidence of any crushing of the Hungarian spirit. Notwithstanding the pressures of a steeply rising cost of living, of poverty and a cruel housing shortage, I found, especially among the young, great vitality. The most powerful safeguard against any attempt to reverse liberalisation was – and still is – the fact that the young wouldn't stand for it, and even the Kremlin won't easily forget the cost of tangling with Hungarians. It seems the Soviets have at last accepted this truth and withdrawn their troops from Hungary. Nagy was reinterred in 1989 and the first free elections since the war have taken place.

'I hate being shot at,' I wrote at the beginning of this book. And yet it seems that much of the last fifty years I've spent in situations where there was plenty of shooting either at or around me. It was certainly not because I was 'lured by the sound of guns', as the *Spectator* once described me: it was partly because I've always loved travelling, as long as there was a purpose in my travels, and so many of the places worth visiting carried also the possibility of being shot at.

Much more importantly, I have spent a large part of my life engaged, like many others, in the struggle against the two most dangerous evils of this century, fascism and communism. My own small rôle in this contest, taking part in or observing conflicts all over the world, has involved me in plenty of shooting. But I have never enjoyed it.

As I finish these memoirs at the start of the final decade of the twentieth century, there is hope that the struggle is approaching at last a happy ending. We are seeing freedom dawn in Eastern Europe – although a pale dawn as yet in the Soviet Union. Soviet-style communism is dead and Marxism discredited. It is well worth remembering that without the firm resolution by free world governments and their people to resist communist expansion and Soviet imperialism, the outcome would have been very different. This thought above all others convinces me that my own efforts were worthwhile and to hope that my life hasn't been a total waste.

But we have also to remember that serious dangers remain. Communism may indeed be dead, but Russian imperialism could still revive, backed by a formidable military strength; so also could aggressive German nationalism. Chaos could replace communism in Eastern Europe, as it threatens to do in Romania; terrorism overhangs us all. It seems that the price of freedom will continue to be eternal vigilance.

Nevertheless, I can take pleasure in looking back on my own experiences. There is stimulus in meeting a challenge, even more satisfaction in surviving it. In spite of the bad times, the frequent tragedy and the significant damage to my health, I can, in summary, only agree with what Horace wrote in his Twenty-Ninth Ode:

> Not Heaven itself upon the past has pow'r,
> But what has been has been and I have had my hour.

Index